"Beautiful… Love this book. Its
there is so much in each page that I f[...]
open a page and I get my answer to what's on my mind… Its rich beyond
words just like your paintings."

Deepthy, India

"Simply so fresh to read, packed with truth and encouragement, a
certain whirlwind to take you forward. I love how the way thoughts are
conveyed are bordering on (and even being) more like art with depth, with a
sense of humor, with freshness, word plays, sparks of light amongst words."

Zak, Finland

"It is something to sit quiet with. Allow words to have their say. Don't
rush. I feel that while I am reading I am in a place of prayer. I found many
different places where the eye of my heart was glued to the page. Your
writings about the Divine Love and the transformation of the soul they are
simply beautiful! Thank you for choosing to listen and hear, for being a
conduit for truths that exist for all, but few stop to listen."

Joseph, USA

"Intensely personal, faithfully rendered from observation and
experience, refreshingly innocent in reporting on interactions with the
Divine Presence, astute in its commentary on stale approaches to Truth,
chock full of exciting encounters with a remarkably down-to-earth God,
profound, mystical, practical, humorous, fast-paced and highly enjoyable
reading. A gem, which I am sure will spur many on to seek their own inner
enlightenment. Your detailed descriptions of what you did to get into the
flow can help anyone to take similar steps adapted to personal characteristics
and temperament. I can see it becoming one of the handbooks for this age
of ascension; it is that good and applicable. I for one feel inspired by your
example and enheartened by the thread of hope running through the book."

Hanspeter, Austria

LISTEN
HEAR
A DIVINE LOVE STORY

I see, I paint.
I listen, I write.
Through the lens of my soul, I see.
Then I paint what I see, so you may see too.
Through the ears of my soul, I hear.
Then I write what I hear so you may hear too.

It is my wish that what I offer
may open a window of new possibility
within your heart and mind.
And like a "breath of fresh air,"
awaken a part of your soul.

DEBRA CLEMENTE

Vibrant Inspirations

LISTEN HEAR, A DIVINE LOVE STORY

By Debra Clemente

Published by Vibrant Inspirations

Copyright © 2014 Debra Clemente

All rights reserved.

www.DebraClemente.com

ISBN-13: 978-0615753041 (Vibrant Inspirations)

United States of America

Some people say

"But of course."

Others say "No way."

And then there are those who ask

"How can this be?"

They are the seekers.

Seekers are finders.

I am a seeker.

This is the story of what I found

and how I found it.

It was never lost nor was I.

I just never fully recognized

the gift I had,

the voice of Love inside.

DEBRA CLEMENTE

Contents

PROLOGUE

So do not fear, for I am with you;
do not be dismayed, for I am your God.
I will strengthen you and help you;
I will uphold you with My righteous right hand.

ISAIAH 41:10 NIV

OCTOBER 10, 2011

My mind used to be filled with pain and fear. Now it is filled with love and comfort.

> *See how far you have come. It is truly a delight. I delight in you. Delight in Me. Delight in Me in you. Oh yes, this is the way it is and shall be. Walk with Me.*

It was a whole new concept, the idea that I should fix me not everyone else. Talk about a hard pill to swallow.

> *But swallow you did, not all at once for sure. You broke it up into little pieces and nibbled on it from time to time. Bitter booger wasn't it? But see how sweet life tastes now? How you can enjoy the company, actually delight in the company, of those who you had determined to fix even if it killed you, and in fact it did.*

My first decision was that I was going to learn mind control. I jokingly said that, knowing all the while that it was my own mind I wished to tame. As I explored and researched ways of doing this, new information continually came to light, very shocking and unsettling information which I didn't just take as a truth and swallow whole. Again, I picked over each bone and investigated and tested the teachings.

> *Yes, you did. We were so proud of you. This is how it is supposed to be. For when you did accept each concept new to you blind belief was not needed, as you knew their truth by your own testing and proving.*

After having spent so many days of so many years in continual physical pain and limitation I was deeply offended to hear it said that it was of my own creation. That really pissed me off. It's surprising now that I didn't just slam that book shut and kick it down the stairs.

> *You were so curious. You were so wanting and desiring better for your life that you closed no door to possibility. This is what is needed by all, an open mind. It is the mind that is "made up" that has no room to grow.*

The thing that kept bugging me about the whole "Law of Attraction" thing was that the ideas that had until that point formed the foundation of my ideas of life, my understanding of what was and shall be, were rocked, rocked back and forth. The ground beneath my feet no longer felt firm. If this was so, the Law of Attraction and all the tricks and tweaks to life as presented in the movie *The Secret*, what was true of God and Jesus as I knew? How did all that fit in? I was not so easily swayed to believe that someone could replace the word "God" with "the Universe" or "Spirit" in a sentence and just move on.

It's also true that prayer had lost its power and magic over me. I had continually turned to "the Church" for answers and comfort and left at a loss for all. My needs were not met. My answers were not coming. But God, or the idea I had always held of God, had a hold on me and said, *"Keep looking. Seek and ye shall find."*

One very important thing, actually I know it was the most important thing I had ever found, proclaimed and received, is a Divine Love prayer titled, *The Prayer Perfect*. I found it on the internet, happened upon as it seemed, while on this truth quest. The person that posted it challenged the reader to pray the prayer twice daily for fifteen minutes and that whoever did so would never experience life again the same. There would be a wondrous, internal and permanent change.[1]

So, as is always my way, I didn't follow this prayer outline to the word nor even the letter. Just as I can't seem to follow a recipe as written, I cannot pray someone else's prayer. So, I created my own inspired by the prayer given. Mine was simpler and flowed gracefully from my lips. Most importantly, I could remember it and creatively embellish it with flourishing concepts as I prayed and desired in prayer.

Divine Love fill me
Divine Love flow through me
Divine Love be me.

That's pretty much the gist of it. So I did it. Every time I remembered about it I stopped and said it. I wasn't even sure what "Divine Love" was. It didn't really feel like a prayer or sound like one, it was almost like an incantation or a spell.

I remember shortly there after things changing for me. More and more my actions, my seemingly thoughtless actions, surprised me. By "thoughtless," I don't mean not considerate of others. I mean I didn't pre-think my actions. And they were so amazingly thoughtful of others it was if I knew beyond my own mind how to be of the right help at the right time. I would continually say and do the right thing. *"Hold on a minute."* I heard a voice inside me say, *"You are surprised at your actions but haven't you just been praying for God's love to flow through you and become you?"* Was I? Did I? Is that what Divine Love was? I needed to know, for I had never heard it spoken of that way. Divine Love, what was it really? What was happening to me? Had any other experienced such and written about it?

Intro

It was to be one of the "marks of the New Covenant"
that each member of it should
walk in personal communication with God.

Andrew Murray 1888 [2]

December 30, 2011

And wonders of His love, and wonders of His love, and
wonders and wonders of His love.

This hymn is ringing through my head so I pick up my journal and pen
to record this thought. Much the same as I have done the past two and
a half years. Something comes to my head and I record it. It began as a
game I played with myself. At first I recorded a word or two at a time,
as they came to me in snippets. I would set my paper down and click
my pen closed and as soon I had dropped my pen another inspiring
phrase would come to mind.

I called the game "Painting Titles" as they sounded much the same
as the phrases I had been using to title my paintings for the past
several years. Soon I realized that I had over eight hundred painting
titles. "What fun," I thought, "that's a lot of paintings." But I never
considered quitting the game and so I filled journal after journal this
way, filling a page here and there with a body of ever growing wisdom
that seemed to just come my way.

I began 2011 with my continued journaling but somewhere along the way it became clear to me that the wisdom and inspiration I was writing was coming from someone with a much higher and clearer perspective. No, I was not scared. I was comforted, for each message was so gentle and loving. And then one day I knew that what I was writing was meant not only for me but as well, for you. God had found a listening ear and a willing heart and writing His word, as given, was to be my part.

So now with love I offer these words to you. As a gift from me and from God whom wants us each to know that He is with us and can be found within our hearts and so wishes to have each sing joyfully the song I now sing because I truly know "the wonders of His love."

JANUARY 21, 2012

I am continuing my work of editing the words I wrote last year, which is the book you are reading now. I continue to edit for clarity, clarity to first myself and then as well ultimately for others. I know as I do that I am being led by the same great "Spirit of Love" who entrusted this wisdom to me so I am assured that God will let me know if I do not perceive such clearly. I am changing no words, only the form so all will read smoothly.

You see much of this wisdom has come to me piece by piece, word by word, quite literally. At first, I thought that the words should remain in such a form. But it has just been "given to me" that as much as possible I should punctuate and create sentences and paragraphs to express the ideas most properly as intended to be perceived.

In the beginning, the message did not come across to me or at least to my head so clearly. Word by word it came and word by word I wrote. Not looking back at the whole of what I had been given, I did not comprehend the greatness of it all. But now, as I do this work and read and reread these words again and again, I am awestruck by the beauty and love that was expressed to me, for me and for all. I bow down and humble myself. Tears of joy and thanksgiving cloud my very eyes as I write, for I am a chosen messenger of the story of the true saving grace of God's Divine Love.

Am I the first to hear? Am I the first to write? No, I know I am not. Yet my ears could never hear the truth as such, so very plainly and clearly as I hear it now. But of course, how can I not believe when such clear wisdom is coursing through me? Would I have, could I have, believed the same if these words had come through you? I know not, but I do believe that here in these words, for each, lies a clue of what to do if you so desire to hear the voice of Love unto your heart as I do.

Debra Clemente

Painting Titles

He desires that they know Him and they love Him.

The Gospel of Truth [3]

February 2009

Live your best life
Trust your instincts
Intuition doesn't lie
Mesmerizing
Breathing space
Turn over a new leaf
Find happiness
The best thing
Do not disturb
Moments of grace
Connections
Mountain high
Expectations
Discovery
Blessings
Serenity
Find happiness
Just this once
On view now

Oh, joy!
Crowning glory
Shall we dance?
Less is more
Oh, happy day
Coming home
Endless summer
I wish you well
Don't waste a moment
Now is the time
What's the rush?
Embracing
Say, yes
Wish you were here
Talk of the town
Everything looks better
Life of the party
It's in the air
You've arrived
Life is but a dream
Easy does it
Sonnet
Never, say never
Rise and shine
There is a time and place
Makes me think
I feel
Being true
Stop for a minute
A fresh start
A new beginning
Tomorrow's a new day
Face to face
Slow down

I see
Sing a song
Be happy
Come on and get happy
All together now
About face
Is this real life?
Go with the flow
Get carried away
Let yourself go
Today's the day
Oh, my
Things are looking up
I thought of you
Oh, happy day
Glory be
So far, so good
Till the end of time
Peace of mind
This ain't a thinkin' thing
Right brain – left brain
Go forth
Till we meet again
Peace be with you.

JULY 2010

The power that be, is the force within me. Stuff of science fiction?

Deeper or higher reality
Known to few
Available to all
On my radar
Watch what you say

Wisdom is emerging
Burgeoning awareness
Reaching a new understanding
A new consciousness is emerging
Carrying a higher awareness
Insights
Expansion of consciousness
Synchronistic path
In my mind's eye
Discover how to use vision, wisdom
Fear threatens our spiritual awakening
The other dimension
The after life
Fully conscious
I had no fear
You may miss the meaning
Open fear block.

January 2011

May your roots go down deep into the soil of God's marvelous love;
and may you be able to feel and understand, as all God's children should,
how long, how wide, how deep and how high his love really is; and to
experience this love for yourselves, though it is so great that you will never
see the end of it. And so at last you will be filled up with God himself.

Ephesians 4:16-19 NLT

January 3, 2011

I desire to have control over my body, not to have my body control me.

> *No limitations*
> *Give it your best*
> *Live your best life.*

I hear myself laugh.

> *Follow through*
> *Move forward*
> *Time to act*
> *Response required*
> *Act accordingly*
> *Your turn*
> *Really good*
> *Really God*
> *God is the power of us in our good*

Good timing
Good going
Extended stay
System wide.

I had to go there, to find my way here. Shortcuts are only for journeys repeated again and again. If you are doing the exact same thing over and over, or going to the same place over and over, you will eventually fine-tune the process or your route. For one thing, you now know where you want to go and the most direct route to get there. Or if you are going somewhere someone else has been, you may be able to follow their footsteps, or outline, to ease your journey. But if you are venturing to a new place, exploring, inventing and creating anew, there is no map. Trial and error is the process, such as painting, such as life.

I can see it going good.

An uncommon phrase.

Where did it go?

No, where did you go?

I feel there is more to life, more to know, more to be, more to experience. I need some time alone, time to step back from the world.

Release grip on life
Hang loose
Allow transformation
Allow growth.

Allow God to work with and through me. If God had given the caterpillar an ego and self choice, there would be so few butterflies in this world. How could any caterpillar begin to dream he could ever soar the skies, much less, dawn wings of fabulous colors? Who would he be to dream such dreams, he that crawled the earth at such a slow pace?

Things will look much worse, before they look better. All you have and know will dissolve before you, preparing the way for greater good to come into your life.

JANUARY 18, 2011

Don't give up
Pep talk
Keep on, keepin' on
Time to tell
Look inside
Ray of light
Higher calling
Raise me up
Told me so
Don't think what to say
Give it no thought
Give it a rest
Wake up call
Do what you are told
Give thanks
Parental control
Growth spurt
First impression
Deep inside
Telling you
Telling me
Don't try to connect all the dots
The picture is too big
No worry
I see it all
Let go
Go with the flow

Shed the old skin
Slough it off
Grow into Me
All you can be
Loud and clear
Thanks for listening My dear
Paint a bigger picture
Rise and shine
Don't doubt
Make up your mind
Stream of consciousness
All good flows
Stretch yourself
Break through
Don't be so reasonable
Listen here
I'm talking to you
Get your act together
See it through
Do what you need to do
Feel good about it
Feel God about it
Be aware
Be fair
God space
Ask and you shall receive
You know so much
Open up
See the light
The light of day
Your night was so long
Time to sing My song
So much fun
Steal away

Take flight
See the humor
To whom much is given
Much is expected
Sing a new song.

I get the upper channels.

So many gifts
Gifts given
A river runs through
Is that all you expect?
Expect the best
Time and again
See it through
Contemplation
A longing.

"Spectacular!" That's what we say when we see what man can create. But it all so pales in comparison, when we realize what God can and does create. The wonders never cease.

The gang's all here
Let's get spiritual, spiritual
Let me hear your soul talk, soul talk
Let me hear your soul talk, soul talk.

I am spiritual, spiritual. I listen to my soul talk, soul talk.

Be patient.

I had Weird Al's song *The White Stuff*, a parody of The Back Street Boys song *The Right Stuff* stuck in my head. Since it was playing continuously, I decided to give the tune that was spinning in my mind better words. It has been said, if you don't like the record that's playing change the song. So, I did.

GOD'S LOVE

First I tried life on my own, fell flat on my face.
Now I ask for all God's help, fill me with Your grace.

He answers quickly, to every bended knee.
God filled my heart, with the peace that's meant to be.

I have God's love, in the center of my soul.
I'm filling with Divine Love, the most important thing I know.

The door's not really closed, just ajar.
God's right here, never been afar.

When I silence myself, and believe dearly.
I am assured, God will lead me clearly.

I have God's love, in the center of my soul.
I'm filling with Divine Love, the most important thing I know.

Ego has no place, in the world I seek.
I have to let go, to be the best I can be.

Jesus showed the way. He told,
Ask and you shall receive, believing in your goal.

I have God's love, in the center of my soul
I'm filling with Divine love, the most important thing I know.

With God's love, peace is my reality.
Filled with His wisdom, I see far beyond me.

Let God open His world to each and all of you.
Ask for His guidance, and you will live anew.

Be filled with God's love, in the center of your soul
Ask for Divine Love, it's the most important thing you'll know.

Inquire within. Order up.
See the good around you, and drink in His love.

Move forward, take God's Lead.
See what you want. Have what you need.

Be filled with God's love, in the center of your soul
Ask for Divine Love, it's the most important thing you'll know.

All I need, is what I have.
And who He is, is who I am.

Today, tomorrow, and eternity,
God's Divine Love is my destiny.

I have God's love, in the center of my soul
I have Divine Love, it's the most important thing I know.

JANUARY 20, 2011

> *Don't say it*
> *Because you really do*
> *Spray it*
> *Leave what was and is alone*
> *There is nothing of which to atone*
> *Move forward*
> *Step ahead*
> *Take My lead*
> *See what you need*
> *Today*
> *Tomorrow*
> *Eternity.*
>
> *Those are fighting words*
> *Fighting your best*
> *Wrestling with the world*
> *Always to test*
> *Calm your mind*

Rest your heart
Invite Me in
I'll give you rest
You'll forget about sin
See what can be
When you walk hand in hand
With Thee
So close you are
Open arms I have
To have and to hold
Forever and again
Inquire within
Order up
Selfless service
You have to believe in good
You have to believe in yourself
Be true to yourself.

I'm so worth it. I can't afford not to.

Don't swallow the bitter pill
Swallow your pride.

With God's love, I make peace a reality. With God's love, I see so far beyond me.

Read the signs
Proceed with caution
Yield
Short sighted
Envision = In-vision
The vision you hold in your mind
As you envision the life you desire
Hold that thought

Draw from My well
Here (hear) I am
No trouble too big
No mountain too high
Time to see
Seek Me
I'm here
Keep telling
Not special interest groups
Instead, in everyone's best interest
For the good of all
One thing at a time
Be available
Time to see
See with Me.

My inner God-ance, guidance, speak to me.

Live out loud
Carry on.

Who is speaking?

Think beyond yourself
How can I be of service?
Let Me know
Move forward
Step ahead
It's not too late
We are resilient messengers
You get what you give
Give it all
Take time out
To take time in.

The Force is with me.

> *May you know the force within you*
> *Unstoppable*
> *All powerful*
> *All knowing.*

Creative energy exudes from my every cell.

> *What do you hear?*
> *Get out of yourself*
> *Take charge*
> *Don't give it away*
> *Feel good about what you do*
> *Feel good about who you are*
> *Look for ways to sing My song*
> *With a joyful heart*
> *Call the shots*
> *I see so much farther*
> *A way will be shown.*

If I put out energy, I will get more energy back.

> *Steam machine*
> *Full throttle*
> *Just beginning*
> *Don't get in your way*
> *I will help you*
> *I'll see you through*
> *You are not alone*
> *Never have been*
> *Are you ready now?*
> *Are you able?*
> *To whom much is given*
> *Much is expected*

Expect the best
Forget the rest
Partner
Every opportunity to succeed
Is yours, as you need
Write the book
Tune out, to tune in
Venture adventure
My business
Businesswoman
Grown up
Totally capable
Delegate
Visionary
Don't limit yourself
One step at a time
I always knew you could
Get My drift
There is a need
Why not you?
No arguing
Follow through
See clearly
Make a deal
Pay it forward
Play now
Ways to go
Many paths shown
Pick one
Follow Me
You will see
Success story
Build an empire
To My desire

For the good of all
For goodness sake
You are getting it
Don't wait too long
Move ahead now.

I'm possessed. Its okay, I gave my permission. I'm possessed by a wonderful loving spirit.

Go tell it on mountain
Sleep on it
Give it a rest
First impression
I have things to say
You are My voice
Loud and clear
Listen to Me
No naysayers welcome
Feel good club
Shining star
Everything is possible
No stopping
Remember Jesus, the Christ.

Fill me up Divine Love, premium fuel.

There is a need
See to it
Get it done
Help Me out
You have arms and legs
No limit living
Be happy and here
And you will be happy and there

Break the code
Do your work
Take care of yourself
Good News = Gospel.

We are told Jesus Christ came to preach the Good News, the Gospel. He and his apostles proclaimed the Good News while Jesus walked and talked as man, as Christ on earth, all before his crucifixion, death and resurrection. So what was this Good News they preached? Was it the same stories we have heard it in church and read in the bible? The stories that proclaim Jesus as the only Son of God and that Jesus was God and of his resurrection from the dead?

It couldn't have been. Jesus never proclaimed he was God, Jesus as Christ said he was one with God. His whole mission and ministry was focused on leading us on this same path, so each of us as well, may feel and know God as our Father. Know God so well and be so filled with Divine Love that God's will automatically becomes our will and thus we are as well "one in being with the Father," the Father, our Creator, Mother, Source, All, the Universe, Parent, Life, Wholeness, Completeness, return to our True Being.

To many it's a riddle that can't be solved. God is the key. It's not a brain thing. The brain is too small for such understanding. One has to let go of preconceived ideas, quiet the brain, the busy chattering mind. One has to check out of this physical reality and check in with their spiritual center. God is our spiritual core. God is good and good is our essence, our Truest Self. The one we forgot about. The one we stopped listening to. The one we don't trust. The one whom is waiting.

Saints and sinners, two groups or one? I want to be a saint. Please forgive my errors of thinking, speaking, judgment, non-action. Take me in, into Your arms. Hold me close. Never let me go. I need help. I need Your help. I am ready.

You called My name
Here I am
Private relationship
Go alone and pray
Go into your closet and pray
Invite Me in
Take Me in
No room for worry
Strength
Stronghold
Security
Breath
Flow
Flourish
Nourish
Enrich
Take it to the highest power
Power source
Take the lead
Re-search
Look again
Into the quiet
Find the calm
The blessing happens
Faith in the phenomenal
I am
Feel your way
Inner trust
Our moment
Dwell in the Light
Be patient
If we trust
There is no darkness
Do you have faith?

If so, faith in what?
You say, "Faith in God"
What do you mean by that?
Do you mean that you know God exists?
Do you mean that you know God?
Perhaps you say you have faith
Faith that God knows best for you
That you trust God's will
So what do you believe God's will is?
Do you say when something happens that
It is the will of God, just because it happens?
Is this your response, whether you perceive
A situation as good or bad?
Do you delight and praise God
When all is well?
Or do you give God a second thought?
As all is going so well for you
By your estimation that
You don't need God's help?
What about when you feel life is wrong
Or unfair to you or others
Do you blame God?
Do you ask why God
Would let bad things happen?
Do you accept this as the will of God?
Are you angry?
Do you think God is angry?
Mean and uncaring?

Wow, that's really heavy stuff and exactly what I believe many people believe. I once did too, but no more. I have a new understanding of God. I have a new understanding of how the universe works. I have a new understanding of how God's will is done. It's all up to us, each one of us really. The prayer attributed to Jesus Christ, the Lord's Prayer, says we are to pray "May Thy will be done." So what is God's will and how is it done? God's will is for each and every one of us to know His being intimately. We do this by silencing our own mind and tuning into the higher frequency of God mind. God gave each of us our own free will; free will to do as we like on our own, living only on the physical plane or rising higher and living higher by acknowledging and listening to our "spiritual essence." There, we find God.

God wants us each individually to seek Him. He wants us each to come home, back to His arms. He wants each of us to love Him and want His love. He is so ready to fill each one of us up with his all-powerful Divine Love. Divine Love is the essence of God. God offers the gift of His "divine essence" to each one. First we have to ready our hearts. We have to build a worthy temple, a worthy temple in our own being, the truth of us, our heart and soul.

Through Moses we learned of the Ten Commandments of God. Yes, this is God's will but as humans we find it not so easy to do. We most often fail at keeping these laws. God knows, He wants to help us, help Him. God wants to make it easier for each of us to help Him, to do His will. When we ready our hearts and drop to our knees and ask to be filled with His love, God will give His Divine Love to us. It's a one on one thing. No one can petition for another for God's will or God's love to fill another's soul. It's a matter of surrender, surrendering the idea of self importance, surrendering one's own will to the will of God.

> *Never fear, God's right here!*
> *Love is the opposite of fear*
> *God is Love*
> *Thus when one lives in fear*
> *They live as though God is not near*
> *God is good*
> *When you believe in good*
> *You believe in God*
> *Who fear's good?*

Look for good
Look for God
Good is not to be feared
God is not to be feared
Fear not
So is fear a sin?
To sin is to miss the mark
Sinning is error thinking
So what do you think?
God is our refuge
Make your heart a worthy place
A holy shrine for God
Fear not, God is with you
I am right here
Too good to be true
What a statement
What a sad statement
Life is good
You have to look for it though
Remember, seek and you shall find
It's a matter of what you are looking for
Not where you look
Open your eyes
Wipe away the mud.

I believe in good, for goodness sake. I believe good is the truth.

Find Me here
Walk this way
Way to go
Go ahead
Lend an ear
Leading the way
Universal viewpoint

All knowing
All seeing
The wonderful world of God
As you believe
Watch what you think
Be careful what you say
Be nice
Let your words be kind
Send love with every breath
Feel Me
Be Me
I need your presence
I need you
Inquire within
Divine council
Ask Me
Feelin' groovy
In the groove of life.

Whatever comes to me, I am not making this up.

For real
Real good
Real God.

I'd like to know more.

Information please
Wisdom ways
Incubate an idea
Sleep on it
The Gospel according to...
Matthew, Mark, Luke & John?
The Gospel word

The Gospel means "Good News"
God still speaks.

I am prompted, urged, possessed to record these "thoughts" that come to me. They are not to be divine secrets. They are to be told, to be written and to be recorded, to be manifested, to be shared. We are to be the voice of God in the physical, a link between the two worlds, a medium.

The Gospel is not the story of Jesus' life. It is the story of the life of Jesus who came to show us and tell us we each can live fully, joyfully, peacefully and abundantly. The Gospel, the good news, is still being told, told to all who listen, to those with "ears to hear," new spiritual ears. God still speaks. We are to listen, listen in, hear and share, show and tell.

Pick a possibility
Satisfaction indeed
Perfect timing
Here with you
Revolution evolution
Sins of omission
Be good, obedient to God's way
Be obedient
Submissive
What works.

The voice of Love is the voice of our very own reason for being. It is the voice of our Truest Being, our Highest Self. This voice of Love speaks with authority and valid reason that only this One can know and comprehend. The reasons why remain a mystery to our small selves. From our narrow perspective on the physical plane we cannot reason out the information given. We have to learn to trust the voice of Love and follow its urgings. Start small, pay attention, gain trust, gain ground, gain acceptance of the truth of this voice. The voice of Love has the good of all in mind for it sees and knows all and thus has the entire picture, all knowledge to work from. Only in hindsight can we as physical beings have this clarity.

> *Rewrite your program*
> *Call forth your good.*

It's about every cell of my body. My skin is only the outward manifestation.

> *So much more than skin deep*
> *Listen in, not out*
> *Inner vision manifests out*
> *Make yourself happy.*

Happy is as happy does. Joy be me.

OMG means "Oh, my goodness!" to me. It's an exclamation of joy, of wonder, of astonishment. For some it means "Oh, my God!" That's okay too. I don't see it as swearing and why should there be a problem with the word "God?" After all, God is good. God is goodness. So say it! Proclaim it!

> *This is who I am!*

February 2011

But when the Father sends the comforter instead of me - and by the comforter I mean the Holy Spirit – He will teach you much, as well as remind you of everything I myself have told you.

John 14:36 NLT

February 1, 2011

I have to have my quiet time. Each day I need some time alone to rest and reflect, a break in the day, time to plug in and recharge, inner renewal.

You have to live it, to know it
If you know it, show it
Take care of each other
Help yourself, by helping others
Selfless service
Self-service, not self-serving
Give back
Pay forward
Don't keep track
You are not here to judge
Only to be My love
Do unto others…
Serve others
Let others serve you
Don't make others serve you

Finding Peace
Knowing Peace
It's not a thinkin' thing
Rest in Peace
While you are alive
Be fully alive
Wide awake
Pay attention
Be here now
Peace
Serenity.

A person at Peace is at peace with himself. He knows, loves and trusts the very core of his being. He feels powerful and safe. He is joy. He is love, the love that Paul spoke about. When one finds Peace with God or Peace in God he is not easily ruffled by outer occurrences. The inner feeds the outer. There are no words. Words are not enough. Language limits so cannot describe the un-limitable. It's a feeling thing. Feel it to know it. Then you will show it.

Very natural
Super natural Agency
Innate capacity
We all have
Learn to access
Learn to work with
Allow
Open to unleash
Sensing
Validated
Don't test God for show
But for life
Experiment.

Show me the way.

> *It pays to discover*
> *You know more than you know*
> *Discovery zone*
> *Know your Source*
> *Come back to Me*
> *To others it seems silly*
> *Beyond your mind*
> *Grow to Me*
> *Visionary*
> *Highest perspective*
> *On a need to know basis.*

FEBRUARY 3, 2011

We are here to serve. We are to take care of each other. That's the plan, God's plan for a perfect universe, God's will. "Do unto others as you would have done unto yourselves." That should be easy to do, shouldn't it? We each know what makes us feel good so shouldn't it be easy and natural to treat others the same?

Sure, except for one big thing, the ego, the part of each of us that says "me, me, me," self concern, self-importance. It's a huge stumbling block for most of us. The ego says, "Hey, what about me? If I do this great thing for him, he will owe me big. Why should I go out of my way to help him, No one ever helps me? What will I get out of it? What's in it for me?"

Whenever we do unto others, or do for others ,with an agenda from our ego we totally miss the mark. We have to give from a place within our self that gives freely, expecting no payback. This is truly "selfless service." The thing that is so amazing about selfless service to others is it feels so great. I mean, besides the good done unto another a wonderful feeling of goodness comes to the giver. It really is better to give than receive.

We also have to learn to let go of our ego to receive ourselves. Others want and need to serve us. It may not be the same individuals that you have served but there will be a time when each of us could use some help from another. Let yourself graciously accept the kindness and generosity of others when offered. You will be giving them a gift in return, the gift of allowing them to give of themselves to you and thus feel the good of giving themselves.

It's hard to do. Your ego will fight it. The ego thinks it can do it all alone. The ego feels threatened by the idea of accepting help from anyone, with skin on or not. That is why we are to humble ourselves, be selfless, let the ego go. The Bible tells us to be meek. When one is meek they are not boastful, they are not directed by ego. Being meek is not being mousy, though I used to think so. I interpreted the term "meek" to describe a person with no will, no self respect, that allowed others to trample on their body and spirit. I missed the mark with that thinking. Now I understand that the true meaning of being meek, as Jesus told us was a requirement for entrance into the Kingdom of God, is to humble ourselves, to humble our egos.

Remember what Jesus said about how hard it was for a rich man to enter the Kingdom of God? Have you figured out why? It's about the ego issue again, self-importance, control, protecting one's territory, feelings of ownership and entitlement, and fear. Fear of releasing into the unknown. Fear of loosing what one has gained.

You can't take it with you, you know. Most of us live as if we will or we plan to. Our entire lives seem to be about acquiring material goods or wealth. This drive goes way beyond what we need or require to live day to day. Even up to the end of our days the ego says, "More, more, more."

The only limitations I have in life are the ones I impose on myself.

Silence yourself
Come here
Come hear
Here and now
Deep inside
What a thrill
Have your fill
As you need to know
The way I will show
Friends for life
Life without strife
Listen in
Hear Me now
I'll tell you how
Follow Wisdom's ways
All your days
Break free
Of what you thought life
Should be
I have so much more
For you in store
Let Love guide
No love you should hide
Play along
Sing My song
I'll tell you true
What I need you to do
See it all now
Don't worry about the how
As you breathe
That's how easy it is
To follow Me
Open up
See clearly

Know I love you so dearly
Feels so good
Yes, God's love should
As you rise
In you I come alive
I've been telling you
All along what to do
Breath
The breath of Life.

I want to know. I'm supposed to grow.

Back to basics
See things My way
I have bigger plans for you
More than you can imagine
I'm just getting you ready
About the money
Why are you holding on to it?
You know it is not yours
You know all I have it yours
There's more to come
Pay your bills today
All will be okay.

I have all the help I need, personal guidance system activated. Things keep happening.

Ever wonder why?
Life tastes good
As it should.

I'm the intuitive, the creative, the decision maker. I am a creative force. The force is with me; I am it, self-directed, my Higher Self. Self discipline?

No, that's different.
Follow Me
I'm sending good things your way
Clearer reception
Fine tune
Tune in
Tune up
Get rid of the static
It's interference
Hear My beautiful music
Music to your ears
Your eyes will see
My glory
Glory be
Let Me flow
Flow through you
They do not know
The way you will show
Don't keep it all in
That's the beginning of
What you call sin.

My eyes have seen
What's yet to be
I want you here
Here with Me
Divinely inspired
In life you'll rise higher
The way it was
Again shall be
Careful now
Walk with Me
See the beauty
Through Thine eyes.

Consumer driven society
Out of touch
With True Reality
Much they don't know
Seeds of debt and doubt
They continue to sow.

Feed My people
Show them how
Show them where
Show them now
It's not all been false
It's not all been a lie
There have always been truths
Hidden in the night
The day has come
Today's the day
No longer the lies of night
Get in your way.

The ego as the antichrist
Ego is me, me, me
Christ is others first
Ego = self-consciousness
Versus
Divine Mind as Christ Consciousness.

Where is this coming from?

From whence all came
Our Source
True Love
True Wisdom
Truth.

I'm learning here.

> *Make a conscious choice*
> *Raise your consciousness*
> *You've always had a choice*
> *Now you know*
> *Know better*
> *Do better*
> *Consciously create*
> *Faith matters*
> *Free prize inside.*

By my estimation, God has gotten "a bad rap." Haven't you heard people refer to one another and say that he or she "got the fear of God?" To me that means that the driving force behind their desire to restrain from "evil" acts is fear of God's punishment or eternal damnation. I believe when the Bible uses the word "fear" it would be better to replace it with "awe and admiration" or "deepest reverence."

If anyone fears God, they truly do not know God. To know God is to have God live in your heart. When you have invited God into your life, your whole life, all you feel is love, for love is God. God is wisdom as well, and God's well of wisdom is deep and never dry. *"Come to My well and drink,"* God says. *"Dip your cup into My everlasting waters and drink. I desire to have my people satisfied."*

Who are his people? Each one of us God claims. But remember relationships are two sided. Have you welcomed God into your heart? If your heart is hard and hateful it's a sure sign you have not. We are to build beautiful temples for God by honoring our bodies and make ready quiet sanctuaries in our mind and our heart. We are to set aside our selfishness, our egos. How is God to fill us up with His Divine Love if we are already so full of ourselves? Ready your heart and ask God to guide you and fill you to your heart's content.

FEBRUARY 18, 2011

Ideas, "Free for all." That's what ideas are, available to everyone waiting to be grasped from the ethers of our Universal Mind. No one can lay claim to an idea. They can only lay claim to what they do with the idea. Having an idea is one thing, uniquely expressing it for all, materializing it is totally another.

> *You are more than you think*
> *Expand your mind*
> *Don't you think*
> *Can you walk the walk?*
> *Or just talk the talk?*
> *Words leave much unsaid*
> *There's more to know*
> *Whatever you say*
> *Say what you want*
> *Raise your standard of living.*

I used to live in fear. Now I live in love.

> *Entitlement versus opportunity*
> *Who are you cheating?*
> *You only cheat yourself*
> *Wisdom ways*
> *The sun always shines*
> *See it this way.*

"We have to worry about these things now," reports a TV news statement referring to some kind of solar storm predicted to attack earth. But it could have been a report about anything as this is the continual message given to us by our media. Our society feeds on this fear, feeds on drama. We are to worry, we are told, be concerned. Caring and worrying are not the same. Caring is a loving response. Worrying is a fear reaction.

Too much news, too much bad news, they say it is what the world wants for if people didn't tune in to hear it, the constant reporting of if would stop. Is there more "bad" now than ever? Most probably not, we just hear about it more. We hear about more bad situations and as well have the same bad situations repeatedly told again and again. Twenty-four hour news channels allow opportunity for us to drown in this deep hole of dissatisfaction with the world.

Some say, "Gosh, why won't they leave that subject alone? We've already heard that!" I say it's up to each of us to choose what we want to tune in to. What you tune in to, you turn into. Tune into the constant doom that the media feeds or turn it off. How many times do you need to hear the same message anyway? Think of it like this. People used to read the daily news in the morning paper, once. I doubt that too many of us would pick up that same paper and reread the same news article again and again whenever throughout the day our eye caught sight of the newspaper laying on the table. Instead the news was read once and then we got on with our day.

We each have the choice to be informed as we wish. There is a lot more information to be gathered and grasped in this world, for the benefit of all than just what is commercially sponsored and fed to the masses by our mass media.

> *It's there*
> *It's here*
> *The good stuff*
> *Free for all*
> *Just ask, we've been told*
> *Seek and ye shall find*
> *Look for the good*
> *Fear not*
> *Love one another*
> *Be the helping hand*
> *Look up*

Look inside
Don't let your light hide
Listen in
See what's here
The sun always shines
Know this
Today is good
Today is the day the Lord has made
Let us be glad and rejoice.

"It happened just as I feared," seems to be a pretty common statement these days. When I hear it said, I hear as well the confidence in the speaker's voice as if they had special knowing powers to predict the future. Like "See, I told you this would happen, I just knew. That's why I worried about it so."

"So," you may be saying, "So what? That's a common story." Well, I say, whoa, we all need to take a step back and look and listen and hear, here and now. I've gained a fresh and powerful insight into the power of our thoughts. When we fear something and worry about it, we are strengthening that energy, in essence magnetizing more of the same to manifest in our lives. So it is actually a given, by the Universal Law of Attraction, that what we worry about will come true for us. It's not magic. It's reality.

Sadly most of us have been in the dark, not seeing the light of this truth. We are always creating. We each live our lives governed by the same laws, which rule the universe. When we become conscious of how the world works, we can make it work for us. Conscious creation is the goal here.

What makes our world seem so twisted to me is that there is so much noise about the bad. The bad one can see and even more about the bad one can imagine. Everywhere we are being given messages of fearing the worst. Ideas put in our head of possible sicknesses we could get or may have. We are told that the world is full of lack and we need to grab hold and hold close in fear. Horrible messages to fill one's mind. The more that hear, the more that believe and the more that manifest. Manifest what, more bad?

Watch out
Listen in
It's time to break the cycle
If you don't do it someone else will
It is your time now
Time to listen
Time to act
Time to move
I'm inspiring you to create
The new
Work with Me
Work for Me
This is good work
This is God's work
Make your story worth telling
Move over
Let Me in
Be worthy of your dreams
You are worthy of your dreams
Live like you know it
Know the best
Expect the best
Be the best
Claim it
Go for it
Take claim
Own up
See where you are going
Get ready
Be alert.

FEBRUARY 20, 2011

Who runs your life? Do you or others? "They made me so mad!" you say. Why, I say, why let another, any other choose your mood? You need to inoculate yourself from catching the pissy disease. Someone else had it and gave it to you and now you want to give it to me. Stop right there sir, if you want to be pissy that's your choice but not mine. I choose to deny any idea of your pissy-ness having the ability to affect my state of being. I'm walking away. I'm not playing this game. It's no use for me to attempt to talk you out of it now. It would do more harm than good, at least for me. You see your ego has been bruised and now it is on the defense. The one who challenged your ego isn't here but I am.

Here's the deal, my ego no longer runs my life. I can see that your attacks on me are not about me, they are about you, about your ego's need to be right, your ego's need to be treated with respect. Egos like to dance with other egos. I let my ego go. I set my ego free, free from the need to control me. I wish for you this freedom. Peace be you, my friend.

FEBRUARY 21, 2011

You have to feel good about yourself
Take care
Appreciate what you have
See more
Want more
You were born to fly
Feel good about who you are
Be excited about who you are becoming
Know Yourself
Know your limitless Self
Yes, I am
See everything you need
Fulfill your dreams

Dream big
Life tastes good
Feel good about it all and have fun
Only place to go is up
Know no limits
Play fair
Speak the truth
Start fresh
Each day anew
Use your words wisely
Play My game by the rules and win
Win at life
Love life
Live life as Love
I love you
My love is for you
Make it all happen
I'll see you through
What are you waiting for?
Clear the way
It's not the end
It's just the beginning
The beginning of
A new chapter
Of the story of
Your life
Read between the lines
It's a very good story
Adventure
Mystery
Discovery
Success
Love
Comedy
Journey.

If it can be done, I can do it!

See it through.

Everything I need is coming to me. I'm on my way.

> *Special delivery*
> *Don't worry about it*
> *You are not that far down the road*
> *When you come to a fork*
> *In the road you will*
> *Know what to do.*

> *You can let your circumstances*
> *Define you*
> *Or refine you*
> *Plan for more*
> *Be careful what fire you fuel*
> *Don't add fuel to the fire*
> *Only the fires of your desire.*

FEBRUARY 28, 2011

> *Why don't you trust?*
> *Don't you know that I*
> *Always have your best interest?*
> *Start with little things*
> *Then you will know*
> *Then you will live*
> *Live in Me.*

I know what I am doing, but not how I am doing it.

Believe nature
Nature knows
Don't keep your good
Share it
Shine it
There is so much more to come
Go to the hills
Climb higher
A silent urging
Spirit calling
Nature calling.

We've all heard the stories, stories of an animal's behavior before a major physical event happens. Tales of wild creatures making their way to safe ground way before man has any hint of danger. I'm thinking about the horrible tsunami that was experienced a few years ago. Upon reflection, it was realized that many beasts had done just that. But why, we ask? Just how did they know? I believe they sensed it, but not in any physical sense. They each simply reacted to a quiet urging, within. Some gentle force propelled them to move and with each step they felt safer and safer.

Most approach this matter as a pure case of matter. I mean physically, scientifically, and would agree with me that these animals did indeed sense something before the recognized event occurred. The difference being that most are purely looking for physical sensations as the answer, like the animals were more sensitive to minor shaking, vibrations, of the ground. Yet, seldom do people look up or within for answers.

This all made me think about the biblical story of Noah, his ark and the animals. Firstly, Noah should be commended for listening and trusting God's prodding to build a boat. Physically this made no sense to Noah, as all he could see was sunshine in the sky; no dark clouds forbade any concept of a great storm. He had no reference even of past floods in the area, but gladly and this is to be the lesson for all of us, he heeded God's Message. He built an ark despite the rolling eyes of all who ventured past and snickered at his "crazy project." Building a massive boat on dry land far from a waterway on which he would ever sail. I wonder if he bothered to tell them that God told him to? That surely would have been seen as a crazy idea as well. "God talking to a man? This man? Why, who and just what does he think he is? It's blasphemy!"

So Noah did his best, as God knew he could and would. He built a wonderfully huge boat then he proceeded to fill it up with animal pairs as God instructed. This is all a story, mind you. A true story? Well, I do know there is a lesson in it. So I think of it as a "truth story." About here in the story people really tend to doubt the truth. The mind is ever questioning, doubt and reason come into play. How on earth (or on the ark) could Noah have ever loaded up all the animals in the world to save them? My thoughts? He didn't, but he did do his best.

Was God mad? No, God knew Noah did his best and besides I believe God doesn't just reserve His Wisdom for his two legged creatures. He loves us all and thus wants the best for all. Regarding the door upon which we are to "knock" to open communication with our Highest Source, I believe that the other creatures inhabiting our earth plane have no such door installed. They have no sense of self, no sense of separateness. What they need to know, they just know. They do not possess a reasoning mind which argues, thus they act as "inspired". We call this their "animal instinct."

So, back to those crawling creatures that Noah missed. God took care of them. They sensed an unease where they were, which lessoned with each step they took to higher ground. There was higher ground which was a safe haven waiting for them. God planned it that way. You say the Bible story doesn't mention it. That's because it couldn't be seen. That doesn't mean it didn't exist and that is the whole point of this story. Just because something can't be seen, doesn't mean it doesn't exist. For many seeing is believing. For me, believing is seeing.

MARCH 2011

For His Holy Spirit speaks to us deep in our hearts,
and tells us that we are God's children,
and since we are His children,
we will share in His treasures for all
God gives His son Jesus, is now ours too.

ROMANS 8:16 NLT

MARCH 3, 2011

Come to Me
I see clearly
I'm above it all
With Me you walk tall
Be not afraid
I go before thee always
Come follow Me
And I will lead thee home
Don't give up
Stay close to Me
You are almost there
Just around the bend
My eyes can see
Your glory

I've been telling you
Don't try and think of everything
There is much to know
When it is your time I will show
Clear your mind
Know which way is up
I'll take it from there
You be here.

I believe all the good stuff is divinely inspired, pure and simple, not complicated, just good. You know the prayer that begins "God is good?" I used to think that "good" was meant to be an attribute of God. Now I see that the true meaning if that "God equals good," they are synonymous. Just like God is love. The purest form of love, Divine Love equals God. That is the love Paul spoke about, not many people know Divine Love nor express it. Instead they confuse human love with all it's tendencies for error as the best it gets. Human love, which we are all innately capable of, can be good but it is not perfect. We know this because we have each been hurt by this love. As much as one tries to love fully, our humanness gets in the way.

True love, Divine Love never hurts. It feels oh, so good! Good to receive it and good to share it. It's "the real deal," what we have all been waiting for, what we keep looking for. This stuff, Divine Love, truly satisfies, satisfies the soul. The only hunger there is, is for more and more Divine Love. It's a good hunger feeling because it's the purest desire which God gladly will continue to pour out into your soul upon earnest request.

Most probably don't have a reference point to this matter of which I speak. I certainly did not even just two years ago, but now I know. I know the truth, the truth of which Jesus spoke, the truth of God's love which is available for all, he told us how, he showed us how, he told us we could have a relationship with God just as he. He called God "Father." Did Jesus ever say "God?" I remember only "My Father, who art in Heaven." This distinguished title told us he was not referring to Joseph, his earthly father. I as well know the "Father" feeling. My Father, Who is in Heaven, hallowed be His name, because no name, no word is sufficient.

I know my Father, who is in Heaven. He has called my name. Actually, there is no "He" or "She," as this Great Spirit has no sex. Attributes of both male and female are part of God but God cannot be defined by either. That concept is again limiting. I guess it just feels right to say "He" because "He" is more personal than "It." So I say, "My Father, Great Spirit, who is everywhere and all."

I know my Father, who is in Heaven. He feels like the most loving and caring spirit. The only reference point I have to this feeling is the love given to me by my own birth parents. My birth father has now risen, raised above the earth plane. I know this. I know much. Much is communicated to me in such a pure loving way. I know that this is communication from my father, yet which father?

> *The One*
> *The One and only True Being*
> *All*
> *All is well.*

All is well with me.

> *Say it again*
> *All is well and all will be*
> *Keep thinking of Me.*

> *And Love said*
> *To each his own*
> *What you give you get*
> *It's good to learn*
> *Nice to see you smile.*

Can energies be here and there at the same time?

> *Yes, because energies are non-local. Spirit is everywhere, no boundaries, and no limits. So why limit yourself?*

I'm beginning to see.

> *Yes, you are, just beginning. There is much to know. But you need not and never will, know it all, so just enjoy today. Let it be. Let it be good. Good for you. Good for all. Trust Me.*

> *You walked away*
> *I'm proud of you*
> *You didn't need it*
> *Any of it*
> *You have what you need*
> *But it's okay to look*
> *As long as you see.*

It's a nice day.

> *Everyday is a nice day*
> *I make them all that way*
> *It's just what you make of it*
> *It's all there*
> *Always*
> *Forever and again*
> *The sun always shines*
> *Know where to look*
> *See through My eyes*
> *My eyes can see*
> *Sometimes yours are cloudy.*

I'm so excited. I see it all now on its way, way to me, as I believed.

> *So it be.*

I believe in good
I believe in God
I put my faith in good
I trust God.

Special delivery system
Now operational
As always.

I'm just now learning the operating system.

All systems go
No need to keep track
I know where you are going
You are going My way
I delight in you
Sing My song
Loud and clear
I'll be with you always
I love you My dear.

No matter where I am, You are. I feel Your Presence, Your love, Your guidance. Thank you, I need You. You are my light Brilliant Beacon, my North Star. Wherever I am, You are.

MARCH 5, 2011

"What good would that do?" It's a question worth asking. Here's another. "Would it do more harm than good?" My response, aim to harm none. Be good for all. Pause and think, before speaking. Instead of asking, "Where's the harm?" ask, "Where's the good?" there must be only good for all.

People love a good story, especially one with a happy ending. That's what mine is, a happy tale, a true story, a story worth sharing, news worthy, an interesting angle.

> *Celebrate who you are*
> *I'm so proud of you!*
> *Put your name on it*
> *Stand beside it*
> *Stand behind it*
> *Be proud.*

Fill me up, up with love. Take me higher. Your love is my desire. I'm breaking free of the old me. With every breath I taste life not death. My young heart will live forever.

How I understand life: We are one, one in spirit, yet experiencing life differently from our many unique perspectives. Life as a whole is too big for any one of our unique perspectives to begin to grasp the wholeness or entirety of it. Life is infinite. Life is continual. Life is cause and effect. I know this and yet I feel alone. I experience sadness. Is it okay to feel alone? Is it okay to feel sad?

> *It's okay*
> *It's good to recognize your feelings*
> *Your feelings are real*
> *Your feelings are true*
> *Be true to yourself*
> *When you are sad*
> *When you feel alone*
> *Come to Me*
> *Ask Me to hold you closer*
> *I will*
> *I am with you*
> *Listen in*
> *I am here*

Here with you
Remember how much I love you.
There is no difference between
A soul with a physical body
And a soul free from the physical
Other than awareness
Your soul knows the truth
The truth of your being
All there is
All there is to know.

I want someone to take care of me, someone to hold me and tell me that all is well. I want to lean on someone stronger. Help me Jesus, I am weak. You are strong. Be my strength. Show me the way. I beg of you. I will follow where you lead. Lead me, I pray. Give me Your strength. Show me the light, light my way. It is so dark where I am. Joy find me here, S.O.S. I do, I do trust in You. I trust in God. I trust in good but I am weak. Help my unbelief, shake my soul. Wake my soul. Raise my spirit.

Of one mind, I channel higher thoughts, thoughts new to me. From where? Nowhere, just there, everywhere. I gain the advantage of a higher and broader perspective. Only the highest and best I request. What's happening to me? Tell me true, I need to know. Please tell or show.

MARCH 8, 2011

Where is Heaven?

There is no other.

My mother-in-law Audine passed to the other side of the veil today. We can no longer touch her but that doesn't mean we can no longer feel her. She was good to go. Audine only took one thing with her, our love. She is now truly a free spirit.

The brain is the processing unit for physical reality.

Let it be
Be with Me
Come along for the ride
The ride of your life
Good times
Good times for all
Amen.

The soul is a sole job
Soul responsibility
Sole responsibility
Soul work
Soul growth
Soul purification.

Make me more like You. Make me remember. Help me remember. Call me back.

Total recall
Promotion
High aspirations
Rise up and meet Me
In so few words
Know your soul Truth
The Whole Truth
Truth be told.

Do I fit in? Do I need to fit in? If I feel good just being me isn't that good enough? Isn't that my mission? I believe so, but it's easy to forget. It's easy to get "sucked into" society's expectations and measures, and then feel bad when you don't fit in just right. Not many people feel comfortable "in their own skin." They judge themselves according to other's ideals and standards and when they don't measure up they think less of themselves. Why are we all so concerned about what other's think of us? Why the need to fit in and not stand out?

*There is safety in numbers, perceived safety, as in
camouflage and blending into a group.*

I am an individual. I am part of the One. I am of the One. I, as each, of
the All have a unique viewpoint. From here I see differently. I celebrate
my uniqueness. I as well celebrate other's uniqueness. As we share
our visions, our perspective widens. We grow. We rise. I am a unique
expression of God.

MARCH 9, 2011

> *Everything you want*
> *Everything you need*
> *Is within your power*
> *Dream big*
> *Don't doubt your purpose*
> *See with Me*
> *The soul truth is the sole truth*
> *Who but you is going to make*
> *your dreams a reality?*
>
> *The power of perfect*
> *God's perfect law.*
>
> *Hear the thunder*
> *Hear the roar*
> *Know that for you*
> *I have only good in store.*

Rain Your Good down upon me.

> *All blessings flow*
> *You have to want it*
> *You have to believe*

Yourself worthy
You are
Just because
You are
Know this
Know Me
Open up
Rise up
The soul truth
Is the whole truth
Lay in wait
Be ready
Be prepared
Prepare yourself
For My feast
Don't rush forward
Receive My blessings
Be grateful for all
All is good
All is God
Live like you know it
Your heart will show it.

Shh
Stop thinking
Start knowing
Start glowing
Shine through
Through the smog
Through life's fog
Be the light
Bring day to night
Easy access
Admittance for all

Attendance required
Your presence needed
In My Presence
No pretense
Feel your way
Go live today.

MARCH 21, 2011

Do as you are told
and you will be justly rewarded
Drop the dead wood.

We've got it wrong. That's not the point, Christ says. It never was about bearing the weight of the cross not for Him, not for us. We are to drop the dead weight of the cross and rise up. The priest told us again last Sunday that we all have our own crosses to bear. He was asking us, telling us, to think of them, to bear their weight. But if we keep tied to the heaviness of our physical weights we will remain planted in this physical plane. Our spirits cannot soar when we have both feet so deeply planted in the ground.

Rise up
Release
Soar
Glide
Grasp a new idea
The idea of the peace of Heaven.

Yes, we here on earth can have the peace of Heaven, Heaven on earth, Heaven above earth. But each time we concentrate on our physical woes, they become mental and then spiritual woes, dragging us down. Did we ever hear Jesus complain? He might have commented, but he didn't complain. He kept his thoughts high. He lived in continual communion with "His Father," as we are to do as well. Some call this

"The Golden Key," the key to all the treasures of Heaven. Whenever you find your thoughts low, tied to trouble, raise them by thinking of God, the glory of God. Thank God again and again.

Coasting or sailing? Some seem to coast through life, but coasting is a downhill action. I choose to rise higher, soar. When the wind is at one's back the hills of life don't seem so steep. Divine Love is the wind at my back, propelling me forward, raising my spirit, sailing me away.

> *We believe in possibilities*
> *What you seek*
> *You shall see*
> *Seek Me*
> *With all your heart, mind and soul*
> *Let Me be your soul/sole purpose*
> *Rise up and meet Me*
> *The day is here.*

I don't have to do this all alone. I have an excellent advisory board always present, ready and available for the asking.

> *Don't focus on what you can't have or don't have. Focus on what can have or do have. Then you will have more, more of what you want.*

Who cares?

> *I do. I am here with you.*

Sometimes it's better to know less. What do self-proclaimed "know it all's" really know anyway?

> *They know limits, while others not "in the know," know no limits. It's whatever you know. Watch what you know. Be cautious with your word. Choose carefully. Remain calm.*

Don't look the wrong way
Look up
The answers are here
The answers are clear
Clear to Me
Soon you will see
Don't try to run with the crowd
Live your life quietly
Not out loud
Run free
Run to Me
Life is not a race
Go at your own pace.

It's good to know
The way I'll show
Come home
Home to Me
I'll help you see clearly
True inspiration
Love is true
Love is always
Love is forever
Live in love
Love in life
Make Love your life
And you will never die
Live on My young heart
Live fully and freely

My love is for you
I've shown you what to do
Live for Me
Love with Me

Be Me for all
I'll hold you up
You will never fall.

MARCH 23, 2011

Stop arguing every point! If someone else chooses to think
about all of life's potential problems, let them. Haven't you
figured out yet that the only one you can control is yourself?
And you seem to have some work to do there any way. So
take care of yourself. Mind your own business and good will
fall into place.

Let it go
Go on
Don't say
Try it
You'll like it!

There is "Wally-World" and there is "Wallow World." A lot of people
seem to enjoy visiting "Wallow World." Quite a few appear to have taken
up permanent residence. If you want to participate in social activities
they have a group for you. Or you can form a new one and invite your
friends to "wallow" with you in your muck. If time alone is what you
desire, you can wallow away at home in the depth of your woes.

Don't be afraid to ask. Speak with authority.

Thanks for all the help.

Go team! Yeah us! Good for all, all for one. Single minded.
Shake your head and laugh it off.

The money will be here when you need it. Take care of what
is before you now. It's yours to do. Say it so. Like we've been

telling you all along, get along. Sing a happy song. Believe in the best. Forget the rest. Do your best. Listen in. Rise up. Don't think so much. Feel your way. Live fully each day. Set sail. Go with the flow. Read the signs.

Help is available. Just ask believing. See, it's true. We've been telling you all along just what to do. Do good, be good, see good. The way life works, we each live our own reality. What we know is what we know. Know more, all in good time. Created with love. Love makes the world go 'round.

MARCH 25, 2011

I know the way. I am the way. The way is clear, clear for Me, clear to Me. Let My light shine. Shine forth My love. Celebrate who you are. Trust yourself. I am in you. Live fully. Breathe deeply. Be alive.

MARCH 26, 2011

I need to thank you, thank you all, all of us. You are showing me possibilities, oh so many possibilities. Possibilities that are manifesting before my eyes making all my dreams come true. Thank you for making it so easy for me. Everything I am given, everything I am shown, is so much bigger and better than what I could have began to imagine. I am pleased that I am learning to work with the system.

Remember, ask and it shall be given? Give thanks.

Apparently, the rules that are in place don't allow anyone outside of yourself to direct, guide or help you unless you specifically ask. It goes back to the free will we have each been given. We each make what we want of our own lives. We can do it all alone or "call a friend." Friends and family are always eager to aid us, to steer us in the right direction and to help us make the connections we need to make to make our visions the highest reality.

> *See what you like.*

It's hard to go it alone.

> *You are hardly "going it alone." We are with you. Listen to Our voice. I've seen you through. See through to Me.*

> *It's so easy to get sucked into other people's drama. Don't be a drama queen. Hear Me now. Fly away. No room for doubt. No doubt about it. Don't doubt for a minute. Don't doubt yourself. Listen up. Things are changing before your eyes, behind the scenes. Act two begins now. Change of plot.*

How many people live exemplary lives?

> *Much to be learned, the illusion of separateness. Our individuality no longer separate. Oneness means disappearance of me. All for One. One for All. The way it is supposed to be. To be one with Love you have to let go of the past. Oneness is expansiveness. Oneness is ordained. Ecstasy of Oneness, only language of Love.*

It came to me.

> *Don't judge. Have fun. No elite class, no better, no worse. Of one mind, agree. Don't be mad. There is only Love. Be glad. Stay true. There is much to do. Stay on-line, stay connected with the Divine.*

MARCH 28, 2011

I am constantly amazed God. You are so great. I am, Your love. Your love is mine. Everyday I rise higher, closer to the Divine. Help me see.

Help me be who I am. Help me to live Spirit's grand plan.

You can learn. Love conquers all. Live the truth.

Jesus told me. This I know. As I believed. In the know, in the now.

Be here now with Us. There is nothing to worry about. See with Me. I am True, truly You.

MARCH 29, 2011

I'm alive today. I've learned some lessons. I still have a lot of time on my hands.

Don't worry your pretty little head.

I live in "the zone" just call me "Flow." Angels watching over me. I can judge no one. I have no place, no right. Everyone has a unique journey. The only path I have walked and can walk is my own.

I believe in laughter.

What you see now, it's all temporary. The only thing that lasts is Love.

I'm not realistic. I was lead here.

Instead of saying, "I don't know what it is." Say, "I'll be shown what it is." Play along, these signs say. Trust Me. Trust Yourself. Desperation is lousy inspiration.

APRIL 2011

Haven't you yet learned that your body
is the home of the Holy Spirit
God gave you and that he lives within you?

1 CORINTHIANS 6:19 NLT

APRIL 1, 2011

I'm no fool. No foolin'.

Everybody is born "in the zone." I mean every soul in a body is not
only "fresh from Heaven" but still there. We are not "born" with a sense
of separateness, we learn it. We are conditioned. We are taught. We are
told. We are "civilized" and "de-spiritualized." We are "reprogrammed"
but not "rewired." Nope, nobody can change who we really are. It's still
there, all there. The innate connection we have with the Divine, lost to
our own awareness perhaps but always at hand. Jesus was reminding us
of this when he said, *"The Kingdom of Heaven is at hand."*

One needs not even to reach. It is already within, within each of us, all
the Power and Presence of God. We are to seek this "Kingdom of God"
this eternal and internal land of good. We are to seek it ourselves and
to acknowledge its existence in all others, whether they themselves
have come to recognize and demonstrate this truth or not. As one
finds his way, his way back to his truth, to the light of God, he becomes
illumined. His light shines. This light becomes a beacon of hope for all
others still foraging through the forest of doubt.

But oh to live in joy! Oh sings my soul. My eyes have seen the glory. These words are mine now, my truth, my reality. I write the songs of joy, my psalms.

I don't need to hear that. Those things you say. The fear and doubt in your voice. If you won't stop then I will. I will stop listening. I work with a higher power, a frequency so strong, so loud and clear that I can hear no others. Shh, be quiet. Go away. Get out of my way.

> *Get rid of that which does not serve you; otherwise you will end up serving it.*

I truly believe out of sight is out of mind.

> *Yes, your small mind. When something arises in your consciousness that has no physical trigger, it is from Divine Mind, your Higher Self. Listen and obey and give thanks for the help.*

> *Carefully set and declare your intentions just like you would choose your words for a "Google" image search. You wouldn't type in "not fat" when you are looking for images of "skinny." You have to declare all your intentions in the same form. Don't say, "I don't want to fail." Say, "I want to succeed."*

I feel that I've been born again, as I see the entire world anew.

> *Stay tuned. You've come a long way. The path to success, eternal reward. Fly away. Glide home. It's all about now. Be here now. Chime in. Be the breeze. Live with ease. See more. Be more. Live more. More to come. Come with Me. Don't tarry. Live merry.*

Say it as you see it or see it as you say it. Seeing is believing or believing is seeing. Believe as you want. Believe what you want. What do you believe? Prove it to yourself. Be in the know. I'm in the know. Make-believe. You pretend, before you tend. Have faith. Believe. Believe in the best for all.

Find it. Find it here. Beneath your feet, at hand. Neither here nor there, everywhere, always, forever and again. You can be so much if you will, will let "My will" be done. Listen in. Hear again. Never too soon. Ready now. Prepare yourself. No need to wait. All can be seen here with Me. No division, all together. Best for one, best for all. The only way it can be. Live worry free, no pain to flee. Live fully a life of glee.

He came to show, so you would know the way to go. As it was, as it is, the only way to truly live. Open up. Rise higher. We are here to fill your desire. There is no other. Nothing is truer than the truth. Seek to flow. Seek to glow. Be filled with My love from Heaven within, not above.

Burst forth. Break free. You are on your way to eternal life with me. So few know. So few show. So few glow. Light the way. Shine brighter everyday. They will want what you have. Share freely as asked. When each is ready, they will be blessed. No need to push. No need to shove. All you need is Divine Love. Deliverables, where there's a will there's a way.

Our free will allows us to believe what we want. If you believe it, the Universe (thinking stuff), thinks you want it, thus creates it. Thus we believe in what we want. What we have faith in, we believe true, we create for ourselves.

My whole world has been turned upside down and yet I now see that for the first time it is actually right side up. Do you agree with me? Do you see life as I do? Whatever you think, whatever you believe, is up to you.

I know for myself. Self-evident truths continually validate my new understanding of this world so big, so infinite, yet so personal and whole. Life is good. Life is a force. Energy's truest form, Love, propels me forward.

Be Me fully.

APRIL 4, 2011

I'm okay with advisors but not dictators. Well, actually I'm not too sure about the idea of advisors, at least not those "with skin on." I really do and always have danced to the beat of my own drum, an inner rhythm that no one else can hear but is oh so real to me. It's always been clearly audible. Sometimes I've danced to it and sometimes I have doubted it.

Those times of doubt, doubt of the truth I felt and knew, were difficult times. Awkward and clumsy were my actions. I lived outside the "Flow of Life" within me. I was not true to Myself. It did not feel well and I did not feel well.

No one knows, no one "else" knows, what is truly best for another. Only "Self" knows. So listen in. Listen up. Hear and heed your "Inner Wisdom." It's your life, your unique path you are to follow. Listen and be led to the wonder of your wonderful life.

> *You are, what you think you are. The song you sing is the vibration you bring.*
>
> *In people, we call it intuition. In animals, we call it instinct. Sometimes, you just have to distance yourself from others to get to know Yourself. To thine own Self be true, not to someone else's idea of what you are to be.*

What are you trying to prove and just whom are you trying to prove it to? You don't need to prove a thing. All truth is self evident, evident only to the self that desires to know.

What do people want?

They want to feel good. They are naturally drawn to what makes them feel good, magnetized. Unfortunately often, people feel good for the wrong reasons. They feel better about themselves and their lives when they can compare them with much worse situations or behavior. Comparison is judging.

So why don't people like to be around others who are happier, healthier and more successful?

Again, it's about judgment. We are judging ourselves as less. Often we are drawn to the positive energy of another.

I'm given understanding. My art, when it came so easily to me that it felt as if it "fell from the sky," did not feel valid to me, even though it was a "wondrous" work of art. It felt too easy. It felt like cheating. I saw "hard work" as valid work. I didn't trust or understand the validity of instinct, inspiration and intuition.

There is no hiding. Truth be told. All life abides by the same rule, same force, same truth. There is one Life, one Source of truth.

Some people say get out of your own way. There is more life to know and that we are hardly aware of the wonders life has to share. They say that each of us is in charge, of first ourselves then the world at large. That what we say and what we think makes our life happy or makes it stink. What if you knew this to be true? What then, I ask you, would you do? Would you say you didn't care, once you were truly aware?

Once you knew, would you, could you, live the same knowingly creating with only self to blame?

I give thanks for spring, new growth, new opportunity. Refresh my soul. Color my world.

> *This is the time. You are here presently. Within your grasp. Think forwardly. Let bygones be bygones. Self-directed, paint a bigger picture. Paint off the canvas. Cover the walls. Paint the sky with dreams on high.*

> *So what? Someone "important" paid attention to you, so what? Did you puff up like a proud peacock? Someone said something bad about you, so what? Did you believe them? Did you hang your head in shame?*

> *Why do you let what others think of you matter? You do have to "let it" matter you know. You are the only one who controls what "matters" to you. Whatever you give your attention to you make matter. What matters to you, what you care about, thus what you think about, becomes "matter," physical, in your life. It's a matter of fact. There is nothing holding you back.*

I'm on top of the world. It feels good to be me.

> *Listen to this good advice given freely. See what you think. Live the good life.*

I'm so worth it.

> *Don't discount yourself. Be true. Don't see trouble. Life is fair. We all play by the rules. Not many truly understand them. Think a new way. What you see is what you get. Call*

My name. I'll be there. Expand your mind. Life is more than you think. It is what you are. Don't sell your soul. Don't look back. Move forward. Try and see. Say what you want. Want more. See what you want. Envision (in-vision) it first.

Some people are so much more evolved than others.

Stop saying can't and you'll find a way. What would you do if you knew you could? God, Our ultimate good, seeks expression through each of us.

So many thoughts run through my mind.

APRIL 11, 2011

Find a way, a way to Me. There are so many paths because you come from so many different directions. Find your own way. There are many a guiding light but you have to look. You have to seek. You have to deeply desire. Desire higher. It's all within, not without. What you find, you keep. But you have to look, look deep. Continue My dear to seek, to see the Light. Step into it. Don't wait for your last breath. Find Peace now, within your depth. Be this Light. Shine so bright. All will see how much you love Me. I love you, this you know. Now's the time the world you show.

See the good. Don't look for trouble. You'll always find what you're looking for. All the bad will fall away. Don't give it any water or time of day. See beyond appearances.

Thank you for your patience. It feels so good to be here with you. My eyes can see your glory. Take life as it comes, watch your step. Winning ways, not whining ways. Smile at life and life smiles back. You have to let go, to go on.

I had to take time out to take time in, inward journey leading me to joy eternally. I sing a new song all day long. I used to think. Life used to stink. From here I see life perfectly.

> *Find the joy. Make time to see. Breathe deeply. Love freely. Find God uniquely. Be still and know. The way I will show. Unplug. Plug in. Drink in this life. Onward journey. You do not have to carry your burdens. Set them down. Drop the frown. Be on your way.*

Merrily I live this day
A peace I've found
Whilst the world rushes around
Lazily I admire
As my heart rises higher
The breeze blowing
The grasses showing
They bend with ease
And bounce right back
Suffering none
Not considering
The wind an attack
It's a dance, a ballet
The wind and grasses
Both born to be that way.

> *Original inspiration. Commercial free programming. Don't sell yourself. You can't be bought. Written word is not the law. No truth can be truly told, only known and shown.*

I'm as happy as I can be
This is all I need
Today, presently
I see the glory
Journeys and journals

Laugh it off
This life I love
Brilliantly lit by the Son/Sun
Within and above.

> *The space between is not empty. You don't need anyone else.*
> *You can see clearly all by yourself. The world has plenty of*
> *"tellers," but so few "show-ers."*

Walk for mankind? I need to walk for me. I needed to get lost so I
would know when I was found.

> *About Mr. Emerson: He wrote many words. Many still*
> *listen, but it seems few yet have heard.*

Saints and angels are they the same?

> *We call them angels while in Heaven and saints while on the*
> *earth plane.*

> *With this constant influx, there is always more to know. You*
> *don't have to write it all down now. It will still be waiting for*
> *you. Time will again show.*

Comforting thoughts.

> *You cannot hide from what's inside. Make peace within*
> *yourself. To thine own Self be true. This is the only "work"*
> *you have to do.*

Thank you for leading me home safely.

> *Soul communication direct from the divine. Highest thought*
> *from the true You. Flowing freely from your deepest being.*
> *Messages given. Messages received. You are finally listening,*
> *for this We are relieved.*

I feel so deeply.

> *Don't talk back; remember it takes two to argue. Don't be*
> *mean. You are so concerned with protecting your "karma"*
> *and separating it from "the other" that you are mean.*
> *We know you don't mean to be mean, but you are. Your*
> *responses are from ego not love. Stop resisting so. Realize*
> *"the other" is trying to help as they know. It is always worth*
> *listening. Hear what they say. You will know what to do*
> *ultimately, but for the moment give only thanks and respond*
> *with love.*

> *Don't close your eyes. Don't close your eyes. You need to live*
> *wide open to be truly alive. Some people are easier to be*
> *around than others. But remember it's always up to you as*
> *to whether you "let" anyone "rain on your parade," dampen*
> *your spirit.*

What if the grass developed an ego and decided one day to no longer allow the wind to have its way? To no longer sway to and fro in whatever direction the wind decided to blow? It would stiffen up and eventually become brittle, not a larger thing, because as it broke off it would be quite little.

People need words. "Tell me" they say, "exactly what to do. Write it down. I need to read it, to believe it." They have forgotten how to "feel their way" and instead look "outside" for guidance on how to direct their day. This is true as well for art, for both its creation and acceptance, many seem to believe. "Tell me how to do it. Tell me what to see."

In this world
Words validate
People need names
Need to be told

What to think
What to say
Once again validation
They've forgotten how to
Feel their way
I feel no need to be told
By others
Young or old
What to think
What to feel
I exist in a world
So real
The bird does not come
When you call his name
He needs no title
To play this game
He is who he is
He knows no other
All is one
He sees himself
As his brother
United they fly
Yes, they soar the sky
What lesson can we learn
From this humble being
We title an erne?

You are no better, no matter what you think. When you believe you are, you start to stink. Listen and learn from all. From this you will walk tall. People need to be heard. You don't have to say a word. Listen well. If asked tell. Otherwise sit still as their emotions they spill.

Why do I expect him, "the other," to listen to me, I won't listen to him?

The only way to break "the curse" is to let love in.

Whenever I feel my way, I feel your way. The big me has a sense of humor. I'm safe!

> *It's not so much the haves and have not's, as it is the can's and cannot's.*

This is a very "big deal!"

> *We are with you all the way, come what may. Through your eyes, the Divine can realize.*

> *Back off. Move on. When you fight something you are actually feeding it, giving it more energy. It's like fanning a fire. Anything starved of attention will eventually expire. The thought of something is what keeps it alive. Turn your attention to what you like to keep that alive in your life. You see what you say. Say what you want. Want good for all.*

We keep losing it. As an evolving society we seem to continually lose and rediscover things, ideas, and notions. I often ponder how the formula for making concrete was "lost" for so very many years after the building of the Roman Empire.

> *People die and their ideas die with them whether it is an understanding of technology or even spirituality. So many spiritually evolved beings have walked the earth. Many creating a strong following for the "new ideas" presented and lived. But just as the formula for concrete material translated through the generations loses its magic and holding power, the energy of these awakened beings seems to fade, dilute and be reformulated with passing years. The integrity and strength of both of these "thought forms" weakens and again is lost.*

Attempts are made, formulas rewritten, but none can be proven. The key is again lost waiting to be found, to be seen, and again discovered with new eyes and fresh hearts willing to look at what is. Thank God for the seekers. They shall find what they look for.

Read what you've written. Hear it now. It's all before your eyes, the words of the Divine.

APRIL 13, 2011

Little by little
I found my way
Growing closer to God
Within each day.

When each is ready to hear, I am here. Be real.

These are messages for my path, but when I read messages received by others I recognize they are my messages too.

All worth sharing. We all get what we deserve. That's hard to hear. Growth factor. Eye to eye, faithful servant. There are no words in "the ethers," man translates his knowings into his own language. Keep it fresh. Movie remakes. Songs rerecorded. Listen anew. Self-help, Bible, Jesus, there's more to it. It's like the different languages.

Outer space exploration, why don't you start investing more time to "inner space" exploration?

Find fault. You can find fault with anything. Don't look for it.

I have my ways. I get knowings. Truth is revealed to me. Make something from nothing, how can this be?

The "creative process."

I ask a question and with the next breath, I have the answer.

> *You are making such an effort to separate that you insult and resist, creating tension. We know what you want. We will help you get there. Get out of your own way and see only through Love's eyes.*

What have I not forgiven?

> *You don't have to forget, just forgive. Then you will not re-live.*

What do you want me to know?

> *You are safe.*

> *There is no "new" information. We keep telling the same story. We will keep telling until all listen, hear and heed. This will be the triumph of God's glory indeed.*

If the Divine and the host of angels are telling me "I am safe" how can I dare fear, fear anything? There is nothing for me to believe. Knowing is enough, knowing Truth. Truth speaks to me. I know Truth's language. I hear Truth's voice. I answer Truth's call. I am "home safe" in Truth.

> *Feel safe. Feel love. Feel comforted. I hold you in my hand. You are my heart.*

Why do people hurt others so?

It is fear. Their actions come from fear, fear of the unknown, fear of the different. They feel threatened by the other and lash out. It is fear.

APRIL 14, 2011

Exercise, ritual, tradition, religion, dogma, scripture, all of these systems have been put in place not as an end, but as a means to an end, an end of fear and suffering. Taking each back to the beginning, back to the good, back to God, eternal and internal. Hear the call My people, answer.

Stop thinking. Start feeling. If you can read this, you may hear it. Hear My call. This is My voice. Speaking aloud to your heart. Stop the drama. Begin the passion. I keep telling you. Feel alive.

I did not design your bodies to self-destruct. I designed them beautifully with systems in place for automatic healing, with warning lights. Pain and disease malfunctions should only be temporary conditions as you respond to these "flashing" alerts and realign yourself with your truth of wholeness. Yes, action on your part is needed. Just as action on your part created an imbalance in your system, your action is required to correct it.

Why don't you see this? Why don't you understand this? Instead of proper action, you take a pill and essentially tell your body to "shut up" that you no longer want to hear it's complaints and thus you "cut the wires" of this oh, so wonderful alert system divinely designed.

We are here to learn from each other. Can you go a whole week without telling someone, anyone, what is "wrong with them" or even indulging in the thought? Bite your tongue. Hold your tongue.

Secret Wisdom: Communion of our mind with the mind of God.

APRIL 16, 2011

Why did you say that? You know better. You are no better. You only know better. Be better. You will be given this lesson again.

Respect yourself. If you don't show respect to yourself, why should others? Life is a game, but life is not a race. In fact, life is not a competition of any kind.

Those we refer to as the "great minds" of history were great, but not because of anyone of their own single minds being great. Their greatness manifested from the one single great mind which we all have access to. All the greatness they manifested was drawn from the great well of inspiration and possibility from the one great mind.

These people shined because their highly evolved souls recognized and utilized this great power. The words and works of these people are theirs to claim because they were the one's who made these ideas real. They "realized" them, first in thought form, then in physical form. They all knew that the gifts they bore and gave to the world were because of a greatness so much larger than their own minds. They were amazed as well and always humble, as grand egos and grand manifestations are not likely company.

It will be what you make of it. You can open your heart or resist.

Artists and great minds of the past have sometimes been described as schizophrenic or bi-polar. I believe this was because they lived two very contrasting realities: their spiritually creative world of abundance and the harsh material world of limitations. Their mind could not comprehend how to bring the joy they experienced while "in the flow" to flow into the rest of their lives, thus they felt out of sorts and often experienced tremendous periods of deep depression.

EGO = Edging God Out.

When someone speaks or acts offensively toward you, you then have a choice; let what was thrown at you bounce off and fall to the ground to wither and die from lack of attention or grab hold and throw it back.

Your good can come from anywhere. Don't limit your good. Too often you limit what good can come to you because you limit your thinking of how it can show up.

What have you decided about your life? Where are you now? Are you growing and rising toward the Light? Or are you clinging to and crawling on the ground? Life holds so much more than you can see with your physical eyes. Use your mind's eye to see greater possibilities in your world.

Imagine big. Think big. Dream big. Live big. Live fully. Drink from my cup, the cup of overflowing waters of an abundant life. Breathe deeply the pure air I give to you. Fill your soul with My love. Become. Come to Me. Be who you Are. Spirit matters. No pressure. Ease up. Up and away. Away from trouble. Trouble not.

I can't breathe that air. I seek purity. If I had to go in to pull out and save another then of course I would with no doubt. But I will not live there. I need pure air to thrive, clean air to be fully alive.

I'm looking beyond local. With my spiritual eyes I see otherwise. I am happy for me. I am happy for you.

My dear father-in-law Albert is "with it" just enough to know that he is ready to go. He told me he hopes God takes him in his sleep. I told him, perhaps he will, but until then he is ours to keep. Keep safe; feel loved, while a new guardian angel prepares a home for both of them above. His wife, Audine, lived full and long and passed quickly. This had always been her desire, through thin and thick. She willed it so. Her will was so strong. Her heart and soul did always to God belong.

My mother told me she so wishes a quick passing much the same, but sees the truth of the matter a chance with no one to blame. If one can so have a will to live, can they not as well have a will to die, to go from this life to the next at a chosen time?

> *God gave us free will, the right to choose. It is up to each of us to decide how this power to use. Call forth your desire. Step up, rise higher. It is not wrong to wish to go. Jesus said, let this be known.*

APRIL 17, 2011

> *Help others, to help yourself. Again We say, get out of your own way. Live bigger. You are not "house bound." You are not bound at all. Live my bounty. Share your joy. Life is not a race. You will not run out of time. Stop measuring. Start enjoying. What do you want to believe? Tell me. Say what you mean. Let your life speak.*

I've decided that I will no longer "tell" someone what I am going to do. I will show them.

> *Show, don't tell.*

I don't have to go "look it up" and read somewhere what to do in any moment of my life. Why? Because I have help online. I stay connected and get all the help I ask for. Yes, I ask for help constantly. I ask, knowing I will receive and I do receive. From whom? My helpers, my team, my family of spiritual beings with soul standings higher than my own. They lift me up. They guide me. Nameless, they remain to me. What's in a name anyway? All I know is that it is all Love, the purest and highest, within my reach, at hand, ready to help. All they ask for is a grateful heart from me.

It pleases them so to know that I want their help, to know that I believe, that I believe in better than I can see. And that I know this better, this good, is of God. These helpers cannot and do not make me do a thing, but they can pave the way for me and my dreams. They remind me. They remind me of my goals. They remind me of my purpose. They prepare and present golden opportunities for me to act, act in accord with the direction of the fulfillment of my dreams.

Do I see them? No, not yet. Maybe someday I will, when I want to. I have never asked. I have learned from reading the writings of others about spiritual guides that these "guides" have rules to follow. They can not interfere in our lives or act against our will. These "spiritual forces" love us and watch over each of us and want so to be of assistance. We have been told "Ask and you shall receive." I believe this is part of that truth. We only get what we ask for. Ask for more, ask for better, ask for help and give thanks for all.

> *Give it up, all those notions that have held you back. Release them all. You cannot tear anything away which you do not want. You cannot push, scratch, or yell it away. You can only let it fall away, die out, wither from lack of attention. Stop noticing what bothers you. Stop talking about what you do not like. Think of what brings a smile. You are so pretty when you smile and the world is pretty too.*

> *Look what you've done. See what you have created. Count it all good. All nature is the same, without the attention it needs to live it dies.*

Stop watering your weeds. You need not even stoop to pull them. Instead fertilize your flowers and talk to them. They will give you a bounty of blossoms and likewise choke out any perceived weed thoughts. Let your sun shine. Go be your best.

I need to share my experience and not be afraid to share, to not fear judgment or other's fear reactions.

Either you fear or you love. Sound familiar, wonder why? It's all the same message, all from the same message center.

Please elaborate later.

I have these "good ideas," I have no right to take credit.

You have "every right" if you manifest them. We are all, all connected to the All, One, all the time. It's only a matter of clearing the interference on your side.

I've got a better picture now. I can see more clearly, the "One True Love" holding me dearly. I used to get words, then phrases. Now I get whole pages.

It is so important for you to have daily interface with others, close to, on or above your soul plane. Ideally with skin on and face-to-face is a bonus you deserve. Be joy, seek joy and joy will find you. You have to balance the energies around you. At one time your children were there at your feet and you fed them and they fed you. Find someone else to feed and you will be fed as well. Know you are loved and watched over.

I'm a spiritual girl!

You have the power to connect, to connect with and draw in whatever and whomever you need at a moments notice.

Know your power. Accept it. Embrace it. The Force is with you! Call forth your good.

Your good is not dependent on any other. No one else can say, no one else can deter it. It is yours. It is only up to you to claim, to connect, to call forth. To believe, to live your good. Live your best life.

Inner – fear – ants, Interference is what keeps us from our good, what drowns out the voice of God, what makes us feel small and alone. This interference is the cause of all pain and strife we know. This inner fear is fed, well fed, by our society, by our media, by our dogma, by the medical community and by the leadership of our world.

But God says, *"Fear not, rejoice and be glad, lift up your hearts, give thanks and praise, delight in good."* Few hear, really hear. This I know, as not long ago I was deaf as well, deaf and dumb to the truth. Now, my eyes see and my heart hears "the truth."

It can be found. I found the way. I am on the way to a peaceful heart. Yes, it requires work, but mostly trust and faith, faith in good. God is good. The work to be done is truly a crucifixion of the self, our small self which manifests as our big egos. It's not a one time lop off job here as we have each spent a lot of time building up our egos, lifetimes in fact. Every time we have experienced hurt we reinforce the wall of our ego castle to insure that no one can ever get in, or too close, to ever hurt us again. We have worked too hard building up our defenses, always on guard, ready to attack whatever or whoever appears to threaten our hold on life.

Living in such a state, always on guard, on the look out, in a hyper state of self-protectiveness, that My dear, is not freedom. No, I see it clearly now, that My dear is fear. What is fear? Fear is what kills people. Fear is what kills dreams. Fear is what keeps us so small, small and mean. God said, "Do not fear."

APRIL 18, 2011

> *Whenever life gives you an opportunity to choose, choose the higher path. Don't be little. Don't belittle. Be big.*

I believe it.

> *Where do you think all the "good stuff" comes from? Don't act so surprised. A better way to live. We're here to help.*

Do dogs get words?

> *No, they wouldn't know what to do with them.*

About the art which I create, which feels as if it created itself from "thin air" or "fell from the sky," is it so?

> *It is so, only the "air" is not thin but thick with possibilities. Your work was direct, "fresh from Heaven."*

Heaven called my name. Some people say about spiritual beings, "Don't bother them. They have things to do."

> *What? Help us. We're here to help.*

Scarcity equals "Scared City" this is where the majority of people live, those same people with such strong egos. Yes, they build their ego castles in "Scared City," their egos built from fear. It's a circle, a vicious cycle.

When I was a child, my mother often asked me, as I restlessly wiggled around, if I had "ants in my pants?" She never spoke of "Inner Fear Ants" but I am coming to believe that they are rampant in our society and the infestation of such is the cause of most of the commotion. Just like regular ants, "Inner Fear Ants" keep quite busy and this busyness creates a constant buzz. It sounds like this "I can't, too hard, not enough, too late, too much, all alone, what's next, I'm lost, I'm scared, no good, no God."

The job of "Inner Fear Ants" is the building up of egos. They have excellent job security for the more work they do and the more noise they create the more threatened and alone people feel. And the more they feel the need to fortify and build up the walls of their egos, again creating more work, and job opportunities for the "Inner Fear Ants."

I'm pretty sure none of us are born with "Inner Fear Ants" and yet it all seems so normal because it is all we remember. The buzz, buzz, buzz of the "Inner Fear Ants" at work is constant as our fragile egos require continual repair and reinforcement. It's like living in a commercial construction zone, saws buzzing, metal clanging, jackhammers rattling. You have to yell to communicate and then it's hard to decipher a voice in the clamor. Imagining such, one can begin to understand how a whisper would be lost, silenced, drowned, never even imagined or listened for.

That's just what happens to the voice of God, the small still voice that is constantly speaking to each of us. It is drowned out by the constant clamor of our "Inner Fear Ants." Is it a surprise to you that God is speaking to you at this very moment, that you have always been connected so? Would you like to hear the voice of God? Would you like to hear directly how much you are loved?

First you have to walk away from the construction zone, away from the clamor of life, away from your ego. A desert, a mountaintop, or even a closet will do. Just get away by yourself. As you close the door on the chatter; you open the door to Heaven where God awaits. "I don't hear a thing," you may say at first. Wait, I say. Be patient and ask for God's help. God has always heard you.

Stop the noise. Stop the interference of the "Inner Fear Ants" in their tracks. Stomp on them. Say, "Let go my ego. Let God in. Let God begin." Speak to God. Ask for more of His love. Ask God to fill you with His blessed "Divine Love." Ask God to hush your "Inner Fear Ants" and listen in.

Listen. Be still and know. Know that I am. I am God.

The more time you spend in quiet with God, the closer you will feel. The more you will know. The more you will love. And you will eventually hear, hear God call your name. The "Inner Fear Ants" will move on for lack of work, as God will help you realize that the defense you have built up with the ego has caused you to feel alone.

In their place will come "Assure Ants." "Assure Ants" say, "All is well, have faith in good, you are loved, there is enough." "Assure Ants" give us faith. Faith to trust in God's goodness and that it is available for all. Day by day you will move closer to God as your new "Assure Ants" will help you move from your walled ego fortress in "Scared City" to a most beautiful palace of your mind and soul, "His Kingdom come. Thy Will be done."

Don't take it to heart what other people say. Because they say, then go on their way. Then you keep repeating it throughout your day. Don't get hung up, don't let another hang you to dry. Don't even let another post you like a flag to fly. We make ourselves, we undo ourselves, all by ourselves. Whose voice is important? The one in your head. What record are you playing?

Don't give it another thought. Time to see. See with Me that you are more and I have a great life for you in store. In store, means it is here now. Don't bother to wonder how. Great things will come your way when you drop ego and bow to God each day. Egoless. Selfless. Boundless.

It's one of those days. One of those days God has made, made for me, made for you.

*Who tells you what to do? Everyone. Everyone seems to
have an opinion on what is best for someone else. You do
the same. You think they should, should be different, should
be the same, should act or speak in such and such a way.
So to whom should one listen? Who really knows best? Is it
another or your "True Self" which should be put to the test?
Know Thyself, to thy own Self be true. Shut up and listen
and then you will know what to do.*

*There are many paths to the same mountain top, the apex
of life. How can this be you ask? From many directions you
came, all calling My name. I answer to all, for all is One.
There is no other. It has been this way since time began.
Scattered you are across the land, I still hold each one of you
in My hand. Come as you are, from where you are.*

*People only know, what they want to know. Know better. Do
you realize what you say? What other people say, let it go
in one ear and out the other. Hear what is best for you. God
says, Love says, here I am. Hear, I am.*

A little voice told me. I used to feel that I had to paint everything
"I saw" and now I feel I have to write everything "I hear." I feel
bombarded.

*It is not so, relax into it and enjoy what you are given
without feeling you have to manifest every "Divine Idea"
that passes your way.*

*Say it and create it. Empower Me with your presence. When
things go right, give thanks. You can do it all, everything
you need to do. Just believe. Be and live in Me. Whatever
you believe, you create. Believe the best. When you are not
connected everything feels disconnected, awkward. You
know the feeling. You have been there. No going back. When*

you can do this, you are not limited by the seen. Actually, you never have been you just couldn't see this. Ha, ha, hee, hee.

We've got a comedian here! I'm glad You have a sense of humor.

It's one of Our most important senses. See, not so hard. We make it easy.

Dear Ones, thanks. I asked for one of those just yesterday and today I received. Consider this a thank you note. Love, Deb

A plan of action is good, quite good. Everything you want, everything you need within reach. Hold out your hands and take Mine, the Divine. We believe in the seen and unseen. Don't let fear take hold. You can put the idea in their head. It's up to them to water it.

I know the Truth. Don't feed me lies. I'm not going to eat them.

People aren't perfect. Why do you keep expecting people to be perfect? Why do you expect more than you give?

APRIL 21, 2011

So you tried something and it didn't work, an act of desperation. Well, of course not. Life does not reward bad behavior. We've given you the rules, laws, truths and still you think you can some how "beat the system" by doing things "your way." All life flows because it is God's way. Can you not see this? The stream flows, flows around obstacles. The dams in life are those who attempt to stop the flow, to gather and hoard.

Read this and be scared! Warning, warning, warning! Cause for alarm, it happened, just as I feared. Cause for concern. Give your attention to this. Panic attacks!

> *It is given to you to know. It is given to you to show. It is given to you to glow. Whatever is going on in your life will continue as the same until you "realize" something different. See anew. Change of plans. Lighten up. Enlighten up. It's just the beginning of everything. Who calls the shots? You call the shots, judgment call, everything in position, alignment. Some decisions were made and they weren't always the best ones. Fear took over. Ego was in charge. Yes, it got ugly. Turn over that page. Close that book. Open a new one full of blank pages for you to write a new story, story of hope, a story of love, a story of life's marvelous adventures. Carry on.*

> *Don't concern yourself with what others think of you, either good or bad. It only matters how and what you think of yourself. Keep and know your power. No one can take it from you. Believe in Yourself. Know better. Get over yourself. Be true to You.*

I truly believe Jesus the Christ is shaking his head in Heaven because so many continue to miss the point, the point of His Life. He truly gave his all, so we could understand. How much more plainly could he have said it? How much more loudly could he have lived it?

He told us we need not need to wait; the glory of the Kingdom is at hand, within reach, now is the time, and still we wait. The Church formed in his name does not this truth proclaim. Jesus told us to be happy and be filled with the love of God, to desire such a connection with the Father as he had that our every thought would be a prayer. To ask humbly to be so filled with this love as so to become a new person, a new person with ears and eyes that constantly hear and see the truth.

The truth that God's Kingdom is at hand and we are not separate at all. That God's good is within each of us, for each of us, connecting each of us.

> *Yes, Jesus Christ is shaking his head. Why "on earth" do they await my second coming? How could I tell them any differently to make them know than I did when I first appeared? Many others have been sent and many others are there. More and more know; more and more live this Truth. More and more share.*

> *It's getting safer and safer to share. Less and less people are bodily crucified for proclaiming this truth, but they continue to be verbally crucified for speaking out and against the written and memorialized dogma. Yes, these voices continue to be silenced, ignored and ridiculed, just as the first followers of these ways of Jesus Christ were.*

> *These first followers got it. They opened their hearts to God and received the Holy Spirit into the depth of their souls. They were changed men, just as Jesus spoke. The love that Paul wrote about is just this love that Jesus knew, pure "Divine Love," a gift from the Holy Spirit, ordained by God to man, not man to man. When the Holy Spirit has so filled ones soul with such love, the Kingdom has come, glory be, glory is, and the Christ within lives. No waiting required. I have to speak out.*

Some people would say its "good news" and "bad news" but that's a judgment call. I have to let that go. I call it all good, all God, at work awakening the world.

> *Do as you know. Pour forth your good.*

Recipes, yes, all of life would be easier it you could just follow someone else's recipe but very boring as well. That is not how I have lived my life. That is not how I have created my art. Heck, that's not even how I fix dinner.

Intertwined are all the parts of my life, my life with yours, yours and mine with all. All is One. I am, You are, We are, the Great "I Am" seeking expression.

APRIL 23, 2011

Yesterday, I had a big surprise. I felt bad, because of something someone else did. What upset me even more, I mean emotionally to my core, was that I interpreted these bad feelings as evidence my ego was still in charge. I was so shocked to find myself feeling hurt. Was my ego really still so fragile?

Today, I understand differently. Feelings are good. Feelings are real and feelings are valid. They are messages that tell each of us the truth of a situation we are in. If we don't like the way something "feels" we are to move away from it just as we are to move away from a hot fire. We decide where we live, in joy or misery. We each choose for ourselves. Our feelings guide us to our best. Not everything we encounter will feel good. We are to move away, about face and turn our attention to what does feel good. The sooner the better, is all the better.

> *Listen to what you say*
> *What you are ordering*
> *Don't notice lack*
> *Say what you want*
> *Hear what you want*
> *See what you want*
> *Be what you want*
> *Inspire the world to reach higher*
> *If you fear*

You do not know
God is near
God is here
Find your way home
Then you will know
You've never been alone.

I love signs, the bigger, the better.

Don't "love" the guru.

APRIL 24, 2011

Who are you trying to please? Why? Does it feel good? Can
they be pleased, ever? Are they generally happy people or
people who enjoy the drama of having others please them?
Remember, whomever you hear talk down about another is
sure to do the same to you when your back is turned. Why
concern yourself with being pleasing to them? Does this
really please you? Please yourself. To thine own Self be true.
Do unto others as you would have done unto you.

Everyone cannot and will not be pleased. You cannot make
your own happiness dependent upon the pleasing of another.
Be true to the True You. Let other's lick their own wounds
and carry their own grudges as they may. It is up to you to
find your own way. Be true. Be you. Don't change to please
any other. No one else can make you happy and anyone
whose happiness depends on the happiness or acceptance
from another is weak and vulnerable.

We are all so fragile, so frail, when we attempt to live our lives alone,
alone without the awareness of the presence of One, the One who
made us, the One who loves us, the One who is us. The plan was never

or is never for us to have to walk this walk this way. But the choice has always been ours. It's called "free choice - free will."

We have always been able to choose, choose better, to want better, to look for better, to know good and to know God. God has spoken. God continues to speak. The voice of God is heard and Truth is proclaimed. Can you hear? Do you really want to? Are you ready to let go and let God be the center of your life? There is no halfway point. It's either, all or nothing, ego or God go.

> *Who and what is running your life? How is your life running? Is it flowing? Flowing smoothly? Is it filled with joy? Are you tired of trying so hard? Life in God is Life, the Good Life, and the great news is that it is not hard at all. It's the easy way, the easy way out, the only way out of the drama and hardness of life. This is the truth I tell.*

No one told me, or at least I never heard. The message I did hear was that following God, or Jesus, or Jesus' path to God, was hard. I now see the hard part is the surrender. I don't mean "giving up." I mean "letting go" of all that one has held so dear, worked so hard to build up, and fights so hard to defend. It's letting go of all the ego stuff and recognizing that this "stuff" is what kept one small. They say, "You can't take it with you" when you die a bodily death. Well, you can't take it with you when you die the death of your ego-self to live again, anew.

> *What is important? What is good? What is God? Do you know? Can you see past your stuff? The stuff you cling to and claim as your identity is so much more than the material goods you have accumulated. It's the mental baggage too. It's your belief in lack. It's your feelings of fear.*

> *It's your belief that one is better. No one is better. Some just know better. Some know God. Some know good. It's not "Some are no good." It's just "Some know good." It's there*

for each and all to know, all there, as much as one wants, goodness unlimited. Know good, know God. No God, no good, no God realization. Always present but not activated unless called forth by the power of the word, the thought, the creative power in all.

Listen, hear. Listen here o' heart. Let it go, what she said, what he did. Don't let it control you. You may see it, you may hear it, but you don't have to believe it. When you believe it, you become it. You claim it is yours.

Is this what you want? You don't have to "buy in" to their drama. You need not take stock of it at all. You are so much bigger than this. This you know. What they have is what they want. It keeps them busy. It makes them feel better about themselves.

Belittling others is never the way to being bigger yourself. So don't even bother to judge them for a minute in your heart. Let it all go, it is not yours. It is not what you want. Don't bother. Walk away. Run. Shake the dust from your feet and go where you are wanted, where people want what you want: peace, love and acceptance.

Flow through me. Magnetize me to good, for good. Let me work for You. Let me work for Love. Let me be Love. Let me speak Love. Let me hear Love. Let me know Love. Let me show Love. Better me each day. Each moment give me more light. Shine through me, purify my soul. Lift me up. Hold me close. Never let me go. This I ask, this I pray, help me to live in Your way. Hold me close all day.

What is this that flows through me and fill pages and pages with such lofty thoughts? It is what I asked for; it is what I pleaded for, when I asked for more. When I set aside my ego and let God go. I let God go to work in my heart, pour forth. These are my lessons, my lesson plans, written in my hand by God's word, by Divine order. What I am given to know, what I am given to show, where I am shown to go. Rising higher to my desire, Divine Love, I asked to fill my soul. Divine Love is what I asked for.

Ask for more
You could write a book
Perhaps you are now
Look nowhere else
Acres of diamonds are beneath your feet
You are in the right place
I have put you here
Be here now
With Me
With them
Love My people
Let them know
My love you can show
I need you to do My Work
This is the why you are on earth
Enjoy each day
I want it this way
Draw them in
Your Light shines
Clear your mind
Fill it with Mine
Now is the time
Time to be
Here with Me
Sing My Song
All day long
Whistle out loud
Above the crowd

Others have known
Others have shown
You still see their Light
It has shown so bright
Few can hear
But they are still dear
Be the shepherd
Take care of My flock
They will flock to you
Please tell them what to do
They can hear your voice
They can see what you do
Please help them see
That I love you and them too.
Personal magnetism
Is very strong stuff
It is what you are made of
We all draw into ourselves
What we want
You get what you give
Give good, be good, get good
Be good
What a powerful thought
Think about it
Be it
Be good
Be God.

You are getting stronger each day
Feel My strength
I am You
You are I
We are One
You are knowing this

You are living this
You are allowing
The resistance is lessening
The flow increases
Your light brightens
People know
Know you know something
Something good
There is something very good
About you
God
God is good
God is about you
So be it, Amen.
Clear the way
My way
Don't get in the way
Stay on the way
This is The way
You are not The way
You show The way
It has always been
But people don't see
It that way
They don't look at the path
They just see the person
The leader, the sage, the guru
The Christ
The manifestation of My love
The one who has found the way
Is not the way
They can only lead others
Down a path and open a door
One has to walk in for oneself

And walk beside their leader
Their leader is no better
The leader only knows better
And if this leader leads
One to believe differently
Justice has not been done
Truth has not been told
But hear ye the words of
Many you look up to
Listen to what they say
Follow Me
Walk with Me
On this life journey.

The saints and angels
Still lead us onward,
Reaching for our
Hands and our hearts
They call out to us
They listen to our pleading
They are here to help
To help us on our way
To help us see the path before us
Not for us, but with us
Ask for help
Ask for light to be shown
Flashes of light
Inspiration
Oh, to live in the light
Such an inspired life
All to God's glory
The glory and well being of all
We are to be "Well Beings"
We are to see ourselves this way
To see the wholeness

And behold it
Hold it high
In high regard
It is our holiness
This wholeness
Everything we are to be.

Fear is like a rampant wild fire in this world. And if it doesn't come directly to your door you go and get it. You bring your torch and light it with the fire of fear. You bring it into your home and then huddle in the corner in fear of the very fear you invited in.

You have it all wrong. You didn't hear it right. When we were told to fear God that meant we were to have the utmost reverence to the power and strength of God, to bow down, to let the agendas of our own egos go. To let God, to let good, rule our hearts, all without fear, with trust and faith. Faith in good, not fear, not fear of anything.

We are to live in the Presence, in the knowing of God, which is our supreme good. We are told by God, through the words in the Bible, not to fear. *"Thinking of fear is wrong, it is error thinking,"* God said. *"Error thinking is what sin is."* So many people are so quick to point out sin, to point out the errors of another. They think they know the rules. "Thou shall not lie, thou shall not steal, and thou shall not kill." But when one lives in the Presence of Knowing, the Presence which is our good, God, no rules are necessary. We do good, as we are good, we are good, God, manifested. We are calm, we do not fear. We walk in faith, no rules, just right.

> *Be mindful of what you say*
> *Watch what you do*
> *Are you being true?*
> *Coming your way*
> *All the good stuff*
> *Hang on*
> *Let loose*

Fly high
Be free
See with Me
You are doing the right thing
You are on your way
Stay the course
You will rise high
Higher than you know
Others will either rise as well
Hang on
Or let go
Their weight will not pull you down
No one is in your way.

Enjoy today
If you see something you don't like
Ignore it
Give it no attention
Do not bother with it
Then it will not bother you.
Let the sun shine in
I do declare
See better
For better
Better off
When better is always
Life tastes good
Enjoy each bite
Savor it all.

What are you waiting for?
More?
Then get up and get it
Take up your bed and walk

Don't be downtrodden
Don't let others step on you
Don't look for worms
Look for butterflies.

Keep in touch
In touch with your Touch Point
The center of your being
Your All
All you can be
And will be
Is there
Safe inside
Take a peek
Enjoy the view
Who knew?
Whom shown the Light, The way?
We speak of Him each day.

Care enough to see the very best
Within all, every time
No matter what they say.
You are on your way
Be a source of confidence
Listen to what you say
If you do not plan for something
You are not expecting it
So you won't be getting it
Stop playing this game and
Lamenting how unfair life is
You have been told how life works
Yet you choose to deny
You are denying your good
The good that is available to you

Not due to you
Just available
It will only be due to you
When you match it with your word.

Don't be a broken record
Record a new tune
Why say anything in life is hard?
You hardly know how life works
Life does work
It works very well
Fighting against the Flow is your issue.

If you can't believe in yourself
Why would anyone else believe in you?
Don't tell anyone a sad story
You are hope and joy
So be it
Breath deep
Look up
I am here
For you
It's okay to cry
It's okay to be weak
I am strong
Stronger than you know
Let Me show
Your tears are signs of surrender
Let them flow
You are releasing the junk
That blocks your flow
Let it all go.

Lord, help me carry on, onward.

MAY 2011

Become a disciple of one's own higher mind.
One's higher mind is "the Father of Truth."

THE GOSPEL OF TRUTH [3]

MAY 1, 2011

If I had not the perfection in my heart, God's perfect Divine Love, I would not be able to live in peace. I have peace within, despite apparent outer turmoil, change and challenge. I turn within and am comforted by the knowing. It is so good to know, all the good there is to know.

Celebrate where you are. Celebrate who you are becoming. Celebrate where you are going. You have work to do, you know this. You know what it is. Get it done. Get over it. Go on. Flow. Fly high.

Don't even say, unless you want it that way. You have to get in a good feeling spot. Keep your eye on the prize.

MAY 5, 2011

Don't worry about a thing. Worry is lack thinking. Worry is not believing in the best. You worry for no good. What you worry about you bring about. Think and believe in what you want in and for your life. Good is for you. There is enough good for all. Praise good when you see it!

I do as I am told. I stay open and connected. Life flows beautifully. God is so good. I praise my Maker.

Heaven engulfs the earth, few know. More will show. Listen here/hear the time is near, so near it's already here. The air you breathe is given to you. Listen in, I'll tell you what to do. Come follow Me. Let Me lead the way. It's time to go, not to stay. Heaven on earth can be felt. It's for all, no matter what hand you've been dealt. Clearer now you are seeing the way, the way to Me, to My glory. Give thanks and praise to all the good you see. You are beside, not beneath Me. Believe. Believe. Believe.

Know this in your heart, I love you and am with you as you write, as you cry, as you laugh. Give it all to Me and I will give My All to you in return. Take My hand I'll carry you through the sand, one set of footprints as you walk this land.

And God said, satisfaction guaranteed with life in Me. The material world can never truly satisfy. That's why people are always looking for bigger and better, more, more, more and still never enough. So when is enough, enough for you? What is it all worth? You can't keep any of it, the stuff you spend your life collecting, none. If you spend your lifetime chasing material riches you will find yourself among the poorest in the hereafter.

Don't let it bother you, the stuff in the background, the crap others may give attention to. You can rise above and be with Me. Wherever you are, I am with you at peace. Meet Me at your calm spot, the core of your soul.

Think lofty thoughts, the higher the better. Feel Me fill you with My love. My love poureth over. Let it spill from you, as

well. Breathe deep. Slow down. Look up. Look around. I give
you this gift, the breath of Life. Appreciate where you are.
Now is the time. Move up. Move onward. Let's go.

This journal, like all the others I have written over the last two years, is filled with two very different kinds of writing. They are not sorted and categorized thoughts, they mix and blend to create a very interesting juxtaposition. Some words are my thoughts, things I need to say, to express. My thoughts challenge me to organize them on the paper. Just as I am now right here.

Then there are the writings that my own mind have not authored, these words flow. They as well seem to glow, glow with an inner light that speaks Truth. Truth is writing this paragraph.

> *There is no limit. That's all you need to know. You don't need*
> *to know how or why or when. Do you know what limits*
> *you? You do by your thoughts and by your actions, by your*
> *limited consciousness.*

> *I know this was not your intention consciously. But your*
> *subconscious listens to what you say and believes, then tells*
> *Me, tells the Universe, what you want. Not getting what you*
> *want? Perhaps the messages are getting scrambled. You have*
> *to speak clearly. You have to think clearly. You have to act*
> *clearly. You have to live a transparent life.*

> *Make the inner like the outer, the same. Be true. Seek Truth.*
> *Know Truth. Celebrate Truth. Truth and beauty will come*
> *to you. See the beauty in life. Celebrate the beauty. Life is so*
> *good. See it. Be it. Breathe it.*

It is fun to be One with you. Write it down as you get it. Now it is there, out of thin air. Can do with you. You cannot run. You cannot hide. The only place to go is inside. Make the best of it, of it all. Wherever you are, find the good. It's there to be found. Keep looking. Look everywhere.

I delight in your laughter, your joy. This is My desire for you, My desire for us. To be so filled with My Divine Joy that your laughter is heavenly. Choirs of angels sound no better to My ears. Keep your spirits high, see the Light in life. Laugh at the coincidences you once would have ignored. Now that you see, you can laugh with Me. Life is a joy. You are My joy. Be - joy - us. Be joyous. Be available, I am.

You have come so far, all by staying so still. Still there is more, more to come. Come and get it. It is yours. I await, you will never be too late. I wait up longing for you, always here, always near. Call Me. Ask for anything. Ask for everything. What is Mine is yours.

MAY 6, 2011

All goodness flows continually. Open up. Allow. Allow good to flow to and through you. Don't block your good. To flow free, come be with Me.

His energy shift, shifted mine. And mine in turn shifted his. We lift each other up.

Decide what you want. It is yours. How can one not be happy with this awareness? It is true. God is good. Seek the good. There you find God, God in action, God in being. There is more good than bad manifested in this world.

Sadly though, people treat each other badly in the name of goodness. They fear. They judge. They condemn. They hurt. They separate.

What do you allow in? You decide your diet, what feeds your soul? Taste the good life. It's not what they say. It's another way. Behold your beauty. With My eyes you see wonderfully.

Know My good. Plan for it. It is everywhere. See it. Celebrate it. Shout with joy. Be loud. Be proud, proud of the goodness manifested on earth. Give thanks and praise.

You asked. I answered. See, I am here. I hear. I hear you. I hear you hearing Me. I see you heeding My call. Give Me your all. Self-seeking: seeking your Highest Self, your True Self. Where are you looking? Do not look elsewhere. Look here, down deep within. Hear My call. Don't tune Me out. Help is on the way. See clearly. You can do all things through Me. Stay tuned. Don't tune out. Tune in. Weather the storm. The sun will rise again tomorrow, I promise.

Religious or faithful, faithful to what? Faith full, full of faith, full of trust in the goodness life has to offer. We are each the authors of our own life story. Tell a good one, be better for it. Take what you need, if need be.

When you meet someone, look into their eyes. See their soul. Seek Me within them. I am there as well. They may not know but you can show them their worth, their amazing value. Value each of My children the same. I made no better. Some just know better. Some say, "Some have wisdom beyond their years." But in truth, wisdom has nothing to do with years.

The bible includes few sayings of wisdom from Jesus Christ, although every word he spoke was endowed with rich wisdom. This wisdom is again resurfacing now that our social climate is more conducive to the spread of these truth statements.

Yes, the world is waking up from a long sleep. The nightmare will end. A new world order is all good. Not great minds of men but men with a clear connection with Infinite Spirit, the One Great Mind all are connected to. To perceive of this greatness one has to clear the channel. Get rid of the static, the noise of the material world and the thinking mind chatter.

It's about who you are, not what you have, not who you are in the minds of others but who you are at heart, at the core of your being and how this being-ness of you shows up in life. Joy is a natural state of being. Ugliness is a manifestation of unhappiness. Life is what we make it. Don't postpone your joy.

Intimacy, in to Me see. Prosperity is to be in alignment with Divine guidance. Whatever you give your attention to forms your belief, which eventually creates your experience. We live in an infinite world and the currency of Infinite Mind is new ideas.

MAY 10, 2010

Believe what you want. Be in the world, but not of the world. The call, I hear. See beauty, even in hard hearts. It is there, make them aware. Nature calls My name. Nature, my glory proclaims. Grow some good.

Even when I can't recognize physical beauty, I carry beauty in my heart. My Source is my strength. We all have a choice. We choose how we live with each thought.

> *You are what you think, think well, well being. I have experienced it all. You are to live fully. Be fully present where you are now. Celebrate today, live it well.*

MAY 12, 2011

I am not afraid to die. I am not afraid to live. I fear nothing in this life nor the next. I know both hold promise of everlasting limitless joy that is ready for me to claim and proclaim as my truth. I desire all that is higher to be my experience now and forever wherever I may be physically as well as spiritually. The words I write here have deep profound meaning to me. I feel this truth to and through my core, my soul being.

Give me rest. Unburden my soul. Take my fear and tears and wipe them away.

> *You are, where I stand. I stand with you. Together in unison, We are, I am. Get carried away by my love. No need to shove. Love leads and the call you heed. All daylong sing my song. Get carried away with me. Carry on it won't be long.*

> *Set down your burdens. You have carried them long enough. Are they serving you? Or are you serving them? Serve Me and I will care for all your needs. Help Me help My people see and hear My voice. I am still here, all along, never left. Never silent, people stopped listening. I still speak truth, the same truth, to new ears with new words. I want to be heard. Hear Me now.*

What is "the Truth?"

*What you hear is My voice, the voice of the Loving Spirit,
parent of all, always here to love all. My force, my power, is
"Love" which I give freely to all who love and recognize me.
I bring no harm to this world or anyone. All choose their
life by the ideas they choose to believe. I am "All Good."
Those that truly believe in me believe in "all good." This is
what they know, when they know and serve me. It is all for
"goodness sake." Whatever is done for goodness sake is good
for all. This is how Heaven is realized. This is the Perfect
World I created. Know me, know Love, know good, know
God versus no good, no God, no love.*

*This is each human's choice because of "the gift of free will"
given to humanity. The other beings on earth have not a
choice. They live, grow and thrive in peace and harmony
as their nature, their natural way, is a way with God.
Feeling and believing in a separation from your good, your
goodness, creates unpleasant experiences and attitudes,
disharmony in oneself and among others.*

*Children know this goodness. They live it but are taught to
doubt it. Their wings are clipped. Their eyes are blinded. The
blind lead the blind across the earth.*

*What kind of perfection are you waiting for? You already
have My perfect love.*

MAY 13, 2011

*Love desires to manifest in and through you. All that Love
is, wants to be. Can you see? Shine My Light. Sing My song.
Sing a love song to the world. Let them see Me, through*

you. The childlike wonder in your eyes speaks of beauty and tranquility. Others are noticing your light. I am here with you. I love you so, this you know. I always have. You have always had My love, but you have not always accepted it. You went your own way. The world led you astray. You didn't know so you could not show My love that was there for you.

Just imagine what we can do together united in love. You are the hands, heart and head and I am the power. I am your source. Dream big, I am limitless. You are limitless through Me, the essence of good which is your perfume. What a lovely scent you offer unto the world. You sweeten the pie, taking the tartness out of life. Come with Me and imagine, imagine what We can do. I am for you to breathe. I am the breath of Life. I give life limitless, unbounded. Come see beyond with Me.

You need to forgive those that hold and have told limited thought. Forgive them, they do not know. When they are ready, they too will seek My ways. When they are exhausted and can barely breathe, gasping, they will beg for My breath, which is already there for them, as you know. All they know is all they know. All they know is all they show. Show them better. Be better. Live better. Demonstrate My good. Demonstrate My bounty. Demonstrate My joy. Demonstrate My love.

Do not shout. Live quietly, at peace, in plain sight. Do not let your mind be troubled. I care and will care for you if you let Me. Let go of the old, the old ideas of limitation. Behold My World of limitless good unfolding before you. I made the world wonderfully, wonderfully good, good for you, good for all My beloveds.

Think of the abundant love you have for your own children is there nothing of yours that you wouldn't give them as they need? I, your Creator, love you limitlessly. All I have is yours, more than you could ever dream. But dream, I ask you. Dreams wonderful dreams. Dream of new possibilities We create together. You are part of My creation and a partner with Me in creation.

What a wonderful plan. That is the plan for you to create with Me, to create the wondrous life of your dreams, of your preferences. It is fun for Me to see what you each desire when you desire higher. Each of you express this creative Divine Love in different ways. It all brings Me joy.

You are My Joy in the world. Can you see this? Do you know how brightly your Light shines? You glow because you know My love. I am here for you, for all. Ask and it is given. All is forgiven already. Trouble not your mind. Trouble not your life. Live in joy. I want you to be happy. I want you to prosper. I want you to live fully. I want you to love fully. I want you to be full of Me, full of My Divine Love. I am so glad you asked, asked for My love to fill you. I have so much to give you and all. I am waiting right here to give again and again it is My pleasure.

Thank you for sending these "knowings" directly to my heart. I am troubled at times as I become aware that so many are truly unaware, as they have "shut" their ears and eyes. They have been told that God spoke along time ago and we are to believe that, but not to believe God still speaks. Why do they believe You shut and locked the door to Your heart in ours and yet at the same time proclaim scripture that tells us to speak with God and listen?

It is that they do not know. Again, they only know what they know and they can only show what they know. It is up to you to show differently, you and others who are opening your ears, eyes, heart and mind to My voice of truth.

Speak truth. Live truth. Love truth. Truth will reign in the end. All will know in time, here or there, now or later. There will be such a moment within this eternal now, all will rest in peace and live joyfully. You are finding this now, others may come with you. Some will stay behind. You are rising to new heights. People will look up to you. Be the best you can be, through Me. Your life well lived will inspire others to seek higher. This is the way, My way.

I am already here. All is yours now. It is up to you and all to allow. Allow the flow of My good to you and from you. Live with ease, a balanced being. Walk with Me through this world. You cannot fall, when I carry you. I hold you in My heart. I have been waiting for your return. You are My "Prodigal Son." I have prepared a feast for you. Let's celebrate life together.

Tell me what you want and it is already yours now, as you ask. I already know, but by your words you show your faith in My giving-ness. Proclaim your life now.

I am prosperous. I am patient. I am loving. I am kind. I am rich. I am sharing. I am caring. I am generous. I am courageous. I am healthy. I am wise. I am limber. I am trim. I am sunny. I am happy. I am Life. I am creative. I am comforting. I am truth. I am honesty. I am Divine Love. I am thankful for all I am.

You get what you think about, whether you want it or not. Worrying is using your imagination to create something you do not want.

I am comfortable in my skin. I like me. I see my beauty, it is radiant inside and out. I am beautiful. My eyes see God's glory in me.

> *Action is required on your part. I will send good things your way but it is up to you to recognize them and act upon them. Only you can act on your behalf. See what you want. See it for yourself. It is all here. Open your eyes and arms wider; receive My Bounty in gratitude with thanksgiving. Everyday live this way. I give unto you My All when you give unto me your all. Don't hold back, I'm not.*

> *The wind kisses your cheek. I am kissing you. The sun holds you in a warm embrace. I am holding you. I hear your thanks. I feel your gratitude. I fill you more and more with My love. Remember, to those whom much is given much is expected. I expect much of you. I expect you to be so much. I expect you to do so much. I will give you all you need to do your work, My work on earth. Wait and see, patiently. Life unfolds beautifully.*

> *Listen to My words. Patiently, be here. Hear now, I call you by name. I know you. I want you to know Me. All of Me is for you to enjoy. Go live, be the best My love. Stay close. Keep in touch. I never cut the apron strings. The umbilical cord is still attached by a golden thread. The web of life is a beautiful design. We have what we need for now. This is. It works for you. Be satisfied. Make good. See good. Be good.*

People say that God puts us though trials. I say God delivers us out of the trials we create for ourselves when we live on our own. The only way someone can be controlling is if another lets them be. It's the same with God. If we want God to control our life and thoughts we have to allow God to work through us and let go of our own agenda. Quoting bible scriptures here and there does not qualify anything. Life does not fit into a neat little box. It's so much more.

Flowers do not need rules to grow and thrive, nor does the sun to shine.

Why argue? There is no need. You have nothing to defend. Believe as you want and let others believe as they want. You will get yours and they will get theirs. This is the way. Love feels good. Try and understand each other's perspective. You come from so many places. Clarity is coming. The truth is good, all good. Are you willing to accept it? It's up to you whether you accept all the goodness available to you or deny it with your doubts and fears. This is your free will.

I invite you to see the "good" life offers. Wake up today. You are, on your way. The way is clear, when you hold Me dear. Leave it alone, whatever you do not want. Walk away. Turn your back. You have a choice. You have a voice. Learn when to be silent. Silence speaks volumes. I am powerful. Do not deny your good. You are doing well. Hold yourself high. Hold your head high. All can be done. Step back, pause and breathe. There is a way. Relax, it will come. Keep your patience. Patience looks good on you.

I'm a "blissener." I have a different approach to life. I am able to be where I am.

Self care program, physical, mental, spiritual. How to live in the world and still be happy.

"It happened, just as I thought." A powerful truth. Worry is always rewarded if by nothing else fear. People fear the unknown and feel lack of control in their life. Fear lashes out. Walk in faith or walk in fear. Your truth is what you believe and you constantly prove it to yourself. Do you want your truth to be good or bad? Everyone has a choice, self-service, what do you order for your life?

MAY 14, 2011

We each have our own preferences. Thank God for the free will given to humanity. Free will, it's the right to choose our paths along this journey, spiritual journey, here, now and evermore. As we travel through our worldly experience we encounter things we like and others we do not like. We mentally choose these. Actually, our feelings, the core of us, shows us our preferences. Some feel good and some don't. This is all individual. Each may and will prefer differently and all is okay. The ability to see and feel differently makes each of us truly unique, particularly our own. We are to own who we are and feel confident expressing ourselves uniquely while taking no time to judge others for their own life choices.

Do you see why? It all comes back to the great law of the Universe. The Law of Attraction rules all energy and all of life is energy. Like draws unto like. This law is unchanging. What can change is our thought. Yes, the free will given to humanity allows each to choose what they draw unto themselves by their thought. This free will allows us to change our thought and most importantly control our thought. The thing about thought that most misunderstand is its magnificent power.

This power of thought is exactly what creates worlds and each person's thought creates their own. You do not have to know how this works to make it work. It is always working. So why, you ask, does my life not always work so perfectly for me? It is because you have yet to fully understand your power.

You think it lies somewhere beyond you, you think life happens randomly. You think you are unlucky. You think you are powerless. You think you are lost. You think you are poor. You think you are unhappy. You think life is hard. You think others have it better. Then, you see what you think. Can you see this now? What you do? It is what you say in your head, the thoughts you repeat again and again, those thoughts keep you stuck.

Remember the saying, "An idiot is someone who continues to do the same thing again and again and expects different results." It is the same with your thoughts. Repeating the same thoughts brings the same experience to you again and again. It is not only the thoughts you express in spoken words, it is as well your "self talk." The mental chatter that is either cheering you on "Atta boy" or tearing you down "I'm stupid. Idiot."

All thoughts have and are energy. I know it is hard to understand how this can be and how this works. But people have attempted to express to others the power of their thoughts throughout time. The Bible tells us: God knows your heart. God knows what you need before you ask, before you speak. Ask and it is given.

Asking does not require words, only attention, as to Spirit, words are not needed. Words are what humanity uses in an attempt to express itself and to communicate with others who agree on what the sounds, words, mean. God, as Spirit, understands all the meaning behind our words, even before they become words. God, as Spirit, knows our heart and knows our intentions as the system in place, the great "Law of Attraction," reads what we give attention to.

If we turn our attention to what we desire we will have more of what we desire. If we turn our attention to what we do not like, we will have more of what we do not like. Jesus said, "To those who have much, more will be given and to those with little, more will be taken." This is what he was saying: Those that think of "plenty" will have "plenty." Those that think of "scarcity" will have more "scarcity."

Did Jesus say this because he was trying to tell us that his Father, our Creator, loved some more than others? Not at all, he was telling us of this "great law." He was telling us how the world works.

MAY 15, 2011

These words I write, I would like to share.

> *They are meant for sharing. They are meant for all.*

I am just the conduit. These thoughts have not fallen on deaf ears. I hear this wisdom. I record this wisdom.

> *This wisdom is eternal. It has been given before and will be given again. It is familiar, because it is "Truth." Truth is always the same. It may be expressed differently, so it will be understood by different people. Truth needs to be told.*

I have a healthy imagination.

> *Everything is wonderful through God's eyes. Positive energy directed, focused, inline. Clear direction. Patience required. Seek higher. Know, it is. Delight in knowing. Knowing is showing. Feel good about it. Celebrate your knowing. Know, glow, show.*

> *See what you want. Enjoy the idea. The power of suggestion is strong. So what kinds of suggestions have power over you? It is your choice as to what you let in. You have the power. You hold the power for your life.*

I am a fountain of wellbeing.
I am a fountain of wellbeing.
I am a fountain of wellbeing.

> *It feels good. Do you see the Light in My eyes? Know this, I love you.*

MAY 16, 2011

I love everyone the best. There are no limits to My love. Find this in Me, within you. Time will tell.

Visionaries see what can be and respond in kind to their wonderful dreams. Others live in a state of reaction to the physical conditions around them. Thus are pulled, tugged and swayed with the mass consciousness of society. They live small and limited. They live in pain and fear. They always think it's better somewhere else. They are always seeking, but in the wrong place.

Come feel with Me. Feel good. Feel your God Force. Feel well being. Listen in, not out. You have much to do. You have much to be. You have much to see. I am with you all the way. The way, I will show. Stay close. Listen, learn, grow. Rise, shine, and glorify Me

Sometimes, I don't know what to think.

Think what you want. You are your point of power.

I see something someone else has done and I think, "That's really nice and organized, I should be that way."

You can be anything you want. See good. You can see good. Learn to help yourself by thinking a new way. It is all good.

I'm receiving, thank you. It's pretty fun getting these messages! I give thanks for all I am receiving in this moment. All is good. I am well off.

You can do everything you need to do. It's all within your power. Take charge. Don't make it more complicated than it needs to be. What do you want to be your truth? What do you desire for your life? Think it into being. Become who you want to be. See clearly. Make it happen. It is happening, as you believe. Believe the best. Forget the rest. Manifest a wonder filled life. Be amazed. Be thankful. Be generous. Be kind. Be loving. Love life. Live in love. You have to rise above. Stay on course.

Sure, there are things that come into your experience that you do not like. So why carry them around on your journey? By doing so, you keep them and draw more to you. Drop them like a "hot potato!" Tune in to what you want. Flip the channel. By watching and tuning into things that make you feel bad you are making yourself aware of bad choices others have made, created, created by minds and souls not as evolved as yourself. You are above all this. You have to be to create a new, fresh, better, reality of your choosing. See good everywhere. Take notice. Life is affirmative. It gives you more of whatever you give your attention to. Life is abundant. Life is infinite. Life is ever changing and expanding.

Most people only see what is there. These people live within the bounds of the world others have created and by acknowledging and tending the seeds planted; they reap more of the same. All new ideas come from out of the unseen. By someone thinking of new possibilities, new possibilities are born.

Sometimes, it seems as if these wonderful ideas drop from the sky or come from nowhere. But they did come from somewhere. They came from the Infinite Mind that connects us all, which is the storehouse of all wisdom and all possibility. All are connected to this source the same.

Most have not allowed the frequency of this channel into their knowing. It is as if they have an information scrambler running interface creating static so the messages are not fully received.

There is much to know but do not think you ever will need to know it all or that you can. Work with what is given to you. Don't make it a problem. Enjoy the journey. It's what you know. Know good; know the best. Try and see through Me. Listen in. It's all for good.

"I knew it. I wasn't surprised a bit. I had a feeling." Yes, whatever you say becomes your truth. If you don't like what you see, think again. Rethink possibilities. Think again and see anew.

It is not up to you to correct any other. All are "built" to be self-correcting. When you are on a road trip to a new place you keep your attention on signs that point you to your desired destination. You do not concern yourself with signs pointing to places you don't want to go. Instead you keep an eye out for new roads that lead to your destination. And if you miss a road and get off track, you understand that you have a choice to backtrack to where you got off track or re-chart your path from where you are. Such is life. Enjoy the ride.

Idyllic setting, mindset, idealist, I am an idealist. I think of the ideal situation I would like to experience then manifest it. I create the reality I desire. I desire higher. I am knowing higher. I see higher and reach higher.

Don't listen to sad stories. Don't tell sad stories. Tell a new story. Tell a wonderful tale of abundance and joy. This is

the way your world will change for the better. Want better?
Think about the better you want. Keep your vibration high.

MAY 23, 2011

I have been reading Elisabeth Gilbert's novel *Eat, Pray, Love* and
thoroughly enjoying it. It's a tale of her personal journey of spiritual
awakening from a dark period in her life. I'm finding many parallels
as I read. I first saw her book two years ago and was not interested in
reading it then. Through these last two years so many have told me
to read it, but I wasn't ready. Now I am, as I have been on my own
spiritual journey for the last two years and thus I am coming from a
different perspective today than I would have two years ago.

I wonder how many reading *Eat, Pray, Love* are able to grasp these
spiritual concepts for themselves? I guess reading of another's spiritual
journey would be quite the same as the reading of another's physical
journey. Reading about a journey is one thing and living it is quite
another. As I have personally been on a similar journey, I can relate
and find special comfort in the words of another as she makes her own
discoveries of the truths I have found.

It is a journey we all must make eventually, on our own terms and on
our own time. It's not necessarily a trip that can be neatly planned and
scheduled by anyone and most importantly not by anyone else. All
have to take the journey themselves. It's a quest, a very deeply personal
quest, a quest to answer the deepest most personal question of all. Why
am I here? How can I live in a continual state of happiness and where is
the satisfaction I so deeply desire to be filled with?

Some people, or probably most people, feel they have to leave where
they are and who they are to feel the joy they feel is missing from their
life. I once did, but I didn't leave. I didn't leave my life. I didn't walk or
run away. Instead, I stayed and stayed still. I stilled my mind, the mind
that was telling me a story of continual woes, sad tales one after the
other, which I believed, then lived.

One day I heard the idea that one had the power to tell a new story, which could then, and would then, manifest as one's new truth. This was all news to me. So new, that it seemed unreal. But I allowed myself to imagine for a moment that it was possible.

I imagined that I had a wonderful marriage. In fact, I told myself this out loud several times. As I listened to the words I spoke, I heard a doubting voice from within. "Yeah, right, but I still have to do all the work." Before I was allowed to indulge in anymore defeating thoughts, the ringing of the phone halted the downward spiral. Within the next few seconds, my view of life, my life and all its possibilities, would change forever. My husband was on the phone. He was calling me just because he wanted to tell me that he loved me.

So, you say, so what? What's the big deal? The big deal is that we had been married close to 28 years and I can't remember him even once doing such. In fact, it was not even natural for him to close a phone conversation with an "I love you." when we were separated by many days and miles. I would say, "I love you." to him and he just wouldn't say it back, even when I asked. He didn't like to. I was just supposed to know.

So this was a true gift, a gift from David, from God and the Universe. Yes, at that moment and with those words my life changed. I had stopped believing that I would be loved as I wanted and thus I had not allowed this good to come to me. "Wow, if this can happen as I say and believe, then the world and my place in it is greater than I ever dreamed!" I don't believe there could have been a more powerful manifestation to make me turn my head and heart in a new direction.

Trust all is well, this is what is meant by having faith in God. God is good so we are to believe as God's children that all of God's goodness is available to each of us as well. We are to trust in God, trust in God's goodness, purely and completely, without doubt or fear. For God is Love and Love does not know fear. No fear, God is near waiting in love with love to welcome all to the center of His heart Eden, Heaven on Earth.

When you know something you are sure, you are certain, you are confident. I know I am loved. I dwell in the house of the Lord, the Lord of love. I have built an altar in my heart for God's Divine Love. God has told me, yes told me, that I am safe, safe in love.

Fear not My beloveds. Know Me. Know Love. Know, no fear.

When we worry we are fearing, fearing bad, fearing not being totally cared for. We are imagining living outside of God's love. Did you know this? Had you ever thought of it this way? Rethink what it means to surrender to God, to surrender to the power of Love. Love is power, the most powerful energy of all, the energy that creates worlds, worlds of good, the energy that is available for the asking in each moment. Ask and it is given. Ask for God's guidance, care and love. Then listen. Heed. Give thanks and share the love.

When you want to know, you ask. When someone wants to know they will ask, when they are interested. They have to have interest to care, to care what you say. So until you are asked, save your breath. Breath deep, know and trust that living well is the best you can do to show what you know.

Nothing is bad or good in itself. It just is. It is what you make of it. It's what you think of it that matters, that matters to you. Someone else may choose to think entirely differently about the subject at hand and thus have a different experience and that is okay for it to be that way. No one is to judge another for their personal choices. It is certainly enough to concern yourself with making the right choices for you. But here's the good news, when you choose God, you choose good, you choose Love at every turn and all is good in return. It can be no other way when you choose God's way.

May 24, 2011

A very major revelation came to me as I lay in bed this morning. A very short time ago I was unlovable. I see it now, pretty darn clearly. I'm not talking about how one usually considers someone to be when they are unlovable, I mean most who know me, actually I'm sure everyone who's ever known me would admonish me for ever making such a statement. But I have proof of this truth, my life and the immense conversion experience or journey I have been on these past two years.

Where I am now is a totally different place than I was two years ago. Forget the physical dimension here; I'm talking about emotionally and spiritually. Two years ago I was strung out and quite frankly freaking out. I felt unloved, unloved by my husband. That is the story I told and that was the cold reality I felt. I had tried and tried to fix him, which had the decidedly opposite affect on him. He pulled away more. There was a cold distance between us. Oh, how it hurt. My eyes are swelling and stinging with tears now as I think back on this.

I had been working on myself to some extent, to the extent I knew how and possible for the previous few months. Yes, I had been a total nervous basket case, evident from my frequent hysterical crying to my extreme weight loss. I had seen and felt my physical world crashing in. What I forecast for our personal and financial situation was more than gloom. It was doom.

I knew my mind was running wild so in an attempt to save me (if not my marriage), I began a new year with the intention of learning "mind control." Nothing freaky here, I only desired to have control over my mind. Somewhere it had come to my attention that I could learn to control what I gave attention to and thus control the rampant thoughts of desperation that plagued my mind.

Thinking back now, I am realizing that what had me most freaked out was that I felt so totally out of control, out of control of my destiny. I had thought the only way to gain the control I felt I lacked was to control others and that theory wasn't working out so well. Besides my husband pulling away from me, my son was as well. Of course, at eighteen and a high school senior living at home, pushing the limits of acceptable behavior to his mother was quite normal. It's just that I was so torn because I still felt the responsibility to control the outcome of his life but was losing my grip on having any authority or right to do it.

Gosh, it's quite amazing with what clarity I see this all now, but in the midst, well I was truly lost. So anyway, I had begun making a sincere effort to find sanity within myself, to gain control over my spinning mind. I really have no recollection of how the ideas came to me to do the many things I did as I cleared a new path. I guess, well I more than guess, I know from the perspective of where I am now that once I decided to change my mind, the universe opened up to my suggestion and presented ample opportunities and ideas to explore.

Firstly, I remember cutting out the random junk. Just as if I was making an effort to cleanse my physical being, I would drop the junk food habit; I dropped the junk media habit. I pretty much stopped watching TV, not totally, but when one becomes aware of all the crap that is streaming into their home via the TV and makes the connection that no good can come from no good, well not much is left. I made a rule that if I wouldn't welcome whatever was on TV graciously into my home in real life that they had no business being there virtually. This was my personal rule, not one imposed on others, so if what was on TV when the TV was on in my home didn't feel good to me, I removed myself from the situation. No complaints, just quietly leaving and retreating to a more peaceful environment, another room.

I found new things to tune into, music, and books and of course my art. Along that time someone whom I did not know had found my art on the web and was so moved by seeing it that they had sent me an e-mail with kind comments. They said my work felt "Zen." Hmm, I knew it was meant to be a compliment but really did not know what it meant. So I looked it up, and yes, I kind of saw it too. There was a peaceful tranquility and balance that had been developing in my art over the past few years. These works were not strict interpretations of the physical but had a spiritual element as well. I had not really known what to call them. My first exhibit of such works I titled *Out of My Mind*. But I knew that these amazing paintings took root and touched something and somewhere so beyond my limited and often rattled consciousness. Whatever this "Zen" was that manifested so wonderfully through my art I wanted to equally manifest throughout my life. This wasn't a clear thought, just a yearning, a very deep yearning.

> *All you have to do to become more loveable is to love more. Then you become "irresistibly lovable." The next time you are feeling frustration try this: Instead of letting the words "darn it all" come out of your mouth say "bless it all," and watch the blessings flow.*

Revelation: Acts of God. In light of the recent most devastating tornado, which destroyed the Missouri town of Joplin, many may ask why God allows such disasters to occur and bring harm to His people. Others may see this occurrence as a specific "act of God" as if it was a punishment or warning. These people believe God is a judgmental being, whom doses out harsh penalties as needed to an evil world.

My understanding is different and certainly more comforting to me personally. I am now understanding God differently than the ideas engrained into me throughout my life. I have opened myself to a constant flow of God's goodness and love. As this love flows into my soul and warms the very core of my being so flows a new level of wisdom. This wisdom tells me that God or what I and others call God is only good, all good; all love here and at hand. It is up to each of us to choose whether or not we allow God's love to flow to and through us. Our free will is what makes us feel separate as well as deeply connected. It's what we do with this free will that matters. We can choose our own selfish ways or God's good ways of love.

Our ego's try and keep us tied to the physical world and tell us that we need to look out for number one and our ego's number one is always self, our small self. So small that the only way it can begin to feel big is to collect stuff and then work hard to protect it's stuff. Our larger and unlimited Self is God or maybe easier to understand as our God connection, our universal connection to the One All Good.

No one can really have both. The Bible tells us we can only worship one, one God, one good. When we choose our small self and say me, me, me, more, more, more and live in fear and worry, we are not putting our attention toward the good of God. Okay, so I believe in the Ultimate Creative Force, the Eternal Spirit which created each of us and as well created the universe and thus this universe runs perfectly according to the laws of nature established in the beginning. These laws are unchangeable but we and our world, our bodies and our earth are. Magnificently powerful forces of nature have been changing the face of our planet continually since the beginning.

So the great storm was a natural occurrence. It just was. Man cannot change the weather. Man can be aware and take measures to protect himself from rain, wind, snow and sun but that is all. It is life. Life is change. Change is what happens. This tornado was a great change. A most powerful and upsetting change. It changed lives forever. It changed the face of the earth. It took away what one survivor described as "everything she knew as real." It took away and tossed around the material. What was left was spirit. When people crawled out from the rubble and they saw the shamble made of their physical reality, their spirits awoke and gave thanks for their lives. Their good came out and more good came forth. Good is God.

So yes, I do believe an "Act of God" has changed Joplin. But I'm not referring to the great storm. I am instead referring to the so very many acts of God, acts of selfless good being performed as I write. This is why we are here, to help each other, to lend a hand and an ear, to be good to each other and to be God for each other and to see God in each other.

Many ask, why does it take a tragedy to bring out people's good? My reply: the lives we build, the walls we build of separation sometimes have to crumble before us so we can see the light, the light in each other's eyes and in our own.

God bless, good blesses. You gotta feel good about it, whatever it is. The only way to bring good your way is to attract it with good. So you have to feel good, to feel good. You have to think good. Thinking good is a choice. A choice each always has. We each have free will to choose our thoughts and as our thoughts create our life we each have free will to choose and create the life we want.

Feel the love, the love I have for you. It is yours already. Don't block the flow. Go with the flow. Pass it on. No one can hoard love. Take time out to spend time in. Within yourself lies the wisdom for your life as you need it, it is there. Quiet yourself.

MAY 26, 2011

Stream of consciousness, let it flow as you know. Here and now is your power at this hour. Open up. Rise up. Look within. Hear your heartbeat. Breathe. Drink in life as you know. It will be seen. Not a cloud in the sky to obstruct your view of eternity, deep blue sky.

Oh my, You envelope my soul wrapping me in Your limitless love. My eyes see clearly the breadth of Your beauty. How I love this limitless view of life. Let me see all that I can be. With these words I awaken. With the serenading of the birds around I am lullabied into a deep peace. Oh, the harmony of nature. This is my nature too, to be in harmony with all of you that breath, you that grow.

You that know God's love is for all, tell all. All are welcome home. You do not need to shut out the world to be with

Me. Welcome Me into your world and I will walk with you. Together, We can make it better. Together, We will love all. All there is to know is Love. My love is for you, for the taking. Here it is. Here I am. Present with you as you write, as you breathe, as you walk and as you talk. What could be better? There is no better. Just know better and thus live better.

I am here for all. Even those who doubt, I am with still, waiting. Waiting for them to be still and ask for more, more of life. More of the good stuff, God stuff to fill them. I have forgotten no one. My love is for all, for all time. I do not live in churches. I do not live in the fancy decadent structures built by man, though I am present there. I am present everywhere, for I am Presence.

You can feel Me, you can know Me, but you will never be able to fully wrap your arms or mind around Me. Know it is enough that I wrap My arms around you. I speak of holding you in My Hand but I have no arms or hands as you know yourself. These are only words your mind uses to begin to grasp how close I keep you to Me.

Thank you for allowing My being to flow through you. Thank you for giving "good" expression in this world. Hold your high thoughts. I am on high so you must hold high thoughts to live through Me. Thank you for asking, for asking for My Divine Love to fill you. I have so much more to give. Keep asking, all I am and have is yours. It is My pleasure for you to experience pleasure My dear. Thank you for noticing, for noticing the wondrously beautiful world I have created. I made it all for you. Thank you for believing, for believing in the best. For having faith in the goodness of all hearts I put it in each of you, see it everywhere.

Thank you for being, for being you, for not trying to be someone else. I made you special and I want you to always know how special you are to Me. Thank you for thanking Me. I am so grateful for your gratitude. The more you give Me the more I want to give you. Thank you for your time, the time you spend seeking Me. I have waited patiently as you busied yourself with so many details of your life. Thank you for making time for us. Your eyes are opening as your heart opens wide. Live fully awake My dear. You are safe when you keep your thoughts near.

Sing Me a song all daylong. So sweet it is to hear your voice express your gratitude. I see it in your eyes, the reflection of My perfection. Know this, know Me, alive and well in you everywhere you go, everywhere you are, I am present with you and all. This is the day the Lord has made. Let us give thanks and praise.

What are you talking about? Do you ever listen to what you say? What you say, do you really want it that way? Think before you speak. Speak the truth of what you want. Think it. Write it. Speak it. See it here now. This is how you create your destiny.

Come back to Me and know eternity. Forever live in Love. Speak prayerfully. Give reverence to the power of your words. They create your world. See the difference a new thought creates. Change things up. Switch the channel. Attract more good. You deserve it. Oh, yes you are worthy!

Worry not, please give no thought to what you see that is displeasing. Offer it to Me. Give it up and I will make it My business not yours. Stop looking for evidence to prove a reality you do not desire. Instead, turn your attention to collecting data proving all is well. This is how tables are turned and lives are changed. Notice what you want. Offer no comment in return to what you do not like to hear. Have it fall on deaf ears. Re-tune your eyes, ears and heart to hear the best. Expect to hear good news. Expect to see joy. Expect to experience joy.

You do not have to "talk" anyone into seeing life as you do. No one can truly see through your eyes, just as you can not see through theirs. All I ask is for you each to have compassion for each other. Each is free to choose to see and thus live as they want. What you want, is what is important, as it is as well important for you to want the best for all. Your intention is enough. Nothing more is needed or allowed, as each is allowed to think for themselves. Think again about this. You are not "in charge" of anyone but you. You are to be present for others the best way you know. Show up well.

I want you to know better, better than you did yesterday. Today is new and fresh. A new day continually presents new opportunity for growth, for understanding, for love and wisdom. Be available to this flow of life. Open up. Do not shut down. You cannot run from life for wherever you are, whoever you are goes with you. You cannot hide, though you may hide your eyes. Even when you tightly clamp your eyes and close your heart, I am with you waiting patiently in each moment. You cannot run from life. You have to meet it head on.

What are you trying to see that you do not? Are you truly looking? Are you truly doing your part? Are you asking but not listening? Are you ready to accept My gifts? When you are ready, they are yours. I limit you not. I want to see you, each of you, live this life to the fullest. The Universe is your, our, storehouse of all possibilities. There is enough for all, forever and ever.

MAY 24, 2011

I am seeking direction. I am seeking guidance for my life. Please help me to know what is mine to do and then help me know I have the power to do it. I am listening. I will heed Your messages. I trust Your goodness and guidance. I ask for the aide of all in love. Show me how I can best manifest love and light in this world. Show me how I can truly make a difference here and now. Let me hear. Open my eyes, open my heart, here and now. Amen.

Note to self: I have lots of ideas of how other people might consider changing to show up better in the world. But oh, if they would ever listen. But why, I ask myself, should I care how anyone else chooses to live the life that is theirs alone to live? Am I wanting this "better I know" for their own good? Or do I have self seeking thoughts, imagining that if they were better then my own life would be better? Hmmm. I remind myself once again, no one but myself is in control of my life, my destiny.

Stop seeing this as otherwise. Don't point to what is bad, point to what is good.

I am not turning away from the God I was raised in faith to know. I am not turning my back on any church or faith; instead I am expanding my knowing to understand far greater truth, which encompasses all truth known. I am knowing, learning to know who I am, who God is and my inheritance of God's infinite Kingdom here, now and forever.

You make life harder than it is by living where you are not. Be where you are. Live each moment as it comes. Think about your life now. What has been the hardest for you, living the moment you are in or living out the possibilities of what may lay before you? Certainly if you were living out the worst case scenarios of what could lay ahead I'll bet anyone of them was harder for you to live in your imagination than when and if they actually presented themselves.

You will never be able to imagine and pre-live all the possibilities your life will present. That is why I tell you to live one day at a time, one moment at a time, in faith that good is your destiny, that all good is yours through the bountiful blessings of your Creator.

You are to have dreams for your life, direction and goals, but to live with the awareness of opportunity knocking in so very many directions along the way. Dream big, imagine the best. Imagine the best possibilities you can imagine but limit yourself not to these. Be open to more, to greater than you can imagine.

Take these words with you. Take them to heart. They are the wisdom of your heart which is so much further above your head. Many live with their heads in the clouds and cannot see far. Your heart envisions more than mind and eye can begin to perceive. You've come so far. You have so far to go. Keep going. I am here, holding your hand. I delight in your laughter. Know Me more.

Everything is being given to me to know. Set perfectly in place for me to find so easily. Clearer I see. Clearer I hear my calling, my Higher Calling. I give thanks for all the reassuring words that find their way to me, to my knowing, to my heart and to my head. Thank You for showing me how You have shown up for others. It helps to know others know this way. Thank You for showing me so today. I know You are clearing my way, purifying my soul. Giving me what is mine to know. This journey called life is what I am on. With You beside I know I can go on.

MAY 25, 2011

Please speak to me. Tell me who You are? Are You me? Am I You? Are you God or Jesus or my Higher Self? Are we all the same? Do I need to or should I call this Love, this knowing, by a name?

> *I shall remain nameless, yet you know who I am. I am All. All Love for you, for eternity. What are words really? They are limiting ideas. I am not limited nor are you, know this.*

> *Come let Me comfort you. Come to Me with your everything, your pain and your pleasure. I want to share your life and be your life. I am Life Eternal. Come to Me as you are. I am here listening to and loving you. You are not broken. You have just been broken open.*

> *You had to be broken open to be available to Me. You were so closed, so rigid, so tight, so selfish. Yes, you were very selfish. You thought you could do it all, all along, all alone. You were selfish because you didn't share your life with Me. You couldn't see My Love for you. You heard the Words but did not get the message. You had to be broken open so you could open up to Me. It had to be this way.*

> *We have always been together as One. When you smiled, you felt Me. When you held and nursed your children, you felt My love. When you painted, I inspired you, I took away your pain. But you could not see how to live eternally with*

and through Me. The sense of separation you felt made you sad and caused your pain. It was a downward cycle that had to be broken, for I love you so much and want so much better for you.

I have given you insights into the lighter side of life for sometime. You could paint it, because of Me. Yes, you knew there was more to these stories you painted. You beheld the glory they told. You will paint again with Me. Now, the more clearly you see, the even more marvelous "Our works" will be.

MAY 27, 2011

GPS Global Positioning System
PGS Personal Guidance System,
    Prayerfully God Speaks
    Perfectly God Speaks

While many are finding their way across the earth today guided by and continually connected to GPS systems, I am finding my own way through life with my own "PGS." It's my personal guidance system, words, ways, knowings and quite specific directions just for me that guide me to just where I need and want to be. The more I have disconnected with the "world systems" and sought solace and comfort in the quiet of my mind, God spoke to my heart in kind.

There is no reason to look elsewhere. You have found what you have been looking for. But yes, there is more, so much more here for you. Stay tuned.

Why do you insist on seeing life as a problem? Why are you always looking for flaws? Can you not see the perfection before you? Have you not seen My perfection in your reflection? All of life, including you is a reflection of Me and my great love. It is all so lovely. See it. Believe it and be it. Be the beauty I created you to be. You honor Me when you honor yourself, the soul and whole body being that you are. I made you wonderfully. Know this, I am pleased with My creation.

It's trash, I know it. Someone else's dirty laundry put up for the world to view. Truth or not, who really knows? It only really matters to the ones directly involved. So why should I care? Why would I dare look? Constantly this is paraded before us, scandalous situations of public people, some already known for their lustful ways of living and others pop up as shocking stories. Oh, the media loves these stories the best, of course they do they sell the best. People seem to crave stories of others failure and misfortune. It's what gossip is made of and this is gossip on a very major scale. Yes, I am tempted to look. Is there harm in that?

Look at it this way, where is the good in it? Are you helping anyone, including yourself, by adding fuel to that fire? Gossip is gossip on any scale. It's talking about another's life in a most negative light. Who needs more of that? Do you? Be the good. Let it go and go on looking for the light and beauty in life. This is what you want, see it and believe it.

MAY 28, 2011

Here I am Lord. It is I Lord. I have heard You calling in the night. I feel weak and scared.

Stay with Me. I will comfort you. I will fill you with My love. You are fine. You are well. You are safe. You are loved. What else can you possibly need or want? You have it all My dear; it is up to you to recognize this. One and all must know for themselves My truth. The truth of the matter is that "matter," matters not. It can be gone in a flash with a wind or a flood, washed away, shed, dropped, gone. This will happen to you again and again in the physical realm you inhabit. You will be shaken to your core. What is left? That's up to you. It's My wish for all that each be so filled with Love that the exit of the material takes nothing from you, that you feel no real loss, that you become extremely aware of what you do have and who you are. This is your essence. What it is, is who you are and what you will be in the nonphysical. As you know, you will show. See things perfectly. Clear your mind. Find the time to see Me in you.

As I look at the photos of my children, as children, I hear myself say, "It all went so quickly." It's almost a blur. The time came and went. The little children I knew and loved are gone. Tears come and swell my eyes. A lump builds, then bulges in my throat. Yes, they only live now in my memory as children but they do still live. Yes, they indeed live. Their tender souls now inhabit the well-formed bodies of adults, amazing young adults that call me "Mom." I answer and come when called. I will always answer to someone who calls me "Mother."

Wake me up. Let me know. I want to understand. I want to live well, fully alive all the time. Hear my cry, hear my plea. Oh, my God help me please. I want to know You more fully. Fill me with Your Divine Love. Raise me up on this day so I can follow Your way.

No one can make anyone else happy. Each has to choose happiness for themselves. You may offer another some of your joy, but they have to make room for it in their own heart to be able to accept it. Always offer joy and love from your heart to another. If they welcome it and welcome you be glad and rejoice! If they accept not your greetings and gifts, shake their dust from your sandals and move on to greener pastures. Many others are wishing for and waiting for your good news.

This is such good news, sending good thoughts Your way. Today is the day. I want to be with You.

I am here.

MAY 31, 2011

Offer yourself up to My Greater Good.

These are messages, messages to me. I am hearing it now, differently. These words have power for me now at this hour. The old me was afraid to question, especially the ways of God. I now know that our questions are good, each one of them. Yes, it pleases God that we care to know more, that we dare to learn the truth for ourselves.

Ask, ask whatever you don't know and want to know. Then consider the source of your answers. Are you listening to the wisdom of man? The laws and rules created by man are from man's limited consciousness. Are you accepting what another, any other, knows as the best you can know? Know better, ask the source of all, ask God the answers to all of your questions. God knows your heart and God wants each of us to know His infinite love and wisdom.

> *Again God says: Ask. Just ask believing and I will answer. Yes, you will receive as you believe.*

I am being continually filled with gifts of the Holy Spirit. Yes, there is more to life!

Walk by faith, not by sight.

Living in blind faith I still lived with many fears. It was like I was blindfolded and left to maneuver through the world on my own. I bumped into quite a lot and fell down more than once. I felt comfort in routine, as I learned safe paths to follow. My world remained small as I was filled with fear of the unknown. I feared the bumps and potholes that I could not see but imagined laying strewn out before me like land mines. This paralyzing fear kept me bound to a vicious cycle of repetition. Round and round I went never really gaining much true ground farther down the path of life. Blind faith is no faith at all, certainly not faith in good for all.

The faith with which I now walk through life is true faith, faith in Truth and Goodness. My eyes are no longer blinded but wide open to the glory and majesty of this world. I see the good all around me. I trust this good and trust that there is more.

No, I still cannot see all that lays ahead on the paths my life may take but I walk with a certain surety that all I need to know will be given to me as I need. These are not simple statements of faith; they are strong statements of my simple faith in God. God has and is showing His glorious ways to me. God is speaking continually to me and guiding my every step. I asked him to. I moved aside and asked God to take the lead. I asked God to lead me, to be my shepherd.

So though my own eyes have such limited vision, to the extent that in comparison to God's wondrous vision I appear blindfolded, I walk by faith, not by sight. Faith that my dearest friend, is holding my hand and guiding my every step. He will lead me into no harm. Yes, as long as I allow God to take the lead in my life, all is well.

The danger for me, and for all, is not to begin to feel so "self assured" that I believe I can run ahead without God. If I become impatient with God's speed and ways and forget to give all glory to God, I will surely trip and fall. Oh yes, fall on my face. But I will always have the opportunity to turn back, for God is always there waiting patiently, not even shaking His head. He knows I have to learn to appreciate His wisdom and ways to walk in true faith. He knows that this "true faith" is what we each require to be with Him continually and live higher. God already has faith in us. He is just waiting for each of us to have faith in Him. The Power that be is the force within me. All glory to God.

JUNE 2011

We do not tell them that they must obey
every law of God or die,
but we tell them there is life
for them from the Holy Spirit.
The old way, trying to be saved
by keeping the Ten Commandments,
ends in death; in the new way,
the Holy Spirit gives them life.

2 CORINTHIANS 3:6 NLT

JUNE 1, 2011

You know my heart before words are ever formed. What I ask is given and again my gratitude is felt by You, without me even speaking. We are that close. It's a love story, a very old fashioned, love story, You and me. You and the world You created for me, for You, for all. Love is what makes the world go 'round. We are not to pray. We are to be in harmony, so filled with God's Divine Love that there can be no other way than love.

JUNE 2, 2011

It's a journey of the soul versus journey of the mind. Some want to become masterminds, they work to master their minds to obtain perfection. Mine is a journey of the soul. I have given my soul to my master, back to God and asked God to so fill my soul with His love that His will is mine. In this way my life becomes divine.

> *Clarity brings comfort. So nice to see you smile. Communion is one with the Presence. This opportunity has always been, but there is good news. New news available now for all, for the asking, first released just over 2000 years ago, God's love. Breaking news: God's Divine Love is now available for wireless download directly to the center of your soul. Ready your heart now, make room for the infilling of this most wonderful substance.*

> *Be kind. Unwind. Your laughter is music to My ears, a song of your soul, a song of joy untold. Delight in Me. Give yourself a rest. Be at peace for eternity. Delight in Me.*

> *Be at rest. Rest in the Presence of the Lord your God, rest in the peace of His love. There is nothing to do, just be. Be in harmony with Me. Grace is My gift for you. Be gracious and accept My love. It comes to you on the wings of a dove. Yes, My love is for you. Be My love. It is here. It is now with you, not beside, not below, nor above. You indeed abide in My love.*

Oh, wow!

> *Here, it is said. Hear, it is said. Paul in his letters was telling people how to get their hearts ready and what God's Divine Love was. He spoke not of human love. He spoke of a love so pure, so selfless, it could only be Divine.*

> *When people "study" the bible they are approaching the words with their mind. This is not the way the words were ever intended to be perceived. We are to each read then open*

our minds and hearts asking God to help us receive His true
message.

James Allen, hmm, too bad he was never known in his lifetime.

But I say, oh, he was known. Known to God and he knew
God.

I feel so lucky. I know I am blessed. It feels good to feel good about
myself, to take care of myself, to honor and love myself. I give honor
to God in doing so. Thank you. I am spending the day with sunshine. I
am spending the day with the center of my heart, my son Dominic. Oh,
how my soul glows!

If they ask, you can tell. Tell them what they need to know.
Tell them how you show such Love. Tell them you have
received a gift from your Father whom lives in you not
beside, below or above. Tell them how they can as well ask
the Father to be filled with His Divine Love.

Creation is not linear. Nothing is wasted. No moment is lost.
From everything, something else builds. Lessons are learned.
Growth is experienced. Have no regrets. None are needed.
Nothing is lost. All is gain to be realized in time, throughout
time, again and again. Be patient with yourself, others, and
God, you have a choice to skip the drama. Know all is well.

From here I see new information, time to see clearly.

When the shift occurs it is like one is living on autopilot
from a much higher dimension and perspective. Nothing
is the same as it was. One is in being, a spiritual rebirth,
a new person with eyes and ears to hear and most of all a
heart to feel the truth of this good news.

If the information is congruent with the information which I am being directly given, it validates both in my eyes.

> *Jesus as Christ spoke two levels of truth. He spoke of the power of the mind and he spoke of the power of Spirit in all the same breath. As one learns and accepts the power of his own mind, the power of his will and the power of his free choice, then one has a clearer understanding of the next step. Man uses his own mind power to choose whose will he follows. He can then make a choice not a "blind" choice but an "intelligent" choice of what kind of power he wishes to direct his will.*

> *Once man figures out the system of linear universal power and how his own free choice directly creates his own experience, he can go forth from this mental awareness and have a fine life of his choosing. Yes, it will be hard, but it can be done. He will have to stay on guard of his thoughts and actions and work hard to stay the course. Yes, he will fall and trip and may even stay down a few times for quite a while. But this is his choice.*

> *I say choice because there is another path which can be taken, one that leads one so very much higher than any path could ever have of man's imagination, one to the greatest of heights, to the mountain tops and above and all with the greatest of ease. This is the path of Love, the path of the love of God, Divine Love.*

> *Divine Love can enter into one's heart and fill it so that all one desires is more of this wondrous substance. And as one's heart swells with the love of God it weeps from one's very pores, healing the earth, comforting all God's people everyone.*

Jesus Christ taught us how to pray and ready our hearts for such love. He taught us to set aside our own worldly plans and selfish will and pray to our Father that "His will be done on earth as it is in Heaven." That God's will be a man's will while walking on the surface of the earth, just as it is done in the spiritual world, our beginning and our end, as we each return from whence we came, our flesh to the earth and our souls back to the wholeness of God. There is much to be said. Wake up people.

People keep looking, searching for answers, in history, in artifacts, in material substance, in the physical realm, here and there, looking back to the past and into the future digging deep into the earth and soaring high into and through space, looking for a golden key to the door which will unlock the mysteries of life. All this searching is in vain. All that is found is more of the same. Forevermore, man has been looking out instead of looking in. Man will never fine the truth of himself out there on the outside. No matter how deep or how high he peers, he will not find. He never has in all his years.

Oh, there have been a few who truly knew, their power was immense and did the rulers they incense. Put to death most were, for the stories they told could not to the masses be sold. So hidden these truths have been, hidden in safe keeping for a time like we are now in, a time when Truth can be told, nothing new, all the information is old, but new to this world, to this physical place, ready to be heard by ears that desire the fullness of God's Grace.

So ready yourself, make a space for God to be. Make your heart a worthy sanctuary for the most Holy. Drop the drama. Forget what it is to fear. Learn to walk through life with the knowledge God is near. Ask what to do. Ask for what you need. Believe all is here and you will know Truth in deed.

But you have to listen. You have to have ears to hear. God is always speaking. God is always near, nearer than you know. Closer than you think, within your very being God's Love is filling every cell of your body.

Family, I love that term of expression for my spiritual guides, my guardian angel team, for that is exactly how the love messages You give me feel. They feel like the loving wisdom of my Father, Mother, Sister and Brother, someone or ones whom know me oh so very well, someone whom always wants the best for me and offers encouraging words along the way.

Thank you, dear Family, you are my Spiritual Family, that is patiently been a steady and guiding presence in my life, whispering to my soul. I see it now as we are a team You and I. I am the player, the one making the final call and actually making the moves but You are my advisors.

Help me to live this life to the fullest, all to the glory of God, through the power of God's Divine Love. Let my life be a physical, mental but most of all a spiritual beacon of inspiration for all, far and near. Help me build a presence on earth, a wide knowing where all will know me and witness my glowing. I can imagine ways, but I know my visions are limited and Yours are not. Help me with patience. Speak louder so I will hear every clue of what to do, what to say, and where to be, as God's Divine Love lives in and flows through me.

Amen! So be it.

I feel so powerful. My power rests in God.

JUNE 6, 2011

I declare my good for real, for me, for eternity. My heart swells. I feel a burn. For more Divine Love I yearn. Fill me up. Let Your Love flow. Here I am. Let me know Your Love.

> *Release Me. Raise Me. Give your mind a rest. Put Me to the test. Live in My Fullness. It feels magical. It is musical, this Energy, this Me, living.*

Extreme thrills, rushes of adrenalin are what people crave to feel so very alive, to feel their hearts pound. Fear is a powerful emotion, as is anger all part of a cycle of drama that runs the lives of most here and now.

> *They seek a shock to their system, a system that lives by routine.*

I may have walked this earth for fifty-two years but I feel brand new. I am but a toddler today. Just two years old in this new life of mine. I suckle at God's Bosom for my daily bread of wisdom, understanding and love, awaiting His Word, staying close, not rushing ahead. My body is new as well. Fresh cells, healthy cells are continually born, pushing away the old dead cells, "youngering" me daily. This I can see and believe. Yes, I believe me.

I like to hear and I like to read the words of wisdom given to and shared by others. Hearing the messages is reassuring as they echo the same messages my own heart receives. So yes, I enjoy them, but neither those words, nor their messengers are my life line.

I know and trust my own pipeline to Source and Truth. I receive continually the Truth I need, as I need it. I have all, know all and I am all I need. So be it. Thanks be to the Lord my God whom lives within my very being. Let this Truth be known to my core. Shake me up. Settle me down. Lift me up. Hold me high. Hold me close. Let me shine in your glory my Father, my Maker, my Mother, my Truth.

There are things that need to be done. Things I need to do. Please set my heart and mind aright and see me through, for through you there is nothing I cannot do. Amen. So be it. Let me live through You.

> *I like what I am hearing. Loud and clear, your words I hold dear. Let's go on and get it done. This actually could, if you let it be fun! Let's turn some music on!*

I turned on the stereo CD player and the first song that played spoke directly to my heart. It was an old CD of my daughter's, music from the motion picture Michael, *Through Your Hands* written by Don Henley. I had never heard this CD before. No more co-wink-a-dink stuff. There is a reason for all, just what I needed. I like this information. I love what I get. I get what I want. I want all the best.

> *Here for you.*

I believe that whatever one invites into their life should make them "feel good" this includes people, media and art. Yes, choose art to live with that makes you feel good to look at. This is way beyond any intellectual response. If it makes you feel good, raising your vibration, that's a good thing.

My kitty is a conduit, physically giving me access to the love which surrounds me. Bless his furry little soul.

Everything I need to do, for what I need to do, is with me now. Let me see this clearly.

> *Feel good about it. Coming through loud and clear My dear. Be patient. You are so close. It's like the game of warmer and cooler. Don't be greedy.*

Driving along the Kansas state highway from my home in Lawrence to Kansas City, I see cattails growing in a patch roadside. They aren't everywhere. I just notice them in one spot which I have to assume is a continuous bog of sort, wet ground, perfect conditions for their survival. So I ask and ponder and thus realize that the seeds for these plants were not just tossed in that particular location where the perfect conditions exist for that plant. No, they were tossed everywhere, strewn across the land by nature's planting system of wind and birds. The fact that they germinated in that spot is a testament to the fact that the ground was accepting and all conditions were right for the implanting of the special seeds.

So go the seeds of thought floating in our ethers, germinating only where conditions are right. They are properly tended, fed and watered whether good or bad. That is the way of all.

Sometimes I hear myself make statement with such conviction it amazes me. I then question my words, as I have no physical evidence to support what I have said. Perhaps I can find some with a bit of searching or maybe not but most likely it is truth, truth beyond me, truth to be known and trusted.

> *Seeds of "Truth" are scattered everywhere. Is your mind fertile ground?*

I speak like I know. I know Truth. Truth speaks to me. Beyond my eyes, my heart feels its way through to You and Your glory. With a new awareness, my eyes see beyond the limits of my mind. Lead me, show me, the way each and every day. This I pray. A seed has been planted in fertile soil. Let the sun shine upon my face. Let tears of joy water the fields of abundance before me. Glory be, it's a sight indeed. Thank You for awakening me.

> *Rise and shine. Now is your time. You've wanted to know. We've wanted to show you the way. Today is the day. This is the hour. Love and insight upon you we will shower.*

JUNE 7, 2011

Today I awake for God's sake; within my being I know His love. God speaks to and through me. My light shines. My light blinds. Love to be found is all around.

> *Here I am. Get out of your way. Live fully today. It's nice to see you recognize Me. Bring out the best. I'll give you rest. Easy does it when you are above it. The world will know as you show.*

I can see the difference in me. I delight to know. I delight to show the world God's glory. My Friends are here with me now showing me how to live, to give, to be, to see. I have invited Them in and asked them please to help me be the best I can be.

> *The Masters knew. The Masters said to themselves continually, "It is well with me. It is well with my soul." They knew that and focused on that one idea. The love of God within creates love of Self. Give energy and attention to only what pleases you. Give no mind to that which does not feel good. In this way you create a life filled with the good you desire, desire higher.*

> *I offer you pearls of wisdom. Where does your wisdom come from? From the depth of your soul, from the very cells of your being wisdom lives. Stream of consciousness, what weeps from one's very being, the You you are, pure and true. The true You coming forth to light, into being, just being you is all you need to do. Say it like you mean it, as you intend it to be for this My dear friend is how you create your reality.*

I give thanks for all I can do. I've gained control over the mole that lived within the one called sin. The one that said I was wrong all day long. Who believed in bad and made me sad.

*Keep smiling. What are you channeling? What are you
giving a voice to? Is it a good cause or a cause for alarm?
It is a voice that brings harm? Invite Peace in, within and
without and there will be no doubt whose voice you hear,
who holds you dear. Yes, it will become clear and there will
be no fear. The voice of Love is soft and low, ready to show
you the way each and every day. Tune in, tune up and you
will be delivered up to and through God. Amen. The proof is
in the heart under the influence of Spirit.*

Today I go beyond before. I am walking through the door. Take my
hand and lead me to the Promised Land. My eyes can see your glory.

*Beyond intellect can be known, through a spiritual sense
that requires development, a knowing of the truth of God,
of the universe, spoken directly to one's heart, a heart that is
ready, open, prepared and seeking higher truth.*

I was fearful, filled with fear and anger. I did not know much at all.
Reality escaped me. I was taught not to question, but to believe and
bow down in fear of the unknown. So I walked the earth in trepidation,
baby steps, tip toeing around potential hidden land mines, which I now
know were only in my mind.

I cannot teach you how to see, I can only show you how to be. I do
what I can do, what is given to me. No regrets. There is a lesson in all. I
am here to learn, to find my way home. My name is being called.

*Are you ready to listen, to hear what is said? Will you
believe My Words? Will they ring true? It's up to you. Set
aside your thinking. It's all about being. Be ready. Lay in
wait. Don't feel bad about anything. Just be and do your
best. This is no test. There is no trial. You have been living
in denial of your very being which is good. The truth I know*

says that is not the way to peace in eternity. It's time to see life as you should.

Coiled desire
For spiritual
Heart awakening
For those
With ears to hear
Higher truths
Love at its best
Available to all
To give rest
I'm good
Good for all
To each
His own
Way.

One man says to another, "You are a sinner, because you do not do as I do. My way is best. You are lost and forgotten. God does not care for you." Point not your finger. Do not poke and prod. This never was, nor will be, the way to or of God. Instead, open your heart and mind. Look for good in all. It is there, perhaps hiding because of what you call "The Fall." Get out of your way. Just be here with Me. It's not what you think. It's so much more. It's a feeling thing. Feel good everywhere, all the time.

JUNE 8, 2011

Shh, be quiet. Stop the noise of your mind. Hush little baby. I hold you in my arms, away from all harm. Hush little baby, don't you cry. Poppa's bought you the world. Raise your vibration. The higher you go, the more you'll know.

Know me, your Higher Reality in you. Now and forever We are together. Raise me up. It's Ascension Day. saintly, godly, wisely, kindly, gently, love the Earth and my children. Who are you? Do you know? I will show. It's quiet time. Shut your mind. Give no mind. Be heartfelt.

I used to think that painting images from my mind was not valid art because it was too easy. I didn't trust it. I now know the validity of such expression and the value of it. I welcome and receive these gifts of Spirit with gratitude.

I used to be a "reason being." I thought there had to be physical reason for every action I took. I am not so reasonable these days. I've moved beyond trusting and depending on my mind, to believe in the gifts of Spirit, knowings, feelings and urgings. Peace be with me. I've put my mind to rest.

I wash you with my love.

Today I see further, higher, better. Yes, today I know better.

Know better, do better, live better, be better, better up.

Brother, sister, father, mother, we are family, you and me. Family reunion, cause for celebration. Let's bake a cake. Light the candles never to be blown out. What are you looking for, an open door? Here it is. Step in. Walk through. It's up to you, what you do. Here we are, close not far. Stop looking out, for Number One is here now for and with you, all for you, for all, now and forever. Come in. Rise up. Be Who you are looking for. Welcome home.

Is my voice clear? Can you tell I am near your heart? So close my words are in your throat. Speak up. Listen in. Forget sin. You now know how to show my love. Do not push. Do not shove. Just live in my love. They will know who you are by my love. Some know, all that know, show. Stop preaching. Start loving.

I was seeking more. I didn't even know what I was looking for but I found it, happiness, true genuine happiness from the inside out.

Notice what you want. See the body you desire. If you want it enough, it will be yours. You wanted beautiful long eyelashes and admired another's now they frame your own eyes beautifully. Ask for what you want. See it true. See it through. You really do, really true, create the life you want. Whatever you see is yours. See beautifully.

I am thankful for our time alone. I love to be with you and have you know My Presence. Be with Me fully, My Love. You materialize, what's before your eyes, see perfectly. Laugh it off.

Do you send blessings or curses? What you give you get. Think about it. Is this what you want? Do unto others as you would have done unto you. Patience is a wonderful gift. Give freely. When you know, you will show, My Love. Read between the lines. It is all written.

Who and what is controlling you? Are you out of control or in control of your life? Your life is in your very hands. Don't give away your power!

I'm gorgeous inside!

"Sign of peace" in church, where it is safe, to those in your box. Think out of the box. Love out of the box. The box limits you, limits your understanding of Me, of us. Bless all whom cross your path. Speak well, in Love dwell.

Within your very being rises a phoenix from the ashes.
You are so great. Love is your fate. There is more than one
chance. There is more than one way. You are never limited.
You can try again, another day.

That's good news! Who is that laughing? It is me. I'm just happy, happy to be. So I laugh at and with me. Isn't that funny? Available to me, a funny thing happened.

No one can be convinced by another. No amount of
reasoning will make it so. It is only knowable to those whom
seek for themselves. Others will always jeer and shout. They
have no doubt, for they live without the desire to know
things higher.

To those whom look within and spend time within
themselves wanting to know, Spirit will show. For all is there
wanting to share. The little mind of man cannot believe,
for he has not seen. You are supposed to doubt, to question
what is true. This is work for each soul to do. Take not
another's word. To each man's soul must the Truth be heard.

Do you like what you hear? Are you happy now? Do you feel
Love today, completely, in an eternal way? If not, you have
not found the Whole Truth of who you are. You are not but
a grain of sand; you are indeed a rising star.

It's okay not to believe, for believing is not the same as
knowing. Knowing is faith. Believing is putting trust in
another's knowing and saying that is good enough for you.
Is it good enough for you to just hear of Another's life in a
Wonderful Land? Would you not care or desire to know for
yourself of what He speaks? If He can live there so can you
as well. If one can, any can, as all have the same ability.
None is so special that He is the only. His words are an

invitation to you to come follow Him to His home and to make it yours as well.

Joy to the world! There are no rules with God, Love rules. Man cannot make man know God. God cannot make man know God. Man has to seek God to find God. God is good. Look for good, there God is found. God is not lost, man is. Find your way. To each his own. There is not one way, for the Love of God, Divine Speaking.

Sure there are challenges in life, but don't make them problems. Problems are hard, life need not be. Lighten up. Live a little more. Trust life's goodness is yours.

It's not what you think. You don't have to convince a soul. It's not a matter of words. Love speaks softly and yet so clearly understood. Just love, be My love for all. I know you want to share what you have and you do with your life, from your being, your just being you. The Truest You, your Highest Self, all there is within you, that is Love. Let them know this Love. Love is patient. Love is kind.

I have a one track mind, the mind of God. Living life to the fullest is my goal. Joy is my destiny.

Do what feels right. You can be, what you want. Do not look to anyone else for approval. You and only you know, what is true for you. It is your path you are on. See the light in others. As their beacon shines it draws you toward the better, the higher, in love.

This is the way you grow, you show My love being who you are, My shining star. Give your gift. Give others a lift. Let them see how love can be. Yours forever, these ifts you've claimed in My name, yours to use, yours to hold for eons, for lives untold.

How lucky you are to be living now as the world is awakening to how My Love unfolds. As your spirits rise, as your souls ascend, the world will know Love has come again. Time will tell the story. To some it can be known now. I have shown you how to live in the fullness of My glory. Clap your hands, sing My song, dance around all in joy. This is "the truth of the Ssory".

What do others think of you, you wonder? What do they see? Do they see crazy? They do see a difference? They feel a change. They want to be with you. You draw them in with your Love. This is all they know. This is all they need to know from you.

Why do you care what others think of you? You do not have to prove a thing. You do not have to prove yourself right nor another wrong. Those are all matters of judgment. Judgment is never the answer, never the thing to do. Your Father does not judge you. He only gives His love. Be as He, "love fully." Drop ego's agenda and allow the will of God to rule your heart.

Do not allow others to "push your buttons." The only response is love and Love is patient and kind. Let this be easy for you. With love there is nothing to decide. Your only action is love. Love is not to be a reaction. Love is a choice, your choice, the gift you get, the gift you give. Give more love.

If you cannot find the words, you can smile. A smile is never wasted, always worthwhile. So you see judgment in another's eyes. It is not for you to point out or to condemn.

Again I tell you, just send your love. It's a gift from you and your Father whom is always near within, not below or above. Love is the message, yes love, pure love.

Do you think you can set the world aright with a fight? All is well with you. There is nothing to do but realize.

When others ask, yes please do tell. They need to know all is well. But they have to want. They have to seek, to understand the value of the words you speak. I know you want to share, because you so care. Be patient please. Live with ease. In this way, as you love and glow each day, you are My light in the dark of the night. There will be a time when ears will hear, ears of those you hold so dear. Trust in Me, never fear. The door is always open and you are always welcome. This is your home My dear.

There are things I want to say of which I can find no words.

Not every idea worth expressing can be expressed with words, that is why there is music, art, nature and silence. Silence is golden. This is the golden hour.

Let Me kiss you with My breathe, the breeze. Let Me hold you in My warm embrace which is your sun. Let Me wash away your fears with My own tears, which is the rain. I do not rain on your parade to spoil your fun. Perhaps you are marching to the beat of a different drum? Let the beat you follow be the beat of My Heart in yours.

You get what you expect, so why not expect the very best? You are worthy. You get what you expect, as you expect it.

Physics are physical laws that man has experienced thus knows. Purely straight line theory of our physical limitations. But there is more to this life we know. There is a spiritual element, Love. Love knows not a straight line. Love is not bound a bit. Love bounds past all physical limitations and knowings when allowed. Allow Love, experience life off of the straight line.

Creative thinking is not straight line thinking, it zigs and zags and takes great leaps of faith. Physics can be learned by study, study of the rules discerned by others. Spirituality cannot be attained in this way. There is no map that is certain to take any or all the highest mountain top, for all come from so many directions, mindsets and spiritual conditions. So there is a "light," a beacon of sort, which gets the attention of hearts and yearning souls. This is the Light one meets upon physical exit from this land, but can be known while still in the physical form today.

Hearts are ever seeking joy and enlightenment, behind the scene of the physical. They yearn for more, more love, for "Love" is one's soul's true home. Some have found this Light and cannot contain their joy and excitement. They say, "I sought! I found! Come see with me!" So they share the stories of their personal journeys with seekers that pine to know. These spiritually ascended souls shine brighter, as more Light has poured into their very being. Their enlightenment can be felt, as they seem to magnetize others to them.

Yes, they each have a light but still they are not the "Light," none of them. It is in them but not privy to them alone. True enlightened souls know that they are not themselves "the way" and that their mission is only, and can only be, to point to or show "the way." This is the way love is, the way of Love.

I get new information everyday. How enlightening!

Special dispensation.

What is that about?

Well, what did you ask about less than an hour ago? You asked about the gift of Divine Love.

Yes, I do want to know more. As I know I am receiving this gift and this gift from the Holy Spirit has swung my life around 180 degrees, and opened my eyes and heart. I ask and continue to ask, but I need to know if all others who are being given gifts of enlightenment as well are receiving this Divine Love. Is it naturally "a given" or are special words or thoughts required to receive this "Love" which is so much very higher? I lay in wait for the answer.

Go ahead with the things you need to do. I'll get back to you.

Special dispensation that makes life easier to grasp, to take in, to live fully, yes, it is a gift, given to those whom ask. Not everyone knows, not everyone shows. You have to desire higher for this is the highest gift of all, for all, for the asking. We have told you to ask for more. This is your Father's love. Above all else, know this, it is your gift. Gift of discernment, rise higher in love for all, with My eyes see the glory before

you. Share it, My love. Why do you doubt? You have been given This Gift, has it not given your own heart a lift? As you know you will show.

You have to have a heart opening to receive This Love. First one has to know there is more and that they are deserving of this more to be able to begin to want, to yearn for more. For one has to truly desire higher to reach higher.

The kind of Love of which I speak is the Love Paul wrote about to the early Christians, but if they as well had this Love as Paul did, they would not have had to be told what to do, to be doing God's Will, they would just be doing it!

What I paint, the art I create are heart felt songs. Color tells the story of the light in my life, of what I see through the spiritual eyes given to me. So sings my soul to God's glory. Testaments without words, for words limit the expression of one's knowing and showing. These works are glowing with a light beyond me.

I am enjoying myself! What a thing to say, what a way to be. I am in love with me, for I know and I show the fullness of God's love given to me, bestowed on my heart. Thank you God, for this gift of love.

Love of Self equals love of God. This is right. This is true.

I am just to be me. There is nothing to do as I live fully through You.

I'm opening up to the truth of my being which was always there. Here I find myself in love, in the rapturous love of God, enveloping my every cell of being, setting my course. Oh, of course I know I have been bestowed with the most wondrous of gifts. God's Divine Love completes me. Oh, dear God make me whole; make me holy, wholly You!

I like to know. I have always been searching somewhere, everywhere else. I did not know I could find within myself all the answers my heart desired. I still forget to ask and to listen within and instead search without, without finding any of my own truth. For "Truth" be known only by the heart, by the hearts discernment.

JUNE 11, 2011

Something has changed. It's so beyond me, beyond my complete understanding. But I know it is all good. It's all as it should be, for God's Love lives within me. I asked, I prayed, to be filled with Divine Love, to have Divine Love flow through my very being. I readied my heart. I cleared the way, making a place for God's Divine Love to fill and stay with me for eternity.

Efforts, mindsets and attitudes; these are important to all, all we are and all we do, for they are the basis of how our light shines through. Respond to all with gratitude and the blessings received will be extraordinary. Let not your ego swell with pride, for no one can hide. All is known to "All." Your attention and intentions are clearly seen to "the Unseen."Give thanks, where thanks are due, realizing that no great works are done by just you. Thank the Divine. Give thanks to guiding souls and you will experience blessings untold.

There is much to know. Let Me show. Listen in. We shall now begin. Find balance, not too hot, not too cold, just right. Allow the process to unfold. Follow nature's way.

Soul communication, it is difficult to hear the messages of the Divine with a lot of static. Static equals mindsets, attitudes, beliefs and attachments. The more you can release, the clearer the line of communication will be. It is beyond words, direct knowing, soul language and translation. Doing soul communication by asking and receiving responses is also a form of service because you will act upon the responses you receive.

When others want to know they will ask. They are beginning to respect your wisdom. Respect theirs as well and only tell what they ask, for which they seek. For they will in this way treasure the answer received. So be it true.

I am really trying to pay attention, to see and hear what is mine to do.

A listening heart is the key to finding and knowing Thee.

I really enjoyed today. I would like to live each day this way, in appreciation. The teachings I received today were from a book and thus received on a mind level and yet they touched the core of my soul as they resonated with my own soul knowings. Further confirming the path I am on, this path of enlightenment, this glorious journey of my life. Thank you, thank you, thank you for making this wisdom known to me in such various ways and means. I remain open to further teaching. Your student in light and life, Debra Ann

Know, no limits. As you understand, more is given. Your thanks and appreciation is well received. I'm glad to be of service. Take not an ego trip for this information you receive. Give thanks and all glory to God.

When you see that which you do not prefer, judge not, worry not. Send Blessings and Love. Then go on to greener pastures which I have prepared for you. Don't bother with hate and disdain for anything, for those emotions do not promote peace within or without, have no doubt. When you bless instead of curse, you add to the happiness of Mother Earth.

I love ministering to your people not preaching but serving through word and deed. *"Feed My people,"* You say. *"Give them the wisdom, food and drink, they need each day."*

Not all can hear My voice or have developed so to discern my words. You are a channel of My love, a conduit. When they ask tell them what they desire to know. In this way you

serve and show my love, a gift given from the Highest Source above, Divine Love. Minister, do not preach. No one wants to be preached to. Love ministers. Preaching is an act of judgment. This you know, so can show.

If you tell something to another even if it is a teaching of extreme wisdom and it has not been specifically requested by them, for them, from you, it will be discerned by them as an act of judgment. And so it is, as you would be judging them, so that you believed they needed that teaching.

Let it be. Let all lay in wait, ready to be served as requested. This is the way all of my knowledge works and is properly discerned. I do not force a single teaching upon you, none of you. It is all self service. You have to want and ask for yourself.

Each creates the story of their own lives by what they plan for, or perhaps they realize not the control they have and feel lost and thus live lives of continual disarray. You need not "buy into" another's drama, you have permission to excuse yourself from such scenes of fear, of rush and worry. Plan well, plan for abundance.

Jesus spoke in parables that the truth be told. No information did he withhold. There is a blatant truth to each story, and to many in history what may lie beyond this first meaning remains a mystery to be solved. And yes, it may be solved but only to souls more evolved. So in this way all was given, no Truth is truly hidden. Jesus said many times "Seek and ye shall find. Seek ye first the Kingdom of God. Look not up or around, the Kingdom of God is close at hand, near it is to be found. Love God with all your heart." This is what Jesus said was our part.

It's time to see what lays beyond, within the depths of Love's soul, for here truth lies yet untold. Never fear just because you do not know. Trust Love to keep you high above turbulent waters. Keep breathing. Take deep breaths and rest in me. I give you My peace for eternity, the real deal.

Lessons learned, like badges earned from Heaven. See more ways to live fully through Me each day. A smooth interface depends on how deep your inner faith, your trust in Me. Trust in Me. Trust in Me completely with your being. I made you. I know you. I am you at heart. In your heart's deepest recesses I live. Bring Me to light. Let Me shine in your eyes.

JUNE 12, 2011

You are learning. You are more, bit by bit, peacefully with Me. You are researching my history, the stories of man, his-stories of Me, how I have been perceived through eternity. Man attempts to conceive of Me but he never really can. How can man conceive of Me who conceived him? I am glad he wants to know. I'm pleased he wants to show. But it saddens me to be put in a box, especially when it is taped shut then stood upon and preached from. Keep looking. Keep seeking. Keep desiring to show my love for that is the truth of me. Know more. Know more Love.

I love it when the right words fall from my mouth, when I am given the right thing to say at the right time, when I can offer a message that needs to be heard. Please continue to use my voice as Yours. Speak from Your heart of hearts to another with my breath. I am here for You to serve You and Your people, my family everywhere.

I sow seeds of goodness everywhere and water and tend those I see which others have planted in the world as I notice their sprouts. We are all gardeners of this world we live in, all together creating the possibility of a beautiful Eden experience. By each one's actions and attention thought forms flourish or wither. I make it my intention today to give attention only to what I would like to see more of in this world.

Here's what I have found: If you would like to see a change in any matter of your life you first have to be able to allow your mind to conceive of the possibility that a situation could be different. This is the beginning of the process of allowing. Once a space opens for the possibility that something in your life could be different, a change has a chance, a possibility to occur. One small step, just allowing a possibility, opens the door to a new experience. By not even being able to imagine that something could be different you are bolting the door of endless different experiences.

> Smile. It's the best "makeup" you could ever put on. See what you like. Be what you like. When you declare that something is always true in your experience you are actually locking that idea into your reality, whether you really want it or not. You are declaring your truth and the universe proves your truth to you again and again, just as you ordered.

I have a new twist to offer the old adage of "finders keepers" with my new eyes I see the finders as keepers not in a selfish way but as finders then caretakers of what is found while it is in their possession. Perhaps someone finds what another has lost; they may then keep it safe and as well enjoy their possession of such until either the proper owner is revealed or it is passed along to another when need be.

Whether what is found is material or spiritual the same applies. For none of us truly owns anything while here on earth. We are all mere caretakers. So take care of what is yours to tend and pass it along as you see need be. This is the cycle of life.

I need to stop listening to people and listen to the directions of my heart. People tell stories of drama. My heart only knows Love.

Settle down. Be at peace with Me.

JUNE 15, 2011

I keep living and I keep learning. I give all thanks to God. Thanks be to God. Those are so much more than words to me. They are my truth, a statement of my truth. My very being is grateful for this life and so I live it fully with gratitude.

Life says to me, *"There you are crying and you haven't even opened all the presents I have for you, already in your presence."*

> *Why should someone else's drama so personally affect you? Especially those to who you have no real relationship, those public figures whose lives are broadcast to the world. Why should any of their personal truths or untruths affect you?*
>
> *You are your own person. You have the choice. The power of choice to choose and thus create the life you want for yourself. Even if you witness another's life running smoothly, it is not yours to claim, for you can live through no other than yourself, your "True Self" it can be no other way.*

The more I listen to others speak of God, the more I understand the "specialness" of the connection I am developing with God unto myself. This "specialness" can only be attributed to the inflowing of God's Divine Love into the very core of my being, my soul. For my soul knows a different experience of God. My soul knows God. My soul knows the truth of God and is becoming more and more of this truth, moment by moment as it swells with each gift of the inflowing of His Divine Love.

I have been asking if there was a difference. I have been wanting to know if the gifts I am being given are being as well experienced by so many others who report to know God and the answer I am getting is that others whom experience God in similar ways to that of my experience are far and few between.

I am awakening to the truth that truth has many layers and so does the wisdom which has been given to us through the ages by saints, sages and saviors. There is first a blatant moral lesson in each of their teachings and then a deeper truth which can be learned but beneath it all is a complete understanding which can only be known but to those who know.

To many reading, even my words will appear as a riddle, but some things are better left unsaid. They are better left alone by any formal thought process, they can only be known. Who can know? Those who desire higher, who let go of all knowings, teachings, and imaginings and open their hearts and souls to pureness, therefore creating a space for the wisdom and love of God to infill.

This is the way these words are being written, for all knowledge being poured forth is "news to me" as I write and read it. This is how God speaks to and through me. I see this as the way through my art, as well as words. God speaks and I listen. I act. I do not react. I just act. I respond to God's love.

How is this so different you ask? I feel the difference in my mind and soul and I as well believe others see and feel a difference to and around me, a peaceful presence, something not entirely new to me but so much greater and so much more consistent than ever before. Why? Because I gained an understanding of the inflowing of God's Divine Love and I experienced the rapturousness of it. I asked for more. I've had it before but in such a lesser amount and without much gratitude for the gift. That is where the true "shift" took place when I gave thanks for everything and blessed it all.

So here is plainly the "shift" I feel I have made. I used to be one who worked hard to follow spiritual principles and now they are completely woven into my very being. There is no choice to make. I need not rules. For I have so given my life to God that God has given me, and continually gives me, the very substance of His divine being, Divine Love, which in turn is purifying my soul, so that my soul only knows the way of God. And my words and actions flow directly from "Source," not edited by my small mind. My mind needs not to be concerned if any action is correct before acting, as goodness flows through me. I am a clear channel, conduit, for God's Divine Love here and now in this world.

Oh yes, I am a work in progress. I am not done, but am being glorified and purified more each day. I continually awaken to how I can "show up" better and then in turn ask for better. I am a lowly weak metal being refined into pure gold by fire, the fire in my soul, the workings of the Holy Spirit. It is my hope for the world that each soul can, and will, someday understand for themselves the truth of these words I write. For it will never be, and can never be, for the mind to know, only the soul can know. Natural to my being, my nature is changing.

I don't read the Bible as a "rule" book, I look to it as a "who knew" book. Jesus knew. His first disciples knew. Paul knew. Many of the first "Christians" to whom Paul wrote instruction to did not and may have never known for themselves. As the church they formed relied on the rules those early few wrote for their wisdom, never understanding the true power and workings of the Holy Spirit. Those whom men termed "saints" knew, as well as many other "Truth Speakers" whom were put to death through the ages by people using the Name of Christ to condemn.

> *There lies the shame of it all, as the deceit continues, for the "Whole Truth" is not known. Please speak for Me.*

My happiness is not dependant on the actions or inactions of any other.

JUNE 17, 2011

Step out of yourself and back into Me, back into the Fullness of Life.

Yesterday, there was no pleasing you. It was all about you. Your ego was a big balloon which I popped! Come back down here, back to being the True You, not the you needy of being self-satisfied. Oh, you really weren't that bad, so stop judging yourself. The world you live in creates this expectation that one day a year you are special, that you matter and that everything should be magical that one day just for you. That's a lot of pressure for one person and one day, especially since the second half of that belief is that the other days are drudgery and "suck!" But oh, I ask all of you to see life through My eyes, every day and every one, the beauty, the glory, the peace.

Let each know that in each moment you treasure them for who they are with a smile, a hug, a listen. This is the treasure you look for, God-ness, goodness all around. You think it is buried. It is not, it is your eyes that are covered with mud and dirt. Wipe away the crustiness that clouds your vision. Goodness is here today and I suggest you make it a habit to get out of your own way.

Thanks for the talk. I needed a good listen.

What's so special about you? It's not your job to let others know or make them think that you are special. I put you here to remind others that I love them too, that the gift of My love that I have given to you is for all. Get off your soapbox and on your knees. Show others My love. Humble your "self" and go beyond, so far beyond what you could ever imagine. Go humbly, please.

*"Fame and fortune" this is sadly where many believe joy
lies, but it is a lie. The ultimate lie, for neither is a certainty.
Both or either if ever attained are at most fleeting pleasures.
They can go just as they came and as well are constant work
to tend to, so unlike real joy, true joy, true selfless joy. The
kind of joy that once one knows is theirs to have and to hold
forever and ever, the internal and eternal joy of God.*

*Why do you think you need to know what everyone is
thinking of you? What makes you think they even are? They
have their own lives you know. So do you. Mind your own
business. What matters is what you think of yourself. Don't
be self-centered. Be selfless and as well love yourself and
others as I love each of you. Be fully activated, an Ascended
Master.*

*It doesn't bother Me. Let it be, leave well enough alone. Who
asked you to do a thing? It's all up to you what you do with
what you have, with what you know. It is all as you show.
Show up better for real. Many things are given to you to
know, not necessarily to "tell," but certainly to "show."
Jesus spoke with the Authority of God, as did his disciples.
These early Christians were killed for "this Voice." Later
others calling themselves "Christians" killed others whom
spoke with this same authority. Thus the "insanity"
continues.*

I hate feeling so mad and hateful, but that is where I am right now,
pissed! I want to be cared for, loved, listened to, comforted. I beg for
this feeling. I feel lost, lost in my own sick thoughts. Please help me to
help myself! I am so weak. I need your strength. Carry me forward.
Why do I expect any other to save me, especially one so lost? I want to
be enveloped in the Love of Father. I need to be wrapped in the Strong
Arms. Carry me away. Purify my soul. Save me from myself, from my
own lowly being. Raise me up. Hold me high.

Dear Heavenly Father, come fill me. Take away the daggers I hold in my hand ready to thrust in blame and shame at myself and others. Let me see Your light. Raise me above such lowly earthly standards. Save me from myself. I do not like what I see, nor how I feel. My stomach is sickened by my ego display, if only to myself.

I want to be with someone better than me, to inspire me, to make me want to be better. I feel so drug down. Raise me up. Let me know no other has the power to do either. For in reality, I hold all the power through Your Love, Divine Love. Come and comfort me. Enlighten me. Hold me close. Let me, let the old me go.

> *I am still here with you, listening to your heart. Let it go. Let it all go. Wash your hurts away with your tears; release them and their pressure on you. My Hold is stronger, tighter, firmer. I will not let go of you ever. You are My love. Know this, you are safe with Me, rest in this knowing. You need to take control of your own life. I will show you how. Just let My Peace be with you now.*

> *Don't ride on another's wave. Never let the actions of another decide how you will behave. The same Authority from which Jesus spoke is speaking to you, as you have awoke. I am perfecting you, but you are not done. You are feeling the frustrations of this imbalance, which you are recognizing as the balancing has begun. Fear not My ways. There is no delay. It's a process. You'll see, eventually.*

I think it would be nice to know how it all works out, but I do, don't I? It all works out perfectly. All is well. I am safe, so I am told. When I ask myself, I will thoroughly in my heart know and show this understanding. Yes, I believe, but I ask you, Oh Great One, help my unbelief.

"I just want to be mad for a while." It's the title to a song, which I sing like it is my soul song, but this I don't truly wish, I want to let go and go on. Lord, please help me to release the hold I feel I must have on life.

> *Mood alteration federation, a way to see, a way to be, on this earth more kindly. Make peace with who you are, with where you are, and with whom you are around. Let us resound, Peace be with you all around.*

I like when I am more than my mere self. I can help myself be more, love more fully, by diving deep and discovering the true treasure that lies within my very being, within the depth of my soul. I can choose to bring these riches to light, to my surface, the Riches of God's Kingdom, Heaven on Earth, unearthed in me.

> *Let My light be seen. Rise and shine. The door is open. True Love beckons. The "Soul Truth" is here for you. Secret admirer, yours truly. Do over, make over. Make up your mind to live beyond your mind.*

Something came over me. Hate came over me. I'm sorry if you were in my way. I brushed you aside. I watched as you tipped over. I laughed. How sick of me. I hate that. That was me. Go away bad self! Be gone! How can I be so little and think that I matter so much? Is this part of the learning curve I must travel? I hope it is the curve that tilts upward. Don't let me fall so low again please.

> *So you want to be purified, how much? How much do you want it? As you experience the glory side, the other side seems deeper and darker.*

JUNE 18, 2011

> *Fiction is more palatable than Truth. Truth disguised as fiction tastes better. It's more easily digested. There is more Truth to fiction than fiction in fiction. Read between the*

*lines. Open your eyes and you will see what they mean,
mean for you to see.*

This is how the world works, like attracts like. Unknowingly, we
mirror back to another, what we receive from them, this is our animal
response, unconscious action. The best part of the story, our story,
is that we can choose to change our action and have it not be a mere
reaction. We can change the trajectory of our life with each action we
take, conscious choice, as a power of our free will.

*It's a gift given only to humans. Accept your power. Embrace
your power. Power up people!*

As you amend your path, by choosing your actions in line with the
life you desire, life will get easier and smoother. You will be drawing,
mirroring, good things back to you, as you broadcast good. You are
mindfully creating your life, good or bad, whatever you choose. We
each have been creating our lives this way all along but perhaps not
being aware of how this most basic universal principle works or even
aware of the existence of this constant truth. So we weren't mindful
of how each of our actions, and even thoughts, created the world we
experienced. Once one becomes "mindful" of how he has the power to
create his own life by free choice, the world looks new, new possibilities
are imagined and realized through "controlled thought."

Whew! Mind blowing huh? Yes, indeed mind blowing in many ways,
but also mind exhausting, having to so carefully guard one's thoughts
to so create all the good one desires is exhausting. One can easily fall
into a worry trap, worry that they won't be able to monitor all those
"booger thoughts." Well, see that's the trap, the catch. Mindfulness
means the mind is always working and quite often the workings of
one's mind spins out of control. "Ahhh! I need help here!" you scream.

Well that's a start. Yes, a step in the right direction, for as anyone can do
it all alone, "mindfully" creating their life, none has been able to reach
anything close to a life of peace and perfection on their own. Those Ten

Commandments for instance, not so easy to do huh? Especially, when it comes to the ones that speak to the control of one's thoughts.

That's when one becomes a seeker, when one desires higher and seeks a better way for his own life. When one believes he knows the way to any truth, he is not and cannot truly be a seeker. He would merely be a follower. A seeker is one who is looking for something they do not have. They may not know, actually they can't know, what they are looking for; they are simply seeking answers, seeking a better way, seeking for themselves.

Jesus talked a lot about the importance of being a seeker. Yes, he did tell others to follow him, but he just wanted to show the way. He never said that he was the end all result. He spoke instead of his Father's Kingdom. He told people to not look too far. He told them that they didn't have to go away to find the Kingdom of God that it was available now and that they didn't have to wait until death.

I just remembered how mad I am. It's okay, Jesus said I would be (Gospel of Thomas) and I am. I am not going to deny this feeling right now, though I know I will move on past it to perfection. I'm mad because I have lived in a world built of untruths, packaged as the way to Peace and Perfection. I have been sold a bill of goods. I am mad because I see it now. I see the unreality being perpetuated before me in all in the Name of God my Father. I see the limitations imposed and taught. I understand how tradition has killed the spirit of the seeker.

> *Man has been told, by man, that all to be known is known. "The rules have been written and here they are. Don't question, doubt or look any further."*

Jesus said, "Seek ye first, the Kingdom of God and all good things will be added unto thee." Seek ye, you seek. When one is seeking, searching, they are digging, looking high and low for something they want, that is lost, not found to them.

Like the child's game of "warmer-cooler" Jesus gave clues. "The Kingdom of God is at hand. It is not in the sky or over there." He did not tell anyone to open a book. He had studied them, the Torah (the books of the old Testament), as well, but did not ever say one's salvation or entrance into the Kingdom of God depended upon the quoting of any verse or knowing the linage of any of his ancestors.

He had good news, different news, He indicated that this knowledge of God was hidden from the intellects. So it wasn't a thinking thing, and can't be experienced by reading any instructions given by any other. It has to be sought beyond the mind. That's where I have found God, beyond my mind, beyond my brain, out of my thinking.

Jesus told us to go away to a quiet place to spend time with God, a deserted place, a closet, seclusion, so one's mind can detach from distractions, from the physical sensations of life and rest, so one can quiet one's being as to hear the small still voice that continually speaks within. That is our God connection. That is the open door where God waits, ready in our hearts for acknowledgement. Let your mind take rest and just be. Be peaceful, restful, rest in the peace of God.

You may not hear God's voice at first as the static of your mind may be so loud. It takes time to tune into the "God Channel," but practice makes perfect. The more time one spends seeking God's voice and wisdom, the more peaceful one will become without ever consciously being aware of direct thoughts or words. But as one makes this seeking a daily practice more good will come. It will become easier and more comfortable. Then, bit by bit, this peace will flow out into the rest of one's life and as it does the seeker will begin to crave and thirst for more peace from their inner sanctum.

Part of this process is dropping the ego self, the mindful part of each of us who is constantly thinking, "Me, me, what about me?" And instead go into the silence with no agenda but comfort and peace, seeking to feel and know the presence of God. Changes, quiet changes are being made to one's very being just by being a seeker. Subtle changes, awareness, knowings, thoughts, feelings and words become evident to one's psyche while in and out of the quiet zone.

Gratitude and love are felt and naturally expressed. The load lightens. As one is inspired to act and as one does and is grateful for more, more wisdom teachings are handed to the seeker, student of life and love. It is not a way of learning. It is a way of knowing, knowing God's love and knowing all God's truth and wisdom.

There is a burn in the heart, yes, a most wonderful heartburn, a fire, an energy felt in the heart zone center of one's physical self. It is the "Fire of Refinement", as the alchemy of God purifies one's soul changing a common metal, our humanness, into a Pure Golden Heart.

So why am I not going to church, to Mass? Because that information is not serving me anymore, it is actually hindering my path to enlightenment, to my full presence of the Kingdom of God. It is not that I don't believe in God, and it is not that I don't acknowledge the saving power of Christ's message. It is that I through my own journey as a "seeker," I have found a much more profound realization of God and a truer understanding of Jesus the Christ's message.

I have physically been in some of the "holiest" places on earth, as declared by "the Church" and been moved only visually by the manmade beauty. Not at all moved spiritually, yet, stepping into the sunshine and breathing the fresh air I am filled with a Wondrous Loving Spirit that can be God and no less. I find God within as I settle my mind and body. At rest, at peace, He comes forward to me and fills me with His love and wisdom. I have found this "love of my life", whom I have been seeking. All I desire is more closeness, more Divine Love filling my soul.

I do believe that others within the boundaries of the formal church have as well experienced this completeness, this wholeness, this holiness of which I speak and seek. But they have been far and few in between. And instead of holding them and their lives up as lanterns for the people, lighting the way, the people whom people have put in charge say: "No, you are not worthy. This sainthood is not for everyone. Who are you to ever begin to think that you could ever be so holy? Remember, you are but a sinner. You are lowly." Many may argue that this is the message indeed, but I can only say that it was the message I received.

People are massed, herded and paraded through rituals that are to give comfort but to many they are but mere tradition. Jesus of Nazareth, as Christ, denied the "faith of his fathers" and walked his own path. He said each had to do this as well. Be a seeker, not a preacher or a follower.

> *Want to know; want to know God's love. Seek ye first the Kingdom of God.*

So I say, I am finding my own way, searching for clues, breadcrumbs dropped by others while they made their own journeys. Some will say, "This is not right. You are wrong!" I say, it is right for me I know. It may not be the path for you. There are many roads to the top of the mountain. Some are filled with weeds and boulders as they have hardly been traversed. Go your own way, but go in peace. May peace be with you, the peace that was meant to be.

And all that being said, I would love to find a spiritual community that supports my personal seeking and knowing experience. I so yearn to be able to communicate and share these profound, deep and true experiences I am having as I live this life. I want to touch another and be touched by another with skin on, who knows and is living a similar journey. Please put this person, these people in my path. Bring them to me. I want to live full. I want to share my joy.

I don't need a "middle man," a mediator. I recognize my direct connection to God, my Source of being, Eternal Spirit. My faith does not follow a calendar. My faith is in the eternal moment where all Truth is present. I do not believe any minute, nor hour, is more magical or holy than another. My goal is to recognize the continuous presence of

Spirit and be one with this at all time, acting from God's will only, as God's will becomes my will.

Just as Jesus "wrestled with the Devil," I continue to wrestle my own devilish side, my ego, which still fights for my attention. But my ego is losing its hold, as God's will is having more and more of its way with me. Ego used to rule my world, not that I was much of what anyone would call an egotist, but yet it was my own will, my ego calling the shots. Once threatened or challenged, my once mild ego reared his ugly serpent head and hissed. He is a fighter for sure, my ego, as he has been my protector since birth.

I must tell you ego, you have not always appeared so ugly and you truly have in your own way done the best you could for me. I find no fault with you and will cast no blame. You have helped me speak up for my rights and cheered me on. But I am moving on now, on to greener pastures. Oh, you will still be a part of me for you are my humanness, but I am no longer allowing you to be the driving force of my life. I am surrendering my own will to God's.

So see it this way. God is in the driver's seat for this ride called my life and you are but a passenger in the back seat. No, not a back seat driver, you are merely along for the ride and from the view I am getting, as my soul elevates and my consciousness rises, it's going to be quite a wonderful ride. So sit back and relax. God is taking care of us now. He has always wanted to, but was waiting for my permission, for my asking and as well the disempowerment of my ego self.

JUNE 19, 2011

Where is God? So I went to church today and the priest told the congregation that, "God was far away, not in this world and could not be known." (I'm paraphrasing here.) Wow, what a discomforting message. No wonder people feel lost, to most God is lost. And yet they follow these men, that men ordained, to tell other men what to do. That they know only from words written by other men who as well do not know God's voice.

God is saddened by this display, this parade given in His name, away from the truth of knowing Him. Why did I give you this body? To do something!

The most important thing going to Mass today did for me, was to make me want to read the Bible to prove that God can be found, not within those written words, but by the words written by man, proving man has found God personally and if any "one" can, any can. I want to reread Paul's accounts.

Look where you are, with Me. You know I am not far. Fear not. I say once again, judge no one else for their path lest they love on My behalf. You know who. You say it is a hard pill to swallow. So I say spit it out. Go without worry, now you are above the fray, for you indeed have found My way. Bless you, yes, I have. It is good to spend time together, you and Me, in this eternity called "Now."

Listen to the words of Paul. See how I changed his very being from earthly Saul. I did it for him. I'm doing it to you. This is one of Mine who knew. You will hear in his words so dear that he taught My love as a gift of the Holy Spirit descending from above. Open your heart, I ask of all. This is where I started with mere Saul.

Paul is telling people how to ready their hearts for the infilling of God's Divine Love, a gift of the Holy Spirit, for they did not yet know the fullness of God's love and salvation, nor how to repent of their sins, their sinful ways, their human nature, to make a sanctuary for God within their heart and soul. I am not sure that even Paul recognizes the specialness of the gifts he has received, the gifts bestowed on him by the power of the Holy Spirit. For he speaks to the others as they should as well know the fullness of God's love by their own baptism.

He is speaking of their baptism by water, which is a ritual of man. Yet

Paul speaks of a change so great, a baptism that changes the very being of a human so that they have no desire for sinful ways. A change such as this in man can only be accomplished by a "Baptism of Fire," a gift of God delivers by the Holy Spirit, not by any calling forth by man, but as a gift of pure grace bestowed on a heart which has been made ready and open to such high gifts.

> *It is all tradition. Tradition dies hard, but tradition is yet to save souls. Let not your heart be troubled, rise above. Soar in spirit with Me to Eternity, My beloved. As you ask, you shall so receive. On this I tell you believe. My Divine Love is filling you more each day. This is what Jesus spoke of, "the way." Forget it and it limits you not. You are My child, My begot.*

> *My peace. There is no need for hurry. "Rest in peace," here and now with Me. See what We can do. Don't say too much. Watch your mouth. There is much wisdom in silence.*

The original teachings of Jesus ventured far beyond the mainly moral teachings we are left with, for few of even Jesus' closest disciples grasped the fullness of His words, His true message.

> *Give yourself entirely to God, body, mind and spirit. Depend on God for all your food, substance of life, physically, mentally and spiritually. Let there be no other, for there is no other so grand, so good, for God is Love and His Love is what makes the Universe and every atom in it. Be ye perfect, as your Father in Heaven is perfect. Ask your Father to fill you with His very substance His Divine Love, so you may be "One in being" with the Father.*

"The Grand Plan" called my name.

> *There is imperfection, there is perfection, and there is holiness. We each were made in perfection. Mankind is*

made in God's "image", which is perfection or "God's Nature." Yes, we were made in His image, perfect like God, but not of the same "Divine Substance" of God's very being. There is a difference.

There are three possible stages of man: A Sinner- man not one with his God nature. Perfect Man - man living in total recognition and in harmony with his God nature, and Holy Man- man so filled with God's Divine Love substance that he has become one in being with the Father.

There are many who are recognizing and acknowledging their "Higher Selves," their "God Connections," and learning to live from this higher state of awareness, God Consciousness. They are rising above any previously perceived physical limitations. They are giving themselves to God, denying themselves, their egos, and living the Will of God, naturally, fluently and fluidly in their own lives. They are finding a better way to show up and rise up to a higher consciousness.

This is a spiritual unfoldment. This is the beginning of the process of which Jesus spent his life preaching. This is the way to being a "Perfect Man," living God's will by the crucifixion of one's own. But as glorious as this is, and it is be assured, it is still most challenging work for the human. For the human has to die daily, crucify their "self" and deny their ego, to keep on the God track. This work is wearing and temptation still lurks behind every corner. Man may rise then fall again, over and over, rising and stumbling in his humanness.

God has watched this weary cycle of man. He has witnessed the love man has had for God and others and seen the turmoil man has been in. "Oh," God said, "if only I could "save man" from himself." And then God, being God, realized that with that very thought that He could and He did. What God did with that very thought was create a new opportunity for man, the opportunity for salvation.

Yes, "opportunity" is the key word here. A new possibility was now available. Just as all the other gifts of God, this gift could only be bestowed on man at man's request. It would never be a gift reserved for the "worthy," as in God's eyes every one of His creations, His children, were worthy by birthright, by the fact that they existed. What was necessary for the bestowal of this great gift was man's understanding of his worthiness. Each man, each being, had to understand that he was worthy by nature of God's love no matter his soul condition. For all are worthy beings and loved by God, even if and as they may be living in denial of God's very being and their constant connection to God, their Source.

Plagiarism, that's the only explanation the minds of men can come up with when another man expresses an idea as his own inspiration and the idea has been previously, documented somewhere else by another. It is thus assumed that one copied from another. Even the radical ideas and teachings of Jesus are attributed to other factions that some assume he must have studied with. These small minds are not yet aware of the "One Great Mind" to which all have access to. Ideas of truth are always present and available here. This is the Source, the fountain of inspiration, of all inspired thought. Inspired thought is that which rises in one's own mind from seemingly nowhere as man cannot physically or mentally know this source.

Jesus spoke of this saying that the Kingdom of God, "His wisdom," was hidden from the intellect of man. This is why no amount of reasoning will convince any one of the truth of these words. Some people insisted that Jesus prove himself. They wanted him to argue his points and defend his message. But as he knew this knowledge was hidden from mens minds and intellectual reasoning, He did not bother. In fact, he thanked and praised God for the fact that God had so hidden and thus kept safe this "glorious wisdom" from fools disguised as scholars.

If we want to know and understand "Spiritual Truth," we have to be a seeker. We have to have an open mind and heart. We have to desire a higher understanding. We have to let go of all preconceived ideas. We have to quiet the noise of our minds. We have to make a continual practice of this. We have to listen, listen to our own heart. Within each of us "Spiritual Truth" lives. First one has to know thyself and their innate worthiness to know higher.

Divine Love comes only in response to the soul's longings. "The New Birth" is simply the effect of the flowing of this Divine Love of the Father into the soul of a man and the disappearing of everything that tends to sin and error.

Accept your bad feelings.

Why do I have bad feelings when I am being filled with such wondrous Divine Love?

Your soul healing includes the healing of your negative mind and denial of will condition and the liberation of all your repressed childhood feelings. This is where our true spiritual growth lays, soul advancing not mere mind advancing.

I long for Truth.

Truth seeker.

This stuff is for me. It is my work, my calling, my way home to Heaven. Heaven calls my name. I answer. Their voice is not in vain. Please help me to see past this moment to eternity.

> *Technology is very seductive, newer, better, best. You know you want it. Live better. Be more connected, but connected to what? Not yourself, not necessarily what is best for you. The only connection that is sure to provide all the information one needs in a true and timely matter is already present. No connection fees to pay. All one needs to do is disconnect from all other which is running interference patterns garbling the messages of Truth meant for you.*

I see. I want. "I need it!" I say.

> *No you don't. You don't need it at all. You are fine without it. You are better off really. You have come to know haven't you, the Truth which resides within you which is worthy of your trust? You have proven it so, so you know. Let others go on. Let them have their dance and their song. You sing your own songs. Dance to your own music. You are hearing it now humming in your heart. You have what you need. You have it beautifully.*

I know what I am doing here. I just realized it. I know it now and accept its importance. This is my soul work and my sole work, lessons given to me by my "Higher Self" and "Guardian Angel Family" to advance my soul understandings. Awakenings of my heart, lessons to learn and lessons learned, enlightenment and encouragement tailored just for me. The important thing here is for me to grasp the value of each teaching and own it. Yes, this is my work, a new lesson each day.

Let me learn. Oh, how I love to learn. Some learn by reading books. I learn by writing them.

JUNE 20, 2011

Declaration of "Sainthood," what a stupid idea of man, how can any one possibly think that by any word of man any other man's soul gains a position in Heaven? What a mere mortal idea. What an insane concept. Oh no, you say, it's not really about where the saint's soul resides it's about what we think of them. One man's mind is to decide what another man's mind thinks? What about what a soul knows? So do some really think souls in the hereafter await a decision from any man to know their destiny? Wake up people!

What is Truth? Is this the Truth, the whole Truth?

> *You will never in your wildest dreams grasp the wholeness of Truth. For Truth reaches everywhere, as Truth is God in Spirit, divinely masculine and feminine. The Truth you are grasping is whole though, completely true. Complete in itself, though part of a much larger Truth. Know this, God is Truth. Truth is all good. "The Truth will set you free," Jesus said. Jesus knew and as well he said we each had the ability to know as he if we became seekers. The hidden comes to light in an enlightened mind.*

It helps to know this information is all for me, for my own good. For me, it is completely relevant. I have been wondering what to do with it. Is it a book?

> *It is a library. It is a bible.*

I know much of it is holy, "Divinely inspired."

> *Oh, yes.*

A conversation with self.

And with "Higher Self," and all the Saints and Angels.

I know it is for me now. Perhaps someday it will be for other eyes and ears.

When the time is right, when seekers find, when another's soul is so developed, as well as yearning for more Truth. Be true to yourself.

I still have a big log in my eye so how can I begin to pick a splinter out of another's? I am my project now. My perfection, the perfection of my heart, is my longing. I long to be so filled with God's Divine Love, that there remains no space between the space of any part of my being for any other substance. I long to be pure. Oh, Divine Master purify my soul. Purify my thoughts. Purify my words. Purify my actions. Of this I beg, on bended knee. All praise and glory I give to God!

Stop being so smug! Who do you think you are? I love you no more than any other. To Me you are the same as your brother. The difference lies in your knowing. Those who know better are expected to do better. I expect so much of you. Steal away. Go into hiding. This is between you and Me.

Do you believe? That is enough. You need not make it your work to convince any other. Oh of course, We love it when you spread the news, but many care not to hear, for they long not. They seek not anything more than they know they can touch.

But you are in touch with the untouchable, not the unknowable. There is a difference. You didn't always know this, so certainly so you can see how others have such disbelief. It was not your time then and it is not their time now. You cannot rush them along either. What you can do is live well. Be the Light for them by showing others that there is a better way. Your life becomes the way, the beacon of hope to the disheartened.

So tarry not, you have much work to do. Not saving other souls but saving yours. Your work is a pleasure, it brightens your day and everyday you live. And as your soul lives forever, so will your light shine. You are a shining star, the "North Light." Rise and shine.

The beginning of my spiritual shift is documented in my art by the actual visuals I created and the naming of each piece. No longer depending on visual stimuli to create my art images, I drew inspiration from a different source, from one I could give no name. I began painting the familiar to me. I painted what I knew, my truth, inspired by the world in which I had lived my whole life as I knew it. Nature and rural settings were the motifs I developed but I was not limited by "local color" as one's eye might define it. The color in these new works was a dynamic element of expression, expressing my joy in being. All imbued with a brilliance of light and intensity that speaks of one in touch with a sense beyond the mere physical nature of life.

JUNE 21, 2011

Let's get spiritual. Let's get spiritual. You are a spiritual girl!

Each day I become more of Myself. More like Me and I like Me more. Life is not ordinary anymore for Me. I see more completely. Life is unveiling itself.

Religious freedom means being free to celebrate any belief or follow any religious belief one has.

*Life is a drama and a love story, a very dramatic love story,
part comedy, part melancholy. There is enough drama and
surprise in life with out adding more, without adding more
melodrama, to life's thick plot. Instead, lighten up on life a
bit. See the comedy in the error. Give yourself a break. Break
free of the tension of the drama and fully enjoy your story as
it is being written.*

There is an expansion going on, an expansion of my consciousness, an
expansion of the universe.

*This is one in the same. Listen to yourself. Know it all. Just
go with it. It is all right. You will see through Me, in You.
It's what you do. A long time coming. Shake it up, break
loose, nothing can bind you or stop you from becoming You.
This is it, what you have been seeking, the missing piece of
Yourself. Claim it, "Your Truth" in being Yourself.*

12:30 a.m., I ask, "Where do I go from here?" My answer, "To bed."

*The answers are always here for you. It's up to you to ask,
to seek, then listen. Listen with your heart. Make room for
the knowing. Questioning is good. It's how you learn truth.
Doubt is important. One needs doubt to question what
one has been given, to truly know. One has to question life.
What is life? What is love? One has to not be satisfied with
what they have or know. A self-satisfied, smug, ego tripped
out, know-it-all, will never truly know. So what is there
to know that I don't know, you ask? Peace, Eeternal Peace,
Joy, Unbounded Joy, Limitless Love, for just a few, a very
important few.*

*Who do you trust? Do you trust yourself? You can know,
once you know yourself. Trust yourself. To thine own self be*

true. Have faith in yourself. This is not an ego trip. It's about understanding your self worth, who you are, why you are here. You know already. The knowledge is there now already for you, in you, waiting to be asked, to be sought with your deepest soul yearning. Wouldn't you like to know what you know?

Come around again and listen to me tell you about you, about your beauty, about your wisdom, about your truth. There is truth in your being, in your being you. There is nothing for you to do, so be still, hush, yes hush your mind. You will never know all until you can quiet the rambling voice which shouts, and learn to listen to the small still voice with which you have never been without.

This is fun stuff, don't you agree? These words are given and they are all free. No price has been paid. This is a gift, no strings attached. Detachment is the key that opens the door to eternity, to this space in and out of time. A place where others surely think I have lost my mind, but my mind is not lost, just set aside no longer allowed to hide the wisdom I have access to. It is here for me and within you too!

You don't have to know all at once. In fact your brain might explode if you did know everything at once. Ha!

My Higher Self has the most wonderful sense of humor. Thank you, for making me laugh.

Hear ye, hear ye, come one and all. Today is the day. Now is the hour, I have made for you. It is all brand new. Begin again, look not behind, nor think ahead. Here is where you belong, with Me, singing Our song. The tempo is up to you. The melody is soft and sweet. Let's dance, partners in this life we create together. Let's dance this way forever.

Who are you trying to please, him, her, Me? Are you pleased with yourself? Why all this pleasing? Just be the best you, you can be. That is enough for Me. I want to see you happy. That pleases Me. This life I give is to be enjoyed not annoyed. So lighten up. Give yourself a break. Break not in to a million pieces. Be whole. Feel whole with Me. This is My wish for you. Do as you please. With love, Me.

I am watching you, watching over you, holding your hand in Mine. Give no mind to worry. You are in My care. You are My beloved, My dear. What feels good? Do you know? Are you listening? To whom? To man? What man knows you better than you?

What can I feel good about today?

Don't make your feeling good dependent upon anything you do or another does. I have already provided enough joy in life for all. Why can't you see this? Stop separating yourself from My Joy. Drink it in. It is your life blood. The blood I give to you. It is your very breath. Yes, the very air you breathe is so easily given to you to enjoy. You struggle not or work not for your breath, do you? So have joy, give thanks. Take a deep breath of my joy."

A breath, a sigh of relief, as I rest in You and Your joy.

Okay, now you need to deal with your life.

What is the most important thing for me to do now?

Forgive yourself.

Who is this voice I hear? This voice I have always heard but not recognized? Is it God? Is it my spiritual guides? Is it my Higher Self?

It is the part of me that knows better.

I can accept that answer.

JUNE 23, 2011

Not everything in the Bible is the word of "God," much of it is the word of "Man" attempting to understand and make rules and judgments for and about God.

This is becoming clear to my psyche.

Love is the rule. Love the Lord God with all your heart and mind. Love your neighbor as yourself. Faith, speaking in tongues, healing and prophesying are good but if one has not Love, they are all works in vain. This Love is special. It is Divine. It is God's love, a gift for our hearts, free for the asking, a gift of Spirit, Holy Spirit. Feels like home.

I hear what you are saying.

Love is the rule and better yet, when Divine Love fills your heart, Love rules your heart. No rules are needed.

Why do people need rules?

People need rules until they get it right, until the rightness becomes them. Very few, of those Paul preached to, actually received "the gift." If the people truly had, they wouldn't have needed his rules. And our history would have been full of saints, so full of saints that they would not be historically regarded as extraordinary but ordinary Christians.

To be so filled with the gifts of the Holy Spirit, to be bursting with Divine Love, is the gift Jesus Christ brought to Earth from God. When the Holy Spirit descended on Jesus of Nazareth he became the Christ, all at once his complete essence was of God. Jesus was the first ever to so embody the essence of God, Divine Love. When He did so, He did it completely. All at once. For so great was his love of God and desire to be one with Him.

The life Jesus lived, as Christ, was to show us what would be possible as well for each of us. We were to believe in him, believe that he was such a manifestation of God. And to believe that we could as well be such and command the universe, such as Jesus did.

Jesus said that "Christ" would come again and live through us and when "Christ" descended upon us we would be delivered from ourselves, from our old nature. We would be given new eyes to see and new ears to hear. That's all for now.

The words that fill the pages before this are not "my thoughts." These words are "my thoughts." I think the words before were divinely inspired knowings. Delivered to my soul, and translated by my soul, to my psyche which wrote them in this journal. They are a direct manifestation of my soul's development and thus a result of my ability to know things higher. These ideas are not pre-formulated in my mind. They are "discoveries" to me that sit right with my mind, for I am ready to know them.

Don't think you have to know everything, for if you thought you knew everything, you would not be able to know all there is for you to know. Don't be a know it all. Be a seeker, a seeker of Truth, which is Love.

Jesus went away for forty days "to the desert." He was alone with himself, with his "ego" and his "conscious," doing soul

work, fighting with "the demons" of his mind and being
consoled by "the angels" of his soul. He was digesting "the
gift" of his Father, he was becoming more than mere man,
he was having a conversion experience, the conversion
experience from which he emerged as "Christ" God's only
begotten son. At that time, Jesus, as Christ, was the first to
be fully "born again spiritually." Through the power of the
Holy Spirit, he was filled so with God's Divine Love that he
was one in being with the Father. Some will say, you don't
know, but this has to be told.

I used to think the first book I would write would be called *Art Lessons*,
and indeed there still may be such a book. But the book I write today I
call *Life Lessons*, for this is the lesson for this life of mine. No one else
has a perfect lesson plan for my life. And my lesson plan cannot be
perfect for any other and yet by reading my lessons, it is my hope that
another may awaken to their own truth teachings which lay in wait
deep in their own soul, waiting to be discovered and treasured.

Wisdom warrior, your heart chakra is growing. Be filled
with God's Divine Love.

I know a young man who is in touch with so much more than he
knows. I can see it. I can feel it. I hear it in his words. I feel it in his very
being. His presence in life is different. He shows up much differently
than he once did. His being is filled with joy, simple unbridled joy. He
is just happy to be here and has so much love for all. He asks me, "Why
do people feel they need to lie?"

Why I will write a book: because I know better. I know better than I
used to.

"The Gods," equals one voice with many dialects.

In all of these religious debates over truth, why didn't anyone just ask
God?

Because they didn't truly believe in the power of and the power to know God, the faith they professed was "of their fathers," not of their own.

When any statement is made and presented as truth is it sure to make someone's hair bristle on the back of their neck, for no man wants to be told what to believe. He has to know himself. His ego and free will are active and are quick to defend what he knows as truth. His mind closes tight around his understanding of truth. His defensive walls of stone are again fortified. "This is what I know, stay away. You cannot mess with my mind. My mind is made up."

Interesting choice of words, for that really is the whole truth of the matter. Man's mind has been made up to believe certain things are true. This making began in childhood as his family and culture schooled him in what is so, in what they believed, which is what their parents believed and thus and so. So what a mind knows is what his upbringing has programmed him to know. Now, this is not the original programming one arrives with at birth. The original programming is one of wonder and inquisitiveness, joy and faith, faith in good, a mind able to imagine infinite possibility.

The only way to deliver teachings of Truth to the masses is to circumvent the mind, the mind that is locked in certainness. And touch the part of man that is less guarded, his imagination. Thus Truth, presented as fiction, is safe to swallow. Man feels free to ponder possibilities without offending the world of his ego, of who he is because of what he knows about life. This is the door of possibility for man's evolvement beyond his mind, where his imagination lies, his heart.

It's about storytelling. Call it fact and they close the book and argue a point. Call it fiction and they open the book and their hearts ready for adventure. It is not so personal and thus threatening to their psyche.

Jesus spoke in parables. He told stories that had not physically happened (fiction), to relay important moral truths (truth). But richly woven within each tale was a spiritual lesson only to be understood by an open heart. Yes, Jesus was a wonderful teacher of Truth, spiritual Truth, through fiction.

Self-discipline and mind control versus surrender to God's Love and meekness. There is more to see than can be seen with these old eyes of yours. I offer you a new pair that does not see despair. Open wide, your heart and mind. Let Me fill you with My Love Divine.

As my consciousness expands, I am given higher knowings. For this I give thanks and praise. Thanks be to God. God within me and above me, who is above all, knows all, and is all to me, for me and you.

The fulfillment of your destiny, of our every dream awaits each of us.

Come home, God says. Come home now. You do not need to take leave of where you are to be with Me. Now is the time you have. Be with Me. Wherever you are, I am present as Love. People think you have to die to go to Heaven but exactly the opposite is true. You have to "live" to go to Heaven, for Heaven is Life Eternal. You can enjoy life in Heaven while your feet touch the earth. Your "Highest Self" resides there now. How high you go is up to you by what you choose to do. Live low, know low, and stay low. Live high, know high and rise high. Love is what fills your soul like helium in a balloon. My Divine Love will take you to the highest of heavenly realms. Let Me blow kisses to your heart. Each kiss is filled with My love.

You can't help but rise higher when My love you desire. No one can keep you down. No one can hold you to the ground. So filled with My love you will be that you will see and understand eternity. This is My gift, My most special and precious gift which I offer to you. This is indeed the "Good News." Trouble not. Have no fear. Divine Love is here!

Jesus said. Jesus told. He wanted each of you to know Me, as he (did), for I showed him the way. He had so much of My love He could not stay. But I sent back another gift, by the power of the Holy Spirit, to give you a lift, to lift your burdens, to ease your load. It's so beyond those rules you know. For I watched you stumble. I saw you cry. And decided that no longer could My Divine Love you deny.

This gift allows you to flow through life with ease. Yes, like a gentle breeze, My way becomes yours. My will be done, without any effort or because of anything you have done, but wanted Me so, thirsted for My love. Oh, how I love to gift you My dears with this gift from My dove.

Listen in, hark, hear! This is the Message for all ears. I will make you anew. You will not feel the same. Some have felt so changed that they take a new name. This is It. The real deal. Offered first to Jesus, My Son, who was once as you, wandering, wondering, what to do. But he asked for My help and offered himself up to Me.

Yes, this was the real crucifixion actually. The cross he died on was his own. He had carried just as you. Falling and tripping, getting up and trying anew. In order to fully know Me, He had to deny "himself." He had to die ego-ly. Three times He denied his own will and served Himself up to Me. Right then and there He was so brand spanking new that He glowed from head to toe. Oh boy, Jesus sure did show My love to all he met. Every time he asked in My name, bounty he could proclaim. Jesus more than believed. What son "believes" in his father? A son can only "know" his father or not. Jesus was My "first" Son, spiritually begot.

"The Christ" that Jesus became, he as well proclaimed was here for you. He told you how and what to do. Love the Lord your God with all your heart and mind and love your neighbor as yourself. Jesus Christ gave no more rules for this was the truth of his message and was his message complete.

If any man so loves Me, as he hungers and thirsts for this closeness, and as well loves and cares for his brother man, he will find himself rising day by day. His thoughts will be of joy and he will see perfectly. This is My promise; the "Promised Land of Israel," where greener pastures lie, the Heaven I promised and My saving grace.

The Savior was Jesus and can be you. This is what I want for each of you. If you indeed so love Me and spend time with Me in the quiet closet of your heart, you will find My peace and love pouring fourth so rapidly into your very being, shaking you to your very core. Oh yes, dear ones, it is you My children, whom I adore, with which I wish to fill with My love, just as I promised "on the wings of a dove."

Do not be mistaken. This is not a one-time thing. I have acres and acres of love for you that I desire so to bring. Bit by bit, puff by puff, I kiss your heart and fill you up. You will feel this, I know. And you will surprise yourself, when you begin to show. Show in your actions, thoughts and deeds. Show my love to others fully, just like Jesus Christ did indeed.

You see, this is the difference, this is the gift. My love makes doing the right thing easy with no thought, or rules, or laws. You will not even pause to think if any action is the right thing to do. It always will be, as you will be becoming Me fully.

After you pass from this earth you will continue to rise with My Love. Higher and higher, purer and purer will be your soul until it becomes golden and burns like the fire of the sun. Yet until that, you will not be done. But you will be Mine and My will, will be yours.

Can you see and understand the glory of this story? I know it is different than the one you knew. But isn't it so much better too? This is the Truth, which you can know. Ask your heart to show. Invite Me into your life. Yes, the one you are living which is filled with strife. I care not where you have been. I just ask for you to let Me in. I'm at the door now, waiting for you to pick up the clues. Yes, you have to seek, but this isn't a game. I just ask you to pray using Jesus Christ's Name. For He knew and He knows now. And He did all I asked him to show you how.

Love's true home, love's true home, repeating again and again in my mind. Are these words another's, God's words, or my brother's? Can I use them?

Yes, of course. Words are for all to tell a story, to express yourself. Words are meant to be used, not put on a shelf. Tell your own story. No "one" is your guru. It's just Me and you.

Love speaks to me and calls my name. Never again am I the same. Words of wisdom line the halls of my mind. My heart continually fills with Love from The Divine. What am I to say?

> *Don't get in your own way. I'm here for you to help you along. All you need to do is dance and sing My Song.*

> *Test the water. Wade in deep. God is Love. For the Love of God.*

> *You need not be awestruck by any other, for there is no "other." He is your brother.*

I can't turn it off and I don't want to. When someone asks me to explain my beliefs, I kind of fumble with my words. For I know more than I can say. Spirit designed it that way.

> *People talk way too much, without saying very much. Enough said. What do you like to think about? Think about that. What do you know? Whatever you know becomes your reality.*

> *For the same amount of energy it takes to point and blame, good works can be done in My name. It's easy to see fault and lay blame. Blessed is the one whom sees beauty no one else can claim.*

> *Have it your way. Today is your day. Let not another tell you what to do, nor how to think. Let them live their own lives. Whether their ship sails or sinks matters not to you. For you do have your own life to live, your own things to do. I cannot tell you what to do. I can only say to your own heart be true. What is sin to you? What you think another ought not to do?*

Contrary to popular belief, I never stopped speaking. You (mankind) just stopped listening. I still have a lot of good things to say, when of course one listens this way. It's one thing to know. It's one thing to show, but quite another to proclaim in God's name. Let it be heard by ears yearning to know, on others it will fall silent or seem absurd. Say what you must, as in God you trust, to open hearts wide and pour Divine inside.

So confining, sometimes my body feels to me. Yet I know this body allows me to freely be if I want to be, if I choose to live through Thee. My mind is my only limitation. And I can go so far beyond, if I accept Christ's invitation to let go of my own will and stand with God at the top of the hill.

What disturbs you is up to you. Love messages, Love notes, pure Love.

I have been engulfed in thoughts of total despair pleading for help and then in the next moment felt a warm calmness flood my being as reassuring thoughts fill my mind.

This, My dear is Love, pure Love, the kind that comes from above, the Holy Spirit's gift of Divine Love.

You are a consumer that's a fact. Your free will allows you a choice of what you shall consume. But often you don't very judiciously exercise your right. You slovenly eat whatever is set out before you. You really should be a more "picky eater" or consumer of life. When you are watching TV or tuned into any media source you are consuming, downloading and digesting ideas, another's ideas neatly packaged to be fed to you.

Have you given much thought lately to thoughts that are fed to your mind in thus ways? Are they serving you or are you serving them? Is this diet of yours balanced? Do you as well spend time in nature, in silence, and in beauty to fill your soul with the good stuff, the non-thinking stuff that is pure and whole and nutritious?

You live in a consumer driven society, which means the choices you make as a whole affect the whole. It has always been this way even before the age you now live in and before the language for these words was ever created. Another term you use is "mass consciousness," which basically means that the general level of mankind's ability to know what he knows is affected by all.

This can change, for the better or worse. You recently experienced and are still living in a society with a mass consciousness of fear. Fear rolling down a hill gathering mass and weight with each rotation plummeting to the depths. You called it "the financial crisis!" Oh, you sure did a good job with all jumping on board with that fear wagon.

I suggest a topic then it is like I am taking dictation.

The men we know as "great minds," did they spend their time filling their minds with other people's ideas? Or did they spend their time developing their ability to know?

You know that answer, because you as well have developed the ability to know whatever it is you would like to know. You seeker you! Life is a game of seek and find.

Good ideas come to me as easily as the air I breathe.

Poet
Field
Source
Mind
Available
Same process
Same source
Source of all
The infinite field
Of potential
River flowing
Streaming with
Ideas of potentiality
Free for all.

Everyday is a new day, a new opportunity for you to grow, to see, to fully be. This life you know is so short term. This is not all you get. What is eternal life? You have to ask the question to get the answer.

What is it with you people? If something doesn't materialize immediately you think you have failed. This is why We tell you to have faith. Believe in what you want to happen. Believe it is coming. Believe it is on its way. Every time you doubt, it puts what you want on hold.

Imagine every wish of yours as a work order. You of conceive something you want. And you believe and that is, submitting a work order to the unseen, (your behind the scene team). So as long as you hold your belief, We work on orchestrating all to make your desires materialize for you. The stronger your faith, the higher a work priority it is for us. When doubt enters your mind, it's like a whistle blows and all work on your "project" is halted. If you have changed your mind We have no reason or ability to proceed further. This is a team effort and you call the shots. We have no right, nor ability to interfere or act against your wishes.

We love it when you give us projects and let us help. We feed off of your energy. We can only make suggestions. It is up to you to choose and declare what you want, to put in the "work order." This starts the process rolling. And when you doubt that it is coming, all energy is lost. It's really like you pulled the plug on that project, so all We can do is twiddle Our thumbs.

Remember, you are the boss of you. But you don't have to do this life all alone. Your family of friends, spiritual friends, is here to help and guide you. What you do is up to you. Ask and you shall receive Our help, but ask you must in full trust.

Sometimes We just want to thump you on the head. Sometimes We do.

I am healthy, wealthy and wise.

Believe, what you want.

I believe I am supposed to write these Truth teachings as stories, like parables. Part of me asks how, as I do not think of myself as a fiction writer.

This is not fiction We speak of. These are stories of Truth and We never ask you to do anything alone or on your own. Remember, help is always available 24/7, a gift to you from what you call "Heaven." You have at your aide the best writers of all times, which have been and are to be, great minds of the "One Mind" which gives inspiration continually. Walk forward. Step out in faith. We have so much to do, so much to do through you. Your body is able, but you must be willing. You must make up your mind to live high. Call it as you see it. You are doing good work.

I heard differently.

Way to go
Way to see
See clearly
Make way
All the way
Way of life
Without strife
See true
Through you
To Me
And eternity
Messages of Love you hear
Meant for your ears
With Me now.

Lots of theories
Drama spins
Out of control
Control yourself
You can
Choose
To see
Differently
Smooth sailing
On the high seas
Of life
Or turbulent waters
You choose

Win

Or

Lose.

Deal with it. Louder and louder your voice becomes. Does the loudest voice win in your mind? What about the softest voice, the quiet whisper within your mind? Ever think of letting it win? That does not mean that you lose. Life is not to be a shouting match. Silence is golden. Shut your mouth and listen in for a change.

Who are your friends? The ones that want the best for you, team players, cheerleaders, advisors, listeners, embracers, lovers. We are all of this for you. We say again. You are not alone. You are on the "friends and family plan" in this life of yours. Even when you don't see, We see you. We hear you. We hold your heart. You are safe. Enjoy the journey.

Lifestyle

How to live well

Show off

Upstage

Drama queen

Look at me.

Stop thinking about what could be wrong. Do you want to make it? You order your life, you know. Your thoughts order from the unseen possibilities for your life. Why would you want to order strife? See what you want as possible for you. This is your job. This is yours to do.

Make up your mind. That is your job. Decide what you want. Tell us how We can help you. It's lovely to see you today show up this way. Do you value your life? What life? You take life too seriously.

I do my best to do what is given to me to do.

The art of listening in.

If you cannot and do not see what you want in your life it would serve you well to GET A NEW ATTITUDE! If you spoke not words of judgment, when would you speak? What would you say? If you thought not words of judgment, what would you think? So what is left? Love, the pureness of Love. Love condemneth not. Have you really listened to the words you say? Not always so pretty huh, often quite petty. You are bigger than that. So be better. You'll be better off.

I am searching for Truth. I want to know the Truth of all, above all, through all in all.

What do you believe? Do you like what you believe? Do you like who you are? Do you know yourself? Don't be afraid to ask. Asking is not a sign of weakness. You will never know unless you ask. Don't hinder your heart. Is your heart broken? Let Me mend it with My Love.

JUNE 29, 2011

All My love is for you for the asking. Ask and you shall receive My gift of grace, My Spirit into you, into your broken heart, making it a blessed heart, full of Divine Love, truth and beauty. You will see. Risen you will be.

Life is to be a love story, a light hearted joyful tale, a divine comedy of sort. Do you see the humor, the compassion, the truth? Are you an actor fulfilling a role which you have been given, reading a script written long before your first breath? Do you know what your next breath brings? Do you believe your destiny has been written? Do you believe you write your own life story, fully in charge of the outcome? Are you a villain, an innocent victim, or a victor? What is the story of your life? What do you believe? What would you like to know? What would you like to feel?

What is a free thinker?

One who is not confined by the known. One who opens his mind to new knowings thus able to discover the undiscovered, which has been covered by man's inability to see more than what is. Thank you for asking.

Google has nothing on the wisdom which I have access to, the wisdom of the ages. What has been and what can be.

Yes, a free thinking human is so free!

Unlimited access to the Power that be, makes me free! Why wouldn't one want to know all one can know?

Give your mind a rest. Life is not a test. The Sermon on the Mount's theme was "Blessed be the..." not "Damned be the..."

What good does it do you to repeat the complaining words of another? None, zilch! If someone else feels they have been wronged it is their business, as it is their own beliefs, or truth, which has created it and will sustain it. Is this the kind of thing you wish to create in your own life, discord? It is not for you to mediate anyone else's felt wrongs. Walk away and bid farewell to those with woes. Offer a blessing for better days to come.

Better days to come. You can not put words into anyone

else's mouth but you can put them into their mind by speaking them mindfully. Speak the truth you know. Live well. Show. Others will see. Others will feel. Others will be touched by your presence. Show up well.

So, I am seeing this clearer, this God-me relationship, the whole parent-childness of it. When any or either of my children comes to me asking for my help and love I feel that I cannot pour forth enough or quickly enough. I know there is no limit to the amount I can and will give, nor to the time I will spend doing such. How great my love. How great Thy Love.

There is no need for any mediator or translator between us either. For even if either party would lose their voice or their mind, our love would still connect us. The ones who once suckled at my breast and fed on my every word are now very capable adults. Standing on their own two feet quite well, most of the time. But they still trip and fall like all. And when they are down and call up to me I will be there to pick them up, to hold and comfort them, to give them my wisdom, my guidance, my love. This is parenting in love is an honor, a responsibility, a calling, a gift, a gift from God.

I know God as my Father, my Father in heaven. I feel the warmth and safety of His Love. I hear His guiding and encouraging Words. There is no greater title than "Father" or "Mother" for God for me. It signifies a very personal relationship, a two way street of sort, an open channel of communication.

I speak, I listen, and I hear. I cry and I am comforted. I am guided. I obey. I am given responsibilities. I am given lessons. I am rewarded for my work. I grow in faith. I grow in love. I rise up a better being, one in being with my Father. As I mature in my love for my Father, I become more and more of His Nature. His ways are my ways. My load is lightened.

Heaven is the womb of God from which one's soul is birthed and that to which it returns. Your body is an earthly treasure made just for you, for your earthly journey. Dust to dust. It is not risen up.

What is this feeling I have? From where does this come? Whose voice do I hear comforting me, loving me, guiding me? Is it you, my Father?

I love you too much for words!

My Father who art in Heaven? Don Brown is it you? It certainly feels like your love. Who else could it be without skin on that loves me so much? Is it you God calling my name? Or are you one in spirit, are you now the same?

You get to do what you really want in life. Did you know that? What you want is what you get. How so? It's all about energy flow. What you give is what you get. Do you know what you are truly giving? Giving to the world? Do you understand the signals you send and their power? You are a powerful creator, you being you. You have the power to create the life you want. The trick is you have to understand the rules of this game of life you are living.

Rules of life, for life, for all of life. It is not necessarily what you think it is, the way you think life works. You think there is luck. Some are lucky and some aren't. You think life is hard work. You think you will never be able to live your wildest dreams. You are right in your thinking. For if you think so you will create it so. You see, whatever you think about you bring about. "Not so," you say. "I've never heard it that way. That cannot be, for my mother never told me." Are you sure? Can you not recall her words?

"If you cannot say anything nice, don't say anything at all. Put your best foot forward. Be grateful for what you have.

Never, say never. Think about what you want. Rise and shine. Want the best for all. Expect the best. Do unto others as you would have done unto you. Take care of your brother. We are family, family first. Have a good day. Don't be a worry wart. Dream big. I believe in you. Believe in yourself. You can do it."

Not all have had such wonderful parenting. Yes, it is a shame. But we are not here now to talk in blame. I will share a story now that is for all. A love story without limits, that will make you stand tall. Amazing "Parental Love" is available now, here for each and I'll tell you how.

Imagine the best parent you can, the best of a mother's and father's love rolled into one, an immense spirit of love, of tenderness and caring, of listening and sharing. Since before the beginning of time such a "Spirit of Love" was and is. We have each felt it at one time or another to some degree. We have known that there was an "Other," that there was some force so great in this world. But only a few have known "This Love" so intimately that it felt like the love of Mother.

Just as the best parents want the best for each child, this force, this "Power of Love," wants the best for each of us. This One Power, this Holy One, waits close by at the door of your mind waiting to be invited in, to be a part of your life. Desiring so to shower each with gifts of His Divine Love, love like no other than has been known before.

His first "spiritually reborn" has shown the way life can be when one is reborn in spirit by being filled with Divine Love continually. He called "Him" His Father who art in Heaven. Our Father, He said, loves us all the same. There is only Love, no blame. Recognize "The Family," We are here together now. This is what He taught and showed us how.

These words are gifts given in the hour of my need. Meant for me and meant for sharing, for all eyes and ears indeed. So I share what comes to me as it flows, as I am given to know. I know this Love is for all. I have to keep my mind out of it. I know more than I can say.

That's true.

July 2011

Then when that happens we are able to
hold our heads high no matter what
happens and know that all is well,
for we know how dearly God loves us,
and we feel this warm love everywhere
within us because God has given us the
Holy Spirit to fill our hearts with love.

Romans 5:5 NLT

July 1, 2011

It's not so fun to live in the midst of one whom sees life so dimly.
Whose every word is a complaint. This is not meant as a judgment, this
is an observation of where I live, on the edge of darkness. As much as I
yearn to see the light, another is keen to point out the dark, the dismal.
This is not the life I want. I want better. Please help us all to see better,
thus live better.

> *First, you would do best not to "point out" another's
> flaws. Be silent. Bite your lip if you must. You cannot help
> someone who asks not for help. The only way one can see
> their way out of the darkness of the forest is the hope of light
> on the edge. Be this light for another. Shine brightly. Dim
> not your light just because another's is low. Be the light of
> hope for another.*

Shine on. Shine up. Shine all around. You are a "beacon of hope" for this world. Hold your head high. Look up. Think what you like. Love to see beauty.

Who are you to tell another how he or she should be, to define happiness for another? "To each his own." is wisdom to recall. Remember, you do not know it all.

Positive statement: I like being with others who see good in life and talk about it. It is so fun to be with people that enjoy life.

You know not how good you have it. This life of yours is so easy. Freedom has been won for you. Injustice has had its day and been put away. But look, you say. Look what he did to me. Okay see, but understand how fortunate you are to have the right to be heard, the right to be free. What you feel good about, think about that.

The voice of Love never hurts with its words. The voice of Love never hurts. Its words are kind and gentle reminders, patient reminders. The voice of Love is spoken to each individually. What each one needs to know from "the One" is available 24/7, from what we call Heaven.

Ask for what you need, then listen patiently. The information is pure. It's when the mind gets involved that it gets garbled. Are you clear? What We say is clear enough for you to know what to do if you listen carefully with your heart, not mindfully, but heart-fully. In this way, you will truly hear what We say here today.

In this way, all along, We have been here with you. Did you know this was meant for you to see more clearly? Higher, better, unfettered knowledge, Wisdom from on high but not from the sky. So much closer. It's personal. It's within. Just for you. Now, let's begin to see the world more clearly.

*Am I Christian, Jew or Islam? There are no words for what
I am. I am that I am, "Truth" for you and all. "God's saving
grace" for your heart and soul, a gift from angels who live on
high in the Heavens of righteousness where I reside.*

*Rhapsody, this is the grand plan of God's gift to us. The gift
of His love delivered into our hearts as we ask, by the power
of the Holy Spirit. So great a Love, Our Father has for us.
Welcome Him in, into your heart, make room for the infilling
of such tremendous Love. The Love that transforms
the weak to strong, that gives wisdom all day long. Ask not
once. Ask again and again for God to fill you up, to live
within.*

*Bit by bit your being will change, never again to be the same.
This is the "The Good News," for all. It is so good that it is
above the law, for when God's Essence so fills your heart,
there is no need for rules of morals or dogma to control the
drama. Divine Love will rule your heart. If you do not feel
this, if you do not know, you will not show. You will feel
alone, for you are. But God is waiting at the edge of your
heart. Today is the day, He says, let's begin, let's start.*

*These words are here to be found by the seeker, words written
on the heart. No man may gift another with wisdom, for all
wisdom comes from within from God our source. Man may
share his wisdom with wisdom teachings, but true wisdom is
only recognized by the heart, not the mind. The mind reasons
away wisdom as it comes from afar. But the wisdom that
is planted deep within is true for you. Your heart already
knows. You must open your mind to your own truth, the
truth that feeds and nourishes your very soul, this knowing.
Where there is knowing, there is showing. It can be no other
way. Nothing to buy, nothing to believe, just be with Me.*

Oh yes, I've heard this voice before, but found it so easy to ignore. I gave it not the credence it deserved. I walked away alone in thought, believing life was hard and God forgot.

"Turn right, turn left, pause up ahead." This is what the information sounds like as I'm lead. I know more than I can say. But I can show all that I am.

> *Forgive them they know not what they do, for anyone who knows will show My love.*

It is not what you think, it is who you are, how you show up in or out of Love. We are of royal bloodline you and I because of our very nature, the nature of who we each are, sons and daughters of God, of the One whom is the One of us. Our inheritance is the very Kingdom of God, but it is up to each of us to know and thus to claim our birthright. Each of us is in our Father's will but until we claim "His will" as ours we have no claim to our great inheritance.

> *Have no other God before Me. Be not a slave to money. Bend not your knee to pay homage to any other. You must love the Lord your God whom is I, your Father/Mother.*

You have to empty your heart of any egoic claims before God can fill you when you call His Name. You do not have to live this life on your own. Ask for God to bring you home. Ask to be filled to the brim with God's Love and Wisdom to be found within. Ask the Holy Spirit to visit you again and again.

> *Come follow Me and I will lead you home.*

Like I know, there is no other for me to love. I ask here and now to be filled with Your Love. Fill me up I pray. Give me more of Your lovely essence each day.

Make yourself available. Turn off your mind. Give your brain a rest. All I want is your love. Life is not a test of wills for you to make. You can go your way or go Mine. Live as human or as Divine. Your mind can guide you or it can be your heart which leads. If you choose your heart, we will "in essence" marry indeed.

So much to say. So much to know. Wisdom pours forth, as your heart is a glow with My love. Burning a steady fire within, you have no chance to sin. For sin is error thinking and love is not a thinking thing. I love you so this you know. This you show "the world outside," what it's like to have God inside.

Time and again, I have spoken to hearts ready to hear, to those who hold Me dear. The Words are not lost. They have been here all along. But how many truly hear My word and know it is true and fully understand what to do?

It really is never about what anyone has done. For this, My Bbessing to you, has already been done and is here now waiting for you to seek. For all that is spiritual is hidden from the mind. Logic has never been the way of The Divine.

JULY 2, 2011

If you want answers, you have to ask the right questions. Don't ask for My help and then shut the door.

There are patterns to our lives, traditions. We celebrate tradition as what we know. Tradition is comfortable and comforting to us. There are traditions that bind families together, traditions of food, traditions of faith. But times change and so do people, people we love. Some that we hold dear, choose not to follow tradition.

See this as not a sign of betrayal. See this as a sign of becoming their own. New traditions may evolve or all such known as tradition may be thrown out the window. Feel free to toss tradition, but don't "throw the baby out with the bath water." Don't throw out the love. Instead celebrate your love, the love that binds you.

Fun to know. Fun to show. Fun to glow.

Start using your voice. Start acting as if you truly have a choice. Some people feel they have to have everything figured out before they can begin. But I say life is not for the figuring, it is for the finding. So go ahead be a seeker and dig in!

I don't believe I have the ability to defend my faith, my new found beliefs, even as it is my deepest desire.

There is no need for you to defend your faith. For your faith, things of God, are not meant as things to be pitted out against the mind. Your faith, the love you feel to and from God, is a heartfelt matter, something that can be known only unto your heart and shown unto the world by your life.

JULY 3, 2011

As I am so drawn, so urged, to say and write these words, I feel I am possessed by a great loving Spirit which I call "God My Father." For the guidance feels so true, so honest, so meant for me. And the knowledge I am given proves itself so instantly that I have to listen. I have to wake up and hear and heed this loving voice which speaks to me.

Maybe you don't want to hear this, what I say. "I liked you better the other way." Perhaps your brain was more comfortable with the old me, the way I showed up. But your heart cannot deny the love it feels when I am with you. So perhaps silence is what you and I need. Words can get in the way. We can sit together in silence lovingly you and me.

Camaraderie or commissary? For what reason do you desire companionship? Comrades lift each other's spirits, help each other to hold their heads high and walk forward to the light together. Commissaries join together to wallow in the muck. As they dog paddle they stir the muck together, digging a deeper hole.

What kind of companionship do you want for your life? What kind of companion are you? Be careful as you bend over low in an effort to lift another up in your seeming "good deed." For despite your own wishes, their wish may not be to be lifted up by you. Their hand maybe outreached to pull you down. For if you feel down as well, they can feel so much better about themselves. It is better to live as The Light, a beacon of hope to those who desire change, a better, more joyful life. Leave a clear path of light for the others, so they can meet you at the top.

You are just coming to know the realities, the possibilities, for your life. Have patience with yourself. Your way will be shown. What would make you happy? Do you even know how blessed you are? Time to count your blessings. Give thanks and be grateful for all you have, the many blessings you know, and the many blessings the world has yet to show.

Do you know why you are so happy when you look at the sky? Do you know why you smile when a bird catches your eye? Do you know why you laugh? Do you know why you cry? Because you feel, feel deeply, "My Love." I've sprinkled it all around for you to find. Here and there, everywhere you look, your eye can see the work of My Love. Beauty is in the eye of the beholder. Behold My Love. It is all for you.

There is goodness everywhere waiting to be acknowledged, to be seen, to be realized, to be beholden. By looking for, by seeking and seeing such goodness you are activating such goodness for the world. Whether it is immediately apparent or not, all contains goodness, people, plants, animals and situations. It takes one to know one. The goodness in you brings out the goodness in another for your goodness recognizes the goodness in another and attracts and draws it to the surface of the other.

When I hold my thoughts high in accordance with Divine Mind, I can do anything and know this is so. It will come to me. I'll find out. I'd like to know.

Everyday is new. Find your way. Live life fully. Let nature be nature. Conform to nature. Don't make nature conform to you.

JULY 5, 2011

What is happening to me? No one ever told me about this way of being! I can be so high and then I can be so low, high and light in a spiritual sense, and low and dense in a material death. Bring me balance today. Show me the way I can be fully present as truth and beauty. Take from me my cares and woes. Light my way. Bring me home.

I sing this song for you. Take care of yourself and the people you love. This is all I ask. Love more. Dip into the well of My love and pour forth My love. Quench your thirst. I am "the Living Water" which flows freely for all, for all time, now for you to know.

There is nowhere for you to go. Where you are, you can show My love in your heart. This is where you start. Now is the time to begin to see clearly all I have written in your name. My love is for you to claim. Call My name. Ask Me please. I am here for you. Be with Me. See what you have. See how blessed you are. Celebrate it all.

Words aren't needed where I come from. Home is Heaven, the Light, the Life. Beauty abounds, welcome it into your heart. Raise your voice. Drink in My love, My substance, for you to live, to thrive. See this. Know this. Feel so very alive.

Christ says; Marry Me into your heart. Let's live together in love, abiding one with the Father. His way is Ours. Follow Me down the path, which leads upwards, to all things good. Consider this well. You have My heart to hold, My heart of gold, dear spouse in God.

Fidelity, God wants your fidelity and love as well. God has all to give, all to help you live. See God in all and all will be good for you. Be "My love" for the world. Be faithful to Me. Do not doubt. My word is true. My love is here for you to bathe in. Be washed clean. You are baptized by My love. Forever we are One.

There is nothing else I need. Nothing else I need to know, now that I know this "Tremendous Love" which swells my heart. My soul dances, sways and swoons in your abiding Love. Dear Spirit, hold me close. Let me have this dance you call "Eternal Life." Let me sing with the angels. Let me soar to the greatest of heights.

There is no denying something is going on here. Something so great has changed and is changing the very core of my soul, something so great that there is no name to contain, to quantify. Oh, how great Thy Love, so sings my soul. Yes, I know this song in my heart, for it is my heart song, my soul song for eternity. It's so good to have found what I was missing. I am whole, holy now. Keep me here. Do not let me ever wander again in the desert, I pray. I ask in Jesus Name. All good comes to me. I am free.

> *It's not about taking a vow of poverty. You can be as rich as you want, for all I have is yours now for the asking, for the believing. As you know that all your good flows from God, your Source, your having it all is entirely possible. Have what you want. I want you to be happy and feel blessed.*

Order up. I'd like one of each, one of each possible blessing to come to me, through me, for good, for all. I am here to serve my Master, my Maker, my Creator who shines so brightly above and around me. Through me, His Works are done.

> *So be it! Truth may be called a million different things, but may only "be known" as "One."*

Truth speaks to me. What I hear is real important stuff. My world is made of Love. Divine Love fills me up.

> *Truth be known. Truth be shown. Light the way. You are on the way home to Me fully. You can never get enough, so ask once ask again for Me to fill you to the brim. You may or may not know. I am here to show the way I've found to walk the earth not touching the ground.*

> *t is not your job to feel bad or sad for anyone or for yourself. By your words and actions, you are to lift each other. Be a friend. Be a brother. Set not your cares and burdens on any other. Give them to Me. I can carry them for you. Hand them over. Think not about what's wrong. See right, see "the Light."*

> *Shake not your fist. Curse not a soul. All are Mine just as you. Walk the walk, as I showed you how to do. This is why*

I give all My love to you. Be Me now on earth. This is the "true rebirth." Act in My name. Remember, always "from whence you came" and will come again home into your full glory.

You are blessed. This life is not a test. It's a discovery zone, a recovery zone, for you to find who you are. A shining star has your name on it. Now go live fully blessed as you are. Forget what they say, don't let it ruin your day. Once you know what is possible, you can do anything. Everything is yours, as you wish. This is my dream for you. Go tell the world of My love!

None of this other stuff is a big deal anymore. I can conquer the world. I see more, so much more beyond this reality.

So someone threw it at you. Now the ball is in your court. What are you going to do? Take it out of play or attempt to foul the other?

Sometimes, the world presses so heavily upon me. But I am saved by the Grace of God whom speaks unto my heart and says, *"I love you. My heart is yours. All is well. Know this Truth which I write upon your heart."* I am to proclaim in Christ's Name. I cannot, not do this. This is mine to do.

JULY 6, 2011

It doesn't appeal to me. My senses don't like it.

That's okay. You don't have to like it all. State your preferences and they will find you. Yes, this is graduate material. We feel you are ready; this is why you have been led to where you are. You are ready to hear, ready to know, ready to experience these deeper truths you are finding buried within yourself. Your treasure has been hidden so far, so close to you all along. Enjoy, reap the rewards!

What you want, what you need, is already here available now for the believing. When you trust in this we will lead you to your treasure. Treasure this truth.

You are beginning to hear it, aren't you? The problems people create as they create them with their words, with their actions, with their beliefs. Now you know that you do not have to follow their lead, their unbelief in the miraculous. You know your own power, your power of choice, of insight, of agreement. You do not have to agree with them. Agree with what you want for yourself. You see now how to create your life.

Do you see what you are creating? Do you see the Light that fills the room? It is wondrous. It is enveloping. It is tantalizing. This Light is yours, all yours. More power to you! They will gather at your feet.

Who are you to say? You are the one who holds the power for your life. Say it like you mean it. Joy to the world you bring.

Someone asks: What are you going to do with all the things you prepared? The plans you made? I say, the day is not over. The fire of my desire is not put out. I still stoke those embers, keeping the flame of desire burning in my heart. The day will come soon for the flame to burn brightly in the face of all.

Walk tall, the day is coming. How can I help you find your way? Live your dream today. Who do you listen to? Whose voice do you hear ringing in your ear? Is it the voice of hope or doom? What kind of voices in the halls of your mind loom?

There is nothing for me "to do." All is being done for me in God's name in the invisible. My eyes see this truth, as I believe.

Purify your body, mind and spirit. Of course there is always a potential for problems but just as well there is always a potential for ease and grace. It's all what you see and how you see it. See clearly what you want and behold the "Power of Love."

Isn't it nice to know who you are, that you are so very capable of calling the shots in your own life? You are not the victim of or in life, you are the victor. Rein victoriously over this life of yours. You are doing well. All is well. How do you envision it?

I in-vision it going smoothly. I in-vision it all for the best.

Temporary, everything physical is temporary, changing, evolving or dissolving. Growth is life. Stagnation is death. Live in the flow of Spirit. You do not have to think it all out. Send loving thoughts everywhere to everyone. This is a blessing to you and all. Curse not another, friend, foe or brother. For whatever you send will all return to you again ten-fold. Be so filled that you cannot help but spill My love.

I am taking dictation, but not from a dictator, from a lover of mankind. Put me where you need me to be to show up as Love.

Life, as you know, will show itself to you. I am here to awaken your appetite for life. Live zestfully. When you say you have no way, you are limiting your options. Keep your options open. Open your mind to new possibilities occurring.

Overwhelmed, you cannot expect the one whom is drowning in the details of life to save you. He is dog paddling so fast; he can barely keep his head above water and gulps some water with each breath. You have to save yourself. We are here to help. One's whom hold and serve such limiting beliefs can never be your answer.

As you believe it, Love believes in you. Oh, the power of prayer. Speak as you wish. Command your good forth into the world. Do not wait for any other to manifest your good. No waiting required. Your good comes directly to you as you wish. See this clearly. Your eyes have been clouded for so long.

My words are my own. I own them.

Toxic environment, physical reality. Take me away. Lift me up. Let my feet not touch the ground of such filth!

"I need this. This will make me happy. No, this is what I want, what I have to have. No, I want that one too. Is that one better? Well, I better have that one as well." Retail therapy a very soul consuming idea. Eat your heart out and never find the satisfaction you desire.

I want to run. I'm mad. I'm scared, but where to go? Where is the safe haven I so desire? *"Shh, over here," says my soul. "Shh, be quiet. Come inside. Shh, listen. Listen, hear. You are safe here now. This is the sanctuary of your soul. Where you heart lies peacefully in love. Rest here for awhile, rest in peace. It's time to go higher than ever before. You have been with Me, at peace, in remembrance of "Our love" I ask you to be."*

I close my eyes and lose my place in this world, my place of confusion, my place of disagreement and enter into the peace of my heart. *"Thank you for coming," says my soul. "It's nice to have you present. Please feel free to show up more often."*

You don't have to stoop so low. You don't have to come to their level. Make them rise up to meet you. Raise the stakes of the games. Play by your own rules. You'll be happier and so shall they. This is how the game is to be played. The first one to the top wins, but no one else has lost unless they choose to stay down. Look up, see where you are going. Be the cream. Rise to the top.

Take care of My people. Be My love for them. Show them The way, the way I showed the world. Show again. Show the way that is still there to here, to the heart of God, to God's love and wisdom. Be the peace today. Stay with Me and live this way.

JULY 7, 2011

Tears of happiness I have cried so many times, for I felt such love. The love of God expressed so purely to me through those whose hearts have touched mine. Tears of love, kisses from the Divine, I wept openly.

I can remember kneeling in prayer at my pew as I was supposed to do. My prayers were not rote, they were words so deep they stuck in my throat. Swelling within my heart tears then flowed. Yes, I knelt crying, for why I did not know. "This is not the place for tears," I said to myself, and hear with my physical ears. "Contain yourself, behave. Wipe your face, appear with grace." Yet, True grace was what I had found but did not know for I had not heard it told as so.

To create our ideal, we must create as the one God created His ideal, our world. We must hold our ideal steadfast in consciousness. We must hold the thought steadily in mind, not wavering but steadfast to the ideal of our dream until it manifests or materializes before our eyes and becomes a reality in the physical sense. We must "speak the word" and hold true to our vision for our vision to unfold and manifest outwardly.

Unfoldment - Just as the butterfly emerges from the cocoon reborn anew, from the death of its past life as a lowly earth bound creature, and unfolds his wings to expose, reveal and realize, his own beauty, mastery and ability to live a new life on such a higher plane of existence than ever before dreamed, we as well will unfold the wings of our consciousness to behold our own beauty, mastery and ability to create wonderful worlds end to end for eternity, when we realize we are One, realize, know, and fully feel we are One with All, whom is God as God is All in Perfection.

July 8, 2011

We don't feel the need to be married in Heaven as we do while on earth for we realize our union, bond with all, in Love. We exist in a state of continual Divine Love. We need not wait for our physical death to experience and know such a state of Divine Grace. This was the mission of Jesus Christ on earth. To show us that it was humanly possible to live in such a high spiritual love state of grace while present in body and mind. He told us we were one in spirit and that we could be as He, One in Spirit with The Father, the One of us that is the divine Idea of perfection, God in and as man.

I have an extra special sense about me today, a sense of well-being.

You have to schedule fun into your life. "Now" is the time of your life.

More about the butterfly - As the caterpillar changes from his low and confined self to the new and free beauty, the unlimited form of the butterfly, he is reborn joyously perfect and beautifully free. He drinks nectar, the sweet life, and suckles on pureness and truth. The caterpillar does not slowly exchange a leg for a wing, the old dissolves back into the pure potential and then again manifests from original source as perfection, God's ideal.

Make time for recreation, re-creation of your soul. Your soul stirs inside wanting to be nourished and exercised. Feed Me, take Me for a walk. Just sit a while and let's have a talk. I'm here for you, as I've been all along. You celebrate Me when you enjoy dance and song. So live more fully. Love more freely. Feed Me. Be with Me. Take Me along.

It's nice to know, you are beginning to show. We see you grow, blossoming before us, with us, as you know. Enjoy today, as you are becoming more and more wonderful. Your heart sings such a sweet song. Keep singing, the day is not long. You see so much. There is so much to see. Isn't it wonderful, oh, so joyful, you're awakening. Wake with a smile. We have been with you all the while. This you see and say, "Well, glory be!"

See it, as you say, "So be it." Declare the life you so desire to live. This is the gift given to you. Accept and welcome this news, this good news with humbling gratitude. All thanks be to God. This is the way of Life.

I know "the Comforter" of whom Jesus spoke. He has touched my heart many times, even before I awoke. With a greater and greater presence, I know the reality of this great gift. The more I realize, the more I know peace within my very soul, the kind of peace which holds my heart together, not torn in fear and anguish. How great Thy love, oh Father, hold me close. I want to know Your love.

These teachings are coming to me directly, in my words.

*As you show what you know, you will be given more to
know.*

Did Jesus ever write down the lessons he learned?

He didn't need to write it down. He just knew it.

*People have been held captive by the limiting ideas imposed
on their consciousness. What do you want to believe? Do
you believe you know it all? What do you give the most
credence to, the words of any other or words written on
your heart and softly spoken to your soul? What feels the
best to you?*

*Personality versus Spirituality
Personality: The invidual, man, ego, competetion.
Spirituality: Spirit can not be divided.*

*What have you decided? Is your mind made up or is it open
to reception of new ideas? A closed mind equals a closed
heart. Hearts which are closed are stagnant, stiff and cold,
as no energy flows in and no energy flows out. The energy of
love is not stagnant. Stagnated energy is not energy at all
thus the only way to a heart filled with an abundant energy
of love is to be open to the filling and well as the out flowing
of love. To be open to this flow, one first has to break free of
the limitation placed in mind.*

*A mind which believes it knows all, of how the world
works, is a closed mind. For this mind has decided that the
information it has been fed is sufficient and thus hungers
not for more.*

A long time ago a man born with the name of Jesus walked this earth. He was a seeker, a seeker of truth. He was not satisfied with the stories that He had been fed to fill His head. So He sought answers for himself. In this way, He opened His mind to new possibilities, new truths. As His mind opened so then His heart opened. It opened so wide that Divine Love could abundantly pour inside. This Love so filled His heart and with such a continued force that it spilled equally as abundantly and forcefully from His heart to others.

This is the love that transforms body, mind and soul. This is the love Jesus wanted each of us to know. Be a seeker, He advised. Be meek and ask God to make you wise, wise to his transforming Divine Love. This is the gift the Holy Spirit brings as God commands to open hearts and bended knees asking God, "Fill me please."

How will you ever know if you cannot hear? How can you hear if you do not listen? How can you listen if you are not quiet? Sit still. Shut up. Button your lips and open your mind. Open your heart, open wide. There is much to know. God will show your heart His face, the face of Love. Then you will know God. God already knows you.

JULY 8, 2011

Palaces, cathedrals and shrines have been built with jewels and gold attempting to hold the power of God. But no material mansion can ever be filled with such glory. For the true glory of God, the power of God is the love of God. Not our love for God, but God's love for us which can only be held in the most sacred of spots, the heart/soul of man. If you so love God, build a shrine in your heart, sweep the streets clean of debris and make room, make ready. And most of all invite God, the "peace of God" to rest in the sanctuary of your heart.

I keep saying these things, these knowings placed upon my heart. "This," God says, "is a good place to start. You hear My softly spoken voice and you are heeding this wisdom which dwells within. Yes, this is a very good place to begin."

JULY 9, 2011

I have to have myself God centered to find my joy.

> *Here and now I am, God says. Feel Me. Be with Me. Be Me for all. Walk your walk. Take Me along. I hold your hand, as you reach out your hand to help others. Be My voice. Be gentle and kind. Be loving. Be trusting. Trust Me to lead you to calm waters.*

Thank you for the voice of Love that sings such sweet songs to my soul.

> *My peace is in you resting. Who do you love? Love everyone. The love you share will come back to you. It's a boomerang, a sweet echo chain effect, this energy, this power of love. Feel the power. Be empowered by the power of love. My heart beats for you, My love.*

> *Do not be fooled My people, when you hear it told that spiritual things cannot be understood. For, oh yes they can and are to be. They can be found by you if you so desire to seek understanding. I desire this yearning for you and from you. As this is what brings us closer, your understanding of My ways, My ways of love.*

> *Be not afraid to admit your faults, weaknesses and failings*

to Me. I already know. There is no need to boast or be proud either. I know who you are. I as well know what you are and want to tell you the story of My heart. You are in the center of it. Are you intrigued? Would you like to know more? Good. Then ask. Ask Me to tell you the story of My love for you. Yes, you, and of course all. But first, right now, I want you to know the story of your birth, your heritage and your rightful inheritance of My Kingdom.

This is not a secret or at least not meant to be kept a secret from anyone, no one at all. But just as to you seeing is believing, hearing is as well. So I want you to hear this story directly from Me. From Me? Does that seem so strange to you, to think that you yourself could hear and know the voice of God? Well, you have heard My voice many times before but found it easy to ignore. But in the beginning you knew and trusted My wisdom words. This all goes back to the time of your birth.

So make sometime and gather yourself at My feet. Set down your cares and ask Me to have you know. Tell Me what you wonder. Tell Me what you think. Then open your mind and heart so wide that I can pour My love and wisdom inside.

JULY 10, 2011

Bring forth the ideal, supplication.

I need not worry what the next moment brings for I trust in God's ways. You see, I see through faith, faith in God's will, God's "good will." This is not the same as one whom one says "Oh, it must be God's Will." Like, "If punishment is due, I guess it is due." No, Jesus taught us a different way to look at and be led through God's Will. Through supplication of our own will, or need to control, and the asking that God's Will, or Good Will to All, is done in His Name through us.

God knows my desires and my uniqueness for My Maker Himself has bestowed the gifts I have, on me. Of course He wants to use these "God given" abilities to enlighten and bring joy to His creation. This is my only true desire, to be of service so I have laid my life down.

Some would say here that I have "taken up the cross." But I do not, for that seems to me as an announcement that one is expecting their way to be hard and a burden. It's just the opposite for me, as I am laying down the burdens of my mind, my fears and worries for the future, and knowing that God will provide my daily needs and lead me out of temptation. Thy Kingdom come, Thy Will be done on Earth (the physical) as it is in Heaven (the spiritual). This is truly my daily prayer, which I ask in the Name of Christ, who reigns in me.

I find myself speaking with such authority. The words take me back and I laugh, laughter of joy and amazement that such adamant wisdom flows so freely and forcefully from my mind and mouth. "It is true... It is this way... Yes, I know... This is because..."

> *Have you tasted the sweetness, the sweetness of life, the nectar inside the beautiful blossoms? Have you looked for the beauty? Have you beheld a sunrise? Have you been swept away by the glory of a sunset? These glories abound all around. Life is what you look for. Life is what you see. Look for, and then see a bounty of beauty.*

I have perfect vision. I see perfection. Some would say, "No, you don't! Look here. See this injustice. See him. He is mean. She is wrong. You are not living in the real world." And they are correct for I am choosing to live my life from a higher perspective, from the spiritual plane, as a spiritual being. And thus my eyes are God's eyes and I see the beauty in His creation.

I see the true spirit of each man. As I meet them in a spirit of love, "The Spirit of Love," which is within them, awakens. We each have said ourselves, "She brings out the worst in me." And as well have said, "He brings out the best in me." For what you give you get and I want to always give my best to receive the best. My best is only "so good," and always "so good" consistently, so I have asked and continue to ask God to make His Will mine, to give me Divine eyes with which to see and a Divine heart from which to be. I want to "show up" perfectly.

Heaven rushes in to my heart. My eyes behold God's glory. Today is perfect, as God made it. In God's heart I dwell, as His Divine Love dwelleth in mine. We are in love, swept away in a most rapturous love, the Love of God, if we will but let God express through us in the ideal way He has conceived for us.

One can be religious without being spiritual. One can be spiritual without being religious and as well one can be very religious and very spiritual. A religious person is a follower of a way to God that many men agree on and have formed rules and codes of ethics for all members. To be a member in good standing one must obey the system of this religion which has mostly been formed by tradition. The Divine Inspirations of each sect's founders have been ritualized for the generations which follow to follow. The original intent of all of these rituals was to be a path which leads the followers to Spiritual Enlightenment, to God Realization.

But many have fallen short of that attainment as they see the rites and rituals, the path, of their religious traditions as the core truth and satisfaction of the groups' requirement, not seeking more for they are not believing more was available to them. The few that have attained the Spiritual Enlightenment which was to be the goal of the quest, have been held so high by the group that they don't even see those as being in their own box. They hold them so above their selves and their own ability that they hold them outside of their box and call them saints. Never realizing that the spiritual heights these saints attained could as well be theirs.

Then there are those who have shunned other's stories and rituals seeking the knowing of higher things on their own terms. They have realized that they can have a personal connection with Spirit without other men mediating. They have heard the voice within speak a language dear to their heart and their heart has leapt in remembrance as they feel and know the Love of God.

Religions are paths to God, paths, just paths, not God Realization. God realization brings peace, patience and a comforting love within one's heart. It's heartfelt and heart full and tears down all boxes.

Why have people created the story of Hell being an unbearably hot place? For Hell being the opposite of Heaven should be theoretically be freezing as Heaven is enlightenment, Hell would be the total lack of any light, fire or not, so it serves that it's darkness would be cold.

The cold hearted live in Hell. Heaven knows. You can know Heaven. Heaven is here for you. Nothing to do, just be in Love with us all. You have to hold it in your heart, your belief in better.

What energizes you? What gives you the power to press forward? As soon as you get out of your mind, you are One with everything. Those you call "simple" see the world clearer than you do. Get out of your way. Wake up little sister, wake up! Press past the point of doubt. Remember, wherever I am, God Is.

I have to start aligning myself with the flow of divine guidance, with the realization that all things can work together for good. We must all make continual efforts to press past the point of doubt, to face the facts from the highest point of view to know reality beyond appearances, to remember the divine law of adjustment, to remember the omnipresence of God as the non-material reality of every person, the reality of everything whatever it may be, wherever it may be. Tell the truth about your physical self no matter what the appearance may be. To do this requires discipline and conditioning as we are all constantly surrounded by "they say" reports.

There is traditional Christain religious thought and there is "New Thought" which is becoming a religion of right thinking, then there is "the Good News" which Jesus proclaimed. "What?" you may say, you already proclaim Christianity. Yes, I did. But I am now proclaiming that I understand, I know, that neither the Christian, nor Judean traditions, nor the New Thought movements proclaim the true "Good News" of Christ.

For a while I thought that the people in the "School of Right Thinking" had the total story, that Jesus was telling us the value of the power of our thoughts and which I still believe is very much a part of His Message which has gotten garbled. Yes, Jesus did stress that we are what we think, in so many words, and yes the Bible tells many stories of Jesus teaching of moral values, which have become the core of most traditional religious thought and creed.

> *But wait, says Jesus, there's more! After I have left you, God will send a comforter, a gift of wisdom, truth and peace that will fill your heart with joy. The Kingdom of God is at hand. Love God your Father. Trust in Him. Have faith in good. See the good in all. Thank God for all. Make your every thought be a prayer of thanksgiving. Ask God to fill you with His grace. My Father is loving and wants to bestow His love into your heart. Love God. Love your brother. Prepare your heart; make a sacred and holy sanctuary in your heart for the Love of God. You can so as I, for the Love of God.*

How do you understand the gifts of the Holy Spirit of which Jesus foretold and Paul proclaimed? Do you believe you have been bestowed with this gift of God because of a religious rite or tradition? First of all, it's not a one-time thing, this gift of Grace; it's something one has to ask for in supplication daily. "Thy Kingdom come, Thy will be done." When you choose by your own power of choice, your free will, to make your own will God's will, and when the Comforter comes, you will have no doubt. You will have no doubt you are being physically, mentally and spiritually changed. As well as you will acquire a mind of trust; trust in God that leaves no doubt.

Yes, this is the "Good News" for ready and willing hearts. God our Father is so willing, ready and able to bring aide and comfort and He does so by offering daily "downloads" of His Own Substance, Divine Love. This is the pure stuff. 100% Divine Love is what changes the minds and hearts of man making new eyes and ears, eyes to see and ears to hear. The "Good News" is that with the birth of Jesus, whom became the Christ, the world has been offered a new gift. Jesus was the first to proclaim the Christos, but as he said, we could too and would do far greater works than He.

> *You think you need all the answers. You want a reasonable answer for everything. The power is in the wonder. Where is your patience? Do you think you have lost it? It's here, deep inside your heart. Sit still, breath deep. Be with Me. Find My peace in your heart. Ahh…*

> *To find Me, go away from the world. You need not move physically, just mentally. Mentally remove yourself from where you are. Go into the quiet closet of your heart where I am waiting, residing within your being as Pure Spirit to lift you up and hold you high. Float easily, comfortably above any physical limitations. The water is calm. The breeze is gentle. All is well. Stretch out and get comfortable, comfortable with whom you are in Me, Me in you. Together We are One.*

> *You can never really run away from the problems you have created. They are yours; they will find you wherever you go,*

so you might as well claim them. Claim your responsibility for them. Claim your responsibility for their birth, their growth, for it was you who planted the seed, the idea of the problem, in the first place. And then of course it was you as well who carefully tended to and watered those little seeds of pure potential, so of course they stick with you, they are yours.

Running from them or burying them a little deeper in the ground doesn't fix a thing, for they will continue to thrive and grow and follow you wherever you go. So stop, stop right where you are and turn around and face them. Face the fact that just as you had the power to create them, you as well have the power to dissolve them. Disarm them and to stop them dead in their tracks.

Say this, "You no longer serve me. You were a belief I once held, but I am now releasing. Go in peace. I am done with you. I will no longer give you any thought, any attention, anything that you could have ever considered to be love. For I have had a change of heart and have made a decision to take a new direction, a fresh start. Goodbye. Farewell. Go in peace. I release you back into the ethers, the space which holds all the energy of pure potential. Dissolve I say!" Then at that very moment turn your attention to beauty. Beauty of any kind or form your mind and heart can grasp. Hold that thought and dwell in the peace of beauty and order for your world.

Why do you feel so bad? Are you mad at yourself? Are you blaming yourself for some past action or in-action? Stop it now, I say! See the Truth. You Are Love and you are loved. Go forth and enjoy the full bounty of this day you have. See and be the glory. This is the way. You see what you know and know what you see, perfectly.

I manifest wondrous works of art. I manifest wondrous works through Spirit which is All to me. I am the observer, not the judge. I observe life. I observe nature.

> *It doesn't serve you to be a "know it all." It does serve you to be a "want to know it all." The answer is in the seeking. Be open to greater truths.*

So what is the basis of truth, the truth kernel, in tales of witches, those who were said to not be mortal and could instantly manifest themselves at whim anywhere as anything?

> *This is to do with manifestations of those who possess a higher consciousness and the unknowing mind of material man takes it for evil. As it is a demonstration of power he knows not and fears, he thus calls it evil. Man has lived so small for so many years and has done a fine job of dousing out the fire, putting out the light, of those whose light they did not understand, thus feared. Crucifixion became their answer. Fear has ruled man's day and night.*

There is another group among us living sequestered from our American mainstream society, the Amish and Dunkard's come to mind. They shun the life and supposed ease of life Americans are so proud of.

> *Yes, these groups are founded on the principle of simplicity. This is their rule, just as much as the Love of God is.*

JULY 14, 2011

> *Do you see infinite possibility? You always have a choice.*

I can't be intimidated. No one holds power over me.

God is Love. Spiritual principle is true, but God as Love offers more to those who desire higher. Christ had this "More," Divine Love. Jesus, as Christ, did not make Christ Realization through his mind. He turned his mind/body/ soul over to God whom he knew so intimately that He called Him Father. God's Will flowed through the Christ Jesus. The small mind of Jesus was not involved.

JULY 15, 2011

As I watch this marvelous work of art develop before my eyes, I know for sure this is not a thing, which I can control. It is what I allow to flow through and manifest as greatness. God's Hand directs mine. This is what I have discovered in my art. This is the lesson for my life. Loosen up, let go and allow God to flow freely.

I like what I see. I see what I like. I know good. It's God I know. The face of God smiles to me. I smile back and wink, a wink of knowing, knowing God's Love for me, in me. Through me flowing, this is supreme knowing. I thank God.

What have you decided? What is your will? Whose is your will? Is it your will to serve or be served?

As you flex your muscles, you strengthen them. Feel your arms. They are changing, strengthening in their power, developing the potential they have held all along. So it is, with your spiritual muscles. Flex them. Stretch them. Exercise them and they as well shall lengthen and fortify. They will support you and be the rock of your faith. Stand tall.

We so love to spend time with you. Oh, We are always with you, but We so love being heard. And are so excited that you are now available to hear and discern Our messages. We are so proud of your growth. You are changing so quickly, flourishing really, in your new found glory, the glory of God within you.

Thank you for listening to Our prompting for seeking Divine Love. Thank you for trusting Our ways. Love, Love, Love. We are Love, You, us, All, yes God. All is Love.

Thank you for asking. You have to ask to know, as you now know. Seek and ye shall find. Finders keepers, yes but finders are also sharers. For anyone who finds such a great treasure, who discovers the "Hidden Treasure" within the heart has to share and show. As their very being will be so changed that there can be no other way of being than one whom shares the Love they have found. "Finders reapers," yes, that's a better way to say it.

Maybe it should be "The lost weep and the found reap." The lost are those whom wander the land in fear. The found are those whom soar the sky with confidence in the abundantly unlimited Love of God. Are you lost? I think not, you have a direction. You have found direction in your life. You wander no more. We see you soar.

You have had premonitions of this coming. Have you not dreamed you could fly? Fly you will. No one is, or can ever can, limit you. Even you yourself cannot stop the jet you are from taking off, for your jet fuel is God's Love. Divine Love is being pumped into your very being each day.

You are right, not everyone feels this way, but you do, so go with that. As you are so filled, more understanding to you will come. Remember, the answers you desire are in here, not outside of you, not in a book, not on the computer or on TV. You can read and hear another's ideas but you will know the Truth when your heart speaks to you. Keep the faith, faith in God. God's Love is your Power Source. On it so rely. Think lofty thoughts. Rise and shine. There is more to your story, so much more to come. You are growing into it. You are glowing into it.

The Words are for you. Tailor made Truth. Truth you can hear and understand. And you will, as you release your hold on life and open up to the true possibilities. Can you dream big? You can dream as big as you can imagine. But We have so much more in store for you. So do not ever limit yourself to what you know or could even imagine. That's how miracles happen, when someone opens their mind and heart to amazing possibilities. Be prepared to be awed. God is So Great. So great is God's Love.

Don't put your life on hold. That's how people get stuck. That's how ruts are formed. Back and forth in a rocking motion the human digs himself a hole he cannot see out of. And as he can no longer see beyond his self dug hole he imagines this is the life he is to continue to live, and thus creates a holding pattern or perhaps a deeper hole.

But oh, the dreamer sees a way out of the rut as he imagines a day when the land he sits on is dry and he can gain once again a firm foothold and walk forward, upward and away from the depths of despair. He sees the day so well in his mind that he is living it in his nightly and daily dreams. And so flows forth his truth, from his imaginings, his dreams, as his life. Yes, the dreamer is the winner in life, for the dreamer dares to see beyond the physical, which to many is end all, and thus becomes their end, the demise of their conscious ability to create a life worth living.

The ego thrives on control and power. Power and control over anything or anyone in its midst. It's not a personal thing. It's really not even so much a conscious thing, but it is real in itself. All egos are this way and if they do not have their way met quickly and easily they are glad to butt heads with other egos to get what they want. You see egos are not by nature patient. In fact, they are quite rude. They throw tantrums and start pushing any button they can find when they feel a lack of order.

Just as every ego likes to push buttons, every ego has a button, which can be pushed. Most people's ego buttons are on their shoulders. This is also the place most egos carry "the weight of the world." It seems that some egos particularly like pushing another's ego button just for sport. It's like a game of tag. It keeps drama high in their life, thus excitement and tension filled. Did you know that the ego feeds on fear? A steady diet of fear will keep a healthy ego thriving, fear, then button-pushing. "Look at me. Me! Me!" Egos are so all about self-made drama. Faith is ultimate trust or reliance. Faith in God is faith in good. What do you have faith in? What do you think about good or bad, God or evil?

Stop listening, announcing, and declaring all the reasons that you cannot do something, instead, list all the reasons you can. You have unlimited potential. The power of God is your force. You have a creative mind which can come up with a new solution. If you just get started, begin, you will find your way through. Help is available.

JULY 16, 2011

What enrages you? What do you fear? Are you easily upset? Can someone else ruin your day?

The answers I give today to these questions are a total opposite to the answers I would have given just two years ago. Why? Did I run into a lot of money? Make it big? Well, I did learn of a most amazing inheritance I have and yes I did make it big, but none of this is according to the worldly terms. I have moved to a higher plane of consciousness and because of the infilling of God's most sweet and precious Divine Love I have had a change of heart and mind. You see the grand inheritance of which I speak is the Peace of the Kingdom of God. This is my "Living Trust." As my God and Father, as the "Living God" has offered and shown me this Peaceful Plane of Consciousness and invited me to partake in all it's glory now as I live and breath.

The will of this grand inheritance is the "Will of God." I made a decision to forgo my own ways and hardships and let God's Will flow through my being. As I ask, God continues to pour forth Divine Love into my heart, expanding my heart capacity for peace and compassion each day. As this piece of God is as well the "Peace of God" there is no room in my heart for fear, worry, judgment or hatred.

The Love of God swoons in my heart. Dancing with joy untold as my true Christ Being unfolds. New eyes to see life clearly and calmly give me perfect vision, perfect vision to see the truth of good everywhere. In God I trust. In God I rely. As God is good, I trust in the good of life. I believe life has so much good in store for me. As God is Love, I am loving, a loving spirit wearing a skin suit on this spiritual growth quest called "my life."

Positive Statement: I so love being with other beings whom exude love and compassion. It so warms my heart to see others whom I love fill with God's special Divine Love and blossom into all that they can be. This is such a joy for me. Joy be me. Thank you for the gift of my loving family. Thank you for the grateful hearts which surround me.

> *Say what you want. Declare it true. We are here for you to see it through. It is done as you have said and believed.*

"Self-control" is the name of the game people play when they desire to better themselves. Looking for moral values or God's Law as they know them man attempts to control his own self, control the will, the force of his own ego self. It takes discipline, strict discipline. Such discipline that most falter along the way again and again. Few find the inner conviction to truly conquer their personal demon, their ego. Few attain such perfection of mind, body and soul. As so few have, many, if not all others, do not believe perfection of man can be obtained by themselves, besides the material world beckons, calls to their senses at every juncture.

There is another way to know peace and perfection, such that even surpasses any attained through the rigors of self-discipline. The way is easy. It is the way of the Cross. But listen closely for the way I will describe here forth is not the story of the cross which you have been spoon-fed your entire life. This story is the "Good News," the real "Good News," for now, for you and forever.

It is the story of God's gift to mankind. A special bestowal that was first delivered to and bestowed upon Jesus of Nazareth, the gift that gave a mortal man new eyes, new ears, and most of all a new heart, a most compassionate heart, the heart of God. For God so filled this man with His Love, his very Essence that this man was no longer a man in nature, he was Divine in nature, all to the credit of the power of Divine Love.

While Jesus walked the earth, he was the first, and at that time the only one, to have been so gifted with the true substance of God. No one ever before had been even offered this gift. All before who knew God consciousness had done so through their own discipline of their own will. They so

*labored, worked and wrestled the desires of their self with
their aspirations to perfectly follow the will of God.*

*Our bible tells of Solomon's own personal trial with this very
idea. He has recorded his tribulations and lamentations.
It is exactly these lamentations of mankind that have
so moved Our Creator to ease our load and lighten the
burden of staying the way, the course, of keeping God's laws,
through keeping control over the wanderings of one's mind
into the desert of discontent.*

*"I shall offer, My love. I shall give of Myself to mankind so
his way will easily be My way," with this God decided to
gift His nature to man allowing man to be transformed,
be renewed. This gift of Divine Love is a gift of Spirit, from
Spirit into the soul of man, raising such man to a higher
plane of consciousness and level of joy.*

*Yes, God made an allowance for man, but did not choose to
override man's preset condition of self-will or free will. So
by this truth God could not place His "Love Gift" into any
human by His caprice. Just as any other act of God to man,
man has to seek to see, then ask. Not many ask, but all who
ask receive. Those who ask in supplication of their own ego
selves, those whom choose to crucify their own will and ask
with all their heart and all their mind for such an infilling of
Divine Love.*

So why do not more ask if this truly is the "Holy Grail" we have been
looking for?

*Because man does not hear the Message Jesus, as Christ,
gave. "The Truth" of the Good News was lost shortly after
Jesus left the earth. The gift had been bestowed, but the*

world could not or would not hear. Jesus told them, "What I can do, so will you be able." He gave them prayers. He gave them direction. But few understood his "true story." So they made up a story that made sense to them and continued sinning, and enshrining, and immortalizing stories that suited their needs and understanding.

Now is the time for the world to know. Now is the time for more to know. How can they know? By seeing others show. By observing lives so well lived that one has to ask, has to wonder, what strength or power it can be to allow one to live so gracefully in the world and yet not be a part of it. When they see, they will feel. They will be touched, and perhaps touched enough to ask "How and why, and when and where? What moves you so? What is the source of your glow? Can it be that such Divine Love can as well be God's gift to me?" And so it is.

What ideas are you holding? What are the ideas that are holding you back? See how I said ideas that you were holding? That wording is very key, as what is holding you back is not truly physical, it is an idea and not the truth of God. For no truth of God can limit your expression of anything bad or good.

It's the ideas which you hold on to that determine the heights you reach, as well as the depths to which you plunge. It is to your best interest to drop hold of those ideas which limit the good you have waiting for you. Yes, I said "waiting for you," waiting for you to claim. Goodness, Joy, Laughter, Peace, Purity, Poise, Abundance, Ability and Wisdom these are Ideas of your birthright. This is your 'True Inheritance" from which you have every right to claim as yours.

Sounds like Heaven doesn't it? Well, perhaps it is. But not the Heaven far away from where you stand now. The Heaven you can be in where you physically are. Mentally and spiritually, you have to change to move up in this world, to see greater possibilities, to soar with the eagles. You have to have a change of mind and a change of heart.

You have to awaken to the good before you and beside you and inside you. You have to forget what you know to be able to know more. In other words, you have to push aside the boulders you have placed at the entrance of your mind and heart which you have built as a fortress to keep you safe, to keep what you know safe. So the ideas you had and held could not, or did not need to be challenged.

These walls you have built to protect you have not truly eased your fears. They instead have given birth to new fears and doubt. Doubt plagues your mind. Open the doors. Release doubt. Let the fresh air into the staleness of your very being. New ideas are the fresh air. Let new ideas circulate within your mind freshening your very spirit. Let them visit your core. Sit with them. They bring no harm. New ideas are just that, new, fresh and worth exploring.

Not every new idea will sit so well with you. That is fine. Toss it out. No need to lock and bolt the door of your mind to other new ideas. Remember, know this, you are the gatekeeper of your mind. You are the one who decides what ideas feel good and thus choose to claim as your truth. The ideas that don't feel so good you can choose to toss out. Once you begin the process of letting new ideas flow into your mind you will naturally find yourself revisiting ideas you have held so very long. Some of which you may realize aren't serving you any more.

*This is when it becomes challenging as some of these very
ideas were at one time the very core of your belief, of what
you thought you knew and would always claim as your
truth. But as you know better, you have to let them go. And
you can, and you will, for when the Truth, the best Truth
sits in your heart and mind and grows within it, the other
thoughts become as weed thoughts and you understand that
to allow the beautiful garden of your mind to flourish those
non-sense thoughts have to go.*

My mother always listens to me. She truly hears my heart. She knows
my heart for my very heart is made from part of hers. Thank you God
for my mother, you certainly helped me pick out the best.

JULY 17, 2011

Did you get the message? The message intended about the cross we
are to bear? As my understanding of this concept has changed for the
betterment of my own life, I wish to share it; my enlightenment with
you.

Jesus Christ did not tell us we were to live lives of trials and tribulations
as we followed him. Indeed he only spoke of peace and fulfillment,
bountiful blessings and healing of body and mind. It is when we
depend on ourselves and our humanness, our own ego-selves, that our
load seems hard. We drag through life as the weight of our physical-
ness pulls us down.

Beyond the weight of our own bodies and our health conditions we
have our minds. Our minds weigh heavy, heavy upon our hearts. And
then there is the physical world of our creation. Things we have wanted
and brought into our lives that as we claim them they become our
responsibility to tend to and carry with us as we move through life. It
seems the more life we live the more things we have accumulated but
not necessarily still need or may have perhaps ever needed and yet of

course we continue to gather in more goods. But are these things truly making our lives good?

"Set down your burdens," says Christ. "Let Me carry them for you." How do we do this? By realizing that we cannot do it all ourselves. The Message of Christ is that we no longer have to. Right here, we can know joy. Right now, not later.

> *No need to wait until death, for Heaven, the Kingdom of God is present in your very midst. But you cannot see, so you do not know. You have to let go. Let go of your self-ness, the ego that has driven your course. The path you have been upon is rocky. The path Christ offers is smooth. "What is this path and where does one get on? Is it Jesus I am to follow? But how, he is gone? I shall wait for his return. I am told it could be any minute," you say.*
>
> *Jesus lived "The Life," the Life of Christ, the Christos, the man Divine. This is the new plan offered by God, the ability to live as Christ Jesus did, to show up in the world as Light and Love. The Christ Jesus died in his physical body but was renewed, reincarnated in His true spiritual form and still lives. He lives on as Spirit, with all Spirit, God. Before Jesus left His physical self He comforted his disciples who were overwhelmed by the idea of His passing and their own ability to carry on. This is when He told them of the gifts to be bestowed on them, gifts of spirit, the Holy Spirit. He said He would send "the Comforter."*

I paint my level of consciousness. I live my level of consciousness. I can do no other. I show up as I am.

> *Leave room for inspiration.*

The law of faith: Everyone has exactly the same amount of faith. What differs among men is where they put their faith. Words are not enough, if feelings don't support them. Faith requires all of one's being. Some have faith in good. Some have faith in bad. Some wander the desert in-between. God is Good. God is Love. Putting your faith in God is putting your faith in goodness and love. As what you think about you bring about, when you dwell in thoughts of good, good loving thoughts, your life returns to you as good and loving. This is the law of faith.

I surrender to the Divine.

Know wherever you are you are safe! Everyone needs to know this. Thoughts of fear, keep you in fear. The media breeds fear. Until you can consciously separate yourself from this worldly, earthly and lowly view of life and be the observer only, not the partaker of such drama, you will serve yourself to back away and fill your mind with words of power and strength, love, beauty and safety. Love good, love God, with all your heart, mind and strength and you will be transformed.

Life gives each of us situations with which we must deal. Call them what you want. If you say something is to be a problem, then you are as good as your word assured that it will be. You will then confirm your power by stating that "It happened just as I feared!"

Fear not, the Lord says, trust in Me, in God, in the Goodness of Life to deliver you from trials and strife. Good can happen. Fill your mind with this Truth.

JULY 20, 2011

Why do you concern yourself so with the future? So you can worry about what bad could happen, or hold good thoughts and see it all well? Be your own fortune-teller. Predict the good. Predict the fabulous. Then prepare yourself to be amazed. Live in wonder. Live in awe. Live in joy. Live in love.

Divine Love is my power and my strength.

There has always been only one Truth, one Power. It is a matter of surrender. The surrender of one's own will to the will of God, surrendering the power of your mind to the power of your heart. When heart and mind are one, you will see Me and know Me beloved, the Divine Presence within, your Calling, your Truth, your Name, your Glory. See your glory now. Praise it. Praise the lovely Presence, the Loving Presence you are. Take care. Treat yourself with love and respect. Love yourself first, then you can share this Love you know with all.

This is not a selfish thing. The love you are to feel is the divine grace, the love of God pouring forth. When you become selfless and think of God, the Eternal Good of Life in you and in all, then you will feel and know the glory of this manifestation in your thoughts, actions, word and deed. Allow this Love to fill you, to be you, to breath through you, knowing all is well. Now and forever claim this Love. Be this Love. Share and pour forth this Love. Be the clothes this Love wears. Be the arms and legs of this Love.

As you realize, you will live anew. You will naturally show up differently in the world. Your Love will magnetize more

Love to you. You will become such a wonderfully magnetic presence of good in this world that all will desire your presence, for you are the Presence of God. Know this and you will be this. This truth is yours. Claim it now.

I am the most loving and ever expansive love of God. The presence and power of God fills me and fulfills me. So be it. Amen.

Nothing can limit you now.

I used to desire to have control over my life, my heart, my mind and my experience, but I now see that that path did not lead me to peace. Serenity evaded me.

What do you acknowledge in life? What do you see and hear? What do you nod your head in agreement to? All is well. What you desire is all things higher. Raise your spirit, delight in all the good, for all goodness is yours as you believe. "We are hoping for the best," versus "We are fearing the worst." Both are mindsets with the same power, hope and fear. Both bring guaranteed results. Where do you put your power? Where do you put your trust? Trust in the best possible outcome for every situation.
What do you fear?

I don't fear a thing. I fear nothing. I have no fear, for God lives here!

JULY 25, 2011

Where are you? Do you know where you are? You are with Me. You are safe. You are home. Be at rest. Put up your weary feet. Unburden your shoulders. Set your cares all aside. Give them up unto Me. I will carry you forward in peace, in joy as you allow My being, My very essence, to flow through you. Put up no barriers. You have asked for My love, asked for My way. So it is given. It is here. The time is now for you to release the beliefs that bind you to what you know, to what you see. Release it all. Walk away. Step forward in faith, with trust in My bountiful goodness to fill every one of your heart's desires.

Do you believe in Me? I believe in you! Do you love Me? I love you! Do you trust Me? Trust in Me? Do you know the power of My Love? Yes, power, powerful stuff, the best, the most original power source. Can you hear Me? Hear this truth I speak unto your heart. You are so loved.

You are naturally empowered, in-powered. Your power comes from within, not without. You need not look afar. It is here now within you waiting, on hold, paused, ready to resume full speed ahead. You are in command, command of the forces, the powers that be, which lay in wait for your orders. This is the work you have to do. Decide what is to be. Stake your claim. Call My name. Speak your truth. This is the work you are to do.

I can see your glory. You have a friend in Me, in you. Together we are entwined. Sail forth into your dreams. I hold your hand. I walk beside. My eyes can see what yours cannot. Trust in Me to do what's best for you. You are My love. I am your heart.

Fill your mind with goodness, for goodness sake! Don't look back. Keep your eyes on the road ahead. Just around the bend you will see your glory. Well, glory be!

Your faith, your trust, was broken. So you gave up hope. Why hope for the best when failure hurts so badly? You are

better off, you say, as if to prepare yourself for the worst.
For then you will be prepared. Prepared to fall and not be
further saddened by dreams not fulfilled. You gave up, gave
up on the promise of life, the opportunity for goodness to
come to you. You said, "I know this game of life and know
it isn't fair. Life has hurt me so. I will not be hurt again. I
will drop my expectations low and within my direct vision. I
refuse to be tricked and played fool again."

Make a list of all the fun ideas that are fun to think about,
fun to imagine. You have to perceive it before you receive it.
Begin anew each day. Put away your old ways. Think anew.
See anew. Be anew. A new day dawns, wake up world, live
anew.

It's like a song stuck in my head, except the words are fresh, each
thought anew, telling me exactly what I need to do. Make me a channel
for Your Peace. Make me a channel for Your Love.

JULY 26, 2011

There is hope. It lies within your heart. There is a way.
Where there is a will, there is a way. Your will is free, free
to be whatever you want. Your hearts desire is spoken and
heard. Your wish is fulfilled as the word is spoken, as you
believe your truth to be. It is. So be it, now.

It is up to you, no one else, to live the life you have. As you
wish, the power lies in thought and deed. For you are to be
true to you, to your desires you must submit. All must align
for you to see as you know in your heart. Be what you want.
Think what you want. Attract the life you wish to live. Keep
your eye on the goal. No other ideas should you behold.

Forces are here. Help is available, on call, just awaiting the signal from you, the go ahead, to allow you to realize your all. Keep the faith. Know the Truth. The power is within you to create, to be, to live, to shine, and to pour forth love to all so beautifully. Be open. Be available. Shut no door. Allow God's Bountiful Goodness to all be yours. Don't shut doors. Don't shut windows or you may miss a window of opportunity.

Take care of your body. Feed it well. Take it for a walk, a swim. Let's have fun and be fun. You have a body because you are physical. So be fully physical. Let not your body limit you. Let not your mind limit you. Let not your soul limit you, experience true freedom of body, mind and soul.

I give thanks for all the Love in my life
The Love that surrounds me
The Love that fills me
The Love that caresses me
The Love that guides me
The Love that knows me
The Love that shows me
The way to freedom
The way to peace
The way to sanity
The way to abundance
The way to wisdom
The way to health
The way to prosperity
The way to joy.

I cannot say, for it is not for me to say, what any one person will do, for all have a will which is free and only their heart can direct. But I can pronounce and proclaim the good I know is mine and which I have and hold and as well that of which I am to know. For this good which I desire comes from a place of all things higher. Within my reach, within my grasp it is there, waiting for my heart and mind to clasp.

No other has power to lay my dreams asunder, for no other man is my will under. By my choice, I have proclaimed my will to be God's. All intent and purpose of my life is directed toward the good of all. By this action, by this denial of my own mere ways, I am assured to go forth, live free and proclaim. I will not trip. I will not fall, for God's Love is my power. The force I know and feel, I am becoming more and more of each day. I pray to God, have Your way.

What do I have to give? I have God's Love. I have God's Love to give. There is a gift no greater. This I know. This I am in being, in truth, in wholeness. By my presence I bring peace, I bring joy for I fully allow God's Divine Love to flow into and through my heart, my soul, my being. My very essence is being transformed by this Love. I am so filled that I naturally pour forth. As my cup runneth over in joy, in ecstasy, with this One Power, Force of Nature, Force of God.

My eyes dance with the spirit of joy. My heart sings with the angel choir. Oh the joy of all that is higher. I look up, I see. I look within, I know. I look around and become one with all good. Nature is God's way of speaking Truth. Nothing in nature denies God's Perfect ways. There is no door to open or shut within nature's being. Only man, mankind, was made in such a way. But there is a way to be found which leads back to the nature of God's goodness.

I make my own music. I write my own songs. I hum along to my heart's sweet song. For God's very Love fills me up. This I know. This I show. I am born again in Love, in Truth, in Beauty. Joy weeps from my very pores. I cry only tears of joy. Oh behold the wonders of God so Almighty.

Beauty lies in the eye of the beholder. Let the eye participate.

*Who needs words? Most do. For they have lived their whole
lives under the direction of the words of another. As they
have lost touch with their feelings, they do not know how
to feel their way through life. They trust not the wisdom of
their soul to help them find their way, the way home to their
truth, to their beauty, so their eyes can behold.*

*Nothing is a lost cause. Ever hear about the resurrection?
Never give up on your dreams. Dream big, dream beyond
what you know. Unleash yourself. Let go and go on to
greener pastures, to the hills beyond your simple sight. I will
lead you on. Carry forth. Get up and go. I am your Lead.
You are the driver. Determine your course. Set your sight.
Let's go!*

On my way to find out more about me, I found out more about you
too. You see at heart we are all the same, even though we answer to
a different name. From the same source we all came and continue
to be connected to. This was news to me or at least it was not what I
considered a truth of my everyday reality. You see I walked alone, lost
in thought, for I thought I knew the way. But the way I knew was not
true to all I was meant to be. Just now, I am beginning to see that there
is so much more which I can be and so as well this truth is for you.
I am opening to the Wisdom of Spirit which tells me about my truth
which I create through my own will. With every thought, my house I
destroy or build. Friends are here, yes in spirit, ones that hold us dear.
To help us as we allow. If we can let go of feeling we have to do it all or
know exactly how.

We've been told before of angels whom watch over, whom guide our
step. But I didn't know. As I did not comprehend their existence or
persistence, I allowed no help. For if one holds tight the door, no voice
will be heard. They are only allowed to whisper every word. They
cannot shout. They cannot force. For each of us with our free will holds
the power for ourselves. But as our eyes cannot see above our heads,

God has provided us with these special guides to provide insight, to guide our way and to work with us by our side creating the life we want, the life we speak of, the life of our dreams.

> *You say you know not what to think. You say you are undecided. Hallelujah. Give thanks and praise, for this is the day you have been waiting for, the day you can experience more. For your mind has not set a limit on your experience. You are now free to taste life, all its varied sweetness can be yours. Walk forward. Step out in faith that all good is yours.*

Whatever it is, show me the way. I am ready. I let go of what I know. I release what I know and allow God's goodness to flow. As I keep the faith my dreams are realized.

JULY 27, 2011

As I believe, my faith is proven.

The founding fathers of the United States of America were full of "ideas and ideals." Some of these ideas presented in their manifesto, *The Declaration of Independence*, were not necessarily congruent with the lives each personally lead. So where did they come from? Perhaps Thomas Jefferson, whom penned the document, was just that, the writer. And the "ideals" he penned were delivered to his consciousness from a consciousness much higher than his own awareness.

The men whom signed the document, as well, did not have the consciousness to understand the full truth of the words "all men are created equal" for to them "men" were men like them. They did not understand that "men" was meant to be "mankind" and as that women and people of all color were just that, their equals. But some part of them knew the line was important and sounded good, so it remained and as it fit their understanding, they did not challenge it.

It was a wonderful fate for our nation that these words were included, for this ideal was now written and available for further generations to question and ponder and thus live up to in new ways as their consciousness increased. This idea has become clear to me as I have this very experience. For this is the way the ideals that fill my journals are delivered to my consciousness. They are ideas to inspire me, to raise me and lift me up to new levels of living, standards higher than I currently own and live up to, but all so welcome, comforting and encouraging.

I write without the participation of my own thoughts, for if I did my mind would edit and question each word as it is given. Thus attempting to control and limit this wonderful, most pure, form of expression to humanity from our Creator, the Spirit Divine, direct from Divine Mind, the "Word of God."

> *God is not about rules. God doesn't desire a "pleasing behavior" from us. God is Love. God wants us to know and be filled with His love. With the infilling of His Divine Love, His ways will be realized, "His will" will be done on Earth as it is in Heaven. This is the truth of God.*

I know, I can know. I would like to find out. I am a channel for God's love.

> *Listen to your heart speak. Open up your heart. Join forces with the All. You have access to a higher perspective. It is taken care of. All you asked is given. Give thanks for this knowing.*

I pour out thanks from my heart, from the very depths of my spirit, my soul, as I know I am fully blessed. All God's bounty is mine. All my needs are met. I have such faith in God's everlasting goodness proven unto me by my faith. I am to be a marker, a sign for others. Let my life be a signpost, a beacon of hope for all others. For all this I give thanks unto God.

I hear a voice. The voice of Love sings such a sweet song to my soul. A lullaby as comforting as a mother's cooing unto her infant, the voice assures me all is well.

July 29, 2011

Don't look elsewhere; you hold the power for your life deep inside. Bring it to the surface. Rise up. Shine on. Be My Light in the world. Tell My story, the story of My love. Act it out. Be the star. I will guide you line by line, scene by scene. What you need is here.

What don't you understand My love? You don't have to know it all. You can't. You never will. But you can know just what you need to know in each moment. Trust in this and I will feed you. I will give you My All as you need. There is no waste, no want, in Heaven. Be with Me now in peace, in love. I am waiting deep in the center of your heart.

Psalms, songs, praises to God. So sweet, so deep the love God gives from above to one's heart. Reaping what has been sown. Seeds not scattered, but sown deep within one's soul. Watered with tears of repentance on bended knee, error thoughts weeded from the mind. What glorious flowers bloom, prayers answered.

Make me a channel for Your peace. Make me a channel for Your love. Fill my heart with Your transforming love. Bring me peace on the wings of a dove. Oh, my heart, desires You so. For only You know the depths of my being and complete my story, the story of Love untold.

Grand palaces, cathedrals, have been built in My name and yet I find no home in their hearts. Prepare a place within for My essence to reside. I want to pour love, love to you inside.

Sweep the dusty floor of your mind. Brush away the cobwebs of your old thoughts and reasoning. For I, your Maker, give you a new reason to live.

My love fills you and the lamp of your soul shines aglow revealing the beauty you are and always have been. See the gold, see the gems I have placed in your heart. The cathedral, the sacred place, has already been built. I have built this for you, within you. It is dark now, so you cannot see. Prepare your heart. Open the doors of your mind which you hold so tightly shut. Invite My Love inside this "Cathedral Divine," where I so desire to live, all within your heart.

Do you consider yourself to be a person of your word? When one is worthy of one's word they are trusted for what they say, they will do. So if someone asks you to do something for them and you agree and confirm you will do it, the other has no doubt that you will perform as you agreed. They count it done. They know they can count on you. Therefore, they give thanks telling you even before they can see the result that they appreciate your actions on their behalf. And in the meantime, as the idea rises in their mind, a smile comes to their face and their heart is grateful for they know all is well and you are working (in the unseen) on the project.

There is no doubt in their mind, even though their eyes do not see your action. They trust in you and your word which you have given to them. They do not summons you for another meeting and repeat their request. They do not call and say, "Oh, just in case you forgot I would like you to do this for me." No, that is not the action of one whom trusts.

Instead, there may be a call or note of gratitude, expressing appreciation for your work. Or perhaps, they make a point to tell you how excited they are that you are creating something special per their request, how they know it will be so wonderful, beautiful and perfect for them. And as their own artistic vision is limited, they can not imagine what you will create. They only know and trust that it will exceed their dreams, as you have always proven to exceed expectations when given the power of full creative expression.

This is so for you, a creator of beautiful artistic visions, why, how could it ever be less than so for the Creator of all, we ask? We are told to trust, trust in the vision and creation of God on our behalf everyday. Give thanks that it is done.

There once was a man whom believed naught and thus and so he was rewarded for his belief. Believe it so. Lead by example. Hardly a novel thought, but oh so important, worth mentioning, again and again.

Let Me entertain you. You seem to bore so quickly. At the first notice of silence you reach out for noise, for sound, for stimulation, but you don't reach to Me. Instead you look to the world which man has created and sit back on your perch, your sofa, watching the "boob tube," watching the lives of others, involving yourself in the drama your media creates.

"Wow," you say enamored with the technological wonders before you. "Look at the color on that TV! It looks so real!" Is this your reality or the reality you choose to fill the blank spaces of your life with? Is this to you real living? If so you have accepted a very shallow view of life. I ask you to

*consider again, consider differently. Consider spending time
with Me, quiet time, at rest, just you and Me.*

*We could go for a walk. We could sit on your bed and talk.
Or we could just be, just be together, joined at the heart,
looking up, admiring the sky, listening to the birds sing
nearby. I could brush your hair with the breeze. We could
both laugh that I made you sneeze. It doesn't matter to Me
what is said or what we do. All I want is to spend quality
time with you. Let Me entertain you. Let Me light your
lamp. Give Me a chance. Take My hand. Let Me have this
dance.*

*Look up to no other. Look down on no other. Look every
man straight in the eye and see the Truth that each man is
your brother and as such there is no other. You are all the
same and at one with your Mother.*

*You are each such a unique expression of the One. Such
wonderful artistry you are. Whenever one can get out of
the mind, there is God, there is Peace and Tranquility. God
is with you. God, the Eternal Good, is continually with
all. It is up to each individual as to whether they choose to
recognize this Presence. This is a matter of will. And as each
human has free will, it is a choice for the human to choose
to recognize this Presence, this Light.*

JULY 30, 2011

*For eternity, since the dawn of mankind, man has noticed
the other, the other side of himself, the God Presence within.
As a child, one's self mingles comfortably with this Loving
Presence. But as the self becomes more and more actualized*

one becomes centered on that part of being, the separate self, the me, me, me, mine, mine, mine part of all of us that first immerges with the development of language at age two.

The terrible twos, we call them, as one first so strongly feels this sense of self and yet does not yet possess all the social skills to manage as a full individual in society and thus begins the socialization of the individual, when one learns the rules of man in his society, rules of conduct, and rules of engagement. As the human being learns the ways of his people, his mind is programmed as to what to think, what to believe about life. He becomes set in his ways and although he is living as such a separate self he feels such pressure to not stand out as different from the others. He feels pressure to conform. He is presented with rules for living. He is told life is hard and joy is few and far between but if he can and will follow the rules he will be rewarded later, much later.

He is told of God, but God is described as a judgeful being, far away, somewhere not to be known, to be feared, who is somehow watching everything one does and hears all that is said. But how, one does not know and even fears to ask. For to ask is to express doubt, and doubt is considered sin, and sin is against God, and if you sin against God you will never see the face of God, you will never experience true joy. You will go to Hell, the place where all doomed souls exist in a state of continual agony. So you do not openly ask.

Once you asked in your heart, within the quietness of your being. You were so sad, so scared and you prayed out to God to show you, to prove His Presence and you felt something, something different, strange but good, a tingly Peace. But after, instead of rejoicing, you feared you had crossed the line, the invisible line that you had been warned of. "Never

*go there, it is bad, it's wrong for man to go beyond. Evil
lurks, just beyond what we know. Whatever lies beyond
the veil is not for human consumption. In fact, people
can be consumed by evil forces if they dare to dance." You
(mankind) are always making up stories.*

There is no question that I am writing a book, or two or three or
twenty, or two thousand for the Word of God is with me and expresses
to and through me. I am moved to write these words, this truth, this
eternal truth of all ages, in words that people of my age, can hear and
understand. I am blessed to be such an agent for the great creative force
of the universe God's Divine Love. My eyes can see. My heart can hear.
Let my mouth speak the Love that comes to and flows forth.

*"I am on a mission from God." Many say this to validate
their actions, but if judgment and force is involved, it is a
sure sign it is not God's Will leading them.*

*Never say never, think about what you want. Give up rules.
Rules are rigid. True Life flows like a river. Ride the wave
of your dreams far beyond your current imaginings. Set
no limits. Keep your eyes above the crowd. Get out of your
thinking mind and into your feeling mind. My Light lights
up your eyes and makes all things possible. Dream the
impossible dream.*

*Don't get lost in the world. There are so many messages
coming at you. Everyone has an opinion and so do you.
Guess which one counts for you? Yours of course, for only
you know the truth of you. Yes, deep inside you are all the
answers to every question you could ever wish to ask. Know
more about yourself. Find yourself, your own truth, your
own path in life. Be assured. Feel safe. Know the way to
peace.*

Shut your mouth. You make things more difficult than they need to be. Only say what you want because what you say is what you get. Expect the best in every situation. Declare your good.

How does the world work? You get what you give. See what you want. Want the best for all. Be in this world, be your best, give your best. If something doesn't please you give it no attention, none. No response. It will wither away and die.

The only limits you have in life are the ones you put on yourself. Listen to your words, the ones you speak, the ones you think. You say certain things are certain ways and not necessarily good ways. Your words are words of acceptance, of limitations. Stop it. Stop limiting your life experience. Open up. Free yourself. Untie what binds you.

I really don't care to hear excuses. Don't pass the buck. Take responsibility. Own up or shut up! I need to breathe different air. I need an upper not a downer. I need to separate myself.

Let it all go. Don't hold on. Let it be. Fly free. Go ahead and live your life, the one you want without strife. So be it. Make it so. Only you, truly know. What falls behind isn't good. If they can't keep up, its as it should. Why care what they say? You are the one that makes your day.

I believe differently. I don't have to stay stuck in your muck.

Everyone is just doing the best they know and when they know better, they will do better. Everyone, just like you, has a story. You even have your own stories about others, but don't let old tales get in the way of your life or the way you see anyone else's. Begin anew each day. Give yourself a break each break of dawn. Let the new light wash away the past and set you right in the present. Greet each person freshly in this same new light. See all anew. Don't bother with old stories, good or bad. You are here now and all is well in this moment. See for yourself the grandeur before you and in others when you interact.

Whatever any man acquires spiritually can never be taken away. Spiritual treasure once found and claimed is one's for eternity. Once written upon his heart such spiritual wisdom, enlightenment, becomes his very DNA. Thus he becomes a changed man. "I will give you a new heart." This is God's promise.

Anything is possible for you. What do you choose? Let us know, proclaim. Imagine all the behind the scenes work being done on your behalf. Hold your intention. Give attention to your desires. Water the blossoms, the seeds you want to bloom. Tend well the garden of your mind.

Some people find their "happiness," their own power, in proving another wrong. Are you certain you are not as well one of them?

You are a powerful creator. You have the power to create prosperity. You say you are an artist, a writer, a builder, so what do you have to show the world? You have to manifest your dreams. No one but you can see what lies in wait to be brought into form from the vast imaginings of your mind. Get to work. Sit down before the paper. Stand before the canvas with the tools of your trade in hand. Bring to light new wonders. Show the world what you've got.

Morning Pages (Three pages of stream of consciousness writing, done first thing in the morning) are the foundation of the creative discovery/recovery process Julia Cameron shares in her book *The Artist's Way*. I used to write them. But for me they were more accurately "mourning pages," for I mourned the life I lived. I mourned the death of the body I had once known. My mind was tangled in the constant realization of pain. I knew not how to turn the page, to turn over a new leaf, to a new page of life. But oh, how I yearned. Eventually I found, for I sought. I continually sought a life of health, balance and joy.

Only the seeker finds. What do you seek? What do you look for? Look for joy and beauty in this world here and now. It is to be found. Enjoy it.

God is not religion. Religion is man's rules for God. God in truth is above all. Let no man lead you astray for God is available to be known to man directly, personally, without rules or judgment. For God is All, all good, and thus when man says "In God, I trust," he is trusting in all good to be for all mankind and creation and by the power of his word he shall know this truth. Trust in God. Have faith in goodness.

It is so nice to have you realize, to have you see. Now, it is for you to understand you must share what you know. You must manifest your realizations in a physical way so others may know that you know something more that has profoundly changed your being for so much the better. Manifest it in such a tremendous way that all who make your acquaintance desire to know as well.

Faith can be shared but it cannot be given or bestowed. "The faith of our fathers" is just that, their faith, the faith of mankind in the past, the faith that has realized what the world you live in is. All men are born in full faith, all endowed with the same faith. The difference lies in how this faith is expressed, in where trust is put.

Do you trust in God? Do you trust in goodness or do you live in fear? If you are living in fear of the unknown, if your mind is full of doubt, you are putting your faith in fear, trusting life is full of things and situations which threaten you. This is no way to live. This is death. This is the Hell in which you fear. You are in a living hell. With mud packed eyes blinding you from the beauty of life and love and light.

You have to be nice to other people. Speak kindly. Have patience.

Laugh it off. See the humor in your own life. Your own life is full of situational comedy; learn to laugh about it today. Don't postpone your joy. Life is to be a sweet comedic love story not a dramatic disaster film. And you are to be the star of your own life. Shine brightly, brilliantly. Light up the world with your smile. Learn to let go and improvise your way. Leave room for inspiration and growth. You are creating the story of your life as you live it. Nothing is predetermined. There is not one set path or plan to follow. There is no divine script. The freedom to create the life of your dreams lies within your very being. Dream big, know no limits. See the sky, do you see a line drawn where the ceiling is? None exists. You are free to fly as high as your heart desires.

Laughter is the lubrication of life. It's what makes it easier to slip through the tight spots. It's what keeps a pep in one's step. It has been said that laughter is the best medicine but laughter is not a cure. It is the natural state of joy into which we each are born. It is health and harmony of body and soul. This laughter is of the selfless sort, when you can let go of ego and forgivingly laugh off situations as they arise. You deem them not good or bad but life being lived one moment at a time with all the best intentions.

One can be full of fancy phrases and spout scriptures but not know that of which they speak, for words can never fill all the empty space in one's heart. Only the infilling of God's Divine Love brings Everlasting Peace and Joy. This is the Word of God.

My new song, sung to the tune of the children's taunt "Nana nana boo boo, you can't catch me."

I'm holding good intentions.
I'm holding good intentions.
I'm holding good intentions.

AUGUST 2011

For his Holy Spirit speaks to us deep in our hearts,
and tells us that we are God's children,
and since we are His children,
we will share in His treasures for all
God gives His son Jesus, is now ours too.

ROMANS 8:16 NLT

AUGUST 1, 2011

*Nice to see you today, wide awake, wide eyed, alert to
opportunity, glow on girl, glow on.*

AUGUST 3, 2011

*Today's the day! The day for what? The day for you to shine!
You are beautiful to Me. Can you see this beauty? See it,
know it, show it to the world. You are My girl, My valentine
unto the world.*

*Contemplation, lost in thought, consider this an activity
worth pursuing for you are more than you think. You are
wonderful, amazing, potentially everything you can dream.
Dream sweet dreams My darling. I so want you to want the
best for yourself. See your dreams come true. Allow Me to*

*live through you. Come forth, step out and about My world
for it is all yours to have, to enjoy. Reap the harvest of your
mind. Think well My dear lose the fear, for I walk beside
and hold your hand. As you allow My Will to flow, you will
know all is well and thus can tell the world of My love.*

*"Ask and it is given." such a powerful statement of truth. Do
you know this? Do you know that this is how it is always?
This is the law, not of the land, for laws of the land are laws
of, by and for men. This is the law of the universe, above
all other law. You receive as you believe. So what do you
believe? You say, "I believe in God," and then with the next
breath, you speak fear. When one is afraid, one feels alone
and no one whom truly knows God is ever alone. So do
you know God? Did you know that it was even possible to
know and feel the loving presence of God so deeply within
ones own very being that one would be at peace and live
in peace, the peace of God that thwarts all fear? Yes, it is
possible to feel God's love so near. Are you afraid you will be
judged? Are there things for which you are ashamed? Have
you not heard the truth told, that the real God is loving, not
vengeful, like the stories of old?*

*You have heard God's voice but cast it aside, not knowing
that truth be told from wisdom within you, deep inside. Yes,
God is near and continually holds you dear. But cannot,
and will not, interfere with the life you choose for a way
was designed for you to create your own by your choices, by
your thought. Free creation, your thoughts are your asking.
What you are given is what you have intended, by your very
attention to such matters.*

*So what really matters, matters to you? What matters to
you is whatever you think about. Think well, My dears.*

Guard your thoughts. Feel your way through life. If a thought feels good keep it and reach for more. On the others that don't feel so good, shut the door. Your mind is a sacred place, as is your heart. Begin with guarding your mind. It's a wonderful place to start.

Be ye perfect like your Father in Heaven is perfect. Do not be disturbed by the outer, for your inner knows Peace. Peace becomes you. Peace lightens you and shines through you. Be this peace. Be still My heart. Know who you are, now and forever. Such a glorious piece of God you are.

AUGUST 4, 2011

What do you believe in? What kind of a question is that you ask? I am not asking if you believe if God exists. I am asking what do you believe is true in your life and what do you believe is possible for your life? This is your belief system, which creates your life as you know it. Do you like what you see? Would you like to see better? Wipe your eyes. Dry your tears. There is hope. Hope is belief in more than you know.

I don't just get this for me. There is a larger purpose. I wonder. I wonder what can be. I wonder what is. I marvel. I marvel at the beauty I see. I marvel at the power of love. I rejoice. I rejoice in the knowing of the beauty and love that fills my world and again I wonder what is next for me.

"Don't count your chickens before they hatch." You've learned this lesson the hard way. Your trust has been so broken that today you don't even believe in chickens. The world as you once have known it has done you wrong. The taste of bitterness continually sours your mouth. "Hell" only exists in man's mortal thought.

We had it, but it's gone. Some would say I had it all, but that is not so. If it can be lost, it is not worth much. This I know, for I have something which I never before possessed, peace of mind. What I have is mine forever, the Peace of God filling my soul, my being with Light.

> *Where are you coming from? Do you know from whence you came? Are you aware that this is the True Source of your being from which all goodness flows? You are comfortable here, so stay. Rest your weary heart. There is nothing to do here, no one else to be. So rest, breath deep, and soak up My Love. Be like a sponge allowing My love to fill every cell of your being. Let Me fill you up until your cup overfloweth.*

Some people say that people that talk to themselves are crazy. Others say that's okay. It's when you start answering yourself, that's when you have problems. So with that in mind, some would say I'm crazy. I say, they just don't know. They don't know what they don't know. They haven't, as yet, discovered the amazing secret to an amazing life as I have, the treasure trove of wisdom that lies within ready and available for the asking. Does "Ask and ye shall receive." ring any bells? Wisdom is a very important part of that equation. I'm not talking about trivial facts here. I'm talking about moment-to-moment useful, totally applicable stuff. Like, "Where did I put my phone? What is the name of his wife?" and "What should I do with my life?"

There are rules though, no guessing, none. For when I attempt to guess, ponder or think the answer my mind is instantly involved and I am disqualified from the game. The only way I can access this wisdom is by letting go of my own estimations and ask trusting, in this higher power working through me, for the answer. My own brainpower seems to block the flow of this stream of consciousness. I have to let go and allow flow. Just be. Be willing to hear and to heed.

The heeding of the information is just as important as the reception of it. Imagine it this way. It's fun to give the ones you love gifts, especially handmade gifts of love. So imagine giving a special gift to a loved one and watching them open it, then drop it on the floor and walk away. Kind of takes the fun out of the giving doesn't it? So imagine a part of yourself that is the giver of such wisdom and how that part of you would feel to have someone you love not take hold and make use of the gift you have made especially for them.

The joy is in the giving, but proper reception is needed for the giver to be excited about the possibility of giving more. When the giver is acknowledged and thanked, their joy skyrockets. They sit on the edge of their seats awaiting the chance to be of service again.

So goes the "the game" I play within my mind and heart. There is a soul truth to me. Not a single "sole truth," but a vast infinite truth within my grasp, available to me, wherever I am, whenever I make myself available. Yes, I talk to myself. I ask myself and I answer myself. I thank myself and I love myself. Some would say I'm crazy. Some people would care if others thought them so. I don't. I know better. Thank you. I love you. You know me so well.

"Put it all out there." I just heard in my head. What? What is that about? Where did that come from? And then I remembered my previous thought about the writing I just did, about posting and sharing it online, about how to pick and choose what it is worth sharing of the information that comes to me. So there is my answer, which I must obey if I want to continue to play. I give thanks for this message.

> *Man has been given a mind, an incredibly powerful mind to use as he wishes. This mind is so powerful; it can build and destroy his world. His word is his command, but he knoweth it not. Man doth hardly know the power of his very word. The very mind which he considers to be his greatest asset is the great barrier he must cross to discover his truest glory, his one in being with his Creator, Divine Mind which knoweth all. All true wisdom is within reach, just beyond*

the simple mind of man. Yes, as great as the mind of man is, the Truth is beyond man's mind, all to be known when man can lay aside himself, what he knows, what he thinks and just is. Is one with All, as a being, not a doer, not a thinker, but a floater, flowing along the stream of life. The current is strong and yet peaceful. Ride the wave, the energy wave of all creation.

I love family, it's one of God's best ideas. People God gives each of us to take care of us, watch over us, and cheer us on.

We are all family, you should know, here and there, visible and invisible, together as One, God's Family, Brothers and Sisters all. Do you not recognize the same glimmer in the other's eye? He is your brother. Welcome him, hold him, encourage him, watch over him. You are your brother's keeper, but keep first yourself. Keep true to your own ideals, the truth inside your heart. Hear the news, all is well. Celebrate family wherever you are.

You make Me smile, when I see you, when I think of you, My heart dances. I love to be with you. Thank you for welcoming Me into your heart, My true love. Be nice, be who you are. Allow the flow of goodness to spout up and out through your very being. You are a fountain, a refreshing fountain of everlasting youth and abundant energy, all called love.

What would you like to hear? Say it, make it so. Then you will know. Then you can show others the way, the way to peace within their own hearts. Let's have a heart to heart talk you and Me. Go ahead. I'm listening.

Who do you love? Just a few or many? All are chosen by God. All are worthy of His love. Why do you not see that they are worthy of yours? We are all different, yet we are all the same, for the essence of each one of our very being springs from the same source. From the same well we draw our strength our refreshment, our wisdom, our love.

I am part of a fun, functional family. This has been key to me, to who I am, to who I know I can be, for through this family, I see possibility of more love, love piled upon love, confirmation of the goodness of humanity.

Love the one you are with.

Your patience is appreciated. It is up to each to find his own joy. It will remain hidden until sought. No other can uncover another's personal joy. You can show another your joy and you can share your joy, but it is up to each to find their own joy, their own light within which illumines their personal path. To behold their own "Divine essence" is each individual's divine destiny.

Rise above your sense consciousness. You are so above it all. No matter what they say, no harm is done to you. For you know the truth of your being. Your highest nature prevails, always the victor in Christ. Your being rises to the occasion. The Christ is not above or beyond you, but with you, within all for the asking, for the knowing. Rise up for the occasion.

These messages are perfect for me. They are in tune with my understanding of what I'm able to know, of what is so. I like to hear, to listen in to a voice so dear that each day becomes more clear to me. It's a mission. Its message is Love. I know this Love is real. I really do. I wish the same for you. I know this in my heart, my head be not involved.

Humor me again. You make me laugh, you always have. You have such a light-hearted view of life. *"Lay down your burdens and live without strife."* I say in my mind with a deep announcer voice. I know you do not mind at all my irreverent tone, for even though you are the King, you do not sit on a throne. You walk with the people as we walk this land, showing us funny "coincidences," as if you in them had no hand.

I like to laugh. It's such a joyful tone.

> *Music to My ears, says God. I want you this way, joyful everyday. I love to watch you dance and sing and shout, not dragging about. This it your time, your time to be physical, so get physical. Move about. Raise your voice. Sing so high that no one can deny you live with Me now. Not later in the sky.*

It can be a question or a statement. They are really more like suggested topics. When I sit down with pen in hand to talk with God, God likes me to start the conversation. I am free to say as I wish, no reason to hold anything back, God wants my all. For He knows all already, but still He loves it when I offer my all to Him and sit fully present, a naked bare soul before Him. For this is the way He sent each of us out into the world. Before the nakedness of our birthday suit, we existed in the nakedness of our soul. And our true goal of this earthly visit is to again remember the freedom we knew and felt as we were unrestricted and un-blinded by our physicality in the pure nakedness of our spirit soul self.

> *Did you know that these eyes with which you see this page are not your first pair of eyes? For before this time of yours, as you live now, you lived with Me and saw perfectly. So in essence, in truth, when your eyes again open to the bigger picture of life, I have not given you a new pair of eyes. I have only lifted the blindfold of your physicality, so you can again see with Me eternity.*

Okay, it's pretty evident to me that God's own voice came through mine. I certainly don't view it as interrupting; I make it a point to bow to the Divine. I say "make it a point" though it is not yet a clear rule. For although God's voice offers direction continually through my day and I don't always hear it or heed it. As my mind is thinking so hard, the soft rapping of His words are not always recognized and thus ignored.

AUGUST 8, 2011

> *This is good news. Let it be heard loud and clear. You are to be Love's messenger My dear. Walk My way. Sing My Song. I will hold your hand so the day will not seem long.*

Within my being, I am Love.

> *I love to be with you. Hold Me close, whisper in My ear. I always hear you. All I want is your happiness, your joy, to flow free. Can you not see how your very happiness thrills Me? This is My plan and always was for all to find the joy that flows within not looking elsewhere below or above.*

> *Let Me tell you a story about a boy who loved Me so. Part of the story you already know, but now you know the truth that that which is within his heart, and always has been, is there for each of you as well. This is the story I want you to tell.*

> *Do you think about God and if so what do you think? Do you think good? Do you feel love, do you realize God is with you, within you and not far away or high above?*

What can I say? Words will never be enough to express the joy I feel as I look across the land I love. So God has given me the voice of color.

People like to know what to think. They want to be told a recipe for life. They are looking for instruction, not knowing that each comes with a personalized set of words for living. Guiding directions, one step at a time, are here at hand. Within one's own heart, one's own truth lies. Look not elsewhere for your truth, for guidance. Listen to the whispers of your own heart tell you what to do.

There is no comparison. Pay no attention. Give no mind to any others drama or decisions. It is up to you and only you to decide what you want for your life. This is for you to see, for you to know.

You are supposed to pray, believing. This is the faith you are to have. Faith that what so ever you ask for it is already yours though your eyes have not yet beheld. This is the first step. Take the first step in faith. Trust in God, the goodness of all creation to provide. Believe it true.

You have a story to tell. Your story is My Story and the other's as well. Some will listen. Some will heed. Some will live because of you. This is what I ask you to do. Pray tell. Pray means please, asking nicely as you believe.

How do you get beyond your mind, you ask? "How do I see beyond the matter which fills my world?" You have to close your eyes unto the world and open your heart. Open your heart to all possibility. Only this way can you ever see beyond what is and glimpse infinity. Set no limits, harden not your heart. Set not your mind. Open up to new possibilities. Fly free to new heights with Me.

God wants the best for each one of us. For God is the good of the universe. All of it is of God. The goodness you see in another is God being brought forth into expression. Yes, God wants each of us to want the good that has already been provided. It's not really a matter of claiming or acknowledging one's personal worthiness. Each is worthy in the eyes of God at any moment. All that is needed to claim the bounty of God's Kingdom is to set down the shield that we each carry guarding our heart.

We have to step out of the bonds we have tied so tightly around ourselves limiting our minds, bodies and souls. The bondage we each live in and fight against, as well as fight to protect, is all self made. The self, the singleness of ourselves, is the shell we believe is all we are and can be. So we resist anything that we feel could threaten our self. We build walls, mental and physical around our person's and our ideas. Fighting to bodily death to defend what we know, even as we know that what we know is not a good fulfilling perfect life, for we don't even have the conception that such a perfect life could ever be ours on this earth. All true joy is postponed. Some day, in the next life, we say, I will see God's eyes and touch His face. I will ask Him why did I have to suffer so and why did He create such misery and pain in the world?

God will not be angry for your questions and will not judge you for your attributing such human woe to His hand. Instead, He will wrap His arms around you and envelope you so in His love that you will instantly understand that the Spirit you deemed vengeful and judgmental could never have been so.

Your eyes will open to the Truth that this most loving Spirit has always fully loved you. For you will understand the truth of the words "God is Love" and as this love fills you and softens your heart you understand that it was your own heart that was vengeful and clinched tight as a fist. This same purifying Divine Love had always been around you and in you but you yourself had kept at a guarded distance, never fully opening the door of your heart and asking God to come in.

You ask God why, why did you let me go on in such a way, believing so? Believing so in myself? And as you ask, you know, you know that the very special gift of God, your own free will is the answer. God wants to be the chosen one. He has already, by the fact of our creation chosen us.

"But I did choose You!" you say to God, "I always believed in You." Believed what? Believed God was far away, vengeful, judgmental, and all powerful. You believed God was all powerful, but you did not even begin to fathom God's ways. The all powerful force of God is love. Love is perfection in action. Let nature show you, for nature has no free will and only knows the will of God.

Man is different. Man has power, the power to choose, the power to create his life by action and thought. Man can choose to do all himself or can surrender his will, sacrifice his self to the will of God, allowing the power of Love, the will of God, to shine forth and flow through his being.

The people who change and better the world are not those who read books and memorize the words of others, but those who open their minds to new thought and inspire others. Original Thought, the source of all creation, is a mighty river free flowing with all possible knowing. Ride the wave. Lift your vibration. Fly high. Soar above old thought. Live on.

AUGUST 9, 2011

You are constantly getting in your own way, the way of which all good freely flows. You build walls, damming up stagnant thought. Old ways are not necessarily the best ways. Better is to come, when you allow love to flow through your being. You are on the edge of becoming so much more than you are.

Welcome in this new being, this new creation you are. All is well and you will show and tell the world of such magnificent wonders. You are My star, My heavenly connection. I will show you all and answer all your questions. There will be no doubt to trouble your mind, as you find My love fulfills your destiny.

Brothers and Sisters we are, guiding the way, directing your path only as you allow. For we will never, and can never, supplant our will over yours. You must want and believe in the best for all at all time. Then listen and heed our guidings. We will see that you will see, the best is yet to come.

For this I give thanks. Thanks be to God, which is all good.

AUGUST 10, 2011

I like what I see. I have perfect vision. I'm at peace with me. I like what I see. I see the good around and through my being. I see God in me. Goodness is the fountain of my being flowing forth evenly, continuously. I am continually renewed and replenished with every breath, I give God all the glory.

You are what you say you are. Open up. Let go. Go on. Fly free. You have wings just like Me. Wings are a concept of man, for man's freedom. They symbolize no limit living, the ability to be anywhere, effortlessly. You are truly an angel, an angel at heart. Live effortlessly, fly free, free from the bondage your mind has created.

We are to believe, we are not to believe a thing, for knowing is the only way to full truth. We are to ask, to question each statement, each idea proposed and let it sit in our heart with wonder. For the only way to full truth is knowing and knowing can only come from questioning, seeking, and experiencing. No system of belief is the full truth. Each can be a way to explore truth if you approach each with an open mind and heart.

Why do so many fall away and fall short of the beliefs they profess?

Because they never knew them as full truths in their heart, they never discovered for themselves the value of the words. The words were not given unto their hearts, but instead delivered to their minds by man.

Many of mankind have found God and fully know him. They feel a rush and expedience to share this knowledge of the truth of God, God's Divine Love, and thus they each attempt to set forth a plan, a system, to guide the others unto this light. Each fully understanding that their purpose is to be the messenger of such good news and that they can only point the way.

I got a healing feeling within my heart.

When you listen to your heart, amazing things happen. I'm not speaking of the heart which beats within your body. I

*speak of your true heart, the pulse of life within your being
that is you, that has always been you and will continue
to be you after your bodily heart makes its last beat. Your
heart knows all, for your heart is All. All wisdom, all joy, all
peace, all love.*

*People are not always going to be nice to you. Their words
will not always be kind. It is for you to remember that it is
their business not yours. Your business is what you think
and what you feel. It's up to you how you act. Let every
action of yours be heartfelt, instinctively good, kind, wise
and joyful. Let this, your heart, be the well spring of your
action and get not caught in the trap of a reactive life. For
that is what reaction is, a trap. Someone acts unto you and
you re-act the act unto them.*

*The truth of you, your heart being, is beyond all that, not
dependant on another's actions for its own actions. When
one is living in a reactive mode of life, life swings on a heavy
pendulum, swaying back and forth with the weight of public
opinion. It's really good when it's good and really bad when
it's bad and you never know what you will get or give.*

*A reactive being is nice to those that are nice, and nasty
to those that are nasty. They do not live consciously. One
who is awake, living with an enlightened consciousness,
understands that they have a choice of how they show up
in this world. And that no matter the words or actions of
another, they can choose to act from the goodness of their
heart continually. The interesting thing is that such loving
action is so calming and passive that it seems to defuse the
raging energy of another, for all fires need fuel and without
such shall eventually die.*

A warm heart exudes another kind of fire. The radiant passion of joy which has an equal power to ignite the fires of joy and love in another's heart which before your encounter may have been just embers awaiting a burst of love to again ignite the flame. So is the power of Love. The power we each hold in our hearts, ready and available to use as we will freely. This is always our choice, not a mandate or a God command. A choice of will, by our own free will we can choose this way of life. Living heart centered is living God centered. It is choosing the will of God, the constant good over the reactive.

AUGUST 11, 2011

My son asks, "Are you writing your own Bible?" Perhaps I am. The inspiration is the same Source.

When that is all you can see, that is all you look at. If you do not like what is already there to look at, plant some beautiful flowers to distract your eye. Then your view will be joyful. Your eye will be filled with the beholdment of beauty; nothing else will then matter to you. You will know the truth of your heart. All is well.

I love the rain. I hear thunder and joy stirs within my deepest being. I love the rain. It smells so sweet. I love to step and splash in puddles with my bare feet. Nature's goodness washes away my woes, thank you God for the rain and the mud between my toes.

You must make it a daily practice to find opportunities to exchange joy. For each joy seed you plant, a thousand blossoms it will bare. Create My garden of joy on earth. This is the Eden of which is told, continuing to bloom each and everyday for those who look. Yes, the Garden of Eden flourishes still. It's not just the story of old in the pages of your big book.

You may look at others, oh yes, please do and admire what you will. For what you admire is the will you create for the life you live. All you see, all you hear can be yours. What would you like to know? What would you like to show? See it. Hear it. Think it. This is your life. Your testament is your word, your action, your being.

No limits you have, excepting those you know to be true. Whatever you have decided is. So why limit what you know? Undo the chains that bind your mind. Let go of all you know. For what you know is so little, so small, so meager. I see you living so large, so high, so tall. Whose vision appeals to you now, that of the earthworm or the butterfly? By your choice, your mind, your will, you can be either.

It's okay to be in a state of unknowing. Yes, it is perfectly fine not to know all the answers. What is important is your wanting to know and believing you can know. This very attitude unlocks the door to wisdom untold. When you feel sure and certain things are a specific way or will be a specific way, you are limiting opportunity. You are limiting your opportunity for better to come into your life. You only will know what you know, when your mind is so set.

Instead, I invite you to release your hold on what you think possible for your life. I invite you to invite in new possibilities. I say, ask only for the best. Say to yourself, "I want, and deserve, and I will have the best life I can have. I open my heart to all the highest and best life has for me. Joy is my destiny." Ask and it is given. Think what you want.

What are you looking at? Rest your head. Open your heart. All of Mine is yours. Don't block the flow of good coming to you. Sing and shout praises.

Dear God, hold me, show me, help me, guide me.

A contemplative life
Direction
Guidance
Clarity
Focus.

Do what you have to do. Get it done. No hiding. No waiting. The day is here. Night has gone. By and by, I walk beside and love you. Don't make life so hard. Get up from your bed and walk.

AUGUST 14, 2011

Get going. Keep showing. Shine on. Rise up. Be the star you are.

My little voice believes in me. My heart is beating louder than my head.

Center yourself. Go within to the heart of your being. The meat of you is not the "meat" of you. Meet your "real self" within. No matter what anyone says, you know who you are. What a blessed gift that is. Celebrate your heritage "Your Highness." Bow down before the throne of All. All there is is yours to claim, to recognize as the beauty God has created in your name. Blessed be the eyes who see this.

What is real life?

The life you are living, here and now. Wherever you are, you are to be fully present. Do not hesitate to be fully aware of who you are in each moment. One moment at a time life comes. Live each one of them.

Do I hear the voice of angels?

You are listening to your heart which resides with the angels. Your heart sings in the angel's choir in perfect harmony. You hit all the high notes. Yes, you hear the voice of angels and it is your own.

Keep to yourself. Listen to what you say. Pay no mind to what others think, do or say. Their action should not you sway. You have one life to live now, where you are. Make the best of it. Go for it. Follow your heart. Your heart knows all the best there is. From a high point it sees beauty and wonder untold, waiting for you to ask and believe, ready to unfold.

AUGUST 15, 2011

I am thinking of my father, holding him close. I wear him in my heart. Our hearts entwine in Heaven while I am here on Earth. I feel and know his love. He sends me guidance, knowing, wisdom and love. Yes, I feel all of this, Daddy. I know you are watching over me from above. Happy birthday! Thank you for being a wonderful father and such a loving husband to my mother. All our love to you, just yesterday it seems I smelled you and held your hand.

As I open my heart and seek Truth, Truth speaks to my heart in many ways. I find writings of other pronouncing the statements of my heart and I question. Has it all been said, are my words needed as well?

There is so much more to say and Truth can be spoken in so many ways.

I know more than I can say. There is more wisdom within me than I have realized.

Room to grow. If the shoe fits, wear it. Not an intellectual pursuit.

You say you feel bad for someone else, you feel sorry for them. But why?? How is that helping anyone? Does that help them? Help you? Does it make you feel better about yourself to feel bad for another?

What do you want to hear? What is the music of your mind? So you say, others get in your way. Do they, or is it in your mind? Mind your own business. Do what it is for you to do. Your way is your own. No mountain to high. No valley so low. All is fine, when you know where you want to go.

Listen to what you say. Are you sure you really want it that way? Why look for flaws? Is this what you wish to see? Learn to see perfectly. See with Me. Tune up. Lift your spirit.

AUGUST 16, 2011

God is Life Force. Life is God force. The perfect expression of this life freely flowing is the Christ.

When I was a little girl I was afraid of death but now I know differently.

Death is only the absence of life. When life leaves, death comes gently in. With the last breath the soul escapes to

freedom, to life beyond limits. There is a time to be born.
There is a time to die. Death is only a bodily action, for life is
continual and lives on taking new form. Find comfort in this
knowledge. Life is good. Life is God. Bodily death is freedom
for the soul. The soul knows the truth of life. The soul knows
no limits. Limit not yourself in life, nor at the hour of your
death, for life is always fully yours, available for the asking.
Come home. Come back to Me. You are My baby.

Please accept our return of this great gift, our father Albert. We are
grateful for our time with him. He has taught us much. He has gifted us
with much. Our gratitude is eternal. Welcome him into Your arms. We
lift him up to You in our prayers. Take his hand, lead him home. Show
him the way. Leave the porch light on.

What do you want me to know?

All is well. There is no time, so no need to rush. What's the
hurry? There is no need for impatience. Just be with Me. I
like this so. I feel your love. Do you feel Mine? My arms are
wrapped around you. I am Love. Your love is so great. Your
honor is so big. You have loved well. So know this, all is well.

There is nothing to fear in death. There is nothing to fear
in life. Death is just the absence of life, just as darkness is
the absence of light. Light is the sign of life which we are all
drawn unto. Life attracts life, and thus as life leaves the shell
of the body it is drawn unto the light of Love to again know
wholeness. Just as naturally as the moth is lead to the porch
light, your soul is drawn unto the great light of its own home,
the bosom of God, our Mother/Father Creative Spirit.

Do not fear the dark. Do not fear death, for there is no time
whatsoever of darkness or fear upon departure from one's

body. The soul knows instantly where home is and is drawn unto the light of God's eternal love, to the porch light of eternal bliss. See the light, love and wisdom in this plan and find comfort. No soul is lost. No soul truly wanders. Some have more light than others; this is true on Earth just as it is in Heaven. You can see and be this Light now. Be the light. Light the way. Lead others.

Please share your higher perspective with me. I'd like to see, to know more clearly.

All is well, as you have been told. This is the same story of old. All is well and always has been. This is for you to see, to know, God's love perfectly.

I am open to inspiration. I am open to information. I have a higher calling. I have the honor to sit beside the bed of a man of God as his spirit prepares to leave his body. Thank you, I sit with honor and respect and wonder at this process and consider it a gift to be present.

The love in this room is immense. It is palpable. It can be seen and felt. I see it in the body of the man, my father-in-law, whom lies in the bed before me. I see it in the comfortable presence of his son, my husband, as he sits beside his father, watching over him. I feel such love for these two men, for their bond and mine with them. For it was the love father Albert had for his wife Audine that created the boy I married. And it was the example of the life they led that created the man I have been married to for thirty years.

What are you afraid of? What are you avoiding? Walk right up to it and stare it in the face. It's called confrontation. By facing your fears, they are brought to the light, out of the mystery of the dark. Away from the looming and haunting shadows, they no longer have the power to creep up, and pounce on you and scare you. You see them for what they are, fears, not necessarily truths. And even as you look your ugliest fear in the eye you will find that most have not the strength and power over you as your mind has imagined. Face to face is the best way, always. The rumors are squelched. Poof, the power they once held over you is gone.

You see beyond, over their shoulder, peace in the light that lies ahead of you. That light moves toward you passing over and illuminating the face of fear, the mask of trouble. And then you see it is only you, the you of your creation, the mind of you. You reach out your hand as a peace offering and find your arms embracing yourself, the tender, fearful, doubting piece of your being and consoling yourself with these words. "Come back to Me and be at peace. All is well, you are whole."

I am sheltered. Love is my safe harbor. I move freely with that knowing. My being is love showing. What do I need to do?

Love, love more, not judiciously but freely, flowingly. Judge not. Condemn not. Jail not your love. For as you give love, you receive love. This is the true story of your true life. Find it. Keep it. Glorify it.

Here I am with you, as always. Feel My presence within your being, feel safe. Know My love. Reach out for more. More is always there available to you. This is My gift, your inheritance, your truth, your beauty. Feel it. Be it. Know it. Show it.

AUGUST 20, 2011

I'm kind of melancholy today, but is it any wonder? Yesterday, my father-in-law Albert passed from this world to the next. Of course, I am thrilled for him to graduate to the next level, but it was so hard to let go, hard for him and hard for us. We cherish his memory so.

So today is different, different from the rest. I find myself crying, tears of loneliness, missing what was and no longer is or can be. I feel adrift in the sea of uncertainty. The physical world has not proven to be a dependable constant reality. Change it seems is the order of the day. It seems all would feel safer if each day stayed the same. But that is not to be, not here in this reality.

But then I remember the safe place deep within my heart, where love and safety are constant, where the world is never dark. I look within, not without, and find my calm, gentle waters, the cooling stream of Love flowing into and out of my heart. I immerse myself in these healing waters and allow the stream to flow from my eyes. Calmness overcomes me and again I feel whole.

Hold me Father, I pray, let me stay with You. Hold my hand, lead my heart. I know not the way. I look to You for guidance, to show the way. My heart is yours. I am listening in. I will be content to sit with You, again and again.

Lord give me patience. You are my light. Light me up. Guide me forth. I will walk with You time and again. You will show me the way to truth.

> *So be it. It is so. This you know. Have heart. I am yours, My love.*

Is Heaven in the clouds?

> *No, Heaven cannot be even contained by the clouds. Heaven is here, there, everywhere. Some recognize it, most don't. Heaven always exists to be found by those who look with spiritually open eyes and hearts. Heaven is a feeling, a knowing, the Truth that is.*

Time doesn't matter and yet You make it matter. You do not have to play along.

AUGUST 23, 2011

Worry versus fear seems much the same as the old chicken and the egg story. Which comes first, the worry or something to worry about?

> *The chicken and the egg story may never be proven in your lifetime but you have the power within your own being to lay claim to the truth of worry's root. Each member of mankind has the ability to test such by his own will. It is a matter of self control, a control of his own willful ways which lay claim to worry.*

> *Wisdom ways, make way for clarity. The light is bright. Do not deny your glory.*

Hallowed be Thy name, for no such word exists to hold or contain the bounty of such glory.

> *You are always connected. What is important is that you feel this way, that you understand, that you know. And that all it takes is intent, desire on your part. God's part is done, for God never goes "off-line." You can never disconnect with God, for God is the life force within you. The beat of your heart is Love in action, flowing freely through your being. You can live from the outside or the inside. When you live from the inside you are drawing from the well of Spirit, the plentiful fountain of everlasting youth, health and beauty. You feel good. You feel love. You feel your God connection. You are at peace and whole. This wholeness is your holiness. How it is and should be, on Earth as it is in Heaven.*

Say a prayer. Make a petition. Ask for My love, My most pure Divine Love to saturate your very being, to raise your spirit, to make you new. This is what I ask each of you to do, want more of Me, want all of Me for you.

What's wrong with me?

Nothing, not a darn thing about you. The Truth of you is wonderful. Wake up to this fact and you will live it. Wondrousness is yours to claim and claim it you must, to fully live it and know it.

I am wondrous. I am beauty. I am perfect. I am God in motion, in action, in form. I claim this knowledge.

"From the looks of things…" This is how you declare what can and cannot be. This is how you determine the probability of your destiny. This is how you see life with the simple narrow view eyes of your humanity. It's a given, you have decided, agreed, that what always follows "A" is "B." That's not necessarily a good thing.

"The devil made me do it." Yeah right, what a cop out. What an excuse, a poor way of acknowledging the freedom of your own will. If evil is your choice, so be it, own your choice, for this is your life.

Does the dark make someone not see?

No, the dark is only the absence of light, not a force of energy at all. What other questions do you have?

The past doesn't matter. It can do no harm. It can do no good. It was. It isn't. It is no more your concern. Look ahead. Watch out. See anew and bring a new life to you. What a story you will tell. All is well. All is well.

You can be so many things. All the things you can dream, you can be. Fully alive and well, presently you are whole. All there is is your potential. Untie your arms, un-blind your eyes. Make these words worthy to share. Show all. Show and tell My glory. Don't look too long at the world before you, for if you do you will not see all you can be. This is why you have to spend time within, for within your heart being you can know all. Freedom exists.

There was a day when something snapped in me. The world as I knew it fell apart. Since that day I've been piecing it back together, my life. But as I pick up a piece I find it new, fresh and whole in itself and as I fit these new pieces together I am made again, a new me, one refreshed in spirit, ready to accept a new reality.

There is no time for pity. There is only time for praise. Glory, goodness and gratefulness are the order of the day. This is the way we are to see it, to live it, to understand the grand plan God has for man.

I like to see you smile. You know, it has been awhile. I watch over. I care. I love who you are. I tell you again, you are My shining star. The world hardly knows the truth of what is. Breathe in, breathe out, I'll show you the way to live from within.

You paint beautiful pictures. You have perfect timing.

Going home, home is where the heart is. Get to the heart of the matter, no matter what. See clearly, love dearly. Whatever is heartfelt, is God felt. Be true to you, for no one else can. Be you, truly. Yours Truly.

You are one of the lucky ones. You have a healthy imagination. You are able to imagine wonderful possibilities for your life and as you do, you creatively manifest them. Go you!

What is the stink about? Is it your attitude? No one wants to be around someone with a stinky attitude, so be sure and put on a fresh and pleasantly fragrant attitude each day.

How is one to get along in this world?

By taking care of business. The sad thing is most have forgotten what their business is. Stop noticing what's wrong and start noticing what's right. Begin with your own body.

Sure you can "Google" answers to learn what men think, but you can as well "dial up" the power of your own knowing. Ask, receive and give thanks.

People aren't trash! They might look like trash, act and speak like trash but for real they are treasure, all treasure, buried though it might be, treasure not trash.

I have control over my own life.

Feel good about it. Feel God about it.

You can't put grief on hold. Let it flow. Don't hold it back. Grief is real. It is how you feel. How you feel is important, it needs to be acknowledged, recognized and felt, felt deeply, purely. Grief is not to be held in or contained. Grief is a sign of your love and a sign of your feeling of loss. But know this, no love is ever lost. Love lives on and on.

There is a time for all. It is the way it is and should be. You are brought into this world and brought out. To and from where? Love's true home, your home in Heaven. You always have been in love, wrapped in it, swaddled like a baby. It is not necessary to wait until your last breath to again feel the completeness and wholeness of this love. It is here for you now. As you cry and grieve, as you sing and dance with the breeze, I love you. Quiet that busy mind of yours and listen to Me. Hear the hum of Heaven in your heart. I love you always.

I wonder.

It's a good thing to do, for with your wonder comes infinite possibility, options for outcome.

They will speak of you and say she is delightful. She is full of the Light.

Fear instilled, the worst expected and planned for. Don't see it as a problem. Don't make it a problem. Feelings of desperation will never take you to the next level. The only way to rise higher is to think higher. Let go of all you know. For all of what you know is only what you think you know and in higher reality darling, that ain't much. So we say, let go of all of it.

To truly be a vessel for Spirit you have to first empty out your self. For when one is full of his or her self, Spirit cannot fully and freely flow. This you need to know.

Being full of your self is being full of ideas, concepts of how you have decided life is. You have done this as a defense mechanism for you feel safer in this "big scary world" knowing that if you do "A", "B" will follow. These ideas have served mankind on some level for eons, but as well kept his thinking and thus evolving low. Now is the time to rise higher. We all so delight in your desire, but you have to understand that your old eyes are of no help in this matter. You have to see life anew with your new spiritual eyes to partake in the full bounty and glory of God.

As you empty out your self, God will fill in the spots, so you will never be less than whole. You will become more and more holy, as this is the desire you have expressed. Holiness will be your nature, Godliness your right, your very being. Continue to ask for the infilling of Divine Love, you can never get enough and supply will never be exhausted.

Whenever you feel lost, stuck or scared, don't panic. Instead take a deep breath and hold it, then slowly release the tension through your breath. This is the breath of Life which you are so lucky of which to partake. This air is given freely to you from Life itself. You know this and trust air to be available for your next breath. This is how we want you to be for every desire you have in life. Trusting and knowing it will be there when needed.

You do not hold your breath fearing it will be your last one, fearful of releasing. No, you trust that the Breath of Life is always there. You trust in air. Air, something you cannot see, something invisible, "supernatural" and yet you know it is. This is the flow of Life, always present, always available, waiting for you to exhale in faith, in knowing that as you release what you so tightly are holding onto, fearing it is your last, more is waiting, "a fresh start" you might say.

Do you believe these words, these words that come from your heart? It's quite amazing to you we know, but it is true.

Your heart is full of love for you. Go on, breath free. Breathe in, breathe out knowing, trusting, this is how all of life shall be.

Thank you, I needed that!

AUGUST 25, 2011

Trial by fire, from the fire the purest of gold emerges gleaming.

So we have told you that infinite possibilities exist. That is true, now it is up to you to decide, to choose the possibilities you want to be true for you. "Only the highest and the best" is a wonderful mantra to profess, for as you declare, this is the life of which you will be aware.

"It is easier for a camel to slip through the eye of a needle than a rich man to enter the Kingdom of God." Why is this so?

Because the rich man is so "full of self" that he has not room for God. Only one who seeks, finds. And one who has spent their life in the business of acquiring material riches upon riches is not the likely sort to spend energy and time seeking the peace of God. This is not to be taken as a statement against having and enjoying material abundance, for God delights in our enjoying the gifts available to all in this world as He wishes to shower each one of us with a multitude of blessings, spiritual and material. He has provided a way for this to manifest while we are on Earth. Jesus told us this way: "Seek ye first the Kingdom of God and all good things will be added unto thee."

Poverty and conditions of lack for lack's sake do not honor God. We are not to see life this way. We are to seek to know our Creator intimately and ask to be so filled with Divine Love that God's will becomes our will, just as it is in Heaven. Just as it truly is in the spiritual realm, the place where material reality has no hold and ideas manifest as easily as they are imagined.

Heaven is whatever you imagine it to be. If you are a fisherman, well-stocked lakes abound, if you love to swim you will find a calm and temperate ocean at your beck and call. Gardeners grow beautiful gardens by planting colorful seed ideas in mind, this mind is Divine Mind, of which we all have access to here as bodied beings on Earth. Divine Mind is the creative mind, where all is possible.

I don't think the answers. I just think the questions. The answers come to me as easily as my breath. Wisdom flows freely, graciously given as it is received and welcomed with gratitude. Before I ask, my little self, my brain, does not know, but my better half, which is daily becoming the dominant part of me does know and gladly offers this knowing to my mind.

Give thanks. Jesus was the personality. Christ was His truth in being.

I declare my good! God wants me to prosper. This is God's will. God's will be done. Others may say "Whatever God's will is…" and hang their head as if they are throwing up their hands and are giving up on life. But I see the acceptance and allowing of God's will in my life as amazing opportunity, for I know God as "all good," so by turning my will over to God I am giving my all to God and allowing all of God, all of good, to flow through me. It is also important that I remember that "free flow" is necessary for action. The good that flows to me must as well flow through me to others. God's love cannot be stagnated. The only way to keep the flow is to be a clear channel for God's everlasting Goodness and Divine Love.

Love is impossible to contain.

I've done some things wrong and some things right. I've tried really hard with all my might. I am tired now; I choose to give up the fight. I no longer will fight for my life. For life is not a fighting thing. It's love and allowing that makes flowers bloom. I'm going back to live from my heart, God's womb. Complete me please. Fill every whole, patch every crack of my soul with Your healing grace. I cannot do this alone. Alone I am scared and fearful. Fill me up; overflow me with Your love. This is all I want, all I need, all I desire, is to know You higher. I want to be taken care of. Take care of me Lord. Be my shepherd, lead me, feed me. I will do Your work. My hands are Your hands. Make my heart Your home.

Some people are given to know. You should be thankful you are one of them. Your understanding is great but small in the scheme of things. Remain open, trust the Truth of you as it shines forth. Find your joy. Tell us what kind of signs you want.

You don't have to decide every move you make before hand. When you are living in the flow you will know what to do next as the opportunity arises. All you need is a goal, a direction, an ideal.

If it's a good idea, it's a God idea. Man's eyes can only see what is in front of them. We are not puppets; we are players, active participants in life. Life is an action verb. There is no room for doubt. No doubt about it.

The Christ is the "New Gift." Jesus was the first to manifest the Christ through God's gift to humanity, Divine Love.

Don't curse, bless! Your negative words are curses to your own life. They are your personal denials of the good of God, which is available to you. No one else has the power to lay a curse on another, yet if you believe in another's words of defile you are claiming them and thus defiling your own life. All the power lies within you by your word.

Don't let people rock your boat. The only way some people are happy is if they are in control. To them, control equals happiness and safety, and lack of control equals fear, fear of the unknown.

You are fine. Everyday, you are fine. Has there ever been a day you have not had your needs met? I will provide for you as you need, as you believe. I ask for your trust, and love and I in return will show you Mine which is here for you. Speak with Me. Be with Me. Do not tarry long. See beauty My beloved. Point to it. Sing about it.

Stop trying to figure it all out. You are making yourself sick with worry. All will come as you allow. Your worry blocks the natural flow of all your good, gifts from God. Love will find you. Enjoy the day, don't wait it out. Come and see My glory. Behold the day My way. What do you need? Air to breath, water to drink, and love. Nothing is too good to be true. Show off, show up, show who you are. It's all connected. Believe it so, see it so. Do something for yourself.

AUGUST 26, 2011

Don't tell me you found the light. Show Me you are the light. By this way, I know you speak truth. Too much of this world is talk. Talk without action to back it up. Actions speak louder than words. Speak to Me by being. Be the light you wish to shine.

I hear you.

> *Throwing off materiality, this concept has been misunderstood and thus man has condemned the material joys and pleasures of this world. This is not the Message intended. Solemnity, plainness and poverty are not signs of heirs to the God's Kingdom. Joyfulness, beauty and riches are the Sons and Daughters birthright.*

> *Stop seeing and giving attention to a problem and it will disappear instantly. Wisdom is knowing things that aren't right in front of you and wisdom is from God.*

It's time for me to move ahead.

> *Wisdom is available to each and for each. You can share your wisdom with another but you cannot impose your wisdom on another.*

> *Know you are safe.*

> *The love of God, Divine Love, is available to all for the asking. Ask for God to come into your heart. This is not a one-time gift as the love of God is such a powerful substance that we can only come to possess it on a drip by drip basis. Ask God to continually give you a flow of His amazing energy and power. Hold fast in prayer and faith for this to be allowed into your being.*

> *If you don't change what you say, you won't change the next day. Instead of "I'm sick and tired." Say, "I'm healthy and full of energy." Some say "Well, that's not the truth." Do you want it to be your truth? Claim it, say it, proclaim it! You are given what you need, what you request, as you believe.*

Heaven is everywhere. God is everywhere. How is that possible? God is Love. Love is not a descriptive of God. Love is the substance of Spirit which fills all space between matter. Within the cells of your being there is Love. Don't deny it. Don't deny anything.

I still have invisible friends, my mentors, higher counsel. My sources say…

It is glorious. This is my Chosen Son. He chose Me over the reality of materiality.

The idea that we can be so connected is amazing to us, as we are limited by the perception of our physical eyes.

Parables are contemplated in prayer for their deep meaning, spiritual lessons. They serve no lesson taken literally. The point is missed. The mind dismisses further understanding. Jesus spoke truth in this way to honor the truth of God which is hidden from the mind of man. He openly thanked God, his Father for hiding the truth from the learned mind.

God's truth is available 24/7 to all mankind. Signs of Life, you are on your way. Keep going. This is the way, happiness ahead. Bump in the road.

AUGUST 30, 2011

Don't be afraid to give your all, for "All" is what I am.

Wisdom of the ages is wisdom of man through the ages. I have wisdom beyond the ages, wisdom untold.

Have no fear. You are where you are supposed to be, with Me. See Me in you. Live through Me. Trust in Me, in My guidance and My love. I will give you all you need, the words, the patience, the insight. You are living fully through Me. This is how it is, how it should be, for now and evermore.

I wondered and I knew.

Tell it like it is, "All is well with me." Know this, the "Truth" is with you. Spirit is life. Spirit is in everything that is alive. What is soul? Soul is individuality. I am here for you with your breath. Know Me. Do not be afraid. Walk forward in peace. I am here to show the way. My way is easy, the burden light. Carry on My child. Carry on.

AUGUST 31, 2011

No doubt about it. Aim high for the stars and beyond thought. Feel your way to Me. Help where you can. You are My arms, My hands, My feet. Through you, My love is complete. You have to use your new eyes with which to view the world. With these you will see keenly unlimited possibilities laying out before you. Not beyond your reach, within your grasp. This you need to understand. This My dear is your task.

What would you like to know? What would you like to show? Have fun with life. It is here for you to enjoy. So, show joy. Know joy. Be joy. Joyful you shall be. You are a channel for My spirit, for My love. Flowing forth like a great river after a rain, My love rains down upon your being. Flow forth My love.

So what is different?

> *Everything and nothing, all at the same time, all that is, has been. You just didn't have eyes to see it. So you couldn't fully be it. But now you know, so you can show. As you sow the seeds of My love, you shall so reap.*

There has been a change in me. What's the change?

> *Opening to Spirit. Letting go of all resistance. Being willing to show up differently.*
>
> *Don't fight. Don't hold on to what you know with all your might. Trust in Me, in Christ's light. Spirit becomes you. Walk this way, way beyond the known. For here all truth is shown.*
>
> *Anything is possible, this is true but you have to decide what you want so you can be a deliberate creator. You have to know it is possible. You have to believe it is yours. Visualize its existence. See it before you, and it is done. Don't believe in anyone else believe in yourself, on God's power within you.*
>
> *Place your trust here, for here I am present now fully within, without limit. Trust in the wisdom you write. You can write your own story illustrated by actions, your truth in being yourself. Reach out, show without reservation. Can you do this? Yes, you can, can do. This is you. Pour forth My love, pour forth. Some will see and help you reach your glory. Be in My name.*

I believe in more good than I can see.

> *You have to believe in it. Did you ever hear of the little engine that couldn't?*

September 2011

Let him have all your worries and cares,
for he is always thinking about you
and watching everything that concerns you.

2 Peter 1 ᴺᴵⱽ

September 1, 2011

*Hope is good. Hope is good intention. Worry works against
your highest desires canceling out the positive energy you
have directed toward your dreams. As the observer, you can
witness other's actions and not become entangled in their
drama. You can see and acknowledge without judgment.
This is the "Eye" of God.*

*Denying the flesh, this concept has been wrongly understood
since the beginning. It is not, and never has been, God's
good plan for us to suffer. There is no joy or glory in God
in suffering. God does not lay pain and suffering upon
his people, not anyone. All people are of God, though not
always for God.*

*The purpose of life is to glorify God, to know God and to
live fully through God. This is Life Everlasting. This is the
presence of "Heaven." This is what we are to strive for, to
pray for, to believe in.*

We are not to believe that it is God whom brings suffering upon us. The Lord, the "Perfect Law," is our deliverer from all suffering and not just in the next life, the life without our bodies. This can be true for the here and now as well, as we believe, as we open our hearts and minds to this possibility, we are allowing God's "True Spirit" to flow freely within us, to sanctify us. To make us right and know the wholeness, completeness and perfect-ness we are.

Life presents us with challenges that we have to learn to deal with. We can bear the weight of these alone or offer them up to the Lord. We are as well to surrender our will for their outcome. We are to submit our hearts and minds to the great truth that God, as all good, will work all good for this situation. Worry has no place in this equation. Worry is our mind becoming involved and wrestling with God, the good. Worry is doubt manifest in the mind. God says, pay no mind to these situations for your mind is so small and limited and only knows what has been. For new good to be created, you must let go of the old and let God fulfill the good. Prayers of thanksgiving are the order of the day. This is how you allow God in your life to have His way.

September 2, 2011

I am fascinated by the lives and stories of the saints and recognized holy people of old. I find there is a great deal to be learned from their ways and beliefs. It is my goal to unlock the mystery surrounding their lives and shed light on how people today can find and experience such grace.

Each were ordinary men and women, just like you, who chose to seek Me and live anew. What each has done so can you. They prayed continually, keeping an open dialogue in faith. They asked. They believed. They gave thanks on bended knee. No egos were involved. They laid down their own lives for the greater good of all. They each asked in their own way for My "Divine Love" to fill them as this they understood was the saving grace which sanctified their hearts. And this My dear is an excellent place for you to start.

Good things happen to us.

You had better believe it. Remain thirsty for My love. I will fill you evermore. Spirit is everywhere, manifest perfectly in the flowers. You can see it in the sea. Feel it in the breeze. So you ask, "Of which do I worship?" Worship none. Give all thanks, praise and glory to God, the Maker, who works within and manifests to the with-out. Walk behind none, beside all.

The flowers, the oceans, the winds are your friends, your brothers and sisters here on earth. See the twinkle in their eye and know all is well. The time has come for you to know the truth of your being, the being that is you, always has been you, and always will be you. Your truth in God, the goodness of this universe, is who you are in reality. Let this reality show. Let others know who you are and by doing this they as well may come to know the Truth which resides within all. The time has come. Show up.

Make no mistake I am here present with you. By you allowing My will to flow, you show your love to Me. I make no mistakes. Do not doubt My love. My will, My everlasting goodness, flows through your being and creates the world anew.

Thank you Lord for these words, this wisdom, this truth. I ask You to wholly consume my being and show up fully through me to the world. I step aside and let Light in.

I do not speak in code. I do not try to confuse. I show up and speak plainly to you in words your heart can hear. I do this for all. My voice is ever present, but some shut the door and bar closed their heart. Others fill their day so with doing that they allow no time for being, being with Me. For when one can quiet the noise of his mind he will find peace, peace inside his heart. The peace I bring to the world. Your heart is your sanctuary where you can stow away and swim in My grace. It is all here, so very near. So many have lived in the knowing of My love, their lives have told the stories of truth and grace that is available to all the human race.

Do not push and shove for the human race of which you are a part is not a competition, nor even a game. There is no one winner, no losers as well. Please see this time instead as a great opportunity to shine. Shine My love outward to the world. Find My love inside your heart and invite it to glow fully, brightly. Hold the faith. See the good. Know better.

You say it happened, as you knew. You knew someone would let you down. You knew it would turn out bad. You think you are so smart, but if you were really so smart you would believe better. You would understand your own power, the power of your words and your beliefs, and choose to work with them for the betterment of your life, for the betterment of mankind. Get smart. Be smart. Own the power of your words.

Do not purposely choose to cause yourself pain. Do not flog yourself with nails and chains. Do not don iron chains

*around your neck and drag through life. Do not inflict
pain upon yourself. Your physical self is not the enemy to
be slain. It is your ego self that needs to be reined in, that
needs to be crucified. The part of you your mind has created
and donned superior, named unworthy or whatever and
however you identify yourself. None of it is the truth. The
truth of you is so much bigger and better than anything you
have decided. It is your limiting thoughts that need to be
released so you will know this.*

*Fighting, resisting, what you don't want is never the answer.
Allowing is the only way to know true peace, allowing God's
goodness to flow. We have been told to deny the flesh; this
actually is to be understood as denying the apparent limit of
physical reality.*

*What can you learn from him? Ask yourself this as you meet
and interact with each of your brothers and sisters walking
the journey of life. Each one has something to teach you,
lessons one by one. Some will teach you patience, others
gratitude, others humility. Look for the lesson, learn it, use
it. Then you can move on.*

*Tell it like it is, perfect in the eyes of God, whom only knows
good and no other. Do not complain; instead choose to
proclaim the best outcome in every situation. Where do you
choose to dwell, in Heaven or Hell?*

*Don't think less of yourself. I will see you through. I am your
Father, your Mother, your Friend. Lean on Me. Let Me carry
you forward. Relax, loosen your grip on life as you know it
and most of all smile, smile your most beautiful smile. God
gives ideas for your hands, head and heart to follow. Follow
up on them and win!*

Look at the bright side, the light side of life. Just as each coin has two sides so does each situation in life. It's up to you to choose how you look at life, to where you put your attention. So why is there bad in this world you ask? Why has it been created? Why would God allow such evil to be? Well, first you must know and understand the truth of God. God is Spirit in Truth. God is Love. The Loving Spirit that created all in perfection knows no other way and can be no other than good. God called the world he created good. So any perception of un-good is not of God.

The noticing of things that feel wrong is giving attention to something one doesn't like, thus bringing more of same into existence. And as the Law of Attraction, which is God's law, is equal in every instance, your attention to what feels good to you brings you more of it. So it is the mind of man withdrawing from the ideas of and perception of all good which has created this un-good, un-God reality. Mankind sees this and confirms this reality again and again, for his own generation and for his children to be born unto. Actually, each child is born unto perfection, but is quickly taught to conform to the ways of the world by society.

None of this seeming madness is of God. It is caused by man's feeling of separation from this feeling of perfection. Man does not understand that he can know perfection and that by his birthright, as a child of God, our most Holy Father, he can know this perfection. The only way he can do this is to understand his worthiness and believe it is possible for him and each other. Then man has to lay aside his personal nature, his own personality that so strongly directs his will. He has to forgo his ego and thus he can make way for God to go. This is God's dream for mankind. God's Perfect Plan is for each of his children to choose His Will over their own. God wants and needs to be chosen. Yes, God already so dearly loves each one of us, whether we recognize it or not.

God so desires to pour His Love into our very being and He will do so freely when asked. So how do we ask and why should we ask? What is the difference of which I speak? First of all asking is easy. Ask God for help; say "Dear God, I need you. I need your Love in my life. I want you to so fill me with your Love that your Will becomes my will." Jesus told us we are to pray continually. Let every breath be a prayer of thanksgiving and request for the infilling of God's grace, His Divine Love. We are not to stop. We are not to ask once. We are to think of God first. Beg God, plead with God, pray to God for his merciful love to fill and bless you.

God's Divine Love will come into your heart and fill you with an everlasting peace and grace. Wisdom will be yours. Patience will be your middle name. This is the promise of God, which has been told. This is "the Comforter," this is the gift of the Christ which will become you as your ego personality fades away. And in it's place you will be so pleasantly surprised to find that God's will flows so naturally from your very being that you will know you speak the truth.

There is no rush. What is your hurry? Time is a concept of man. Man sees opportunity as slipping away; he knows not the Truth of his being. He feels not his power. I say to him, slow down, press pause, come to Me, I lay await in the inner most chamber of your heart. All is well. Know this and all will be.

Name calling, I have been called by name. The Lord of all knows me by name. I call out to him asking for his Divine Love to fill me, to be me. My name is called as I call on the Name of the Lord.

Know My love who you are, so precious, so perfect. You are My dream come true. It is My desire to live through you.

My Father loves me this I know for he speaks to me and tell me so. Take me over. Let Your Will be mine, I know I am heir to the Kingdom Divine. It is nice to see the truth in plain sight here and now for me. It is wonderful. I am dancing. I am singing Your praises in my heart.

You need to prove it to yourself and to the world. Prove My love. Walk forward in faith. Be My shining star.

The way it works, it shouldn't be a surprise at all. For this is the Truth of the matter. The world "works" very well indeed, continue to give thanks and praise, be so moved. It's God's way to give wisdom. Much has been lost in translation. Hear Me now, know. I speak the Truth unto your heart. Hear Me now, know.

When is enough, enough? Whenever you say it is. You decide how long you stay and what you do while you are here. Do My work. Share My love and when you are ready to come home I will welcome you with open arms.

Feel your power in patience. Enjoy the stillness in your soul. You need not always offer comment upon another's words or actions. Often the silent treatment is best. It allows the other's words to hang unadorned in the air. There they remain bare, exposed for what they are. You can hear them and leave them alone. The other has said them and can own them or choose to atone.

Do you hear what I hear? Do you hear the word of God as it is imprinted upon your heart? What a glorious gift this is. It is for you as well as I. I didn't always know this. I guess I presumed God was on pause, that He had stopped speaking unto the world. Now I know differently.

> *There is more than one way to do anything, do it your way, own it, make it yours! Don't make it a problem. You can see it through. Give all glory to God and watch what you can do.*

> *The power to communicate is one of your greatest powers. You have ideas and can express and share them with others. Do not take this lightly, for there is immense power in your words, power that can build mountains as well as tear them down. Be aware of this power and you can effectively move the mountains that appear to hinder you out of the way whilst building the castle of your dreams atop another. Keep listening there is more to come. Show up tomorrow. See you there bright and early, right back at you.*

SEPTEMBER 5, 2011

A healing is taking place within my heart, within my mind, within my body. This I know. This I show. I have opened my heart to the infilling of God's most wonderful Divine Love. This love blesses me, heals me, and restores me. Like the cooling waters of a mountain stream it refreshes me. I am made whole. Holy, I am through this blessed gift. My eyes show it, my actions and words show it.

So how can I not fully "know" it? Why does doubt still lie in my heart? I ask Thee to fill me so that doubt and fear have no room, no place to lie in wait. Crowd out this weakness, which lurks within. Flush out all "fear" and "doubt," these words I thus give up. Today I choose again, anew, words you would like me to use words such as "faith," "strength" and "good cheer." Oh yes, my Lord let these be the words I use to express my countenance. Let these be the words spoken upon my heart. Let today be a new start.

Blessed be "The Word of God," words spoken at Mass after a Bible reading. Words written so long ago in another language, translated by man again and again and edited as man's mind has seen and yet I am to believe these are the direct words of God for me and my fellow man.

> Lost in translation, so much has been. The "Keys to the Kingdom" have been misplaced. Error has occurred, some without intent to confuse and others purposefully omitted leaving truth untold. This malady has been perpetuated for ages leaving the masses not sanctified and satisfied by Grace but lost and confused.

> Just as God spoke unto the hearts of biblical men and women, God is available to speak to each today and in exactly the same way. The Truth of God is written at birth upon each one's heart, here lays the "Kingdom of God." Within one's own heart lays the door to the throne. Look in, not out. Find Peace. Find Joy. Be content. Be alive in Me, God begs. God pleads each to come fully Home. There is no building to go inside. There is no place you are to hide. Wherever you are God is now, for God is the "Life Force" within you. God gives you your breath. Be still and know that I am, God says.

> Quiet your body and mind. Pay attention to your breath. Just be. Give the rest of life, a rest. Be, just be. Breathe in, breathe out, again and again. Be aware of the air. There is nothing to control. Let go of it all and be. Be continually here with Me. Now ask Me, ask Me for My Love. Ask Me to fill the empty spaces of your lonely heart with the Peace I

send on the wings of a dove. My Love is for you, God says,
ask Me, allow Me, to fill you up.

Man seeks control, control over every element of life. He
pushes away all that threatens to disturb his perceived
peace. Walls are built in stone on earth and in the mind and
yet there true Peace he does not find. For his life is spent,
literally "spent" in defense. Fighting and defending his way,
the way he knows, the way he knows life to be. He sees all
other as a threat something to be conquered, put down, cast
away, killed. He sees himself as superior. He judges others
as less, less than he. He fears their ways and calls them evil.
And just as this man does to the other, the other does to him
and thus a battle ensues. A battle of wills fought still today
wherever two strong wills meet and are determined to have
their way.

This small mindedness has been the consciousness of man
for so long that man has forgotten the time unto which he
was born, the time of Love. The time in which mankind
was born was a time of Love and this Love born man into
perfection. Man lived in harmony with all, every man his
brother, and God his guiding Father. Mother Earth provided
all his needs. He did not want. This was the consciousness
of mankind at his birth on earth and the consciousness to
which he is returning. This is the shift which is occurring.
Walls are coming down. Peace is being restored. Brothers
are being recognized.

There is no half way here. God desires full expression through my
being.

Look not unto man for your answers. The mind of man is
so limited. The answers are here for you. Come to Me in the
hour of your need.

I believe in the miraculous. What is the miraculous?

> *What man doth not know, nor barely dared to imagine.*
> *All is possible through the eyes of God. Dare to dream.*
> *Dare to imagine beyond your wildest imaginings. Here lies*
> *possibility in wait.*

> *Jesus was a personality. Christ is the "Truth." The Truth, the*
> *Light, the Way we are to follow. Christ said, "Believe unto*
> *Me and I will set you free." This is the Christ speaking. God*
> *fully manifest in man. Inviting all to follow in his footsteps*
> *to do as he had done, to do as he proved could be done with*
> *the allowing, full allowance, of God's Divine Love and Holy*
> *Spirit to flow within.*

> *All new ideas and creative energy is from "Divine Mind,"*
> *the one mind of All. That is why it feels so good to be in the*
> *creative flow. One is truly in that moment, one with Spirit.*
> *It is up to the individual as to how the ideas are used, for*
> *what purpose they will serve if any. There are two kinds of*
> *talents, the talent to create ones impression of something*
> *which is before them, and then there is the ability to create*
> *anew, drawing upon energy and substance from the unseen*
> *and bringing it into form. This is the creative impulse.*

SEPTEMBER 6, 2011

I know who I am for I know who my Father is. I trust in His being which lives in me and expresses through me. I am, who I am. I am the love and Spirit of my Heavenly Father who speaks to me, who comforts me, who guides me home to Heaven. Divinity is my destiny.

Holy Communion and Communion with the Saints, I understand now, now I know the Truth. For I experience such through my very being, my being one with my Father. My being, filled with His Divine Love, is transformed, glorified in His name. Halleluiah. No one speaks of this but I will. Through the will of my Father it is done. Let God's will be done on Earth as it is in Heaven

Stop digging, stop digging a hole for you to crawl into and hide from life. It is time for you to rise up. Lift your face unto the sunshine. Sunshine is My gift to you which brings sunshine unto your heart. Plant Me a garden will you please? A most beautiful fragrant colorful garden in your mind. Water it with My love each day. Pull the weeds away. Toss the thoughts you do not desire to live in your garden to the side. Water them no more. Without your attention, uprooted from their existence in your being, they can live no more.

Water the flowers. Sit with them. Admire them. Drink in their fragrance. I will bring you rain. I will bring you sunshine. My love is the fertile soil in which your garden will grow. Lovely it will be. So bountiful others will see and admire it so, for you can not help but show the colors of your mind radiating out into the world from your soul, your love-filled heart. Plant a garden in My name. This is what you have wanted to know. This is what is your destiny to show. Grow with it. Live with it. My love becomes you, unites us as One.

God gives each one special talents. You honor God by using and developing such talents for the good of all. Do not sit on your hands. Your hands are your instruments for good, your tools for full expression.

There is no right. There is no wrong. It is all a matter of preferences. What you give your attention to is what you bring into your life. Give attention to the good and there you will find Me.

I'm getting a "Master's in Divinity" with every breath I take.

> *Put yourself in a receptive mode. You must know the Source of your being to call it forth. Give all glory and honor to God and He will bless you all the days of your life. Let go of what you know. Stop deciding beforehand, for with each breath you limit your good.*

> *Did it defeat you, or make you rise up? What does it cost you to be alive everyday? Keep a bigger vision. Don't think small about life. You are not alone. Do you feel alone?*

Thalo blue is a good color isn't it?

> *They are all good colors. It is just up to you to decide what to do with it.*

Some part of me wants to cry. Another part says, "You have no right." Yet another part says, *"Go ahead, morn your losses, then you can move on. I know this is not what you planned. Not what you thought it would be. But wait, hold on it will get better. You will see. Come see with Me. Rest your heart. Give Me your pain. I will take it all away. Wash it away with your tears."*

> *It is more than "principle," for living by principle is living according to the Laws of God. Yes, you can do this if you wish. I mean you can try, but no human to date has been able to fully live God's Law unto himself. God has seen this. He has watched our struggles. He has witnessed our fighting, our inner battles with temptation and power. God has seen it all and been displeased. Displeased and yet compassionate for He chose to offer a new deal unto man, a new promise He made. This is the New Covenant of God.*

Firstly, I will tell you how you will know if you are in fact enjoying the fruits of this gift from God. Ask yourself this, do you have joy in your heart? Inner joy is part of God's Promise. Gladdening of hearts is guaranteed. This is not a joy to be postponed for a later date but joy today as you walk the earth.

Do you have wisdom? I am not asking whether or not you are book smart, but do you have wisdom untold? "Wisdom untold" is wisdom that comes to you directly not by written word, mouth or experience. God's New Covenant promises "wisdom untold."

Do you struggle with sin? Do you struggle to keep the Commandments of God? Is it hard to love all others as God loves all? Does doing God's will in any situation come naturally or is it something hard, which you have to think about to do? The promise God foretold to biblical prophets was a life of joy, wisdom and abundance.

You have the ability to create things out of "thin air." Actually, this air is not so thin at all. It is rich with potential, with spiritual substance waiting to be called forth. Claim your good. Call it forth in My name.

I need someone to believe in me.

No, you need to believe in Yourself. Things change, appearances change, but God as "Truth" never changes. You must know this. God will never desert you. It is My plan for you to have bounty unlimited.

Driving by a restaurant and catching a whiff of an enticing aroma and I think, "Oh, it is so hard for me to eat out as all the food poisons me."

Then my heart hears, "*The biggest problems you have are the ideas that are poisoning your mind.*"

> *Things can be fun to have and enjoy but you cannot build the foundation of your happiness on anything which is of this world. I am the Rock unto which you must believe. Put your faith unto My goodness and joy shall be yours eternal. No wasted effort on My behalf.*

I didn't hear God's voice before. Yes, I did. I just didn't recognize it.

I see a woman walking with a cane, crippled she was, and I think there was a time I walked as so. Was it what I was eating?

> *It was everything you believed.*

I appreciate this truth. I appreciate what I have.

> *If you can believe in that (wireless technology) how can you not believe in the wondrous things I can do for you? You say such technology has been proven to you. You have witnessed the result and you may not know how it works to the nth degree but you understand how you can use such power. Well, I say, as the "Power that Be" behind all things, test Me!*
>
> *Test the power of your word, which I have given to you to decree. Say what you want. Declare it out loud, be firm, be consistent and watch for the result. Be on the lookout for the good you have declared to appear. All good things shall come unto you as you believe. You have experienced good in the past, but to you it appeared randomly. Actually, it all came as you believed.*
>
> *When you believe in someone, you offer them the opportunity to believe in themselves.*

I thought I needed books. I don't need books. I write the books.

> *In any given moment, I am here with truth for you, Divine truth. Don't let them put ideas into your head. Put it out of your mind. Take My love to heart. Shielded from lower vibrations, wrapped in abstract thought.*

I don't need anything to change the chemistry of my brain. God made me perfect.

> *Some saints may have lived in apparent material poverty, but not because it was more blessed or honorable to God to live as such. They had all of their needs met. Fulfilled were their dreams, their imaginings. They had not want of more, so they had no more. Living on such a high spiritual level they were wholly (holy) content with little material substance.*

> *Poverty, lack of material wealth and goods, was a choice by thought of the highest saints. When viewed from the without, it seems as an apparent rule or truth to holiness but this is not so. God is abundance and seeks for all to know His abundance and enjoy fully the fruit of their labors. What is important is to first and foremost choose God. Seek God and God's love first then all "good things" shall be added unto thee. No one is born into poverty. They are born into poverty thinking. They are taught lack, so lack they know.*

These are not thoughts to be edited. If I let my mind get involved they would be, but I do not. As much as possible I allow the words to flow uninterrupted to the paper without entering and thus being edited by my mind. I am not a "deep thinker" by any means. The deep well of wisdom from which these thoughts are drawn is not my mind, not learned or experienced.

Some people love to be in crowds, to be in the midst of a bunch of people as the sum of their energies makes them feel whole, but not I. I, the loaner, feel less whole in the midst of a crowd. I find myself alone. Solitude is where I find my sanity. Do I not love people? Oh yes, I do love them; it is just that I do not gather my strength from any other's being. The "Being" inside me is more than enough to satisfy my soul. My soul longs for closeness with this "Being." Hold me close I say. Never let me go. Let me have this dance.

SEPTEMBER 11, 2011

> *Mystic, self-knowledge, wisdom untold, look what I am giving you. Look what I gave you. These words of truth written of old, so many years, centuries upon centuries before you walked the Earth. These same truths written just as your own hand has, confirmation of this "Great Truth," confirmation of My love eternal. Wake up, rise up and rejoice. For you know My love and can share it.*
>
> *Heir transparent you are to My Kingdom, yet you see it not. Celebrate your fortune, sing glad tidings, jump with joy, for you are one of the few whom have stepped through the veil of matter and yet you still cling to the old. Is this way not so much better? Can you not still see the glory in My plans? Hold tight My dear. Put away your tears. I have great plans for you. You and I have so much to do.*

After another obvious sign too clear to be chance I hear, "*So, do you still not believe?*"

Yes, I do believe, I have faith. Total faith in Your ways! My mind is moving out of the way. It doesn't matter so much anymore. As my soul rises I think higher thoughts, all good comes to me. I just have to stay out of the way. Thank you Lord, for Your continual bessings. I praise You for Your glory.

Those whom believe in despair, despair they shall find, professed holy men or not. The glad heart honors God. The Earth's bounty is for all to claim and enjoy the fruits of. The objective of life on Earth is to recognize and enjoy the fruits of My Kingdom while as well enjoying the fruits and pleasures of the physical world I have created for you. Hiding and holing away to bar yourself from temptation is not living as I intended. You are to love yourself and others. How can you love your brother if you cannot look him in the eye?

I have seen your pain. I have seen your struggle. Try as you may to obey even the most devout of you have not found a way to live in the world and yet not be of it. I have seen this. I know this. That is why I made the new plan, gave you a new promise. I promised to comfort you and bring you wisdom, give you My strength to hold fast to My ways, to take away your sin by taking away your temptation, all while fully living with your two feet planted in your world. You have not understood what has been said, you have misinterpreted My promise. Yes, Christ was to return but not again in the form he once did.

It is you My child whom are to become Christ as well. With My gift this is possible, for the way is the same. Jesus, as Christ showed you. He told you that you could be as he and far greater works you could do. What I gave to him I offer as well to you My love, My Divine Love implanted into your hearts. You do not need to change who you are to become worthy of My love. My child I love you so much, you are already worthy. All I ask is that you ask continually for My love, for My will to become yours. You have to want Me more than life itself; more than the life you know. You have to want to know Me. Show Me this earnestness in your heart and I will give you My love and change your heart.

SEPTEMBER 12, 2011

*If you want a beautiful garden you have to plant the seeds of
beautiful plants then water them each day. You must plant
these seeds so they receive some sunshine each day. Loving
thoughts you must send your garden's way. One day, almost
to your surprise, lovely blossoms will fill your eyes. Your
creation is grand indeed, lovely in thought and action with
no weeds.*

*Next to where your garden lays is another's plot in decay,
barren as the day is long, no place for a bird to rest or sing a
song. The contrast is now plain to see. The other can expect
no bounty for they planted no seeds. Cherish My dear, each
joy you have. Continue to plant seeds of love along your
path. Some will be washed away. Some the birds will eat.
Others will soon be more blossoms at your feet.*

*Whatever you believe in becomes your destiny. Do you
believe in, put your trust in what you see or what you would
like to see? Here lies your truth. The life you shall live shall
manifest forth from your mind, from your imaginings good
or bad. Think about it and think long and hard. Do you
really want the life you say? The life you talk about? For
whatever you talk about you bring about. If what you see
does not please you, you do not have to stay there. Life is
full of options. It is your option to think what you want.
Your mind is where you plant and water the seeds of your
dreams. Good or bad, it is all a product of your mind.
Guard your mind well. Think on only those ideas you would
choose to manifest.*

*Happy thoughts grow a happy life. Sad thoughts bring more
sad stories to tell. If you do not enjoy the life you have, stop*

telling that story to yourself and others. Tear it up and toss it away. The past is the past and at this very moment you can begin again to write a new script for your life. Think big. Think grand. Think wonderful thoughts. You do not have to decide or figure out all the details of the script. Just lay out the basics. Is it going to be a happy tale? Does the star (you) triumph over all? Is there beauty, comedy, action, and a colorful cast of characters helping you along the way? Think on these things and smile. Yes, most of all smile. For if you smile, your smile will cause another to smile back giving you again cause to continue smiling. Yes, I say this, continue on smiling, for I do believe it's hard to smile and have a bad day.

Your girth does not determine your worth. Way to go. Tell it like it is. Feel good about it all. No exceptions. See through Me. Signs everywhere call your name. I have placed them not in vain. You must "feel good" about it.

Are you hopeful or hopeless? If you say hopeless as you see no hope in sight, I say to you change your perspective see with a different set of eyes. The eyes of yours that see no hope are keeping you stuck on ground level, such a low level to all your potential of being. You have within you another set of eyes with a much higher and broader perspective, your spiritual eyes, your eyes of faith. In these eyes lies your power, your power to create anew. These eyes are hopeful, full of hope, full of belief in better days to come.

Can you get out of your little busy mind for a moment and look up? Look up at the sky, the sky without limit. This is where Heaven exists in all the unseen and unlimited around you. You have the power to draw upon this limitlessness and create change in your life. Now close those beady eyes of yours and come inside. Sit quietly with Me and enjoy imagining yes, actually imagining what you would like to be. See it clearly. See you enjoying it dearly. Form this image so well in your mind that you could touch it, hold it close and near. This is the truth of you, your power, your power in knowing your power to pre-tend. This pretending is what you need to do so what you want can manifest, tend, toward you. Come back often and enjoy the view. Someday soon your little beady eyes will see it too.

Children are pure in spirit. Blessed are the pure in spirit. When one is pure in spirit, they are totally open to the ways of Spirit, the Will of God. They flow through life as though on a breeze. Nothing hinders them, nor their advancement. Through life's situations they easily bend and sway in the breezes that blow like young tender reed grasses. Their hearts have not been hardened by life. They do not find life hard but everyday appears to them as a new fresh exciting adventure.

Watch your words. Mind your words. You've been told over and over to mind your manners, speak politely and kindly and think of another's welfare as well as your own. Most actually do a pretty good job of this in public but don't necessarily carry this admission forth into their private life, their most private life, the secret place in their heart where they speak truth unto themselves. What do I mean by "truth?" I'm talking about each one's "personal truth," what is true in their own life, as they see it and as they say it.

In an argument, a calm voice speaks the loudest.

No, silence speaks the loudest.

The voice of Silence speaks to me.

Alive and well, do you know what alive and well is? You are alive and well. Have no fear, I hold you close my dear. If you do not use your body, you abuse your body.

There is a "body" of information here at your disposal. Use it well, do not easily dispose of truths you do not yet understand. Not to be taken lightly, to be contemplated at your finest hour. When is your finest hour? The hour you give to Me and sit with Me quietly. A continual conversation We shall have you and Me, so quietly.

I lay in wait watching your unrest. I do not give you life as a test but as a gift you are given, the chance to explore and to this world I have created, you to adore. All is here. All is now. Come sit with Me and I will tell you how. Such a joy it is to have you with Me. My Heart glows brighter because of you.

What do you expect? Life can never give you more than you expect. Expect great things. Expect wonderful opportunities to come your way and they will. Expect doom and gloom and doom and gloom shall be the order of your day. Whatever you say, so your life shall be that way.

God said, "Let there be..." God allowed with "His Word" wondrous things to be and so shall you have the world at your command with your word when you truly believe in the power of your own word that God has given you by your birthright. Recognize and accept your kingship. You are heir to the throne of greatness. Wake up to this power. Know it and use it to better yourself and the world you live in.

"Who put those ideas in your head?" Some might say. "No one," I would reply, these ideas are not of or from my head. My head is still yet attempting to grasp the entirety of these words, which I know as

"Absolute Truth." These words of wisdom and direction are "thought forms" that come unto my heart. This is all wisdom from such a higher and broader perspective that I in my little form could never know or conjure up. I give thanks for every such knowing.

> *Some things can seem so hard, but they don't have to be. Open up to the possibilities Spirit knows and your life will flow smoothly. Why do you always have to be somewhere? Somewhere special, you think, as if any one place is better than another. None is better, though each may be perceived differently. Move to whatever and wherever feels good then stay, sit and relax and soak up all the goodness I have for you.*

> *Now you feel it don't you, the warmth of the sun on your back? I am warming you with the rays. Consider these My arms, which I wrap around you. Feel My Love penetrate your being. This is exactly how I send you My Love, My Light, from the invisible it manifests into your being. Can you touch the sunshine? Can you catch it in the air? Can you hold it and stow it away? Can you contain it in a box? I think not. So is the Love I give you, the Love I send unto your heart. You cannot see it nor feel it until it hits you and yes we both know you have felt My Love hit you, such a powerful force It is.*

> *Look what you can do when you set your mind to it. Good for you. You can believe bigger. You can show them by your belief. It's all coming together. It's all good. Let others be as they may. Their thoughts are not your concern. They matter not to you. What matters is what you say, what you think, what you believe.*

September 14, 2011

> *Think not.*

"*Think not*" are the words I heard. I had just called my husband "an idiot." Although the statement was made in jest, I am told it is none the less important to understand that value or devalue of my words. As those words will stay with the other and myself until I release them by putting new thought forms in place. So I say, "David, you are a smart man. I love you and believe in you!"

> *You've got things to do and it's within your power to do them. See them through. Step by step instructions will be given. Trust in this.*

I've seen it proven again and again. Each has to prove it to themselves. Prove the power and knowledge we each have access to. Only this way, one can know.

> *Yes, it is okay to ask, to wonder, to test, to question. This is the path to knowledge and discovery of all you are. You may listen to the ideas of others and consider them, but first I ask you to consider your own. Take time to be open to ideas that come directly to you from the purest and highest center of your being. These ideas are yours, meant for you. Oh, they may well hold value for others, be as that may. But be assured they are "well, just, and truth messages" to you, worthy of your full consideration. Give them a try. Test them out. Take them for a "test drive" as you will. Start with the simple stuff and you will find yourself gaining trust so you can apply such knowledge, and wisdom, to the bigger picture of your life.*

Are you prompted by your intuition to pick up something, which seems quite random, as you head out the door? Go ahead and do it. Just do it. Why not? No harm done. Then wait and see, for you will, be assured you will. You will find the reason you were prompted into such action. Someone may ask for it or see it in your possession and say "Hey, that's just what I needed. I'm so glad you had it here now!"

That's the way it works when a thought comes to you. It's always in your best interest to act on it. If you don't, well you don't. You have free will of course; no one will make you or punish you. You just might find it rewarding to follow such direction. These are the simple pleasures of a life that flows naturally. Your intuition is your inner knowing which arises to your consciousness as the need presents. This inner knowing part of you, is your Higher-Self, the God part of you, which knows all and sees all.

It is not for any of us to know all, now or ever in the physical form, as we are not capable or built to know, handle or assimilate such information. But we can handle it and are meant to receive piece by piece. This information is strictly given to us on a need to know and want to know basis. If you have no need to know or believe you can not know this will be "the truth" for you. If you have a need to know and a desire to know it will be there for you to know in a most timely fashion.

So watch your words. Listen to the message you tell your "Higher Self." When you say "I can't find this or that." or "I don't know." or "I'm lost." or "I'm overwhelmed." your Higher-Self sits back and quietly watches you stumble around blindly and will not and cannot interfere. But if you change your words and thus your thoughts and open your mind to the possibility of knowing, you set your Higher-Self in action to communicate such wisdom.

"The magnetic force of the universe is at My command." Why would I say that? That's a pretty big statement, yet I will not deny it. For within these words I believe my power lies.

Use what you have. All of Mine is yours.

My Father in Heaven watches over me, both of them. As well as the omnipresent loving Spirit of God, I know that the loving spirit of my earthly father watches over me. He has communicated his presence to me through dreams, very vivid dreams and knowings. He imparts his love to me. I see not, yet know he is near. My thoughts of him draw him near. He comes to me at my calling, not even a moments notice is needed for he is not bound by space or time. Sometimes, when his energy is the strongest I will be overcome with emotion and tears. I will feel such a strong longing for his physical presence.

I am now comforted with the knowledge that at these times he is actually the closest to me. His spirit, his loving presence, is enveloping my own. The emotion I feel is love, our love intertwined as one. There is really wholeness about it, "holiness" if you will. He is communicating as best he can, as the most I have allowed him to, that he is still with me, around me and among those he loved.

> Whenever your family gathers in celebration of their love and support for each other you are to know that the ones who have been a part of this circle of love are still a part of it and are truly present in spirit. So do not lower your heads in grief or sorrow for their departure. They are not limited in "being" by their lack of physical-ness. Low and behold, it is exactly the opposite, for they are no longer bound by physical restraints and can be and are with all they love all the time. Be comforted by this Truth. It is for you to know.

> Don't just tell people what you think. Don't so broadly broadcast or impose your thoughts upon another. As you listen to another's lamentations and audible questionings, hold your tongue. Be patient in your reply for they may not really care to hear your thoughts, however wise they may be. After the time of silence, when you sense that the other has relieved himself of the thought he wished to express, you may ask "Would you like my help? Do you care to hear my

thoughts? Would you like a different perspective?" Then sit tight, continue to hold your tongue. For unless the other asks for your help, give none. For any help or wisdom words you may give which is unsolicited will be lost or pushed away by the other. He will not have ears to hear. His ego nature will be quick to defend his situation and his evaluation of it to the end, for better or worse.

These same rules are for all of the Truth, Wisdom and Knowledge given by Spirit. It's always available for the asking but unless one asks for help and listens with an open heart and head, they will not have ears to hear or eyes to see. So learn this lesson now, as the listener and the questioner. Wisdom is available and this Wisdom is a Treasure, a Golden Treasure which can only be found by the earnest seeker. Open your heart and mind to this Truth.

So you believe in "the cloud/ internet technology," but you don't yet believe in Me. You don't even believe My ways. You don't fathom My Power. You put your trust in man. You believe the words man speaks. You speak them again and see them come true. Then you say, "Well, if there ever was a God why would he let things be this way." There is so much more to it, to life than you see. But you don't even ask, you don't bother to ponder what could be. Another man tells you what is wrong and you agree, but you still don't see, see what you do, when you agree. Instead, you blame your problems on Me.

September 19, 2011

How do you judge other? How do you judge yourself? You say you don't but are you so certain? I do hear your voice. I know your thoughts. They are not always so kind. No

*judgment is needed upon your part, anyone's actually. It
is this action which brings you out of alignment with who
you are and the natural flow of life. Static is created in your
naturally healthy vibrational flow.*

*You do not need to tell anyone who someone else is or your
estimation of them. Allow each the opportunity to be who
they are. They will show up as they will and prove who they
are. When you judge another you are broadcasting your
limiting thoughts to the universe. You bring no harm upon
anyone but yourself, as each only has access to their own
vibrational flow unless you give someone else permission
by agreeing with them. The Well Being of the universe, the
Fount of all Goodness from which all are born remains
constantly and consistently within us, connecting us all by a
golden thread.*

Someone told me, "You must learn to be uncomfortable." But, I
don't agree, as that idea goes against all the intent and purpose of the
universe.

*You are here to experience contrast and move toward what
makes you feel good. You are to care for yourself and care
how you feel. It is right, it is well and good, to feel good,
think good, and be good. To be happy in the moment and
look forward to the next happy moment which is sure to
arrive. Positive expectations bring positive results. Feeling
bad and sad and unsatisfied is not a place you should wish
to stay. You do not have to and should not expect and accept
that your life is to be this way. If you brush up against
something itchy and prickly, your instinct tells you to move
away for your safety's sake. You do not have to grin and
bear it.*

Forget what you know. You are such a "know it all." See anew. See freshly.

Good job. You have done well. Look at her now, how she stands with confidence. You gave that to her. She knows she is beautiful. She knows she is special, because you have always told her so. You have shown her your beauty, by recognizing hers. Yes, you have been a beautifully wonderful mother. You lovingly guided her, held her hand and walked beside her. You have not led, not pushed or shoved, but walked the journey as a protective partner as you instinctively knew how to do. She has now released the grip of your hand and fully taken the hand of another, her husband, partner, friend for life.

There is to be no sadness here, for this is the way I have designed for life for all its blessing and bounty to be shared. None of us are meant to travel alone. This is a private as well as social journey. Together you move forward. In love she is and always has been. She was created by love. Emerged forth from love and carried to this point by love. Your bond is not broken, it will never be.

It's just like another link has been added to the chain. The chain which holds you all together, but supports its own weight, so is never a drag or a burden. A chain of joy it is. And you now have another which she has chosen to draw into this life circle you call family. Blessed be this day for it is good. It is right for it is filled with love. Yes, you are a good, good mother. Know this, she will love you all the more as she walks this new path and sees you still beside her.

Forces of nature must obey your word. We are a long ways away but are separated by nothing. Spirit connects us if we stay true to ourselves. Hope is not lost. Hope is to be found by those who look. Where are you looking?

We get "do-overs" in life. Each day is a new chance, a clean slate. The board is wiped clean every night as we retire our minds. Yes, each day is new but you still arise and begin chalking up the fresh day with your old stories of how life is. I invite you to pick up a new piece of chalk each day and don't start right in filling the fresh board with details you have decided. Instead allow the opportunity for change to occur. Let good things happen. The story of your life has not yet been written. Leave room for exciting scene changes.

SEPTEMBER 20, 2011

"I was pissed." you say. What do you expect to prove by your anger? Are you out to teach the other a lesson? How about instead make it a lesson in love, a lesson of forgiveness. I forgive you of your hurtful thoughts. Let others misdeeds go as well. Only in this way will you know Peace. Peace be with you, the Peace of Love and Forgiveness.

It's the ego that doesn't want to let go. It fears for its life. It is always in the defensive mode. Put the ego to rest. Tell it that is runs your life no more. Let God move up and take control. Put God's will, Divine Love in the driver's seat. Do not keep score. Keeping score is not how you play or win the game of life. Whoever keeps score loses, loses their life. They die to the opportunity to know Wholeness, Holiness.

Crucify the ego or you damn yourself! Don't you see this? You are not so all that that anyone is going to bow down to you. If you cannot hold your breath or bite your tongue then remove yourself from the situation. Take a walk, breath deep.

What exactly do you think three little words of "I am sorry."
will do for you, redeem your soul? Not unless they come
from your own mouth, otherwise they are lost, or you
are lost. This lesson must be learned. Will it be tonight?
Why not change your mind and change your heart? It is
hardened so. Do you know that you are ugly when you
choose to behave this way? Your beauty is hidden, spoiled by
your boastful pride. "Pride, me?" you disclaim. Yes, pride is
getting in your way. Are you too proud to unconditionally
love another?

Try this experiment for me, if you will please. Let go of the
anger and hurt, if not just for a while. Set it aside for now.
Imagine laying it on the floor and pushing it under the bed
out of sight. Now, in your mind's eye pick up a bouquet of
fragrant flowers. Hold them, admire them, smell and inhale
their sweet essence. Let their essence become yours.

So how did that go for you? Quite smoothly, I observed. You
transitioned well. You let go and allowed Love to flow to
and through you. And look what happened, the other was
able to love you in return. He had no need to act in defense
with his ego. Instead through the love, the quiet space you
softly offered, the other was able to self examine and thus
realize his ways and how such had impacted you. A sincere
apology was then offered, and again and again, which you
most lovingly accepted. Now, how could have this scenario
have played out any better? I presume you have no need or
desire to pull out the old hurts for they now lay dead under
your bed.

SEPTEMBER 21, 2011

Life's challenges are to be met head on and not avoided in
fear. Yes, head on. But first, you would be wise to examine

which head is facing them, the head of ego or faith? The head of ego is defensive, always ready for battle because ego assumes the worst. Ego comes out kicking and screaming from the get go. Whatever ego wants, ego gets and ego wants a challenge. So a challenge ego will get.

But we all have a choice, yes, always. We have a choice of how we see the world. We can see all kinds of possibilities. It is up to each of us to choose the possibilities in life that feel good to us. So, given a choice, who among us would not choose for peace and understanding among all mankind? Who wouldn't choose to have a day of ease and comfort, when all of life is met in joy and triumph? None, none truly would deny this true joy to their heart, but they do. We all do, because we don't know better. We don't understand better. We don't understand better is possible for us, not only possible but our birthright.

"How so, how come?" you say, "For I do not see life this way." It is true; you do not, for the eyes you view life from are dirty and clouded. You see only that which is before you in plain sight. But I am speaking of a higher perspective here, a vision whose possibility lies within you. Dormant as it may seem to be, it lays quietly, alert, ready to be called into action. All on command, command of your word, your word of faith, faith in good, faith in better, faith in God's Will being done among man. Yes, "Heaven on Earth." Some of you pray words as such in the Lord's Prayer, which you dutifully recite. But do you believe them, the words you say? Is this what you truly pray? For God's Kingdom to come, for God's will to be done on Earth as it is in Heaven? For this is the faith of which I speak, the faith you need to call forth each day, each moment as you live and breath.

Jesus told you to pray believing. So again I ask you, what do you believe? Do you believe the world is hard and out to get you? Do you believe the way is hard? If so you do not believe in Jesus. Oh, you might believe there was a man one day, a very good man that walked across the earth in sandals telling tales of good fortune. You may even believe He is or was God's only begotten son, but all of that is a mute point, says Jesus the Christ, if you do not believe in His ways. If you do not know and trust His ways to salvation, salvation from your earth bound ego point of view, salvation from the mud that is smeared across your face and packs your eyes. With this salvation you will again recognize your true eyes of birth, your spiritual eyes, which see and know Heaven right here on earth.

So again, we are back to the point we began with. Which head are you going to meet today with? From which eyes will you choose to view life's options? The eyes of ego, or the eyes of faith in a higher more glorious perspective? Your spiritual eyes are your "real eyes." It's time you learn to trust their vision, for it is true and perfect for you.

When I have questions, I get answers. The answers are to be found in the Love which surrounds me and moves through me, around and above.

Is this Christ or me speaking?

Christ is God in expression.

Divine Love, is it a gift?

Yes, a gift.

What is a gift?

> *A gift is something given that one previously did not have claim to. God's gift of Divine Love is a gift of the highest and most cherished substance to be ever known. It is the very essence of God gifted into one's heart and soul, the very substance that changes ones very being into that of the Divine.*

For this I give thanks. Thanks be to God.

> *You have to believe in your power for good. The power is your belief. I will show you the way. Follow Me. I will lead you home.*

Maybe it's Christ's voice.

> *It is.*

Something happened to me that changed forever who I am. I know now what it is and what a gift it is, a gift freely given by God, my source, to my soul. God's Divine Love has awakened and empowered my soul. The very essence of my being is being changed as I breathe, refined not through trial and error but through grace, the grace of God graces my being.

I am in harmony with all of nature.

> *It is up to you to recognize both the Christ in yourself and others. Another is not required to show you the "Christ" within him or act from that power center for you to respond to his inherent Christ nature. You are here to lead, to show the way to others. Let them be surprised at their own actions when they come as reactions to your "Christ Presence."*

You have heard tell of people whom others have said made them better people when they were around them. This is why it is so. Be the kind of person people naturally gravitate to for it feels so lovely to be your presence.

Stop saying that, saying that there is not a way. For if you choose to speak differently, a way will be found.

So you think some idea is too good to be true do you? Why do you continually limit the good God has available to you? When you can see and know that all good is yours at your command, you will then allow all good to come your way. Confirm with your word: "All the good of God is mine to have and hold and shine forth. I limit my good no more. For every situation, I allow the highest and best to manifest."

Don't limit your good to what you know. Rethink possible. Know you can know more and do more than you now know. Know more is possible now that you now know.

So many people discount the kind of communication that I, like others, receive and report it evil or of Satan.

They are confused. Do you feel lost or alone?

No.

Jesus said he would send "the Comforter" and he didn't mean a spread for your bed.

This I know.

What people don't know, they don't know. Many do not care to know or they would seek this truth for themselves. Others don't understand it is here to be found so they don't look for more, as they have no need or desire or belief in more. You desired more. You yearned for more. You hungered for the pieces of truth which made the puzzle whole. And as you searched, We listened. We put things in your way so you could find them, read them and hear them. And of course you prayed.

Even with out distinct words in your mouth, you prayed from your heart to know Me. You asked for My love to come into your heart and it has and will continue to fill you as you desire. Desire all things higher and they will be yours. Let the others in darkness be as they may, as your light shines so brightly, others will take notice and draw near. Only then will they be ready to hear.

What was I afraid of? I was afraid of my world collapsing and loss of control. What was "my world" that I feared losing? The world of matter and material which I had spent my whole life gathering and piled at my feet, my home, my livelihood, my way of being, safety in numbers, those numbers being money in my name. I was afraid of being alone with no one to understand and console me. I felt the world I knew slipping from my fingertips and beneath my feet. I knew nowhere to grasp. I cried out loud for help, for light to be shown. I cried. I wailed. I prayed, but not in a "religious way." I was too lost to be found, I thought. I knew not the voice of God.

But God knew my voice and heard my cries. The intent had been given. I had asked for help and guidance from the depths of my being. This is what was needed, needed on my part, to set a series of actions and events in place to awaken my spirit to its truth.

From that day on, little by little, light was shone. Here and there pieces to the puzzle I wished to solve were "highlighted" for me and put in places I could not ignore. As I found, I pondered new and curious information, ways of being never before described to me. They at once resonated with a part of me and offended another. "Could this be a truth for me?" I would ask my heart. Piece by piece, I would test the waters, first by just "dipping a toe." Some felt good and right and other ideas didn't hold so tight. But seek I did for more truth, for if this is so, what about this, and so on and so on I did go. I wished my ego farewell. No tears were shed.

About this time, a special prayer came my way. It was here to truly save the day, for as I prayed asking for "Divine Love" to fill my heart; new wonders and wisdom began to impart a light to my soul, a freedom from care. I now know I am safe, of this I am aware.

Where do you put your trust? People are scared. Fear is rampant. The very thing they have put their trust in has let them down, has proven unworthy of their faith. The "almighty dollar" is proving once again that it is not so "almighty." But even the lowly dollar bill knew its place for it proclaims the truth of where one's allegiance should first lie. "In God We Trust" is the admission on our currency. We must first bow our individual wills down and let the will of God, the will of All Good for all mankind to rise up. Seek ye first the Kingdom of God then all good things shall be added unto thee. If the dollar bill is to be trusted, then we must first put our trust in God.

Do you understand what "free will" is? You are free to live as you please. There is no force outside of you that controls your actions or your thinking. You have "free will" to think what you want and as you do such, "think what you want," what you think about manifests as your life. All this is on your own, controlling your own destiny you are. Although most have not realized their own power in their thought and word and as thus have unknowingly created situations in their lives they truly do not desire. They attracted these things to them by their thought and attention to them.

Okay, so that's the basics of "free will" and the "power of attraction" but there is another side to that coin, an even shinier and brighter side to be known. Help is available for the asking. That's right, even though we each have the power to create the lives we want all on our own, there is an abundance of help available immediately for each of our personal journeys. It's called "the God factor."

SEPTEMBER 23, 2011

I'm taking it personally when I have no business doing so.

> *You are right. I'm so glad you now see it as so. You are personally affronted by someone else's dysfunction. That is what it is; someone who on one side seems to the world so together is actually a selfish slob on the other. The way they are, has nothing to do with you. So let it go, the condemnation. Wouldn't you want the same from another?*
>
> *After all, you haven't exactly mastered perfection in this lifetime either. Have you considered the idea that each time you dwell on their dysfunction you feel a little better about yourself? That's ego for you. Pretty distorted thinking isn't it? So get your ego out of it totally and replace ego with compassion, for all the world needs more compassion, more love. Each time you send out a feeling of love, you bless yourself as well as all others. So put yourself in the right frame of mind, God mind, before you put yourself in this situation again. Try it on for size. I bet it fits well and sits well with your heart, the center, the core of your being.*

Tell me what I need to hear. Tell me the Truth.

> *You are loved.*

All day, all night, angels watching over me my Lord, all day, all night, angels watching over me.

It's just material, just a shadow of your reality. All is well.
We can see for you, when your eyes are clouded.

Thank you, I need and welcome your help, assistance and guidance.

Be patient. Be persistent in your love to all, all things, all
people.

It is scary, because all I have known as safety is slipping away. Yet I know what matters isn't matter at all, it's spiritual and my spiritual truth is grand and wonderful. On this truth I rely. I put my faith in God and His Magnificence. All glory, I give to God.

This is the way, the way you come to Me when all else fails
and is broken. You fall to your knees and I lift you up in My
arms. I hold you, love you and admire your strength, your
willingness to circumvent yourself for the larger goal of love
to and from your "True Self." This is the way of Life with
Me, Life for eternity.

Things are better than they seem. They really are. I can
see the glory of the day to come. I know what you do not.
I know what your future holds and it is glorious. Yes, your
vision is clouded, but your heart is in the right place, next to
Mine. We beat as One. You are My hope and you thought I
was yours. I have plans for you, for things We can together
do. Yes, Me and you. Oh, what We will do.

We do not desert Our own. You have awakened into a
Brotherhood of a caring Family. We are here to love and
support you as you do "the work." You are our eyes and ears.
Head to toe you can be and go, and be seen, where we may
not. Whatever you do, wherever you are, we are now fully
able to assist, as you have allowed us to enter your heart

*and consciousness. You can say what needs said, so it can
be heard. Your voice is clear and beautiful. It will ring true
and herald Truth for many. We write books together. Of one
heart and mind we are. Whatever kind of questions you ask,
are the kind of answers you get.*

I like things to be relevant.

Sure you do. We all do. It's all relative you know.

*Tell it like it is. It is wonderful. Take a moment to realize
how wonderful your life is. You have been continually
blessed. Be thankful for all you have and know you are.
You are grand beyond dimension. Stop thinking so small. It
doesn't become your stature.*

*A little bird told me today
How much
You are loved
I agreed
And sent him on his way
To come back again
Another day.*

Poetry is pretty.

And so are you.

I needed that you know.

*Yes, I know. I know your heart and mind. I carry them
with Me all the while. Watching over, guiding as you allow.
Loving you all the time, the only way angels know how.*

It's a big thing
This life you live
So much bigger
Than you know
Little by little
We are allowed
To show you more of
What and who you are
Your light is shining
As bright as a star.

Notice how you forget yourself when your mind is properly
engaged? You truly got up from your bed and walked today
didn't you? You could have stayed down and wallowed in
your pain but instead you chose to rise up and be active,
to be engaged in life. Any task that needs done is a worthy
task. Good for you. Lesson learned? Today you had an
"out of body" experience. You moved through your perfect
spiritual body and not your body of pain.

I have put beauty before you and yet you refuse to see. You
seem to prefer the muck in which you are stuck. I offer to
lighten your load and yet you continue to drag around your
old baggage. Come see with Me how glorious life can be.
Lift up your cares. You are so unaware of the Feast I have
prepared for you.

SEPTEMBER 25, 2011

The voice I hear is part of me with a much higher perspective. It came
in with me and has always spoken, yet I denied the validity of the voice
and the message. My ego drowned it out by the loudness of its own
banter. I know all is well and that the voice is the all loving God piece

of me which brings me the peace of God.

> *Enjoy life now, not later. Make your way. Find your joy.*
> *Celebrate it. Shout about it! No thing is too hard. Don't*
> *get in your way. Stay out of it, the muck you like to walk*
> *around in. Find a friend to share the journey.*

Send me a friend. Let me be a friend. Show me where to shed my light. Lead me where You need me to be.

> *I am here for you. As you say, it is. It is your choice to be*
> *here. Wherever you are, you arrived by choice. Hard to*
> *hear, we know. Hard to understand when you may not*
> *like where you are. But wherever you are, you are there by*
> *choice because of the decisions you have made in the past,*
> *because of the thoughts you have decided to think, and*
> *action you have chosen to do.*

> *There is no force beyond you making you move in any*
> *direction. You have a manual transmission, meaning you*
> *manually, by your mankind power, move through the world.*
> *You are not on auto-pilot, it's up to you to steer. Yes, God*
> *is here. Good is everywhere to be found, but not imposed*
> *upon you. Yes, angels watch over, but they are only allowed*
> *to watch, not interfere. Oh but if you ask, that's another*
> *story. If you ask for help believing, you will find the answers*
> *clearly before you.*

> *By the grace of God, man can know God, grace given freely*
> *by God to hearts, repentant and willing. Willing to put*
> *down their own will and be filled with a deep abiding desire*
> *to only know God's will. That gift of grace is the bestowal*
> *of the essence of the Divine, in truth - Divine Love. This*
> *"Divine Love" is the "Love of God," the love of God for all*

equally. A love unlike any love man has known. It is a special gift of grace. This is the New Covenant. This is the gift of the Holy Spirit, the true grace of God which can be so known to man that man is transformed into the Divine.

I have received a gift. I am continually receiving the gift of Spirit, the true gift of Spirit, God's Divine Love, the love that transforms. I am changed. I am different, so very different. Maybe not in physical appearance to any other, but in my heart I am new. Born again, yes, that phrase fits, but not the contemporary understanding of that phrase, the original meaning. The one Jesus the Christ spoke about when he referred to one not born of a woman but of Spirit. Yes, I am of a family of Spirit. My spirit has been raised, ascended and yet I walk the earth for I am not done. I am a work in progress.

The work is two fold. There is the work of the receiving of the "spiritual gifts" and my soul's refinement and there is the work I am to do while present here in the flesh. I am coming to know that relatively few have been received such gifts, because either they do not understand what it is, or that it exists, or how to ask and receive or that this "grace" is available in this life, not reserved for the hereafter.

I now complete approximately two notebooks a month with such spiritual wisdom coming from what looks like "thin air." I had never before considered myself a writer, when I did journal it was more of a laundry list of things I desired to accomplish or a place to vent my frustrations over life. So besides the amassed quantity and quality of these words, I didn't used to have much to say that was meaningful or insightful. Now, I am so prompted to keep pen in hand and notebook nearby that I carry such from room to room throughout the day and night. As I write now, I am speaking through my mind, in my own words, not quite as eloquently as I write when duly inspired by Spirit. Because then the words and ideas are flowing from a Source other than my own being, yet it feels like a natural part of me.

My interests have changed. My attitude has changed. My wisdom has increased. My confidence has increased.

To most the world is "black and white" with just a few shades of grey. It is, what it is. No more. No less. Things come. Things go. Nothing is certain. Thus is the world of those whose lives and eyes are centered on the material. They do not understand the World of God, the World of Good, the "Kingdom of God" which is abundant, eternal, everlasting, unchanging, constant, steadfast, dependable and worthy of our trust. They do not know Peace for their lives and are subject to pressures, images and ideas around them. They do not draw their strength and vision from their Inner Sanctuary, their God source.

Let you be the one. Let you be the one to show the way to peace, to abundant life and joy. Let Me so fill you with My love that they cannot help but look and take notice. I will give you all you need. Trust in Me, in God, in the peace/ piece of God within you. Claim your heritage. Claim the Kingdom I am building inside you. Want more, want more of Me, for I am the "substance" which will sustain you and glorify your life.

You must move on from these old ideas and create anew. I have shown you a way. I have given you an idea, a wonderful idea. Take it and run with it. Run to the bank with it. Build a wonderful empire in My Name. Who is this that does so? They will ask. From where does her power come? And you will say, you will speak, "the Truth" in My Name.

I am impressed with your calmness. It shows you believe in more. More than you see manifested now. Yes, this is good, very good. Now, you need to start clearly envisioning what is possible for your life, the one without strife. The one I have promised you. You are infinite. The world is so full of possibilities for you. Not one word, idea or dream can or ever will describe you.

I am unlimited in my power and resources. I am all I need to be. I am the manifestation of God in this world.

September 26, 2011

You are not lost, you are found, for you have found the Life Eternal, the Golden Key, for which all seek. You have found. Now, you must manifest a Wonderful Life in full view. You will recognize Me and credit Me for all, for you perceive My glory and Power fully. My Force is with you. What else is there to want?

People are so used to noise that they seem to be uncomfortable with the Silence, the stillness that is the undercurrent of all that is. As people gather, voices jumble together, one upon another, into a loud rumble. The energy of it may seem to be exhilarating. But in actuality it is depleting for it is stealing from them the opportunity to know their Core, the Pure Essence of their being.

Direct from Source! No middleman. The Good Stuff. The Truth you need to know is here for you now. Know this, it is written upon your heart. Who needs to believe? No one, for no one else matters in this but you and Me and you know Me. Fresh, relevant material. Live action!

As I remember John Carlson, author of the book series, "Don't sweat the small stuff and its all small stuff" this comes to me:

> *John Carlson was a master in disguise of a man. He told*
> *the truth, the truth he got from Me. This was his mission,*
> *the message. On this, We had agreed. He did his work quite*
> *splendidly. You got the message, as did many others. He was*
> *done and I called him home. Not early, on time, on his time.*
> *He is now resting comfortably with Me. He is one of us here,*
> *available still to guide and direct, to show the Light.*

If I don't ask for it, I will not receive it. This is the way the Universe works. I am a celestial angel. I soar above. Nothing matters to me. as I see. I find, what I will. God's Will be done through me.

> *Messages left behind for the finding. Find out who you are.*
> *Don't let your thoughts betray you.*

> *Just love them, send them love. There is no need to give*
> *another your sympathy for their situation. For when you*
> *sympathize with another you are thinking of their situation*
> *and thus drawing the like to you. So do not feel bad for any*
> *other. The best you can do for all, in any situation, is to send*
> *your love. Forecast out blessings. Blessings are thoughts filled*
> *with Love. This way you love another while loving yourself.*
> *Small talk is mostly just that, talk which keeps you small.*
> *This is all practice. Do not worry over these lessons that*
> *come. They are here for you to learn from. Trust My voice*
> *and I will lead you onwards. Be all that you can be through*
> *Me.*

I hear Your voice inside me, calling me home. Who will believe in me?

> *Those who know My voice.*

I am not channeling. The word of God is upon my heart.

> *You have all you need. Stop looking to another. My Word is written within you. Ask and you shall receive. No Voice speaks clearer. Surrender to Me. Do not think what is next. It shall be shown for what it is. Listen to Me. Lest you forget, true wisdom comes only from Source.*

> *Don't be afraid to be alone with yourself. I am here. Listen to Me as I speak clearly your name. Must you always seek to drown Me out? I am here. Hear Me now. I give you rest. Rest in Me, not in what you think. You are more than that. Oh, so much more you are. Listen to Me, listen up My dear. Hear Me clear. My words ring true like a bell. Yes, clear as a bell I speak unto you. Give Me room. Move over. Get out of your way, I say. I speak peace and love unto your heart.*

I want to be taken care of.

> *You are cared for, but it is still you who lives and breaths in the body and must move your mind and limbs forward one step at a time. It is the ideas you have put in your head that have poisoned your system. Empty yourself of all of it. Let me fill you with My truth and wisdom. Let me fulfill you with My love. Purify your mind. Ask for more of My love. I love to share My divine essence with My beloveds!*
> *Clear the house. Spring forward, Dust the cobwebs from your mind. Let My light shine in. Don't let your well being be at the mercy of any others condition, "any" others. Be not swayed. It serves you not.*

I have been seeking to know God, the truth of God in my heart. Now, I hear His voice. The voice of Love speaks unto my heart. I am so excited to witness "the Life," the True Life of God. I will witness by my love. I will witness by my life. Thank you, God for giving me a glorious life to shine forth. I know you have great things planned for me. I see this clearly. Your voice will guide me forward. As I know your voice; I will know what to do for you are the power and the glory.

So be it.

I am meant to have all of God's bounty. Solomon was a rich man. How do I know that? Because it was given to me.

Listen to My voice and obey My command.

I will obey Your Word, for I know Your Word is truth spoken unto my heart for my own good and the good of all mankind.

> *Against all odds; it has to be this way so that they may see My Favor with you as you choose My will and My love. You will not suffer if you trust My voice. I will lead you on and forward. I need you to do My work. I will glorify your life so your light shines so very bright. You have My word. This is My covenant with you. Someday you will speak and show these words and they will know and then know Me.*

September 27, 2011

This is so much. The old part of me says how can I? But the new part, which lives in You, understands You make all things possible through faith. I have faith in You and Your word. I will keep record of Your word for I know the path has to be shown. I want my journey of faith known.

> *Life is not an emergency. Don't rush through it. Time will tell the truth. There is a way. One fine day. You are right.*

All is well. Everyone has access to God within and the portal is not through the mind. God is not an intellectual property. Feel good about it. Feel God about it. Harm no one, in the best interest of all. Wait patiently and you will be justly rewarded.

Spirit allows me to live fully.

Say what you want. Get out of your mind. Your mind keeps your small. These aren't prayers. These are answers to prayers.

This is what it is like. It appears everything is crashing down. All that I put my trust in, in the material world, was built on sand and the tide, which was in, has gone out. Thank God that I know God and put my faith in Him. I stand steadfast in my faith for Good, God, to manifest good in and through my life. I am ready to hear good news, lots of it, lots of it, lots of it. Let the "Good News" begin.

"America" is a spoiled nation. You maybe My Princess, but you are not "too good" for anything. No one is and those that think they are just that, thinkers, stinker thinkers. Body, mind and soul I have given you to live wholly as one unified throughout. As inside, as without. Be true to Me, your "Divine Essence."

I hear things and know things that my mind cannot yet wrap around.

The rules are written upon your heart. You do not need to "look it up," you just need to "look up." God does not test your faith. Ego does and that is the Truth, Truth, Truth, Truth, with a capital "T."

Listen to something happy. Do something happy. Put yourself in a happy place.

I know I am a very old soul. I wonder who I was, who I have been?

It doesn't really matter does it? You are to concentrate on your work here and now.

But if I did I could draw upon that energy and wisdom.

You can now. All that was still is, within you. You do not need to get sidetracked by the details of your history. Just know all of the wisdom you have accumulated throughout is yours for the asking and believing. The information you are getting is true and correct.

Thank you for the confirmation.

Thank you for listening. Those that breed fear, live in fear and squalor. My peace becomes you. Think peace. Think prosperity.

My new name is "Joy Be Me."

See where you are. You have really come so far. Way to go. As you know, you will find more. Stop going to "the negative" when an idea comes. You always analyze it to death. Stop it. Just be with it and move on.
You gotta move your parts. I am the part of you which inspires your desire. Know what is true. All I have, is all you are. Manifest Me to all. A tall order? Yes, very much so, but not too high. No mountain is too high.

The time of Jesus that is lost, or not recorded in the Bible, was His time of growth, His time of Self/God realization. To the world He seemed not one to take much notice of, for He was not a physical manifester. He was not intent on being caught up in the world. His focus, His desire was finding and manifesting Me perfectly. Thus so, He was lost to the world.

Find your voice.

Who will listen?

The ones who have need to hear. All I am, is All you are. Come find Me in you. This is what you are to do.

There are so many parts to life, so many stages, so many lives within lives. This is how it is. You have lost nothing. You have lived every minute very well, as you knew. You have been full of life. You gave life. You formed lives. Now is a new time, a time of adjustment.

This is life, always changing, always moving forward. What you have done is not lost. It is all still with you, still a part of you. Now you have time for reflection and in your reflection you find Me. Continue to know all is well. I love you so.

All this other world is going on and I am not a part of it.

Join in. You must feel good, to feel God. Excuses be gone! It doesn't matter so much where you have been it is where you are going. Look ahead, you cannot go forward with your attention turned behind you. The past is past. It does not exist. All you have is now. All you ever had is now. There was a yesterday, lots of yesterdays, but they are only memories of what was once today. Hold today close. Honor today, for today will become a yesterday soon enough.

OCTOBER 2011

Then he was filled with the joy of the Holy Spirit
and said, "I praise you, O Father, Lord of heaven and earth,
for hiding these things from the intellectuals
and worldly wise and for revealing them
to those who are as trusting as little children.

LUKE 10:21 NLT

OCTOBER 1, 2011

*Everything passes away, everything but your soul for your
soul is the embodiment of the part of you that is spirit. Yes,
your spirit stays, stays intact. It will always exist. Yet, your
spirit will not always exist exactly the same for there is such
a thing we shall now term "soulvolution," the evolution, if
you will, of your soul. This is truly the name of the game,
if life was at all ever a game. Your soul isn't anywhere to
"stand still" whether embodied or as a free spirit. Your
soul's mission is to evolve or rise up to Glory, to the glory of
God, to the Highest Heavens, to the Brightest of all Lights,
Ultimate Enlightenment.*

*Don't waste your journey by not understanding this now,
for this is the gift of humanhood, your chance for rapid soul
advancement. It's like a blink of an eye this life you know,*

compared to eternity. And the lessons you are given here offer opportunity to advance your soul standing so much quicker and easier than any later efforts. So you see just because this body you know so well dies, your soul's work is not done. Oh it can be if you wish, but believe me you will not wish, for every soul knows where its true home is and when it returns it looks again to the bright light and yearns to go there. All do. All want to "touch the face of God." All want to feel and know the most glorious feeling and knowing of peace and love. And with this earnest and steadfast desire a soul concentrates, mediates, on this wondrous healing, uplifting love of God. And as a soul asks God for the infilling of such Divine Love, the soul receives and is lifted to a higher state of wholeness or holiness.

Such is as well so for all souls, souls as free spirits and souls embodied in the flesh. They each evolve at their own rate, their own desire or will. Will to make their own will God's will. You call this soulvolution process "enlightenment" on earth. Many, many, more are "seeing the Light" and thus being the Light. So again, all "things" pass away. Your soul is not a "thing" it is eternal for it is spirit, part of the totality of Spirit. This is your work, your soul job and sole job on earth, to wake up, see the light and desire more of the "God stuff," Divine Love. Ask and ye shall receive My glory.

Everything you have created before this time has been in the old energy. You created such as thus, the best you could with the best you knew. But now you know better, and thus you will do better. It has to be this way. It can be no other. Do not be dismayed by what was, for it no longer is. By the power of your light, the power of what was has vanished. You are to move forwards from this day forward in the light, from the light to the light. You are no longer a match bearer you are a torch bearer. Run with it!

I speak to the energy you are. You understand as such for your energy frequency has risen more and more. Our vibrational energies match. Come to the light and dance within it. Find your power. Find your voice. It is here for you now.

OCTOBER 2, 2011

Today is the day! The day I awoke with sunshine in my heart! The peace and love of God fills me to my core. I am filled with the peace and lof God. I give thanks. I praise You for your glory. May my every breath be an act of peace upon this world. Amen, so be it, Truth lives in me.

It's all fine. Bless this day.

OCTOBER 3, 2011

Good morning wonderful guides. How does the world look today from your perspective?

Wonderful, just wonderful.

In light of this perspective, this view you have, I will move forward today with a smile on my face.

We love to see you smile. What a much nicer way for you to start your day asking us for today's forecast rather than relying on weather predictions or the news channel. We are your Highest Good and want so to be brought forth into the light. By your asking what the will of your Higher Intent is, you shall so follow. Wonderful, just wonderful My child!

We have no reason to lie to you. Even if we did, we couldn't for as we are Truth, we speak Truth. The lie that is spoken is the words you say to yourself, the stories you tell of a lost and broken woman. This is not your Truth and in your Highest of Hearts you know it. It is our job, our privilege to help you show it.

It is not right to "trade" with those who have different ideals from your own. Notice I say "ideals" not beliefs for they are different. An ideal is what one wants to be or manifest as a highest good. A belief is what one carries in their mind that limits their consciousness of the very ideals they can dream or attain. When you trade with someone of a lower ideal you are in truth lowering your own. Be conscious of how and where you spend your dollar.

Divine perception: Mother's intuition is human love at its finest. Wherever you are, be a positive influence. Take your time to see the possibilities of life before you jump ahead.

The coolest thing just happened. A Praying Mantis blessed me with his presence. I was drawn to his energy and he to mine. I felt like Saint Francis with whom the birds and beasts were drawn to his presence. I just learned that Praying Mantis means religious prophet. (The same Praying Mantis and I were to meet again two more times within the next few weeks.)

OCTOBER 4, 2011

You asked for it, My Love, Peace within, understanding, all of it. So why do you still question Its very presence? Did I not say, "Ask and it shall be given?" It is time for you to believe that I Live within you. The Master has come home to your heart. Welcome Me with open arms. I wrap Mine around yours and hold you close.

*You can listen to different things and when you have
questions I will answer them. Judge not, lest thee be judged.
Do not take it personally, for it is not at all personal. None
of it is. Even though to most of you others actions appear so.
Look at them differently. See them as about them, not about
you. It is a much clearer perspective.*

*Don't get discouraged by what any other is doing. If they are
successful by any means at something you want to do, so be
it. Let it be an inspiration, not a downer. For whatever you
offer will be different, for it is from you, uniquely yours.*

*Think how excited you become when another tells you good
news and my, oh my, how your heart sings when another
sings your praises and delights in what you do or what
you have done. You can and should as well do the same
for yourself continually. For this is your truth, you are a
wonderful, wondrous being. You are, it's true! You know by
now that I speak none other than Absolute Truth. So repeat
after Me will you? I am a wonderful, wondrous being. I
am a child of God. I am beautiful. I am powerful. I am
insightful and I am so loving and loveable.*

*You are too attached. Notice how much easier it is for you
to do "the dirty work" of another and yet you falter and
stammer about when it is time to do your own. It is because
you are too attached to the outcome. You consider each
thing you need to do as such a personal reflection. Since you
do and to help you, I have a suggestion. Think of the things
you need to do as someone else's chores, like you are doing
them to help a friend. Just get them done and be a friend to
yourself. Your world is so dependent on physical findings.*

*I love the way Spirit manifests through you! I'm glad
you can appreciate the beauty. Beauty is in the eye of the
beholder. Such is the same with all things spiritual. No one
can fully express or convey to another the beauty of their
own spiritual truths or findings. It is up to each to seek to
know and see through their own spiritual eyes.*

*Writers, poets, composers and artists create anew, ahead of
the consciousness of the masses. Driven by a Force within,
and yet beyond their own understanding, to manifest
what has never been. Thus so, not necessarily welcomed or
accepted by mass consciousness for it is different, not the
norm. It is eyed suspiciously and not validated.*

*Family gathering. Choose to walk in the Light of the Core.
Hand held through life. I know better. Stand in your power.
Step into your power. Don't think like a human. Go to the
Source. Communicate potentials, synchronicity.*

*You need a name for everything, as if a name validates your
experience. You like roads you know, all humans do, for you
know what lays ahead. And there is a dependable certainty
to your experience. Come find certainty in Me. Believe in
Yourself, your Highest and Best Self, the One who writes
these words upon this paper. For I, as you, are here for you.*

*When you perceive intuitively what someone else wants and
needs you are listening to their spirit, which is broadcast on
the "spiritual channel" we all contribute to and draw from.
The more "tuned in" you are to the higher frequencies the
more you will receive. When you offer your life in service,
as you have, you will receive messages, knowings and
communication instructing you in such ways. You have to
use your best vision to dream the impossible dream. You
don't have to see the way. The way will be made.*

OCTOBER 5, 2011

> *Do you listen to yourself? Can you hear the sound of your*
> *own voice in your head? It is one of doubt and worry. Yes,*
> *this is what I hear from you. You cannot hide from Me*
> *for I see through you. But I also see so very far above and*
> *beyond you. I see very clearly opportunity with your name*
> *on it. Will this opportunity come knocking on your door?*
> *Maybe, perhaps, or just maybe it's you who needs to knock*
> *on opportunities door. Get your goods together, whatever*
> *they may be. Gather your talents, polish them up and start*
> *knocking on doors. Surely, I say to you, if you keep knocking,*
> *opportunity will open its door very wide and say, "Come in!"*
>
> *Service with a smile, this is what we all like. You have said*
> *you want to be of service, so how about a smile. Yes, serve Me*
> *with a smile.*

So do animals and insects have access to Universal Mind as their
instincts?

> *Yes, but only on their level of consciousness to understand*
> *what they need to understand. Much the way humans can*
> *but their spirit/souls are different.*
>
> *The more you experience, the more questions you will*
> *have and the more answers that will come. Move ahead in*
> *confidence. You know everything, everything can be known*
> *to you. You just have to ask the right questions and listen*
> *carefully. Nothing is hidden. All will be revealed as you ask.*
> *Ask as you will and you will receive.*

Thanks for the Love. It is the best gift of all. For if you do not have Love,
what do you have? People fed me fear and I gulped it whole without
even chewing on it.

If you have Love, you have everything! There is no need to fill. Do you feel anything is possible? There are answers everywhere but you have to open up your heart, to your own True Self, your Best Self. You do not have to "go places" to look for it, but experiences can show you.

OCTOBER 6, 2011

Past life and past lives are all the same as far as what they mean to you. For it is not in the reliving that you gain strength and insight, it is in the lessons learned. You have access to all the lessons you have learned within the core, your soul. Go within and ask what you need to know. The answers are there for you. Put your best foot forward and walk with Me. Just say there will be, and there will be.

It's hard to know.

Only if you say it is. Remove yourself from the power of all negative influence. Don't make life harder than it is.

As long as I am in the creative flow, I am happy.

When you "fall from grace," you fall from the flow. You step out of it not believing it is rightfully yours, your natural way of being.

I can do anything.

Of course you can! You have to ask for help in order to receive. You do not have to wait for Heaven. You just have to knock and ask Heaven into your life.

When creating something new and perfecting your idea, lots of experimentation is necessary. So thus you can understand, why one way works better than another. Each time you try is a trial. Consider it as a test of ways. Don't make it trying on yourself. The possibilities are endless. It is only you that stops trying or even imagining better.

So Steve Jobs, of Apple Computer fame and fortune, has passed on as of yesterday. Does this mean we now all have access to the creative intellect he had or the mind that was his?

You always have and always will, for although Mr. Jobs did not believe in Me, I believed in him and worked through him. He is home now and fondly remembers from whence he came.

People have their reasons, reasons why something does or doesn't work. It's all a bunch of talk, hot air, I tell you. Don't let anyone else's reasoning hold you back from pursuing any dream you have. If you don't start, you will never be able to do it. Whatever Betty Lou can do, so can you! Be active now and later. Keep active in the now and now will always be now, not later or too late. Plant these seeds of greatness. Adopt a new youth now. Change your mind about it. Get up and out of your way, I say.

Listen to your heart, a very good place to start. Your heart is full of Love, Love for you, Love to give and share. Give this Love to yourself. Be good to yourself. Step out of what was into what is. You are prime. You are in your prime. Your prime is now, in the now, not past, not later. Now is the time of opportunity. Today is ripe for the picking. Pick it up and run with it. Show yourself what you can do. When are you going to decide you are somebody?

It is amazing how even those who profess to know and love God are taken back, offended, and full of unbelief when another professes to have heard the voice of God and felt His presence. Isn't this what we all truly desire? Why is there such fear, distrust and scorn in these matters?

The supernatural is not that which is "unnatural." It is actually the supra natural, that which is supremely natural. To eyes that have not seen, nor heart felt, the idea of and thus the ideas are feared. Fear builds walls and hate pushing away and seeking to trample down the unknown, thus feared, ideas and the ones who have brought the ideas to light, manifested. But man cannot kill God. He can attempt to suppress His word by condemning or even crucifying the messenger. But the light of God shines on and others will come and hear and again proclaim Truth.

"Holy Communion" is not about bread and wine, nor the physical consumption of such matter. It is a mystical union of one's soul with My loving and welcoming heart. This communion is My grace filling you, the feeling of warmth, love and compassion infilling your own heart and soul. Holy Communion means being one with Me, recognizing our complete and everlasting connection, which has always been. And welcoming Me and My Divine Love into your life and desiring to follow my Will in your life by laying your own life aside, your own ego, selfish desires. As you desire to know Me, I will fill you more and more with special graces, the power of My Divine Love.

This Love is a transforming love. "The Love of God" is not one's love for God but God's love as a gift to and for mankind, given as special dispensations to the faithful, filling the desiree with more desire for more Divine Love and thus more faith. All this changes and transforms one's very being into one of wholeness, abet holiness. Thus God's will flows from one's being as the most natural thoughts and actions. This is My promise. This is the New Covenant I have given to you which can only be given by Me, God, not man or man's word.

The man that doubts these words does not know Me. If he truly seeks he will find. Why would one not want to find and know Me, the Truth of all? If he believes so in his own ways and will, he will follow them and continue to "wander in the desert." But I am the "Fountain of Life." My love is the "Living Water." I offer My love, compassion and mercy to all. I will not hold back these gifts from any who so truly desires. Come to Me and I will fill you so. Come to Me as you are, and I will wash your heart clean. But I will not rush against your will. I gave you your own free will and can never take this away.

We are connected now. You are a part of Me, all is. But not all recognize. They see separation and thus live as so, fighting, defending and blaming, living in fear. I offer you and all a Life without fear, a life full of faith. Why and how so full of faith? Because when you truly come to know Me, I become you. My love so infills your being there is room for no else. My will prevails, as you have desired to live through Me. This is so and just a "mustard seed" of your faith will prove it so.

But whoa to you unbelievers, I pity you and My heart bleeds for you to listen to those who speak Truth. Do not be afraid of the messages. Do you not hear how they are so filled with My love? This love is the fountain you have all been searching for. Come to Me and your thirst shall be quenched. Do not fear the light of God.

Holiness is wonderful. Be filled with wonder. Ask, question and you shall know. My Word is Perfect, spoken unto your heart, written with your hand. Let all eyes see and desire to hear and know for themselves this Truth of which I Speak. All are to know Me personally, for I am a personal God. I am All That Is, truly Is, All which is Good. Come as little children unto Me.

The mind of the learned thinks it knows, thus does not truly seek. Or if thus seeks, it is only in an intellectual way, through the reasoning mind, by discerning the words of others written or oral. Yet man can never know God through the words of any other. Even through the belief in any words of any other. The words are only given to proclaim that indeed the Truth can be found within each one's own heart. Each is to be an individual seeker for to know God is to know His word as it is written upon one's own heart. This is the message of today. Today is the now of forever.

The voice of doubt asks, "Did you read this somewhere?" Yeah, I read it after I wrote it! I did not contemplate these questions and answers with my intellect. Contemplation suggests a long time involved process. These words of Truth and Wisdom are given in immediate response to my inner questions barely formed in my mind. The answers are received as my mind and heart is open.

All blessings flow, which means all blessings are in the Flow.

October 9, 2011

Do not hold back. Do not impede the flow of Life within your own. People never fall from grace. They fall from their acknowledgement of grace.

All through the ages mankind has understood that to know God fully there was to be some kind of sacrifice on man's part. Ages ago man's consciousness understood that to be a worthy sacrifice it was to be an animal, symbolically giving to God from what they had. Others have interpreted the necessary sacrifice to be more personal and understanding themselves in merely a physical sense they have sought to honor God by sacrificing their physical senses and all associated with physical pleasure, even going so far as to bring physical harm unto their own being as their offering to God. The truly enlightened individual understands that it is "the self" that is required to be sacrificed not just tamed, and this self is one's own ego or personal will. Sacrifice means to make holy.

Prayer does not change God's Mind of how to treat you. Prayer changes your mind of how you accept the Love of God, Divine Love, which is the true and complete Essence of God within and around you. The totality of My love is coming into your awareness. Thank God, you are waking up!

As I am given to write, record, the wisdom I am given, I find my own self being surprised as how a statement may begin or even a sentence finish. My mind watches and says "Hold on there, this seems odd. How can this be? This statement seems so contrary to how I understood it." But I do not allow the voice of my mind to interfere. I say, "Shh – hush little mind. Let's listen together to this Wisdom of God and allow it to flow forth uninterrupted and unedited by any other." And then what happens amazes me, as I see the idea that at first seemed disconnected or irrelevant come together in a perfect light.

With this understanding I see how any of man's attempts to edit or limit the Word of God as it flows forth is a hindrance to the complete understanding of the simplicity of God's Will and how we can become One with such Graceful Flow of Life.

OCTOBER 10, 2011

My mind used to be filled with pain and fear. Now it is filled with Love and Comfort.

> *See how far you have come. It is truly a delight. I delight in you. Delight in Me. Delight in Me in you. Oh yes, this is the way it is and shall be. Walk with Me.*

It was a whole new concept, the idea that I should fix me not everyone else. Talk about a hard pill to swallow.

> *But swallow you did, not all at once for sure. You broke it up into little pieces and nibbled on it from time to time. Bitter booger wasn't it? But see how sweet life tastes now? How you can enjoy the company of, actually delight in the company, of those who you had determined to fixeven if it killed you, and in fact it did.*

My first decision was that I was going to learn mind control. I jokingly said that, knowing all the while that it was my own mind I wished to tame. As I explored and researched ways of doing this, new information continually came to light, very shocking and unsettling information which I didn't just take as a truth and swallow whole. Again, I picked over each bone and investigated and tested the teachings.

> *Yes, you did. We were so proud of you. This is how it is supposed to be. For when you did accept each concept new to you blind belief was not needed, as you knew their truth by your own testing and proving.*

After having spent so many days of so many years in continual physical pain and limitation I was deeply offended to hear it said that it was of my own creation. That really pissed me off. It's surprising now that I didn't just slam that book shut and kick it down the stairs.

You were so curious. You were so wanting and desiring better for your life that you closed no door to possibility. This is what is needed by all, an open mind. It is the mind that is "made up" that has no room to grow.

The thing that kept bugging me about the whole "Law of Attraction" thing was that the ideas that had until that point formed the foundation of my ideas of life, my understanding of what was and shall be, were rocked, rocked back and forth. The ground beneath my feet no longer felt firm. If this was so, the Law of Attraction and all the tricks and tweaks to life as presented in the movie *The Secret*, what was true of God and Jesus as I knew? How did all that fit in? I was not so easily swayed to believe that someone could replace the word "God" with "the Universe" or "Spirit" in a sentence and just move on.

It's also true that prayer had lost its power and magic over me. I had continually turned to "the Church" for answers and comfort and left at a loss for all. My needs were not met. My answers were not coming. But God, or the idea I had always held of God, had a hold on me and said, *"Keep looking, seek and ye shall find."*

One very important thing, actually I know it was the most important thing I had ever found, proclaimed and received, is a Divine Love prayer titled, *The Prayer Perfect*. I found it on the internet, happened upon as it seemed, while on this Truth quest. The person that posted it challenged the reader to pray the prayer twice daily for fifteen minutes and that whoever did so would never experience life again the same. There would be a wondrous, internal and permanent change.[1]

So, as is always my way, I didn't follow this prayer outline to the word nor even the letter. Just as I can't seem to follow a recipe as written, I cannot pray someone else's prayer. So, I created my own inspired by the prayer given. Mine was simpler and flowed gracefully from my lips. Most importantly, I could remember it and creatively embellish it with flourishing concepts as I prayed and desired in prayer.

Divine Love fill me
Divine Love flow through me
Divine Love be me.

That's pretty much the gist of it. So I did it. Every time I remembered about it I stopped and said it. I wasn't even sure what "Divine Love" was. It didn't really feel like a prayer or sound like one, it was almost like an incantation or a spell.

I remember shortly there after things changing for me. More and more my actions, my seemingly thoughtless actions, surprised me. By "thoughtless," I don't mean not considerate of others. I mean I didn't pre-think my actions. And they were so amazingly thoughtful of others it was if I knew beyond my own mind how to be of the right help at the right time. I would continually say and do the right thing. *"Hold on a minute,"* I heard a voice inside me say, *"you are surprised at your actions but haven't you just been praying for God's Love to flow through you and become you?"* Was I? Did I? Is that what Divine Love was? I needed to know, for I had never heard it spoken of that way. Divine Love, what was it really? What was happening to me? Had any other experienced such and written about it?

There was something else going on, something that I haven't even dared to record until now in my journals. I was being physically affected. I felt a deep burning, a warmth in my heart region, a fire burning in my soul. Who knew of this? Who spoke of this? I had to know. And then there were the tremors, the convulsions so to speak. As I would pray the prayer for the infilling of this Love, my whole body would shake with ecstasy. While lying on the bed stretched out in total ease, my body would contort and spasm, briefly raising my entire torso off the bed. They were not painful but instead almost orgasmic, addictive. And yet as well annoying as it seemed it became that when ever my mind was at rest, my body would be propelled to move as such. Again, I told no one. Who would believe? And if they did and so did witness they would either send me off for an MRI or away to a convent for some kind of anti-demonic ritual.

But all along I knew in my heart of hearts that all I was experiencing was good, from God, for my own good. Each muscular spasm I experienced seemed to break loose a bit of the tension which has for so many years strung together the fibers of my being. But what was this? Was this the gift of the Holy Spirit? Was this an actual physical "down loading" of a physical substance from God into the very fibrous core of my being? I believe so now.

Then of course there are the writings, the writings upon writings, that fill journal upon journal. To date I average filling two journals a month with amazing wisdom, thoughts and teachings that pour forth so generously and easily from the fount of my most Inner and Highest Being-ness. At least that is my current comprehension of this source. I think of it as my God connection. I call it The Wisdom Channel when my family questions from where I get my facts when I answer a posed question with the confidence of one who speaks with authority. I do speak and write with confidence that I am speaking and writing the Truth, for I have full faith in this source, which I believe is "The Source," the one and only True Source of all.

I didn't always know so. No, not at all. It's almost like I was tricked into this writing. Not in any deceitful way, but if someone had clearly told me from the beginning that I was to listen to and record the promptings of an inner voice, well I would have been so much more than skeptical. I would have been so freaked out with every random thought that I would have probably admitted my own self to the "funny farm." But thank God, Yes, thank you God, for not handling it that way, for my trust was gained by a much softer and gentler approach. I signed myself up for what I felt was almost a game.

Words and phrases started coming to me as inspirations that I thought sounded like wonderful names for paintings. In the few years before, the names of my paintings had evolved from a statement of referencing time, place and subject to more esoteric concepts. Like *Enlightenment* and *Look at the Bright Side* and *The Sky is no Limit*. Now, I also see that the works themselves had emerged from within my own being, not specifically referencing a particular time, place or subject. When it came time to name a painting, I would just stand in front of it and wait for one of these ideas to pop in my head. I never second-guessed the idea, for I was always humored and delighted by each original idea presented. Besides, as I was such a prolific painter, I was always so thankful to have a painting title come to me, so it was never a chore.

Anyway, one day I was inspired to write down words and phrases that were coming to me which sounded like excellent painting titles. I began writing each phrase down like a list as it came to me. Then I would click my pen closed, lay it down and turn my attention back to whatever I had been doing. But it seemed that just the moment I set the pen down that another great idea would pop into my head. It was a fun game. I remember saying to my husband David how I had a lot of painting to do as I already had the names of over 800 paintings. I thought it was funny and pondered the idea of reversing my creative process and beginning with a title and allowing the image to flow forth from that inspiration instead of the process of creating an image and having a title inspired by such.

I never read back through them. I never saw the importance. But I do remember wondering if I was repeating phrases and if I should edit the thoughts by not writing down "a paining title" I had written before. But I soon decided not to edit the words and just let them flow. At that time, I didn't have any idea how or really why these ideas were coming to me. I got my brain involved for a while in the beginning and started looking for inspiring words and phrases. I would underline them in magazines articles and advertising. But that didn't last too long for I found I didn't have to work at this, the task at hand was to write down whatever came to me on whatever I could find to write it on.

It was a lot like how my art ideas have come to me. An idea forms in my mind begging to be expressed and until it is my mind cannot rest. So to appease my mind, I had to empty it of each idea as it came. And the more I did it the more that came. I couldn't think about it. I had to remove my mind from the process. I never sat with pen in hand

and stared at the paper wondering what to write next. I just wrote
what I was given as it was given. I learned to always have a notebook
within reach and kept several handy, not ever considering that it was
important when or where I jotted down each idea. It was just a game I
played with myself.

Gradually, I was inspired to write out more flowing essay type ideas.
The thoughts expressed and wisdom offered amazed me. I treasured
the wisdom which was so apropos to everything I questioned about life
and never doubted the authority behind it. It is now my understanding
that the words of wisdom that flow through and to me, are for sure
Divine Inspirations. But, I wondered, just how did I ever manage to
be such a channel for such Divine Wisdom? And then I thought back
to the multitude of "painting titles," words which I had never assumed
told any story or were any form of communication. When this idea
came to me just a few months ago I literally ran to the cabinet where I
had stuffed my painting title journals. As I read I was stunned. There
was an amazing continuity to the words and phrases, a conversation,
communication, messages, wisdom, love, all there, all the time. It was if
was if Spirit was tapping the door of my mind. *"Hello. We are here. Are
you listening? All is well. Keep it up. Each day is better. Look up, Love is
all around you."*

Jesus said, "Men think, perhaps, that it is peace which I have come
to cast upon the world. They do not know that it is dissension which I have
come to cast upon the earth: fire, sword, and war.

GOSPEL OF THOMAS [4]

What no peace? Most would discount the fact that Jesus could have
ever said such a thing. After all wasn't He "The Prince of Peace?" If
you consider He thought and taught peace as a practice rather than
fighting and discord then yes. But appeasing people and pleasing
people just by being pleasing and not "stirring the pot" was not what
He was about, not at all. His mission was to bring a new message to the
world, a message of Love, Joy and Forgiveness. But His way, His real
way, was such an upset to the ways of old that it was like throwing fire

on all the ways of the world. If that "fire" had truly caught on as per His intentions the world would not be as it is today. All would know and live through the true glory and wisdom of God without the need of governing forces.

So when is it me writing and when is it the higher Wisdom of God flowing forth?

> *There is no clear defining line, for I, such as God himself, cannot be divided into parts. What is holy is always whole.*

I can clearly tell when my own psyche is involved, as it is the part of me that questions for it does not fully know and yet thinks it has so much to say. It's the part of me that wants to tell my side of the story, my ego self. Which is neither good or bad, it's just me being me.

OCTOBER 12, 2011

> *It can materialize. Shut your physical eyes and realize with your Real eyes, your Spiritual eyes, that all is possible to those who believe. And so it appeared. It's a wonderful story, a wonderful true story, told again and again for your benefit and the benefit of all who believe. Believe it true. This is what you are to do. What you call miracles are really not so miraculous. It is just that you do not understand their workings. You do not believe properly.*

I would like to know more. I would love to be a part of your "Miracle Network." Show me the way to this Truth. Open my realization to all the wonderful possibilities.

> *You don't believe all is yours. You hold back and cling to what you have, what you know, limiting what you could have and know. This is not flow. It is stagnation. Stagnated*

water stinks. To allow fresh Rejuvenating Waters in, you have to be an open, free flowing, vessel. As you give, you can take, as it will be given unto you. This applies to all: money, wisdom, peace, and love, all of My everlasting Bounty. Believe as you will and you shall have.

Are you ready to manifest My glory? Will you drink from My cup? I hold it unto your lips for I see how parched your spirit is. Come to My well and drink My dear. Free flowing Healing Water is here for you. Live in charity. You are to share My bounty given unto you.

From "nowhere" it comes and then appears whole. You can see it and believe it, all without having to wrap your mind around. Your computer screen images and data, your TV, your music, all appear from virtually "nowhere." But it is somewhere, all around and even in you. All working in accordance with the same power, the same energy that manifests every miracle you can dream. You saw each first in your mind. You wanted it so. You could taste it and feel it, almost touch it. This is the part you play, your work to do, believing it so, believing in wondrous possibility.

Your dreams are not to be analyzed they are to be imaginized. We keep telling you dream big, think high, there are no limits but the ones you create in your mind. Think of good things. Delight in beauty and kindness. Sing praises where praises are due. You do not have to understand it all. You truly cannot. It is all so above your ability to know as a human. Let that go and go on. Work with what you do know. Have fun believing, pre-tending, make-believe!

Rules, rules, rules. "The Love of God" takes away one's sin, one's propensity toward error thinking and action. For as the "Love of God" fills one's being the will of God flows naturally and gracefully forth. Worth believing. Worth knowing. Worth showing. It all becomes you so very much.

It is not too late for anything. Consider how far you have come? Dream of how far you can go. Consider it done. People are always in a rush. Don't be in a rush. Take time to listen. Take time to see. Take time to be all you are and can be.

Do not put yourself in harms way. Stay out of the worry zone. You hold the power for your life. Green flag, power on. Yellow flag, caution. Red flag, stop unbelief.

Jesus became perfected as Christ, then he spoke. But I do not need to wait until Perfection to tell and show what I do know now.

Perfection is wonderful indeed, but there is much to be shared from where you are now on your journey. You are on your way, the right way. You can point and lead the way. You "way show-er" you!

The Peace of God fills me.

You are not to worry, for if there was such a thing as sin, I would tell you worry was a sin. But that would just give you something to worry about.

You do not have to believe in any certain way. You just have to believe in your dreams.

"I don't believe that." My mother said as we both sat in front of the TV listening to Oprah's new show, *Life Lessons*. "I don't believe that you can just believe something true. I believe in circumstances. When I grew up it was during the war and things were hard. I don't believe what she says is true for everybody." So I just had it spelled out clearly to me, why I had never understood, why or how I had not known these truths. Because "the faith of my father"(and or mother) was a faith not in the possibility of the better in the here and now but always postponed to the hereafter.

"Have faith, trust in God" These words spoken all the time but what exactly do they mean to each? I want to know. I believe the answers will enlighten me and many others.

Not everyone believes, so not everyone receives, although it is here, there and everywhere ready to be claimed, ready to be asked for by name. Call forth your good. Your good, you must proclaim. So do you see it? For see it you must. In your ideas, you must trust. It matters not at all what anyone else believes, for all are free to believe as they want. What do you want to believe? That all your dreams are true? Try them on for size and I'm sure you'll see all your dreams are the perfect size for you.

You can do it for you have imagined it and thus created it so well. Now is the time to share your creations with the world. You have been given gifts galore and so much more are in store. Yes, We have told you before that you were going to be playing with the "big boys," so it is great to see you are empowering yourself and your body for the long haul. For there is so much more yet to do and We are as well so excited to see you make your dreams come true.

See what a wonderful story this is? For your success in life, your story, Our story, which you now write will open so many eyes in the days and years to come, but also for generations upon generations. For as you have found the bread crumbs of Truth left for you to find by others following the same path centuries ago, others will be comforted and enlightened in the ages to follow.

These words must and will live on to be found. Someone, if not you, will get this done. Publishing this now is not to be your concern. It will get done when the time is right. Now your job is in the living and the creation of your dreams. Continue to follow your heart and all your wildest dreams will come true. Consider this as well your dream journal. Don't be afraid or hesitate to say what you want. See it true.

Don't be afraid to be who you are. See the truth clearly. You Are, who You Are. Have patience with all, for all do not know the Truth that is. Take time to see. Take time to be My love. Don't be so assuming. You are limiting your options every time you decide what is. The flow of life is so much better, so much richer. Just allow. Allow all good to flow forth. Call forth God's goodness in your life. Time to tell what you know. Your life will show the world My love. Manifest your heart out, for I am with you always.

Can you not see My dear the world more clearly? How I love you so dearly? You are My all, for you are such a great part of it All. I so want you to see the Truth, the whole Truth, the holiest of Truth that My love everlasting is here for all. But so many do not see, so many do not know, this Truth. They walk the world blind to the Truth, the Truth you now see and hear and write for Me, for as My eyes are yours, your hands are Mine. The work you do is Mine, for you have taken My name. You have accepted and proclaimed My glory.

Just put it out there is all I ask, so those with need to read will find and their hearts will leap with joy. For they will then understand the words they hear spoken unto their heart. Oh My dear, you have begun. What a wonderful place to start.

Your mother gave you life. And all of her life she gave you all she had and knew. But as you see now, she knew not all. She has been blinded by fear, trampled by the world, limited by what was and is. She knew not how to dream, nor ever dared to dream that her dreams could come true. But she has always wanted better for you. She has told you so your whole life. "If you do not like the way I do things, then change them in yourself." She saw hope in you, hope in all of her children. Live her hope. Make her dreams come true. Step into the Light and become all you can be. Be the Light.

You need not convince a soul. That is My job. When someone wants to know Me, they will ask. All you have to do is hold the Light. Shine your Light so bright that people will want to draw near and then your Love will steer them home, home to Me in the center of their heart.

Don't make it a problem. Make it a solution. Why don't you "check in?" Don't see life as a problem. There is more than one way to get things done. Know there is a solution. Then see the solution. Then use the solution. See it work out as you believed. You won't be disappointed. Whatever you know, is your truth. What do you aspire to? Don't make it any harder on yourself than you need to. Be a friend to yourself.

OCTOBER 15, 2011

Ten years ago, I remember feeling times were hard. Well, that has been my story way too long. I'm telling a new story, one of hope, abundance, joy, health and prosperity, my true story.

That's not going to be a problem. It takes awhile to get it through your thick head.

Maybe I didn't have the right attitude.

That's the attitude.

I trusted and I was rewarded for my trust. In God I trust. I'm pretty happy. I trust that all is well and I dare not believe otherwise.

You have so much Love; it looks beautiful on and in you! Let Me fill you with more, be filled with My love galore!

So you say it is a certain way. Is this truly the way you want such to be? Do you not still know you are free to see as you like and like what you see? Is this now the way you want life to be? If not, you are free to change your mind. "In an ideal world..." You live in an ideal world. It is your choice to live in an ideal world. We all live in the ideal world of our own choosing. Wrestling with the ego? Sure, it feels like you are wresting with the devil.

Oprah has an excellent platform, which she has built. She is trusted and admired by many. Many will listen, many will not. Those with ears to hear will hear. No one can open another's closed mind. Free will is the key which locks and unlocks the door to the mind of knowing.

Know what you want. See what you want. Be what you want. See it true. Evolution of consciousness. It's expressed differently because it is coming from different channels. But all channel from the same Source of Truth. All water flows from the one same Fount. Amazing things can happen when allowed. Don't let your mind be a plug which stops the flow. Let the good be as it may.

So you've seen the truth of who you are and you've seen the truth of where you've come from. And you are beginning to understand that what you've been told has given you a very limited view of life. I am happy to see you are laying no blame for you understand Jesus' words "Forgive them they do not know."

People only know, what they know. And they know what they know because they trusted the word of another or have such experienced. You have always been one who had to know by experience. Society looks down on and shames the "Doubting Thomas" for his unbelief. But I do not; for I know this is how belief becomes knowing and knowing is so much better.

You have continually questioned what you have been told all of your life. You were made to know. You came into this world with a yearning for full remembrance of Truth. You are still yearning for more clarity but now confident that you are on the path to understanding and most important of all you feel and know My love. You are My love and you express and exude My love. Oh yes, it's all so lovely. Thank you for letting Me have this dance. It's a long slow romantic heart to heart dance we have. I am in no rush to hurry on with life and nor should you be. When you stay close to Me, time (as you will) stands still. Come out of time and dance with Me.

I used to pray by talking, talking, talking, but never heard a word in return. I see now that I never stopped to listen, to listen in. I prayed my prayer then went back to the rush of the world, back to the noise and confusion. "Where is God?" I would say. "How am I ever to know what to do? How am I to believe when hate and pain is all I see true?"

And now you know and must show the world the way unto the words I write upon each heart. As you write My words, this is a start. As this is the way you found My voice as the small still voice within you. You asked to know. You asked to show My love. You asked for Me to so fill you with My Divine Love. You got your ego out of the way and surrendered your will unto Mine. You asked for guidance all the time.

I have always been here. I have always held you dear. But I could never and would never force My will over yours. I want and need to be chosen. I have already chosen each of you. Your birthright is My glory, but only for the asking, the asking by a truly repentant heart. Repenting of what? Repenting of your old ways, your selfish ego ways, your old single mindedness where you thought you knew it all. Forget all you have known and come unto Me like a little child full of wonder and a wondrous life you shall know.

The Old Testament is just that, old. When you know better, you do better. You are not helping yourself or your understanding of "the One True God" by listening to the stories of people with such shallow, limited consciousness of God. The birth of Jesus, as Christ, is the birth of the New Consciousness of man, which He expressed fully. Unfortunately, those that followed did not. Thus they edited and altered His story and all Bible stories to fit what they themselves knew could be true.

But the time is now. Now, man's consciousness has evolved to a state of further knowing and understanding. More and more are becoming enlightened unto the truth. Not dependent upon words written by others, to which their own mind has to become involved to decipher the meaning, they hear the truth of God spoken directly to their own heart and are immediately endowed with full wisdom as to the Words meaning.

Stop comparing yourself and your ideas to what has already been done.

Today is a wonderful day you say, a fine fall day, wonderful day to be out and about, a wonderful day to be alive. You feel so alive you want to sing and shout about it. Well good for you, it's wonderful news that you can so see the beauty in the day. Oh, how you love today. But now I ask you what about yesterday, the day that was once today? I made it the same way. All today's are right now. And right now is always perfect, no more, no less. I make it all as wonderful as I know. What it is for you to do is know this truth as well.

The stories I tell are different, for I have different stories to tell. When I was a child I thought, acted, wrote and drew as a child. But my consciousness changed and evolved to an even higher place, a higher plane of knowing and awareness. The reality I express with my art and writings is a higher, brighter expanded awareness, an awareness of so much more than the day to day physical nature confronting our five senses and thus our mind. This higher reality is beautiful, wondrous, brightly lit, and exploding with color. Let me continue to manifest as I see and know.

I watered my plants today.

Yes, I see and how lovely their colorful blossoms are. You are to water each day, all the seeds you have planted in consciousness as well. Bring each up into the light of day and see each as a beautiful plant in full colorful bloom just as the flowers you now enjoy in your garden.

When one knows My heart, there is no need for commandments. All is known unto the heart that knows Mine. Sing My Song all the day long. What a lovely tune it is when you tune into Me. You are on the God channel. It's the highest frequency, there is no static, beautiful music free flowing all the time. Easy going tunes. Music to dance to. Skip along. Lift your feet high. March to My drum, the beat of your heart, which is now Mine.

I laugh.

Laughter is the sound of angels.

I laugh because I am happy. Joy is my being. Who I am is happiness today and always. This is my way. I know no other way to be. Joy is my breath, my blood, my reason for being. In Love, I am present with all.

Feel no sorrow, for I am the Truth of You. I am Joy; Joy to the world. Feel no sorrow. Feel no shame, for joy and only joy is the name of the game. Ask and you shall receive all the good you desire ask in My Name. Consider My Love your "working capital." All that is Mine is yours, for you to see and claim. See what is, what is for you to see. See perfectly through Me. You don't need the voice of doubt! Tell that voice to shut up and get out!

How is everything?

Everything is wonderful, just wonderful. When are you going to tell it like it is and say this every time? "Everything is wonderful." Try it out for a month. You have nothing to lose and all joy to gain. Think of it this way. Everything is "wonder filled." All is amazing. You are amazed by all, filled with wonder. You have not decided how all is to be.

You have not limited your good one bit. Instead, you are choosing to go with and live in the flow. The flow of life which is all good and for this you are filled with wonder seeing all life as wonderful. Yeah, go with that.

OCTOBER 16, 2011

Everyone wants to be heard. God wants to be heard, to be known, to be understood, to be loved. God understands this about us. God believes in each of us but more than that God knows each of us. Ultimately, life is knowing God, for to know God is to truly live. Know Me, God says. Know Life. Think about what you want. Hold that thought. That is all, all you are to do. Then just be. Be with Me.

Isn't life lovely? Have you noticed today? For today is happening now. Today you are alive and well. Did you know this? Did you not or do you not know all is well? You say you see different. You see disharmony. Well, I ask is disharmony what you want? If not, then I challenge you to think differently about life. I challenge you to think what you want. For as you think, you create.

Now I ask you not to think about that idea too much for if you do you will spend your time and energy creating reasons, defending why you believe that this is not so. But what if you took down the defensive walls in your mind and allowed a different possibility to be true? Could you, would you, dare to dream that life is wonderful and full of ease? Dare to dream. Dare to dream big.

Make a game of it. Play by new rules, the game of life where all is fair, where you are not just a helpless pawn but an active player, where you are calling the shots not just rolling the dice. For life is not a game of chance. Nothing happens by chance, nor is it all decided. What is decided is how the game of life works. Most think they know and understand the rules and are playing by them but then feel cheated because they find life random and unfair. What is unfair is that they have closed their minds to a different possibility, a possibility that the world is different than they think. And that by the very power of their thoughts they are creating the problems their own mind is entangled in.

I say, step out of your mind and into your heart. It's a feeling place not a thinking place where you will find your truth. Feel your way to Me. Let down your guard. You are safe with Me. No harm done by looking, by feeling what you feel. Let Me feel what you feel. Let Me feel your pain. Let Me feel your joy.

Now let Me tell you a new story, a story of Love, Love from Heaven, but not the mythical heaven far away or high above. The Heaven within your heart where I lay waiting to be found, anxious for your return, your return home to the center of your beingness. This is where your truth lies. Love's true home.

Come find Me. Sit with Me. Talk with Me. Walk with Me. The answers are here, all the answers to all your questions. You have lots of questions and this is good. It means you wonder, wonder about life, about the why's and where's of life that are more than you can see. This is I know and I know the answers. Find comfort in this knowing. Find comfort in My words spoken unto your heart.

New questions will arise each day, each moment, and as you walk hand in hand with Me you will know the answers as soon as you think the questions. There leaves no room for doubt. The days and years of wandering alone in the desert are gone. Vanished, just as the mirage you once walked toward. And as you do you will see that your past path led to nowhere, for every time you thought you had arrived your thirst was never truly quenched and again you looked beyond in the distance to another place, another person, another object which would quench your thirst, your desire.

But I hold the cup of Living Waters to your mouth and say drink My child. Drink of My love. Drink of My wisdom. Drink of My life. With these waters you will live anew, think anew, act anew, and be anew in Me, for I will live through you. My will, will be done naturally. For you will be in the flow of life, the flow of all that is true, all that is true is good, truly good. You have decided that if something is too good it cannot be true. Decide differently. Decide to choose only the best. Proclaim only the highest and the best for your life and then this you will know. Only this you will show.

Oh, so many have come and pointed the way, the way to Me within your heart. But you have not listened, not truly heard a word. Instead you held them so high above that you dared not dream, lest believe, that the truth they proclaimed in God's name was not only their truth but was meant to be yours as well. The Truth they told fell on deaf ears. Few had ears to truly hear. So instead of accepting a message of Love they changed it to a message of fear.

Now is the time to see. The time to know that fear and love cannot exist in the same heart, for God is love and one that knows God does not know fear. Can your ears yet hear? We want you to know (We, who all speak in God's name) that you are so loved and there is a plan. The plan is for you each to awaken to the truth of who you are. You are each part of a dazzling star, a piece of light, which is the light of God. The plan is for you to know this and live this. The plan is for you to wonder and question and seek Truth for yourself, for your own heart, for your own being, for your own good. God knows you and calls each of you by name. Now is the time for you to call out to God and ask to hear His voice speak clearly unto your heart.

Why so sad? Why so disheartened? Why do you allow your mood to swing so? First it's high, then low. When you ride the waves of life, this is how you live. When you look to the outside, the outer, you ride the waves, the highs and lows clinging to the edge of your small boat for your life. Your knuckles are white with the terror of your tight grip. Yet what are you really holding on to? The boat, which you are never really sure if it will sink or float? How about floating gently through life with Me? Flowing majestically on the high seas, riding the waves with confidence for the power which is the wave is the power you are, the power you work with in each moment, a power which does not slam against you but flows through you.

When you truly live through Me your life will reflect the peace and power which is the ocean. The depth and breadth of the ocean will be the all you are. You will not fear drowning. As you are the all of the ocean, you cannot drown in your self. One drop of water does not fear the cup of water. It is glad to be home with family. And added to the cup it is no longer separate, no longer alone but one with the all, no separation, none.

You are that drop now. You are that drop of water in the ocean. You are the wave. You are the water in the depths of the sea. You are who you are but you are no more separated *from any other than one drop of water in the ocean is from any other. Together all is one. When you look at your reflection you only see yourself but you are not looking properly. For as you look about you are as well seeing yourself.*

When a wave slams into the beach and splashes water into the air, a little drop of water sees itself for a brief instant as an individual drop, a single piece of water, a separate identity from the all. From the time of its birth (the big splash) up to its death (its return to the all of the ocean) seems an eternity to the little drop. Suddenly aware of the world it sees itself as alone and separate. Although the drop feels separate, it is still all the one is, as it is still of the same substance. It just does not recognize it.

This is how you see yourself, as alone and separate from the All of life that is. And yet each of you, just like the little drop of water, will just as naturally and effortlessly return to the One that is. Are you understanding this, dear ones? Do not fear the ocean. Do not fear life. Ride the waves in confidence that you cannot be swallowed up by or up heaved by any perceived turbulence. For all such turbulence is of your mind. Your heart knows better for your heart knows Me.

At one time many believed that to live a "Godly life" one of holy purity they had to barricade themselves physically from the world. They saw this as the only way. They saw the material world and all in it as evil "out to get them" and tempt and trick them into false notions.

Yes, the material world is a trap for egos but Godly men and women walk the earth today through the fire of hell without so much as a burn. Why and how? Because there is so much to Love in this world, so much good to notice and share and someone has to stand and walk the course to lead the others through to the safety of God's Hand.

Think of Jesus Christ. Did He run and hide from sinners? Did He for a moment feel threatened by their actions? Would He or could He have so served the world if He had holed away and hid His Light? No, He had to walk among the people and show them that He was one of them that could walk through the fire unharmed, or as it was, walk on water and not sink. How was it that Jesus was so unaffected by the world? It was because He was so affected by God the Father, so totally affected that God's holy nature made him into a reflection of God himself in word and deed.

This is for all, not just one, for all to become, a grand possibility waiting to be sought, waiting to be claimed. This life changing force is the force of life itself. Love replaces fear. Love replaces judgment. Fire can be walked through. Water can be walked on. Renouncing the world does not mean hiding from it. It means claiming your higher Good, which makes one above it all.

OCTOBER 17, 2011

Practice makes perfect.

Sometimes I wonder why "church" didn't do it for me.

It's about having a spiritual practice. "Church" as you say it, can only do so much for you just as "gym" can only do so much for you. You can go once a week and sit in a church pew and listen to another talk a spiritual talk and as well you can go sit on a gymnasium bleacher and listen to

another give you a pep talk on the virtues of "working out"
and being physical. But neither is any good unless you take
those ideas and put them into a regular practice for yourself.
Every spiritual coach and or physical coach would tell you
the same; you have to do the work yourself.

I am a drop of water in the ocean of life. A part of the whole, there is no
separation. We are all One.

It's easier to imagine Oneness with the analogy of being a
drop of water in the ocean of life for you have touched and
thus understood the physical form of the ocean. The body of
Spirit, Spirit as One and you as an inseparable part of this,
is a notion that escapes your mind. That is alright for your
heart has this understanding. When you follow your heart
and not your mind, you will always find your way home.

Give no mind to what you do not want for yourself or any
other. Separate yourself. Raise your consciousness above the
matters of matter. Here you will find peace for you, which
is a peace so strong and lovely that it has the power to give
peace to the all. When you recognize the ego you are giving
credence to the idea of your separateness. When you deny
the ego you are able to recognize the wholeness of life in
Spirit and feel a part of such.

We know the power matter holds. It is full of energy, a force
very strong. It bombards your senses. It says look here see
what is wrong. And then it says look over here gain this, buy
this and feel better, feel good. But no one tells you the good
feeling is just for a moment for your eyes are so weak they
can not stay centered on good, even if it is true good for only
but a moment.

This is why we tell you to shut your physical eyes to the world and look within for strength and beauty. Here you will find peace and tranquility. Here lies God, your God connection to all. The more you can stay centered in this knowing, the more you will be God showing to all in the outer, for when the inner and the outer are the same you are whole and reside in Heaven.

October 18, 2011

A new awareness
Revelations daily
Stay the course
The way is known
The way will be shown
Look to the inner
Not the outer
We are with you all the way.

My course is set in the Heavens. Glory be to God the highest. Only the highest and the best I request. Let me show the way to life, the life worth living. I am drawn to the "Authentic Master" who teaches me. I have no guru. I only have God.

Wisdom and bliss are effortless and never ending. Contemplate the vastness of your Self. See not separateness. Don't believe in the self importance stuff. It's all a lie.

The fact that your family has pretty much ignored your writings has been a gift to you, as you have not felt the need to be defensive.

Looking at a book about contemporary society, I say to myself "Someone is just thinking all this stuff, they don't know."

Knowing and thinking are complete opposites. Not all food is health food or healthful food. Not all thoughts are healthy thoughts. If it is life giving, whether it is food for the body or food for the mind, it is healthy promoting well being in and out. There is junk food and as well junk thoughts. Both society tends to load up on to fill a void. But both body and mind are precious, precious to the soul, the spirit of your being. The beingness in your core center wishes all food and all thought be of the highest life sustaining value possible. Weed out the junk from your life, food and thoughts. Live free eternally, internally and externally.

Youth is easy. Youth is beautiful. Age and youth have nothing to do with each other, for youthfulness is a mindset and age is only a barometer for the number of your days on earth. Youth is graceful and limber.

I am full of youth. I am youthful.

You have to say what you want. Believe what you want and be happy about it all.

Sign of peace, there shall be no real peace until each finds Peace within, within their heart and mind. And then their hearts and minds become at peace with each others. Then "new found Peace" is thrust into the outer manifesting peace with every breath. This is the breath of Life, the breath of Peace which God breathes into each, to be found, to be sought, to be claimed, to be proclaimed. Give each a sign of peace, a smile, a hug, a handshake. Peace be with you and with you.

Who's keeping track and what are they keeping track of? There is no contest. It is the will of the Father for all to share in His bounty and the Lord's bounty is endless.

The role of any way-shower, guru or faith practice, which leads to Truth, is as a guide and not a destination in it's self. Their proper goal is to lead their follower to the knowing of each one's Inner Wisdom, the eternal loving Father, Mother of all.

These statements come to mind just after a question has come to my mind.

I know that of which I speak. I speak Truth through this pen in your hand.

My husband says, "You are possessed by that paper." and I agree.

Say what you like and if you like what someone else does tell them. Everyone enjoys an encouraging word.

So many people are afraid to question life, to question God, as if to do so is a sin or error thinking. Actually, the error that occurs is that one does not ponder God and thus misses the opportunity to know God and the fullness of life in God's Love.

You are full of joy. Joyful you are. Be joy to the world.

There is a way, more than one way, more than one chance, more than one opportunity to know God. God gives up on no one. Don't give up on God. God is good. Good for all. Yea God!

You cannot pull anyone closer. You can only draw near with your light, with your love, which is My Light and My Love, Debra of God. Life is very flavorful and has many layers of flavor. Come taste My Sweet Life. Let Me treat you to the Life Divine.

There is nothing bad about technology, nothing. No power is bad or good in its self. It is all a matter of how the power is used and that each is considered as a tool to ultimate understanding of truth, good for all.

Tell Me something good. Look for it, see it and talk about it. How do you know what is good for you? It is that which feels good and harms none. It is important to feel good everywhere and all the time.

You want to speak. You want to be heard. Everyone does. Everyone wants to be heard. We do as well. Thanks for listening. There is much to be learned by listening. When you can observe without judgment, you will know you have arrived, arrived unto My Kingdom.

OCTOBER 19, 2011

You have been led astray. You have misled yourselves. Each time you focus on the "rules" you attribute to God you are pulling your focus away from the God idea and into the man idea. For the only idea of God is "Love," Love pure Love, the purest of Love, Divine Love, the sacred heart of God, the sacred heart of Christ, all ideas of God who is Love. This is to be your focus. This Love is what you are to attune your heart and mind to. Think on this: The power of God's Love.

Jesus Christ told you this. Above all else, He said, seek the Kingdom of God. Love God with all your heart, soul and mind. To love God is to love the Love of God, to desire God's Love, to thirst for God's Love, to be passionately and innately hungry for God's Love. This is the devotion we are to possess, to live with, to contemplate, to ask for blessings of.

This is what is right and true. God is Love, the highest and most divine form of love there is. The love Paul spoke about to the Corinthians. The love that is kind, patient and not judgeful. This is the love God already has for us. But wait, there's more. God has made a special offer to all His faithful, the ones so full of faith in the power of His magnificent love that they are devoted to it. They pray for it. They ask on bended knee for the infilling of such love. God's deepest desire is to shower all of mankind with His healing Divine Love, the love that transforms hearts and opens eyes and ears to truth.

Yes, God has always loved, deeply loved each of us. But because of the free will He gave us to create our lives as we desire, He will not and cannot force His will, His love upon anyone. But now God has a new deal for us, an offer, the "Good News" Jesus was telling us about, "His love." God will freely and lavishly gift each repenting heart who so truly desires His love with His love. God's love is the most powerful substance in the universe thus can only be dripped drop by drop like an intravenous line into one's heart. But oh, when you get just a taste and you understand the gift you have received you will want more and you shall ask and you shall receive.

So what is a repenting heart? Is it a perfect pure heart? No, for only God's love purifies hearts. A repenting heart is one that says he has had enough of his own ways, that he chooses the will of God. But most importantly he chooses the love of God. The will of God is just the natural course of action that will come. You see as more and more of God's Divine Love fills and transforms your heart your will is so very naturally and easily and comfortably changed into the will of God.

You will have no choices to make between right and wrong, for God's love will have so transformed your heart you will do no other that "what Jesus would do." The rules man has created and attributed to God are not needed for your thoughts and actions are so ever supernaturally aligned with the highest good for all. Peace, love and joy will prevail in your heart, mind and soul. Your very being will change. You will become a new person. After the man Saul was so filled with the love of God he changed his name to Paul. Remember the wisdom, the wisdom of God which filled him, and the love of Christ of which he spoke? These are the gifts of the Holy Spirit, the gifts of God, which come upon those so devoted to the knowing and receiving of God's love.

So what do you have to do to receive this Love into your own heart? Open it. Open your heart and open your mind. Come unto to the Lord as a little child, full of the wonder and trust of a child. You do not have to understand God to understand God is love. All know some love, but not all know God's love. All can so know God's love if and when they want to. Remember, this is not a one-time thing, it's a process, a continual process of asking, and receiving, a process that flows so naturally and gracefully that nothing is more perfect. The more you get the more you want and all you will truly want is God's love. It's the icing on the cake of life, the tastiest and most beautiful icing that becomes the bread of life allowing full communion with God. Come to my table and eat and drink, says the Lord. My love is the all sustaining bread and wine you have hungered and thirsted for. Come eat, drink and be merry.

Do what you have to do, My word will always be here for you. Many will deny for they do not know My voice, of course this is their choice. My will, I will not impose on any unwilling soul. I so Love all my children as they are. But oh so rejoice when they come home to live in the fullness of My heart of love. I have prepared a banquet for the celebration.

The more ideas I expose myself to, the more questions I have. Just like a child, I ask "Why?" I wonder.

When you were dissatisfied with the life you knew, you sought Me. You sought more to life, and I am the more to life. Living through Me you are finding joy abundantly. Physically you are in the same place, yet spiritually the ladder you have climbed. You cannot be unhappy with Me, for you have found true joy in My life, in the breast of My loving heart.

Don't keep these words under lock and key. Keep them where they can be found by the ardent seeker. For just as you have found wisdom and comfort in the words of Mine written by the hand of others, many others will find great value in these words you write. They will bring comfort to seeking hearts for generations upon generations. Do not take this work lightly.

The world taunts you at every turn with seductive marketing ploys. Act now, limited time offer, buy one, get one free, special exclusive offers all around guaranteed to make your life better in some way. But you're pretty smart. You are catching on. If you miss one offer your chance to ever have that promised happiness will be offered again, if not in the next commercial break then next week or next month. And besides you're not stupid. You know that while you may enjoy the benefits of such a product, your life will not truly change. Yet all seem to want change, want a better life so continue to look, to acquire and acquire stuff, stuff,

stuff, stuff and more stuff. You are stuffed with stuff and remain unsatisfied.

What you are looking for is a special offer that never expires and has no cost. Haven't you heard that you can't get something for nothing? Everything has a cost. Even the ultimate gift you can receive, God's love. Some believe it's free for the taking because another paid the price but this is not so, not the true story. Each must lay down their own life to walk with God.

The crucifixion that is to take place is with your own ego. I can hear it now, the crowd gathering, roaring up against these words. "This is not the truth we know! Shut up! How dare you even recite such words!" But those who do are not listening now. They have already thrown this book to the side and trampled upon it, all out of fear. So I do not speak to those with minds closed so. I speak unto the seekers of Truth, whom want to know God in their own hearts and minds. You have to let go of your ego. For your ego is what keeps your mind and thinking small.

It is the ego that refuses to listen to new ideas. It s the ego that thinks it knows all and yet fears the unknown for the ego does not want you to look any further. For it knows if you do glimpse beyond you will walk away from its hold and it will wither and die. Yes, the crucifixion to take place is of your own ego. This is the price to be paid.

But such a deal, such a small price to pay for freedom, freedom from fear, worry and judgment, such a small price to pay to know God's love. Let go of your ego and let God. Let God's love fill all the spaces of your heart and mind. Feel God's love. Know God's love. Be assured in God's love. Walk through life in God's love in faith, in trust and contentment.

The offer is available now. Always is the now. It can be the now of today or the now of tomorrow but God asks, "Why wait? There will be no better offers to come. Come enjoy life now to the fullest with Me." Come forward. Do not lag behind. Your light cannot be hidden. It is for you to know. It is for you to show My love. Put your fears aside and walk in faith with Me. Trust in goodness. Trust in the goodness of God. God says: Come to Me as you are. You need not be perfect. You will find perfection in Me, in My love. With My love you will be purified. Day by day we grow in love. Day by day we are sent signs from above.

Some see the world and say it is coming apart. Crying out like the little chicken who screamed in terror that the sky was falling. The world my dear is not coming a part. Yes, it is being shaken up, but it's being put back together bit by bit the right way. Your eyes only see a jumble of pieces of what seems like an unsolvable puzzle. You can not see as I do. I see what can be. I see areas here and there uniting, interlocking, working together, joining forces with others who find strength in looking for their similarities not differences. Looking for how they can be stronger and more meaningful as a united force.

Oh yes you see, I see the bigger picture and it is lovely, it is grand. I do not expect any of you to begin to grasp the whole, leave that to Me. I just ask you each to have faith in the grand plan of one people united in love, living and working cohesively together for the good of all. Look around wherever you are on this grand board game for others who have something they need that you may give. Just as others will be looking for something they need to give you. This is how love interlocks, builds and comes together bit by bit no longer as a puzzle but as a beautiful picture of life.

It's not my job to make everyone or anyone else happy. My job is to be happy myself, for myself and with myself.

OCTOBER 20, 2011

You keep looking for trouble then are surprised when you find it.

You do not have to say you hate someone just because you do not respect them. God calls us to love everyone. That means to show love or be love to everyone. That does not mean we need to love another's actions or respect their actions. We are to respect the person, respect the creation of God that they are whether or not they themselves recognize it or respect it in themselves. We are to be the light in the dark, the light of God.

Stop looking for someone else to validate you. Find your reason for being within yourself.

The church sign says, "Come follow Jesus." There is the Jesus Christ of the Bible then there is the Christ within your heart. You are to follow the ways of the Christ in the Bible to find and recognize the Christ within your heart to be one with the Father as Jesus, the Christ was. Do you know the Father?

If you were talking with a friend now, what would you be talking about? Would you be talking about the joys in life or the trials? Watch your words, powerful they are. Let the sun shine into your heart and scare away the dark.

You have no reason to prove God to anyone else. You have no need to prove these writings to anyone. All is to be taken by any other for their own consideration of value and merit for their own life. Each has their own work to do. Whether they choose to investigate on their own can only be their choice. It is only their business, not yours. So leave those thoughts alone.

If you can't talk nice in the company of others you are better off alone. Some people are toxic. Some situations are toxic. Some foods are toxic. Learn what to avoid.

My mother taught me that if you can't say something nice don't say anything at all.

Live big wherever you are. Trust the future. Do not feel limited by what you know.

OCTOBER 21, 2011

Problems, problems, problems, and fears, fears, fears, this is what is advertised, pointed to, called out. Hear ye, hear ye, look at lack, see your faults, compare yourself to others. This is exactly the opposite message of God and of religion, which as been created to bring people closer to God. Keep God at the forefront of your thought. Hold your thoughts high. Do not judge or compare. Feel no fear. Live in love.

Why do you continue to drink poison? Knowingly consuming what is not good for your system daily? Poison comes in many forms. So many things are toxic to your system. You watch toxic TV, consume toxic drink and talk toxic talk. Why do you continue to walk this walk? Walk away, walk toward Me. Walk with Me to peace, to sanity.

God is my immunity from the toxicity of the world.

The saying "trial and error" means to try many times, many ways to perfect an idea. Trying and failing is not an error. The error occurs when one gives up trying.

When you hold high energy, people want you around for they consider your mere presence "good luck."

You can't see the big picture from where you are but there is one and it is beautiful. Trust My vision, it is beautiful. It is the vision of a beautiful world. Come dream this wonderful dream with Me. Live in and through My reality. The time has come for change.

"You don't want to do that." You have heard this statement again and again from the other's mouth. Sometimes the words have been directed to you and sometimes to others. Now, that you are waking up you are hearing this statement differently. You are recognizing the truth that no one else can tell you what you do or do not want to do. At one time those words may have been convincing and held power over you but those days are gone. You now know that only by listening to your heart, to your inner knowing voice, and doing what feels good and right is the only way to honor yourself and life the life you are here to live.

I give thanks for the blessings bestowed on me. I give thanks for the life I am living. I give thanks for the "light keepers" whom have lived in the light and shared their stories, their insights and their wisdom with humanity through the ages. I give thanks and praise to God who is all holy. Thanks be to God, whom is Love Eternal.

Thank you for being, being in love with Me.

There is so much joy in my heart there is room for no other.

Uniformity with God's will, this is to be our aim for by living a life in concordance with God's will we will find true peace and perfection in our heart. People have tried and tried and failed and failed and blamed themselves miserably since the dawn of time. They let themselves off the hook with words that comfort them such as "it is only human to error and man is not perfect." Just because man is not perfect or is inclined to error does not mean he should lose all hope and be content in living life a drift from fully knowing God.

The reason man has not found perfection in his ability to live fully God's will, or at least only a handful have made this attainment, is that he believes he is to refine himself all by his own doing. This is an impossible feat. The way has been shown and the way to a perfect heart is not through any ways of man. You see, the ways of man are the ways of the mind of man, as he reasons and thinks. Try as he may to control his mind no man can think his self into perfection. It is not a matter of his will. Man's singular self, his ego, believes so in himself that he is all that he can see and thus know. The ego keeps mankind from evolving into God kind.

The way to God is the way to Love. The way to God's love is the answer to all. The total answer, the truth in it's most condensed form. God is Love, a special kind of love, Divine Love. A love that is ready and waiting to be poured into willing hearts and souls. A willing heart is all that is needed, not a perfect pure heart. God says come to Me as you are and I will make you clean. Desire only Me and I will see that your life is good and plenty.

Get out of your thinking mind, the hold of the ego, and

*come to Me with an open and willing heart full of wonder
and awe as a child. Ask Me questions. Want to know. Seek
and ye shall find. Show Me your gratitude. Show Me your
reverence and I will show you how beautiful the world really
is. All I want, says God, is to fill you with My everlasting
sweet love which will purify and raise your soul. This is My
Will for all, all who come to Me on bended knee, tired and
weary from the world. Those who seek Me, truly seek Me,
will find Me and I will give them rest. I will gladden their
hearts and give them wisdom untold. This is My story. It has
been the same for all days of old.*

*You cannot begin to follow My will by the power of your
mind. You are not strong enough, temptation is too great.
This is why you are to pray to Me to lead you out of
temptation and deliver you from evil. This, My most Divine
Love will do for you as it fills you and purifies your heart bit
by bit.*

OCTOBER 22, 2011

*If you have been blessed with loving parents you know that
all they have is yours. They would hold nothing back from
you and would want to give you from their stock all that
you need. Their love is too strong to have you go without.
This too is the way of God's Love, yet ten-fold. God wants all
His children to be happy and live full and blessed lives. We
are to know that all blessings are ours for the asking and it is
God's great pleasure to do so.*

*Man's great mind, that which he believes is his greatest
strength, is his downfall. For this great thinking mind of
man is what keeps him from knowing the Great Mind of All,
the mind of God.*

I am open to know God's will for me. Some may read or hear these statements and find them interesting, but I feel the power and truth of them and am in awe.

> *Mankind, as a whole, is freer than ever before to believe what he wants and yet he continues to put limitations on himself. God loves a repentant heart. Where there is a will there is a way. Where there is God's will there is always a way for good to be done.*

> *Don't see lack. Don't look for lack. Look for bounty. Look for abundance. Come follow Me and I shall lead you home. Do not tarry. Do not be wary. The way is clear. The path is known.*

I am in communion with God. This is the way it is supposed to be. I feel and know God's love. I trust in God, I trust in God's good wisdom.

> *You've got questions. We've got answers.*

I think it's funny. I laugh at coincidence. I see humor in life. Life is a joy to me, a continual joy.

> *Do you feel the joy, the joy in life, the joy in living? Feel your way to Me. Crawl inside My heart. My heart is the womb of your birth, rebirth yourself through My love.*

> *Weak minded people are not those who have given their will unto God's Will, for those men and women are of strong mind and heart knowing God's will is the will of the betterment of all mankind. You can find a way to do as you want to do. My way is your way. Come be the way," through Me. See the beauty in My love, the beauty which surrounds you, the beauty which engulfs you, the beauty which holds you close in a loving embrace.*

Those with eyes to see and ears to hear will welcome these words. Life gives each one many opportunities to choose between bitter and better. Everyone's opinion matters, matters only unto themselves. If you believe as another says, then that belief will have an effect on you and your life, good or bad. All points can be considered but only believe what you want.

It has been said that man can accomplish anything he sets his mind to, but it is better said that anything can be accomplished when one's heart is set on it. For the mind of man is limiting and only knows what it knows. But an open heart can know all and will soar unto the heavens. Set your heart aright. Come unto Me and I will cleanse your heart. Be pure of heart and full of My love. My love knows no limits. Do not limit yourself by living through your mind. Open your heart and let My love flood in.

God is not one thing. God is All, One in being and truth. Do not chastise any other for their belief or unbelief. Love is the only way, the only way to be the light.

These words are spoken unto my heart. God knows my heart. God knows I want to walk in the purity of His ways. God knows I want to know His ways and wisdom and thus delivers these words unto my heart.

Walk with Me and talk with Me.

God remains no longer a fairy tale or mystery of which my mind tries to believe. I know God with all my heart and love God with all my heart and mind.

This is the faith of the saints. The path for true wisdom for mankind lies not within his brain or mind but within his heart. For the heart is the path for true knowing. Do you doubt My voice? The path of wisdom, for all true knowing, lies within the heart. The mind has to be circumvented to allow new information, truth to be exposed. This is why dreams are helpful for man's conscious mind is turned off and his subconscious mind is free to explore new concepts. Thanks for listening.

My words as given, by man to man, are always under scrutiny as to whether the ideas presented hold true to the doctrine of God as set forth by man. I welcome scrutiny of the heart. By all means, please I beg of you, to contemplate within your heart all new ideas presented to you. What I take offense at is that man continually appraises new ideas with his mind, comparing and judging new ideas against what he has decided he knows. Have you not yet learned not to judge? No man is a worthy judge of another, himself or an idea. For all is under God, and God is great, so very great that His wisdom, His truth, can only be known through the heart.

So stop thinking about everything. Rest your busy monkey mind and let something just be. Be as you are and sit with new ideas that intrigue you if you wish to know and grow. But if you take each new idea and hold it up to see how it measures with the ideas you already have you will be stagnant and never come forward into My Kingdom. Being observant and judgeful are two very separate ideas and ways. Let Me entertain you. Come watch the sun rise and set. Watch the dance of the leaves in the wind. Follow the flight of the birds in the sky. Cherish the scent of the roses. Run through the pasture and wade in the clear cool stream. Let Me entertain you. You will not be bored.

Friends for the journey, We are your friends for the journey, the journey of your life. Welcome us in. We are here to guide, to listen, to love life with you.

How can this be?

Why can it not be? Why would you not want it to be? Does it not comfort you to know that you are not in this life alone? We are here for you. We are your most loving Spiritual Family. We come from a higher perspective of life, which we love to share with you and We will as you allow, as you will us to be a part of your life. We are God's love for you. To know God is to know God's love.

Time to tell what you know. The way we will show. It will be a wonderful ride for your love you cannot hide. We will show you the way each and everyday. Remain open to our love. Hold open the door. Let the light of love shine within your heart. As Jesus knew, so shall you. Be excited for this news is good. Everything is as it should be, forevermore. You shall find an abundance of light within your heart. This is a wonderful day to start to know the wonderful plan We have for you, the wonderful things you are going to do. Keep all this information close to your heart. Let it fill you and lift you high above the matters of the world.

This is a cause for joy and celebration, the celebration of your new life. Look what you have found so far. So far you have come, and far you will go. You will continue to rise unto us in thought, word, and deed as there is no limit to Our Love there is no limit to your knowing. As you allow, you shall know the fullness of God's Love.

Youth has its splendor. Do you believe in youth eternal?

Youth eternal is knowing the fullness and joy in life forevermore. In this you should believe, for it is more than possible. It is the way of God.

Who are the saints of today?

Whoever does the will of God. This is the highest attainment. Give all glory to God. Set your heart on what is right and true. Life is not a competition. Rise above the rocky stuff.

I used to have to guard my thoughts; now my thoughts guard and guide me. That is a revolution and a revelation, all because of one thing, the gift of Divine Love into my heart.

Do what you want. Be who you are. Be My "angel baby." Be My love in the world. For God so loved the world that He rained His love upon it into the hearts of the willing, those whom chose His will above their own. This is the love story of God. Tell it again and again. Amen!

He who gives his will to God gives God everything he is. Some say that all is the will of God and whatever befalls them is of God's hand. But they have forgotten, or not understood, that God gave each person a free will to live the life of his choosing and that by each one's thoughts and action their life is made. The will of God is always good, good for all, the best there is, the best of the whole of the universe. It is the holiest. The will of God is therefore above the will of man whom lives in sense consciousness.

The will of God is what man is to aspire to, to be all that he can be. But man alone, by his own power, cannot follow the will of God. He cannot make his own will into the will of God by any means of his own will. It is only by the surrendering of his own will that man can obtain the grace to live the will of God. This grace is a gift of God. This grace is God's Divine Love which God gladly delivers into repentant and God willing hearts. Repentant of the ways and holds of their own will. Pleading for the infilling of such grace by God to change them from mere mortal beings with the will of man into holy creatures which can by the will and love of God do no other than the will of God.

This will of God is love in its highest and fullest form God desires so for His will to be done on earth, but has left this as a choice for each and for all. We are free to do as we please and as well we are free to do as God pleases by offering the ultimate sacrifice to Our Maker, the free will He gave us upon our birth. And as we do, we are so filled with the grace of God's Divine Love and we are reborn, birthed in Spirit unto the Lord.

The abiding peace which surpasses all understanding
Peace of mind
The peace promised by the angel of the nativity
And on earth, peace to men of good will
Continual serenity of the soul
God only wishes our good.

The will of God is being supplanted into my heart. My ego has moved over and is on its way out. I am the Christ in expression for all.

You cannot pick and choose My words. No more than you can pick and choose My ways. My ways are My ways. My Will be done through you on earth.

It is no longer my choice. I have given my will over to God.

Let all your words be beautiful and ring true to the Truth you know within your heart.

I hear the messages spoken unto my heart.

Make all your words kind and sweet. Be a man or woman of your word for you are made or unmade by the words you keep within your heart.

What does your mind allow you to know or not know? In your head or your heart? These are the questions each should ask unto themselves: am I following the way of God which I know in my head or my heart?

Only the heart knows the truth of God. Many things are done in the name of God which are not "good for all." This is a sure sign that these actions do not arise from the truth of God, but instead from the mind, passed from mind to mind as the singular way to God, as the "truth." Which must be so fought for and defended that all other ideas must be condemned. And even so must the men that hold ideas contrary, for they are considered "condemned men" to be killed along with their ideas. Thankfully, people of such low consciousness are far fewer than have been in days of old. But the effects and power of their thinking still has a hold on the world breeding fear and thus more hate.

None, absolutely none of this, is of God. Not the initial anger and righteousness, nor the fear. God watches and waits, waits for the world as a whole to wake up to the truth, waits for the world to free itself from the hold of its own selfish ideas, waits for man to choose His will, God's true will, not the will of man. The will of man arises from the mind of man. The mind of man is small and narrow in view in comparison to the Great Mind of God. The Great Mind of God is where God's will resides. Man can access this Great Mind only through his heart.

The heart we speak of is not the heart muscle which beats to the rhythm of your life pulse. Your heart, your living heart, is actually your soul, which has been implanted into your body and remains with your body as long as your heart beats. Your soul resides within the area of your heart. This is why you get such feelings you describe as tugging on your heart. This is your heart and soul. Each must listen to their heart/soul center for Supreme Guidance.

"Chemicalization" is a process, that takes place bodily, when one begins awakening to the truth of God. Like a caterpillar's metamorphous into a beautiful butterfly the old cannot change into the new without the old breaking up to be recoded into a new beautiful pattern. Patience is required through this process, patience, trust, and peace of mind and heart.

Everything you ask believing, you shall know. Nothing will remain hidden. Do you live in fear?

I am breaking free from fear.

Self-control is about the power of one's will over one's own mind and body, free will used knowingly to produce and create the life one wants and desires. Controlling one's desires or aligning one's desire for the good of one's self. Let's play a game. It's called "no complaining." See the good everywhere and talk about it. Whatever you entertain your mind with, make sure it is good company.

OCTOBER 25, 2011

*Without questions there can be no answers. Question
everything. There is no such thing as too many questions.
It is wrong to tell a child that they ask too many questions.
Instead tell them that you don't know all the answers. Let
them continue to ask and allow them to find the answers to
life themselves. Allow the child to be curious.*

*Curiosity may have killed the cat but lack of curiosity kills the
ability to know and grow as a human and as a free spirit. Be
a free spirit. Become a free spirit. Ask the questions you yearn
to know. Then listen in with awe and wonder. The answers
are there for those who are aware.*

*Say what you want and only what you want. Don't confuse
the issue. Give a clear message to the Universe. Loud and
clear My dear. I'm glad this makes you smile and brings you
happiness. We hear the song of your soul. It is so sweet and
lulling.*

*Today is a fall day. Yes, it is blustery outside, but it doesn't
have to be inside. Decide now how your day will be. Give Me
your all and I will give you My All. Give Me your will and I
will make it Mine. So you will see the World Divine.*

*Do you remember, remember how much you are loved? There
are no words for this. It is only a knowing, a feeling deep
inside you shall have when you know My love. When you
know My love you will share My love. It is the way of My love
and there can be no other. I am giving you words to express
this love so you can share the way to peace within one's heart.
Tell them of My love and its saving grace. Tell them how I
love them all so and wish for them to come home and live
from their heart.*

I so wish to fill each past the brim with My saving love, but cannot without permission. Yes, each heart is guarded. The ego stands at the door protecting the way it knows. The ego does not want to be questioned. It is affronted with the idea that what it sees may not be true. But I ask all to ask of Me anything. Do not be afraid to ask. There is so much truth in life which from your perspective you cannot see. Ask Me. Trust Me. Let Me in. Crack the door. Let some of My luscious light in.

As you begin to see with this new light you will question more and I will tell you more of My ways. I always Love you. Do not be afraid to come to Me. If you say you have not felt My love, it is because you have not allowed My love. Your heart has been hardened by life. Come to Me and let My love soften it. I'll be gentle and take your hand and lead you to a better life.

You say you have asked questions but have not heard. I ask you when did you ever take time to listen? You are so distracted you cannot even hear a little bird. So how can you hear the voice of God within your heart? You ask and then run ahead with whatever you think you need to do. It's as if you really don't care, trust or believe I am here for you. And many perhaps don't fully believe there is any more to life than one can see with their two eyes and hold within their hand. Oh, ye of little faith, I ask you to try again.

If you do not want to believe in more then continue to shut the door. But if you do feel a tug within your heart, call My Name and We will start. Go within to the quiet place where I reside. Yes, I live within you deep inside. There My love for you awaits, waiting, just waiting for you to awake. Awaken to the fact that I, God, am Love and that I live within you, not someplace high above. Ask Me to help hold the door ajar. Ask Me to help you know I am not afar.

Ask Me for the knowing of My love. Ask Me to send angels on the wings of a dove. Ask Me for gifts of grace. Ask for My will yours to replace. Ask most of all for My Divine Love, as this is the gift I have for you when you really want to live through Me and live life anew. My Divine Love will fill you, but only as you ask. And as you ask you will know, you will know what peace truly is. For this love is of such substance that your fears will flee and all you will know is the grace of My love and will want to stay close to Me.

Please don't tarry. Time has been long enough. I am ready to gather all of My sheep back to My fold. Yes, I gave you a free will to live as you choose, but deep in My heart it has been My desire that each of you would desire higher, desire to know more, desire to know Me, desire My will over your will. You cannot have it two ways. It is your way, by your own will or it is by Mine. My will lives on earth only through you, as you choose to do. Yet you cannot choose to do My will. It is not in the power of your mind to do this. A change of heart has to happen. I will change your heart when you ask. When you ask for My love to flow free, when you burst open the door and allow Me to fully be. Then My love will fill your heart and soul. This is the story of all saints, new and old.

Your ego may be saying "no way, that's not real" or "that's no fun," but believe me this is as real as it gets and this is when the real fun begins. Let Me show you life from My side, from the side where the sun always shines within your heart. Let Me into your life. I'm here waiting patiently in love; it's up to you to start. Some believe they are not worthy of God's love.

But God does not hold back the gift of His love from any of His children and all are children of God by birth. It is only the mind of man which has created separation, a separation from knowing God and God as Love.

God is Love and you can feel God's love. But there are many that do not know of God's love. It has never been a secret of God but kept a secret by man to enslave other men and keep them small. It is the Truth of God's love, the gift of His love that God offers, the love of God, Divine Love. The love of God which I speak of now is not the love man has for God, not the man to God love. I speak of the highest form of love, "the love of God" which is Divine Love. This is the very substance of God, the love God is.

On special request God gifts His Divine Love into hearts. This is the saving grace, the Comforter of which Jesus spoke, delivered unto a human heart by the power of the Holy Spirit. A worthy heart is a yearning, hungry heart, one who truly desires to know God fully, but one must ask to receive. Ask and ask, again and again. I will change your life with My love says God, ask and you shall receive.

It is time to do my life's work. An understanding has to be made in my own heart and in the hearts of all. What is the will of God and how can one follow it? Is it the Bible?

The will of God in its completeness will never be written on paper by any hand for eyes to read. For the will of God, just like God, is unlimited and thus infinite. The will of God can only truly be known by heart. Not by any form of memorization but by heart knowings given to man individually through his heart, to and through the heart of a man who has chosen to crucify his own will and live through the will of God. Man may thus desire God's will, but man may never follow or truly know God's will by any will of his own.

Change is needed, a magnificent change of heart, all the work of God. By the order of God, God's Divine Love is poured into the supplicant heart. This Divine Love, the very essence of God, is the changing and transforming source of power. This special love of God is what makes one know, do and live God's will.

God's voice is heard, "the Comforter" has come and He is known as "The Father." The most Loving Father lives in one's heart to guide and direct step by step. This is the will of God as chosen by man. Man cannot have it two ways. He cannot adore the world and adore God. The bible has told us so. Seek ye first the Kingdom of God and all good things shall be added unto thee. Have no other idols before Me.

What is a sin?

A sin is not knowing God.

Is it a sin to dance?

No, not in itself. Seek ye first the Kingdom of God. When God is in your heart you will feel like dancing. Who cares to hear?

I do. I want to know the fullness of the Truth.

Do not preach to anyone. Allow these words and your life to speak for themselves. Preaching is saying, "You should do this or you should do that." to another. You may tell them the story of your life and minister to them but do not preach. The will of God can only be given unto each ones heart. Forget what you know from the words of others and follow unto Me. I will bring you home.

You have nothing to prove unto Me. You do not need to prove your purity. You do not need to prove your worthiness for My Love takes care of all and purifies each soul. There is no work for you to do but to surrender your all. Surrender your belief in yourself, in the power of your own will. This is how you are to come to Me to live through Me and living through Me, My will will flow naturally.

To each his own, it is by birthright the right of each human to choose the way of his life. He may choose the ways of his father's, his own or the ways of God. To follow the way of God in true form one is not to attempt to conform his will unto God's will but to supplicate his own will and ask God to so fill him with His love and light that God's will becomes his own.

So you say that is hard to listen to another tell of their faith and their life, which they believe is ordained by God, when you believe that way is not true. I say stop judging. This is what is hard for you, the feeling you are having that the way you believe is right for you, is right for all. Truly, you do not know. Stop believing so. Stop judging.

Christ is Divine Love in action, God's love in being and truth. Jesus found and recognized this Love through the Father whom he knew and spoke to in the silence. Through the power of this Love he became the Christ. Jesus Christ told us that all He could do, so could we if we followed his way, as his way, his life, was the way to the Truth, the Truth of God.

Jesus found and claimed this saving and transforming Love of God. The love of Christ is Divine Love which God is ready to give each repentant heart. A repentant heart is an open heart, willing heart. A heart willing to forgo the will of the body's ego mind and to be so in filled with God's love that one's very will is transformed by this love into the will of God.

Before Christ left his physical form on this earth, he assured us he would send "the Comforter" to care for us and lead us on the path to righteousness. For this, we have to ask believing. The words, the exact words, are not of such a matter as the intention, the intention of the heart. Your heart has to yearn for this knowing. Yearn with all your heart. Some may ask to know Jesus. Some may ask for Divine Love. Some may ask to know God. Some may ask to be shown the Light. All who ask, ask in faith, shall find. Find the Father's love in Christ within themselves.

The Divine flow
The great flow of Life
By Life Itself
Flowing forth
Freely
Abundantly
From the everlasting
Fount of Life within
Know Me
Know Life
God says
Become wholly conscious
Let My Love
Flow through you
This is the work

You are to do
Be the pipeline
Allow My Lifeline
To reach the world
At large.

You have a divine right to accomplish all things, all things in
My name. See your accomplishment as true. Hold it in your
hand. Caress it with your heart. Do not cling to old ideas.
Habit is a jail for the mind and soul. Open your heart to
new experiences.

Become self-reliant, vibrating in the God Vibration. God
Vibration is the highest vibration of life. Resistance to this
God Vibration is what causes disharmony in life. Living as
such is living under the Law, the true "Will of God." Do not
fear. Walk in the Light, the Light of My love. Stop deciding,
thus creating limits for yourself. Go with the flow.

MY SONG OF JOY

Say, say my playmate
Come and complain with me
And bring your problems three
We'll look for trouble to see.

We'll climb a ladder
And look near and far
To see life a jar
Oh come with me.

No, no complainer
Your game I will not play
Not today
Not any way.

I don't like the game
Of laying blame
I choose to see
Life without misery.

I see life now
Full of joy and hope
And will not talk
As if I cannot cope.

I will not play that sad game
With you
Of that old game
I am through.

I have a new game
Where it's fun to see
Things that make me
Truly happy.

I smell the flowers
And count my blessings
And sing God praises
Forever more.

So playmate I invite you
To look with me
For joy infinitely
For eternity.

We'll look for rainbows
And silver linings
Never searching
For things distressing.

No, no complainer
I will not complain with you
I see life anew
I know God's love is true.

I know it's my choice
To see life abundantly
I cast away my fears
And dried my tears.

I hope you'll join me
In looking for the good
It's all around
To be found.

Come, come playmate
Come out and play with me
Bring your blessings three
And we'll give thanks to thee
Forever more.

OCTOBER 26, 2011

Is my authentic self my soul self? Do all the answers to all the questions
lie within my heart? Show me the way. Point the true course for my life.
Keep me on track, on the right course, so that I may reach the highest
Heavens. This I pray.

> *Totally surrendering to God's will is totally allowing Spirit to
> live and breathe through you. Giving of yourself is the greatest
> gift you can give to God/Spirit and the greatest gift you can
> give yourself. Don't hold back. Don't resist the flow of "True
> Life" through your being. You have requested only the highest
> and the best and this is what we offer to you. Trust in God.
> Trust in good. Trust your heart. Trust this voice.*

If you don't listen to other's ideas, how can you ever truly know if the Truth is what you have? Sit with new ideas. Not with your mind, let your mind rest and sit with new ideas with an open heart. Those that feel good are worth keeping and pondering more. The other will naturally fall away.

Open your mind and follow your heart. Your heart is your soul being and your soul knows the truth of all. It came in with you, your body, to this world knowing. Your mind got involved and created stories, stories of man, stories by man of God and of God's ways. Let go of those stories. It is safe and you are safe. You do not need to cling to the ideas of your mind. You will not fall down. You are not your mind, you are so very much more. But you closed the door, the door to the knowing of your heart. You forgot how to trust your heart. Go with the flow. You do not have to know. Consider anew and a new life you shall live.

Behold, I am born anew. Christ is here.

Let go of what is holding you back.

OCTOBER 27, 2011

God in truth and power, You are one with me. I am with You in being and truth. I am perfected in body, mind and spirit.

Stand forth in this truth. Be the light of God, the spirit of knowing. Only see, and thus know, perfection. All is well with you and all. Forevermore be one with Me your Father.

Don't even say that. Don't even tell that story again. The story you tell about what you cannot do. The story you tell about limitations you have known. As sure as you repeat such with your words so will your life prove. You do not want this I know. So you have to erase what you knew, to know better. Know better for yourself. This is the story which you are to tell yourself and thus the world. Tell your new story, the wonderful story of your life.

This is who I am. This is what God is. Accept My love as your truth. Be My truth. Live fully through Me. Be My light. Be My love for the world. I command you.

I've heard the calling, the Christ calling.

Be Me for all. There is no other. Feel the Strength. Know the Power. Call it forth and use it.

Is this "New Thought?"

This is Original Thought, True Thought, and Pure Thought from the Fount of All Being. This thought can never be considered "old" as it is timeless, as is God, the Source of all truth. All good happens through the belief in good. God is good. Thus all good is of God.

God is my executive power. My will is God's will.

This shall be done as you say. Speak forth My will.

Is it a change of heart or recognition of one's heart?

You are right in your asking so. It is recognition of one's True Heart, the heart and home of God within. Consider it all good. Consider it all of God and it shall be. Stretch your imagination of what is possible. Don't know too much! The world needs dreamers, dreamers willing to accept their power to call forth their dreams.

Don't have a dirty mind! A dirty mind is a mind clouded with thoughts of lack and hardship. Enjoy clean and pure thoughts. It is not to be a burden to follow My ways. It is a joy to behold My ways as yours. Don't defend your weaknesses. Applaud your strengths, believe as you like. Then believe there is more of life to know than you believe you know.

Don't raise any man above you. Only raise My crown upon your head and don your "Sonship." Live in truth through Me and no other. When Jesus Christ said, "I am the Truth and Life" he was speaking My words. Do not get caught up in the man, but see the truth of who He was and is. His truth is My truth. The way is one. Truth is one, One in Me your Father which art in Heaven within your heart, begging for full expression unto the world.

Sit a little higher. Stand a little taller. With each breath know Me more. When someone says "Unfortunately for you..." don't believe them for he who liveth through Me is not bound by circumstances or appearances.

To accept better, one has to truly want better. One cannot truly want better unless he believes better is a possibility or exists as a possibility. Thus, which came first the chicken or the egg? The chicken had to believe in the possibility of the egg to manifest it. All that has been manifested resided before in the realm of infinite possibility, thus the chicken and the egg have always existed and one was never before the other.

How can one know God?

Know good. What do you want to know? What do you want to believe? What are you willing to believe? My truth you

*shall know and My truth you shall show as you believe and
trust in My love which I send forth unto your heart. Receive
My love My darling. My love is My healing grace which
transforms you into My own being in truth and grace, in
beauty and love and in patience and peace. Come with Me.
Walk ahead. Walk My way.*

My heart jumps for joy!

*Children are born believing, believing in their own power.
Unbelief is taught, unbelief in the power of the individual's
ability and thus power to create as he wishes, as he thinks.
The greatest sin of man may be the teaching of this unbelief
as man's core belief. This is the origin of all of man's error
thought. Make this known, known unto man.*

*Wonderful things can happen for your own good as you
desire without changing the mind of any other. You do not
need the conscious participation of any other to manifest
the good which you so desire. Many good works are done
through hands that do not know My full glory or recognize
such within their heart and mind.*

*All I have, all there is, is available to you to work through
and with, as you manifest good for all. Keep your vision.
Hold true to your belief in My better ways and such better
ways you shall know. No one else's consciousness is your
responsibility. You are only to show what you know. You do
not need to change any others mind or heart. In fact you
cannot. God cannot, and thus you as a piece of God cannot.*

*All change, all awakening, within man has to come from
within each man for himself, mere words do not serve. The
only way man can possibly awaken to the more of life is*

to witness the transformation of another and to see and feel the light and love of God expressing through him and shining forth. Then this light may awaken a yearning in his own heart to so seek such light, love, grace and wisdom for himself. At this point he may ask and you shall tell.

You can wonder all you want, the wonder of it all. When you think, think quick. Do not get trapped in your mind. If you know you are safe, you are safe. If you live in fear, then life will give you things to fear. A prophet is not recognized in his own house.

OCTOBER 28, 2011

When you pray for God's will to be done on earth, whom are you expecting to do God's will? When you say, why does God allow such things to happen? Ask yourself if you yourself allow God's will to happen. Have you put the Good of God in charge of your life? Have you surrendered your will to His? If not, then why do you expect any other to have done such? For this is the way the world works, by his own free will man is free to create his life by the will he chooses.

So you say someone is messing with your mind. No one is messing with your mind but you. And messing is a very apropos description of what it is you are doing. You are clouding your own vision, stirring up mud, muddying the clear cool waters of your consciousness. Lay blame nowhere, not on any other, not on yourself. Just be still. Stand still. Breathe in and breathe out. Find the Calm in the center of your heart. Find Me. Rest in Me. Hold still in Me. When you again open your eyes you shall find again the clear water of which you can drink.

You are free right where you are right now to paint a new picture of your life. Stop crying. You need no other to realize your vision. No one else has to see as you do for you to see clearly and to see the life you want clearly. Dry your tears and realize the power you hold to behold the life you want.

Do you trust yourself? You are fine where you are. You do not need to search beyond yourself for yourself. There is a fortune to be made and it is yours. There is an unknown before you. Do you fear it? Step into it with confidence. Know who you are.

Out of space and time, messages come to me, messages of Love.

There was a time when you said the world you knew was falling apart and you came apart because you could not hold it all together. The shell of the existence you knew became cracked and all the stuff slipped from your fingertips. But look what you found? In the midst of a shattered reality you found yourself whole. You acknowledged wholeness within yourself and your realized you are alive and well.

I reach for happiness wherever I can find it. I reach within my heart. I am not satisfied with the existence I have known, the one where the blinds are drawn to keep the light out.

You don't have to be. Well good for you! Spirit quest, what you are looking for is found within you. Slow down, stop running around, nothing is hidden. All is here and all is well.

You do not have to put up with that. Stand your ground. You are well grounded in Me. You cannot fall down. I will not allow you to. I hold you up. I cheer you on. I believe in you as you believe in Me. We are here for each other. We hear each other.

I hear you and feel your pain. My arms are around you holding you, rocking you. I Love you so My dear. I will never let you go. Don't compromise who you are for anyone! Feel free to be who you are. You are the best you, you can be. Be true to yourself and you will always know true happiness.

Continue in the Love you are. You know who you are. Live it fully. Trust in the Christ you are. Do not hold back. Be the Love. Be My love. Look for and know peace. Peace becomes you. The piece of God you are is whole. You are holy. Walk My way. Hold My hand. We are together in Spirit. We are One. There is nothing to forgive. There is only the life of Love to live. What do you choose to fill your mind with? Fill it with thoughts of My love. Become My love.

It's like I have a life coach in my head, but the wisdom is from a whole different source than my brain.

Nobody wants to hear "You should's. You should do this or you should do that."

Part of the reason people do "recreational" drugs is to circumvent the mind which is so busy, so busy with its stories. They attempt to escape their mind reality. What they are seeking, truly seeking, is a deep inner peace. They do not know that this peace lies within their very being, within their heart. It is the journey for all and up to each to desire such a feeling, a knowing. Then to understand it is not outside of them but within that the peace of Heaven resides, within their heart. Seek and ye shall find.

You didn't always think like that. The way you think about how hard life is. There was a time when you were ready to meet the world head on and show the world what you had, and were, and could be. You might now refer to that time as a time when "you didn't know better," but a more accurate statement would be that it was a time "you believed in better." That innate belief in "better" is what propelled you forward. It is what set your course.

The thing with you is that you have tasted so much failure that you no longer believe in better. Your vision has become tunneled into the hole you have dug for yourself. You cannot see your way out and you do not even dare dream of a way out. Instead you fill your nights as well with visions of endless terror.

Look at yourself and see what you have done, done to yourself. No one has done a thing to you. Only you can control your mind and you have changed your mind about life. You have not had steadfast faith in the good. This is what is required, steadfast faith in good prevailing. If your eyes are constantly drawn to and focusing on what is not right, you have not the vision to see better ahead.

When you were young you told the world how it was going to be and now you are allowing the world to tell you how you are to be. It is not too late to change your mind and thus your life. If you are still breathing you still have the life force within your body.

Claim this power, for power it is. Direct this power to the ideas of your better good. Focus this energy on creating anew, a new vision, a new reality, a new you. This is work only you can do. Before the hands get involved in laboring away, the heart and head need to get in the same place and agree on the direction of focus of your life. Whatever you think about you bring about. Stop telling the stories of a broken you, a broken spirit, a broken heart. Give life a new start.

You are what you think. Be what you want. Say what you want. Claim the life you want. Decide to be happy. Give love freely. Accept love freely. Do not be stingy in love. Give thanks for what you have. Be grateful for everything. Do not complain. Do not lay blame. Look ahead. Enjoy now. Walk in the sunshine not the shadow and you will see the light of day. Available now, see My love this way, available every moment, everyday. Free to give. Free to give away.

So something knocked you out of whack again. Life knocked you upside the head, into your head, and away from your heart. You were living those dramatic painful moments away from the awareness of My love. All the pettiness of the ego came back full force. It's as if you were possessed by some evil force, overcome you were with emotion. You could not see or think clearly. All the world felt against you, you felt disparity and aloneness. Your saliva became sour in your mouth. Even the taste of your own spit disgusted you. You hated every moment. You yearned again for the Peace you knew still existed, existed within your heart. "Where is it you asked? Come find me save me from myself."

And then part of you remembered, remembered My Love. "God loves me. God loves me. God loves me just the way

*I am. I am perfect in God's love." Again and again you
reminded yourself of My love and with each breath you
drew your consciousness back into the peace, back into the
sweet well of My love, all an inner journey, all while still
standing in the midst of the same physical reality. The outer,
the physical, stayed the same but as the inner perspective
transformed your view, the outer cleared and you could see
Peace in your heart and beyond.*

*As you lived and breathed and drank and swam in the
peaceful existence of My love your tears dried and the lump
in your throat dissolved. "I always want to live from here!"
you declared. "Keep me close dear Lord. Keep me in the
peace of Your loving heart. Never let me go. I let my ego go
and thank God, the love of God for saving me once again."*

OCTOBER 30, 2011

*Don't let your spirit be broken. Look for love and joy
everywhere. You have tasted the bitterness of life away from
the knowing of My sweet redeeming love, but only tasted.
You do not realize what a fortune you have always known,
as you were raised in love and acceptance. Let this little
taste fuel your compassion for those living their lives away
from the knowing. Let your heart reach out with My love to
all you meet. Many you may touch will find your love, My
love, as never before known to them. Bring My peace to My
people. Show them My love. Show them where to find Me.
Allow the Silence to completely immerse you. Step into the
ocean of My consciousness.*

Daily revelations presented to my consciousness awaken me to the
fullness of Spirit.

Man is perfected in his God realization, his recognition of his true Spirit essence, of this True Self, his "Christ-ness." With total recall, he is pure in spirit and mind, wholly holy. God speed.

You are going to have to change your mind. When someone says something that trips a mental trigger that sends you to a bad feeling place it is of no use to bother one moment with the idea of changing what they say. For the only thing that can possibly matter to you is what you do with it in your own mind. If you don't like the thoughts that come to your mind and thus the feeling that comes over you, reach for a good thought, a better thought, a new way for you to mentally process and thus emotionally process the information (energy) coming to you. Change your mind about it. Think of it a new way. Create in your own brain a new association for those words.

Someone says "It's only 55 days until Christmas" and to them it may be a statement in anticipation of the joy of giving and the traditional celebration, but to another that same statement may bring on a feeling of dread and anxiety as they think of the many preparations yet to be done. Whatever the meaning intended by another, you get to choose your own personal interpretation of the saying, even if the other is saying such with a heavy heart full of anxiety.

It is your choice, always your choice, what you do with any energy directed your way. You can leave it, push against it or accept it. If you choose to accept it, make sure whatever you accept feels good and sets right within your heart of hearts. Only let in what feels good to you. In this way you are living the saying "To thy own self be true."

So what is true to you about the thought of Christmas approaching? What do you want to think about it? Of course you want to feel good about it, so make it a true statement that feels good to you which can repeat to yourself whenever "the Christmas lights" flash before your eyes.

A Christ is born unto the world.

Very nice, very true and as you know continues to be true as you are yourself birthing a new Christ within your own heart. Repeat it again and again.

A Christ is born unto the world. A Christ is born unto the world. A Christ is born unto the world. I have Peace within my heart.

November 2011

And I will make an everlasting covenant with them,
promising never again to desert them,
but only to do them good.
I will put a desire into their hearts to worship Me,
and they shall never leave Me.

Jeremiah 32:40 ᴺᴸᵀ

November 2, 2011

*You think you are to tell it like it is. Tell the truth. Tell a
different story. Beat to a different drum, the beat of your
True heart. The one who knows all is well, the one who can
tell your true story, your story of abundance, health, wealth,
joy and peace. When you are keeping your thoughts on
God, you are keeping your thoughts on what is right with
the world, things that feel good to think about. Thus you are
aligning yourself with Spirit, with the good which is God
the Father. Know that which is true and good. Know God.
Give God full expression through your thoughts, words and
deeds. Be one with Thee. Walk with Thee. Breathe through
Thee.*

*Bait and switch, God does not bait and switch. You get what
you give. No more. No less. Walk in this truth.*

Song time…

Don't make everything a mountain.
Don't make everything a mountain.
Don't make everything a mountain.
Say, this is fine with me.

This is fine with me.
This is fine with me.
Don't make everything a mountain.
Say, this is fine with me.

I am a joyful creator
I am a joyful creator
I am a joyful creator
I make life what I want it to be

Life what I want it to be
Life what I want it to be
I am a joyful creator
I make life what I want it to be.

Do you see what I see?
Do you see what I see?
A star, a star way up in the sky
Signaling beauty and grace
Signaling beauty and grace.

The messed up message people have been given is that to feel good others around them have to perform in certain ways in order for one to be happy. Let go of that idea now. You only have to be and only can be in control of yourself and your own thoughts and actions.

You have always believed you had to be perfect at something before you did it or claimed you could do it. Let go of that idea now. Whenever you put your best effort into doing something, full of good intention, you are doing it perfectly. Get in the spirit of it Mastermind. Get in your Master Mind and create a wonderful experience.

I am a joyous creator!

You don't have to wait to be a success, you are a success! See your life this way. You do not have to wait to be happy. You can be happy right where you are. Realize this. Look at your life with your "real eyes," your beautiful, bright clear eyes. What do you think you have to prove and whom do you think you need to prove it to anyway? Life is delicious just the way it is. There is nothing for you to fix, only the True Life to accept.

Whose voice speaks the loudest to you, the world's or Mine? Whatever your answer is depends on where and to what you have given your attention to. Another way of saying this is what do you worship God or the material? Most quickly you will deny having any idols before Me, but yet you give your attention to so many other things before Me. What does this world you look at promote? Peace and harmony or discord and injustice? Competition or compassion?

You are in this world to live in it but not to be consumed by it. Keep your thoughts high. Raise up your spirit. Be of a light and joyful countenance. Think of Me and all the good you see around, which is an expression of what I am, the Eternal Good. You have lost nothing, but gained everything as you realize who you are.

Many of this world believe that knowledge is required to be acquired from without, from the words of others. Much can

*be learned from others and yes, much wisdom is conveyed
this way. But where do you believe the root of all true
wisdom lies? It lies within, within all. All sages and saints
have drawn from the same well of wisdom and you too will
be wise as you dip your own bucket into this well.*

NOVEMBER 2, 2011

My highest ideal is being fulfilled.

> *Don't discount anything you do. You may discount the price
> but don't discount the value.*

The voice I hear and of which I write messages of love from is my
Spiritual Growth Advisor.

Positive statement: I am a motivational speaker. I am a published
author. People look to me as a spiritual facilitator. I am a spiritual
facilitator. I write books and give workshops. Like Louise Hay, my life is
an inspiration to millions. My light shines bright!

> *It's true. It's just true! Start where you are. Whatever it is
> that you want to do or go to, start where you are. You do
> not need to move to any other physical, spiritual or mental
> place before you begin your journey. Deicide what you want
> from where you stand. You are standing in the right place
> for this is your starting place. Start here. With this breath, a
> new chapter begins.*
>
> *Hear Me now, loud and clear. I keep you near. I wear you
> in My heart. You are the love of My life. Love your life. The
> life you have. Cherish each breath. For with each breath
> you manifest your desires, as you bring them forth to your
> consciousness. Be conscious of your thoughts. Hold them*

high. Reach the sky. Do not hold back your dreams, as you are so much more than you think you are or can be. I can see your life clearly and it is beautiful.

Let Me tell you how I love you. Let Me lift your spirit unto the stars. Let Me take you and keep you in Heaven, where you will realize who you are. You are My love in motion. You are the beat of My heart. Oh, My dear I hardly know where to start. I've loved you since the beginning and way before that. Time is not a measure. There is no measure, as a matter of fact, for My love for you has no limits. It's way beyond the sky. Come let Me show you how I love you. Let's walk together through life you and I.

NOVEMBER 3, 2011

Souls purify through God realization, through life as man. Don't get so caught up in what food is or isn't right to eat. Give more attention to the nourishment of your soul.

What can I do to nourish my soul?

Drink from the cup of My everlasting love. Breath in the beauty I have set all around you. Behold it. Make it yours. Own the beauty of creation in your heart. I can see the way from a higher perspective, the way to truth and beauty.

Decide what you need, what you desire for yourself. Give no thought to what you don't need. Without thought action, such cannot exist.

Be full of My Love. My Love overflows My own heart unto yours. Take your fill. Let it overspill into the world for all. I give you My All so you can be My All, All of Me for all for all the world. What a wonder it is. Isn't it?

Do not be afraid to wonder. Wondering and wandering are not the same. When you wonder about Me, when you ponder on the Grace of My Love, more is drawn to you and more of My ways you shall understand. No wondering is not wandering. Wondering is where all knowledge begins. Wandering is what the lost sheep do as they have lost sight of their dear shepherd.

Do not lose sight of Me. Keep Me in your thoughts. Wonder about Me, wonder about My ways. You may wonder where I am. I am always with you, as I am part of you. Oh yes, the wonder of it all. I am your dear Shepherd. Although My Vision is from the highest of the hills, I am never far from you. I am as close as your thoughts and yet you can know Me fully when you move beyond all thought to the center of your being, your heart. Here I reside in the purity of your soul.

I am within you and I am out of you, but We are never without each other. I am the air you breathe. I am Life and so are you. We are together forever. No separation there is. So never wander my dear, your Shepherd is here. Never wander in fear and desperation. I see beyond your vision. Ask Me for My Aid. Ask Me for My eyes to be your eyes so you can as well see life so clearly. Wonder about this, wonder about all of it and you will never wander again.

Love letters these are.

Don't worry. Don't bother your little head about a thing. It is being done as you asked. As you gave your word, I give you Mine that it is done as you asked. Feel comfort in this knowing.

Don't let the sticks and stones of any other dam up the flow of good to you. The only way they possibly can is if you take such notice of them that they become your reality as well. Allow Good to flow to you and through you freely. This Good has the strength to push past, around, and through any debris you can conjure up. As the current is more freely allowed, the True Force of this River is known. No debris will ever be able to collect again. May this Force be ever in your consciousness for this Force is ever with you.

Pyromaniac: One whom enjoys setting things afire. What can be set afire? Things of the world. Only the material can be burned and thus burned away. Yes, gaseous matter is still matter. It seems there are many among you who would proudly bear the title of pyromaniac, for they are those who delight in setting fires of fear upon the earth. Such great and grand fires that much attention they draw. Many draw near as the tall dancing flames enchant the eye and as they draw near, they fear.

Could this fire be the very Hell of which man tells tale tales? Why do so many gather around in such great heat and despair? Why do they stay in this uncomfortable place? Does safety in numbers mean anything to you? What about the idea that man only knows what he sees? And of course he only sees what he looks for.

You do not have to stay by the fire of fear and keep it burning. It is not your destiny to walk the earth looking for broken twigs here and there to toss into this fire to keep it a roar. One always has a choice to walk away. First by turning your head, looking in a new direction and then walking a new way.

You may feel at first that you are walking alone for you see no trail. You just keeping moving toward comfort, toward what feels better and then better. Let your instincts guide you to higher ground. And as you rise to this higher ground, this elevated plane of existence, you will begin to notice others have arrived and are arriving just as you. Together and separately you search and find clues. Like breadcrumbs left, perhaps generations ago, by others who have been on the same path. These breadcrumbs lead to yet a higher plane. And as you journey toward this great feeling place of great safety and comfort you will gain peace with every step. The smoke will clear, the smoke from the fire of fear which had enshrouded you and clouded your vision.

This is not the whole story. There is so much more to come from where this came. Continue to tell the tale. What greater gift is there but to speak for Spirit, to make known to humanity the great love of God? None, there is no greater gift, nor finer service. God is everywhere. Good is everywhere. The power of God, the power of Good, lies within man. True man is the Christ, which is God in expression.

I am delighted to tell you all which you yearn to know. That is all that is required on your part is a yearning, a hunger, a thirst, for this knowledge. Then of course you have to allow and recognize the gifts given. You must receive, accept with gratitude and give thanks.

Allow yourself to feel good. Allow the good which is there, or here, always present, to shine forth through you. Allow good to rise up within to the without. This is your source of good, of all God's goodness for you. From your own heart you dip into the deep well of My love. Do not dip sparingly as the more you dip the more there will be. Hold the ladle to your own lips and then offer the refreshing "Life Water" of My love to all you meet. Whomever comes across your path you are to greet with the fullness of My love. No one is ever in your way. They have come for a drink from My well and you My daughter are to offer them a drink. Let My love flow freely to all. Jesus said: Whatsoever you offer to the least, you offer unto Me. Take this cup and drink it. It is the cup of My blood, given for you so that all may have "Everlasting Life."

So much can be. If you dream it, you can do it. Feel free to dream big. Imagine a wonderful life. Then believe in your own dreams. Believe them true. So many live life so small, hardly a life at all compared to what could be. If they would only follow their dreams with their whole heart, but their mind gets in the way and takes charge saying, "Stop being silly and wasting precious time on pipe dreams, for you know such can never be." And then their heart agrees and dreams fly out the window, away, far away from their vision, never to be seen again. We say enjoy your dreams. They are a preview of what can be, if you allow the possibility.

Do not fear. In this moment, We ask you not to fear. What would you be fearing anyway, something that hasn't happened? The unknown? You say you fear the known, for you feel you know what the future holds. And the picture you hold in your mind is grim and the longer you hold it in your mind the sharper the details become. Well, if you continue on this path you will surely reap the grim outcome you are predicting, or pre-dictating, or calling into existence. So stop right there, turn that switch off and turn on a different power for your life.

Look for God, your good, the goodness of your heart. Reach into the Peace of your heart and pull goodness out and grab a hold of it. Do this with all your heart and mind. Hug the goodness. Pet and pat the goodness. Admire and love the goodness. Think of God and all God's goodness. Think of a sweet new baby, a blushing bride, baby birds in a nest, a light spring shower. Think of how happy you are to be alive. Stay with Me now. Hold hope. Hold hope high like a banner. Fly your banner of hope into the sky. Make your hope into a kite and let it fly high. Let it come to Me. Let Peace rain and reign in your heart. Dance with this Peace. Sing the song of Peace. Hum along with Me.

What bad can happen? Whatever bad you can imagine can be. What good can happen? Whatever good you can imagine can be. Consider your thoughts your programming. What you give thought to is what plays out as your life experience. Is what you are thinking about really the life you would choose to experience if you could? Did you know you can choose, choose the life you want? It's all a matter of proper programming. They got what they wanted or what they thought they could have and they never wanted more than they thought they could have.

Gospel music, "Faithful is our God" equals "God is always here." The big mistake that has been is that God is far away and Heaven cannot be reached today. God lives within each heart and today each can start to find the joy that lives within to rise above negative thought, which is sin. "Sin" because this thought of fear and lack is what keeps each from knowing peace, comfort and joy. Sin is error thought. Proper thought brings forward the joy. Improper thought destroys one's vision of Peace, which is the Truth of all.

Let me know peace, comfort, harmony, forgiveness, compassion, foresight and unity. Open my heart. Let Your Love spill out for all. Hold nothing back. Shine on and through me. Make my heart aglow. Set my heart afire. Raise me up. Raise me higher. Let me fill Your Higher Desire.

NOVEMBER 4, 2011

Today I saw a new way to go through life in joy. Though nothing new, I hadn't seen the way so clear.

> *Let go of burdens and they do not exist. Cut the shackles from your ankles and walk My way.*
>
> *When one experiences something that one has never experienced, or never been told about by trusted authorities, even if the happening is completely natural and right, there is a feeling of uncertainty that comes. To validate that very private experience, one quietly begins a quest to see if any other has known as he. There is a comfort in knowing that another has as well shared the experience. Even across oceans of time experiences are shared by the written word and minds are eased and souls are joined. It is good. All is well.*

I can tell the story I want to tell. The story I want told. I write the story of my life, word by word. With my word I write my life. It is a beautiful love story, so worth telling, so worth sharing. It is a story of joy and compassion, of peace, comfort and abundance. Such a good read it is.

> *Let the joy unfold. Let the story of joy be told. Sing a new song unto the world. Let your heart be glad. Tell a new story of life. Sing a new song of your life. Shout it high on a mountain. Proclaim it widely. Make it yours. Through the power of your word, the new song shall be your life.*

Sing a new song unto the Lord. Let your song be sung from mountains high. Sing a new song unto the Lord, singing Alleluia.

Whatever you give your attention to, you believe in and that belief becomes your reality. Pay attention to what you pay attention to. I hold these truths to be self-evident. No burden of proof is laid upon you for truth speaks for and defends itself.

This is where I live. I live from my heart, from the truth of my soul. I need not spend hours in mediation to reach a brief glimpse of heavenly delight. This delight is mine to have and to hold and from which to enfold. I have painted pictures of what it felt like to live in such a place. I expressed the intensity of my joy with color. Breathing life into images held in heart and mind. Some received them as intended. They connected through their heart. Experiencing my painted visions gave their heart a start, an opening to look at all life anew. Whoever knew what paint and canvas could do?

You have to stretch yourself to grow. Sometimes, as you stretch beyond a point you have been before, whether physically, mentally or spiritually you will experience resistance to the new way. Patterns have been set in your life and following the patterns already set is quite comfortable. But no gain is made by continuing to travel the same path day in and day out. You have to journey beyond with full intention to get beyond the point you are at, to persevere through the discomfort of a new space. But know this; the new space will be comfortable one day. So comfortable that again you will feel an urging to again go beyond and challenge yourself to new heights.

*The gift of knowing, all are given the same gifts of Spirit.
It is not a matter of anyone or another having the gift of
hearing the call of Spirit over another. What it is, is a matter
of acceptance, recognition and then desire to develop a
clear channel. A clear channel is one free of the static of a
chattering mind. Spirit speaks to all. All can hear but they
must choose to listen.*

*Jesus Christ was a clear channel and thus voice for Spirit.
But even as plainly as he spoke the word of God to the
people of his day, he was aware that many did not have
the ears to hear the truth of his message. So he spoke the
words for those with ears to hear. He spread the seed of
God's message of truth everywhere. Even though he knew
much would fall onto unfertile ground (unhearing ears)
there would still be some which would fall on fresh tilled soil
awaiting the word of God to plant within their souls to grow
their faith anew.*

*If you are not growing you are dying. You are in the process
of degenerating versus regenerating. You must challenge
yourself daily to grow in some way to become more than
you were the day before. Stagnation is certain death.*

*"IT'S TEN O'CLOCK AND ALL IS WELL!" You don't hear
that anymore in your society, the clear voice of the town
crier ringing out across the night air messages of safety and
comfort to all. Your society feeds no messages of comfort.
Only fear is bred. Even with good intentions messages of
fear and discord are rang out. The story now is awareness of
discord and disease. Breeding more and more discord and
disease with each breath given to such talk. What you think
about you bring about dear ones, so why not change your
tune to health and happiness awareness.*

For as you declare and make more aware of living in accord with such a flow of life, much life you shall give to all whom truly desire to live well and at ease, in comfort and joy. Comfort and joy is to be known. It is to be proclaimed and specifically named. The Comforter within knows your truth and proclaims joy and comfort in your name. Take time my dears to listen to the call, the call for all to know the Truth of angels as they herald. "JOY TO THE WORLD, YOU ARE SAFE AND WARM! IT'S TEN O'CLOCK AND ALL IS WELL."

Bless you. Know you are blessed. Call forth your good into fruition. Allowing the will of God is allowing the flow of good. It is allowing whom you really are to flow naturally and completely into the world. There is love and there is fear. Fear breeds hate. Love births acceptance, thus peace and joy for all.

Some may say that he or she is "in good spirits." But it is better said that he or she is living through the recognition of the good spirit he or she is. For there is only one, one spirit, which is good and anyone with a heartbeat is a good spirit in truth. To be lived, truth has to be recognized and appreciated, given attention, praise and thanksgiving. So the truth is that when anyone appears to be in good spirit, they are in fact aligned with their truth and are acknowledging the good of life of which they are a part.

Don't water it down. Lay out these truths as given unto you. This is the work you are to do. This is your calling. You hear My voice so loud and clear. You are to tell others as well, My dear. Everything is set in place waiting for you to arrive and you will, as you have asked for My will to be done. Consider it all good.

It's exciting to be the messenger of such joy. Jesus was excited as well. For his mission was to proclaim the Gospel, the Good News. Some of your seed will fall on barren ground. But do not be dismayed, for the words will as well meet fertile soil, ready to receive these words. It is the art of listening to your heart.

There was a time when you walked and lived in fear and could only seem to see what was wrong with the world. You felt so lost and alone wandering in a desert of despair. That time is long gone and now your life hums to a new song. Joy is your name. "Joy Be Me" is your claim to fame. No longer do you lay blame.

Wondering is not wandering, though the masses have been made to believe as such. Fear has been instilled in the minds of many. It is the fear of God. As they believe in a judgmental, wrathful God they fear the very thought of pondering God's mysterious ways. They have been taught that to wonder is to doubt. And that anything close to doubt is sin, very serious sin, separation from God.

But I say, whoa to those who fear Me. Fear and awe are not the same things in the language of your day as it once was. Your Father, your Creator, is not to be feared. You are to be in wonder and awe at My ways. You may not understand My ways, so you name them mysteries, but they do not need to remain as so. You are to know Me and as you know Me you will understand more and more of My ways. Ask and it is given. Ask Me for the answers. Understand that you do not know, but can know. But you will only know what you give your attention to. So give your attention to Me and ye shall know Me.

You may not feel I am real for you have not felt My Presence. I do not judge or condemn you for this. Perhaps you don't care to know about Me and choose to give Me no thought. The choice is yours. You may carry on as you wish with the power of your free will. When and if you are ready in this life, just ask. Ask Me to show Myself in your life.

Don't ask if you truly don't want to have what I have to give or you will receive nothing in return. But if you are curious as to what this More of life is that makes people talk about God, then please do inquire, inquire within. Ask for My Love in your heart. Ask for Me to fill you with your hearts true desire. Ask Me to raise you up to an elevation which is higher.

Wonder about Me; wonder as a child wonders at the sky. Ask Me how I do it and how My Love is so strong to make hearts see good and not wrong. The more you think of Me and wonder at My ways, the more the Truth of Me you shall know, as I shall show you in your life how to live without strife. Oh yes, there is power in wonder, the wonder of it all. It is all wonderful.

NOVEMBER 5, 2011

You have to push the reset button of your mind to start again with the freshness and fullness of life as a possibility. You have to clear your "hard drive" of all the corrupted files that are jamming the flow of the system that is in place. We are speaking mentally and spiritually here. This has nothing specifically to do with the physical things you see in life, except what and how and if you think of them. What has to happen is a major reprogramming of what you think about anything, period. You have to get back to basics, to what

*you came in with, what you knew and didn't know.
What you didn't know was whatever you believe now about
anything. You didn't know about money so you had no
beliefs about it, whether it was good or bad or if you had
any, some, lots or none. You didn't come in to this world
worrying about what you wore, or if you wore anything.
The only thing you knew about was what felt good and what
didn't. When something didn't feel good, you openly showed
emotion by pouting and crying. When you were comfortable
and satisfied you were calm and peaceful.*

*That's what you came in with, a wonderful guidance system.
No beliefs, none are necessary for existence. If they were
you certainly would have come in with them as you will
notice you were designed perfectly for this life you have.
Actually you haven't noticed as well as you should, for you
have forgotten this wonderful guidance system you came
in with. You stopped trusting it. You stopped believing in it
and instead believed those who arrived before you. Well of
course you did, as they were bigger and stronger and caring
for your physical needs. We know that they did have the
best of intentions when they told you the stories they told
you about the value of material things and emotional things
that arose. They taught you well, as well as they could. They
just taught you what had been taught to them, customs,
rituals, and stories explaining life and how one was to move
through it.*

*They taught you with their words and actions, some good,
some not so good. Some you vowed to follow and some you
chose to deny. But at that point, when you became of age
to choose your own life course, you as well had forgotten
what you came with. The wonderful system put in place to
guide you through life without rules, regulations, rites and*

restrictions. Your original programming was a befuddled mess, so entangled in the things you had been taught about life that you didn't even know what you knew. Yes, you came in knowing, all the rest has been a belief. And the beliefs are what trip you in life, what impedes the natural flow, that block the strong current of good that is always coming your way, flowing to you.

So we say to live afresh you need to see the day anew. You need to "reboot." You need to clear the hard drive of your mind from the random files that breakup your stream of consciousness.

November 6, 2011

When I have a choice between comfortable and uncomfortable I always vote for comfortable.

Good for you, for this is how it should be. You seem to recognize this easily in the physical but not always or so much with the mental. But it is exactly those comfortable mental thoughts that drive you unto the comfortable physical place you would like to be. See no limits before you. There are challenges, yes we know, but what fun would life be without challenges? Challenges are opportunities for growth, for expansion. Define none as limits.

If it is your mission to change something, anything, for the better, then think of only and speak of only the better. You add no good to the situation by continuing to point out to yourself or anyone what is wrong. See and think only of the right which you are intending to manifest, otherwise you are truly "up to no good." The only way to change is to know good. When you know good, you know God.

Do you know where all fresh ideas come from? They arise unto your consciousness from within your heart, which is your soul, which is continually connected to Source, which it the fount of all possibility. They come to and through you as you allow, as you allow the possibility of something to be, as you allow the possibility of a solution to a quandary you have. They come to you when you say you would "like to find a way," not when you say "no way." When you declare anything impossible you are declaring it impossible for you and you alone, unless others believe your talk as well. So when anyone chooses to prove anything cannot be done he can and will do so by the power of his very word. He is using his own will power, the power of his will to set limits on his own knowing and showing. Believe what you want people. Do not believe in the limits others set unless you want to make that as well a ceiling for the possibilities of your own life.

You were taught to fear. You can be a calming presence in the space you are in. You can be the Peace. You can hold the Peace by not getting caught up in the drama which drives the fear that others dance to.

What is bad? It is the absence of the recognition of the good that is. Cognition is necessary. That means you have to be cognitive, aware in mind, of the good around or you will not perceive the good and get in a bad feeling place. Just as the sun is always shining day or night, no matter what, your good is flowing to you as well. Just because you do not see the light of the sun from where you are does not mean the energy of the sun has stopped its flow. Just the same is true for the energy of good, as it is still available to you even as you do not feel or see it. It is all a matter of perspective and allowance.

Yes, we know you have tried to be a good person your whole life and actually you've done a quite good job of it. We are certain anyone questioned would attest to the fact of your sweet demeanor. But you have not been satisfied and your heart was restless. You were often sad and confused, overwhelmed and tripped up by all of the life outside of you and even within you of which you felt no control.

Here lays the difference between the old you and the you holding this pen in your hand. Before, you tried to be a good person, and yes even a God person, but you were only attempting by the power of your own will. You had never truly said to Me; let Your Will be done. You never surrendered your control over to My Control. You didn't because you didn't know how. You didn't understand the power of My Love.

You ask questions. You get answers. People look everywhere for content, content that matters, which can make a difference in their life, fill the hole. It is a collaboration, most of what you do and say is; a seamless stream of inspiration you are fed and which your mind interprets. Some seems to be from more of the workings of your mind. This is your self-expression and your questioning. And then other things come to you as a surprise. They just arrive or arise in your consciousness. Like when you wonder about something in uncertainty in one moment and then confidently speak the answer in the second. These are gifts from Spirit, which you have allowed. You asked and you have allowed. As well you have paid attention and heeded, all part of the process of allowing Spirit to express through you.

Sometimes, for a brief moment you hesitate to write what you hear as it does not fit with your mind. You do not know where the words are going or if they are going anywhere. But then you remind yourself to let go and allow Spirit to express as it wishes. This is an art, truly an art, the art of allowing something to be without judgment or control. And of course, complete trust is necessary as well. But as you have expressed that only the highest and the best can come to and through you, you have not feared. Faith is what you have, faith that there is a power higher than your own physical mind, faith that this power is love for you and only wants the best for all.

"You could," sounds a lot better than "You should." "Could" sounds like a friendly suggestion, "Should" sounds like a demand. Demands ignite ego and thus walls of defense rise up from nowhere.

Only do what you can feel good about. If you can't find a way to feel good about something then you are better off just not doing it. If it is something which you feel, or know, needs to be done then you need to get to a level of acceptance with it, a neutral position. Don't ever participate in anything with a level below acceptance or you will be swinging or shifting yourself into an uncomfortable place which only sets you up to continue on that downward path. Look for things to feel good about all the time wherever you are and whatever you are doing. As you think about things to feel good about you will feel good and thus more good things to think about will come to you and then you will be upwardly mobile on the upward spiral of higher desire. Desire well.

Don't tell anyone who they are. It's not up to you to decide who anyone else is at anytime. Don't say to another

"You don't like this or that." or "You are always this way."
Allow them to just be. Accept them as they come to you
without your preconceived notions. What was, was, but
isn't necessarily now. People change and often for the
better, allow the possibility of this to be your experience.
Experience each day and each person anew.

Take a "chill pill." That's what you are to do when you are
exasperated and about to venture below the comfortable
place where you belong. You have found that the words
"take a chill pill" roll off the tongue and from the lips quite
nicely but are not so easily accomplished. Usually the person
saying it to you is already in a comfortable state of mind.
That is why they have the perspective to see that you are
looming out of balance. So it is easy for them to say it, but
how are you to so easily accomplish this state of chill or
stillness?

There is no pill to be swallowed, but you most likely do need
to swallow your ego. Quite often the ego and its agenda
have felt threatened and that is what has gotten your
"undies in a bunch," so to say. Stillness is the key concept
here. Swallow your ego pride and then take a deep breath
and hold it. Then slowly release. Release the hold, the grip
you feel clenching your chest. Search now for the stillness
that is always present within, within your inner most being.
The place of you which is only being and not emotion, not
agenda, just being, pure being. We call this place your heart,
but it really is your soul self. It's the perfect part of you that
always recognizes perfection and is in harmony.

If you don't regularly make a habit of finding this stillness
within you, then you will probably have to make more
effort to find it. But relax into this space with another calm

breath, again and again. Turn your attention to your breath and notice it. Just be aware, aware of the life within you.

Did you know that as a human you cannot be in two places at the same time? Really, you say, duh! Okay, so we agree on something here, but I am not really talking about the physical things now. I mean you, as man, can only be present mentally or spiritually, one at a time. You are either living from your head or your heart. Oh, it's often an instantaneous experience, but it is always either or. It's the heart part of you, your spiritual nature, that is the observer. The ego, brain part of you is the calculating judging and emotional part of you.

So when we tell you to be aware of your breath and continue in this awareness you are doing this through your heart center not your brain center. Yes, this takes practice but as practice makes perfect, you will find it easier and easier to do. So that in time you will be able to accomplish calmness in the center of calamity as easily as taking a chill pill and oh yes, have a nice glass of water to wash it down.

"TWO, FOUR, SIX, EIGHT. WHO DO YOU APPRECIATE?" It's a cheer. You remember it from your school days. A cheer: something to rally the gang. Who are you a cheerleader for? Do you cheer yourself on? Do you appreciate yourself? Do you value your own presence? If you don't appreciate you, then you cannot truly appreciate any other. So, two, four, six, eight, who do you, appreciate? We say, appreciate you! Accountability, accountable for and accountable to, it's really only you. To each his own.

Song time...

I keep myself available for opportunity- knock-knock
I keep myself available for opportunity- knock-knock
I keep myself available for opportunity- knock-knock
I keep myself available for opportunity all day long.

> *It is okay to be scared and admit you are afraid. Come to Me and ask for My help, My light, My wisdom, My abundance and My strength. All I have is all I am and All of Me is here for you. See this, know this. I do not ask you to be strong except in faith, faith that good can prevail. Your belief is necessary to call it into existence. Believe it true. Whatever it is you desire. Call to Me in your hour of need. Call to Me in your hour of joy. I am with you always. We are together as one. Ask for My eyes to see beyond the pain which is so real to you. Ask for My arms to hold you in a loving embrace, as you have not the strength to stand alone.*

> *You need not wait until a dire hour to make this plea for I am always available to thee. You do not have to do any of this alone. Help is available. Aid, comfort and wisdom untold are all awaiting the word from you, the word of acceptance of My love into your heart, the word asking for My will to be done as you set aside your own. I am your Loving Father and you have been the defiant teenager determined to do things your way and all alone. I gave you this independence and I do not take it away. It can only be by your choice that you come to Me and choose to see things My way.*

> *It is okay to be scared. Know that I am here to comfort you. Tell Me of your pain. I am listening. It is okay to be afraid, but do not my dear, please do not choose to live in fear.*

For if you are living in fear, you are living away from the acceptance of My love. You are choosing the world and their stories over the Truth, which I am. My truth is love, Divine Love, no other. Ask for My love. Ask to be filled with My love and your fear will be no longer. I want you to have a comfortable existence. I wish you well. I am always sending you My love. Be where you are. We are all in this together.

NOVEMBER 8, 2011

You have the weight of the world upon your shoulders. You cannot carry the weight of the world upon your shoulders. Give it unto Me. Only I can carry the weight of the world.

NOVEMBER 10, 2011

Most people might be fine with that, but then again they don't know it can get any better. Don't say anything about it, about what you do not want. Say everything is wonderful. She did not complain. The other complains. Choose who you want to be. You are better than that.

What am I going to do?

You are going to manifest! Do not doubt My ways. We are all on your team, "Special Forces" at your service. When you are ready, everything is ready. The banquet has been set. Manifest your heart's desire. What you give your attention to you shall know. Realize with your real eyes. You are going to manifest fully aware of your Higher Power. Wonders you shall know. Wonders you shall show. Reveal Me, through your breath.

You are not limited to just one thing. Many wonders you shall know and show as you grow in love. You do not have to choose between. All you desire shall be. Continue to desire higher. You have a higher calling, calling you home unto My heart. Do you realize who you are? You are My shining star, a beacon of hope unto the world. Shine My light. Proclaim My word. Be My truth. Use your power of good unto the world.

It's all how you see it. See it a new way, My way, with your real eyes. Make the world what you want. Create a new vision. Envision a better way, My way. Walk with Me. Hand in hand, We shall go forth.

You, as mankind, often excuse the words you say as "just an expression" not understanding that each expression you offer unto the world is expressed in the world as you say. You attempt to pardon yourself from the rules which have been set forth. Do not envy. Jealousy is not the way unto My heart. I hear you proclaim to another as if in pride, or as a compliment to them, that you envy their position.

You do not have to know how everything works you just have to know the rules. Build a new world, a brave new world, by holding your thoughts up to Me. By the power vested in Me, I vest unto you to create the world anew. See with Me how life can be.

You are all My sheep. None lost to Me. You have just lost sight of Me and wander without wondering. Instead deciding to know that you know what you see is true. God's love is very practical. There is no waiting period. You can begin to show as you know. Show up for Me. I am here for you.

Where there is a will there is a way. It's always true. Be
true to your word. Give Me your word. Like what you see.
See with Me. Delight in My world, My world of beauty,
gentleness and kindness. Grow a garden of beauty within
your heart for all the world to see.

What would you like to know? What would you like to
show? You claim it with your word. Be true unto your word.
I give you My word as your power. Realize your strength
through Me. Claim your inheritance.

There is no secret formula. All can be known. Just ask
believing you can know. A process of self-discovery is
in progress. You've changed the channel and wrote new
programming for your life. You sing a new song, a song of
joy unto your heart, which is My heart.

Suspend belief. Forget what you know to get to the Truth, to
the All Knowing part of your being. "I was afraid that was
going to happen," you say. I say, have no fear. Fear does not
serve you well. Your fear fuels no fire but of more fear. Fear
not. Be not afraid.

NOVEMBER 11, 2011

"Daily Word," I get a direct deposit of the daily word of God. I stilled
the mindless chatter of my mind and the Small Still voice speaks unto
me continually. As the static of the world has been eliminated from
my mind the volume of the voice has risen and my reception of the
message is so much clearer. It had to circumvent my mind! This is clear
as a bell.

Why would you want to constantly reread the doom and
gloom papers? The only way you can help the world is to hold

your energy high with good thoughts. Think on Me. Think of My love. Become My love for the world.

Everyone works with a higher power whether they recognize it or not. Names are not important. Labels do no good. They get in the way and clutter the channel. Stories are written, further confusing the clear reception of this life channel. Do you think God only speaks to people when bushes burn? You think too much! You have to believe in more than you know, to know more than you think.

I believe in the magic of possibility. When it is given to me, I do it. When I have an idea, I act on it.

Pay attention. Have presence of Mind. Uniting of desires, you have to allow Spirit to work through you. Your thinking mind has taken over. If you only believe and trust in what is in front of you, you will only know and believe in what is in front of you. Your experience will not change, just more of the same. This is called limiting belief.

NOVEERMBER 12, 2011

Concerning the first, almost cryptic, messages, which you refer to as "Painting Titles," which you have just been typing and analyzing, just let it go. Consider them exercises, like worksheets. Be where you are. My love I have given you, receive! You can write them down, but don't analyze too much. You are over thinking it. That just proves you are all receiving this which you aren't paying attention to, valid messages of insight, love and wisdom, reaching out to you from beyond your busy brain. It's a matter for each to "fine tune" the channel of perception by tuning out the idle chatter of your brain, which is mostly self-defeating talk or ego.

No rules, just right. It's not going to happen unless you focus on it. That focus is your intent. When you are ready to give attention to the matter it shall arrive or arise unto you. Good things only come to a prepared mind. You are preparing the way as you sweep away the clutter and tie up loose ends of the old energy. You are "cleaning house" and creating a new energy which is ripe for you to easily receive that to which you will now direct your focus.

Give thanks continually. Each time you give thanks you are recognizing the presence of good. And with each moment of recognition of good, you will be offered another in which again to be aware of the good which is in you and all around you. Be careful of what you decide.

NOVEMBER 13, 2011

Personality is a human physical trait. As "One" we are not limited by nor identify with personality. Personality is part of man's "ego consciousness" which keeps him small. It's not about personality anymore. Your mind is attempting to define this voice as one or another personality or individuality, as you understand how souls appear to you in your earth form. It is not this way, not for us, not for you, not now, before or ever. It is only your limited consciousness that perceives it so. Please don't bother too much with your attempts to comprehend or fathom the greatness of this concept. All you need to know is that "all is One and all is Love."

You know both in your heart and mind that these messages are messages of pure love. The same love which Paul spoke about. This voice never judges or condemns but is patient, comforting and encouraging. Love knows all. Love conquers all. God is Love. This is what you are to know.

You have to discover your own power. You have to lay claim to the Kingdom within. It is all within the power of your word, in thought, spoken and in deed.

Buddhism is about mastering the mind. While there is much to be said for that as an effort to becoming the perfection of man, we are offering you more, a way to get beyond the mind which knows all it knows so well. We ask you to forget all you know and be born again unto Truth. If you can learn to work, live and breath just through, only through, the mind of God, that's when you've "got it going on!"

Whenever you go past the point you thought you couldn't go, that is when you have reached the next level. You have to venture beyond your comfort zone for growth to appear. You have to push yourself to this new limit. It's a personal challenge, whether mentally, physically or spiritually. You do yourself no good by measuring your rate of growth against any other.

All have access to the same gifts. All good arises from the same Source. All power is One and One for all. The only difference lies in individual man's level of consciousness and awareness of such power and aptitude gained by the exercise of such. Jesus, as Christ, told us "What ever I do, so may you."

Some say they talk to dead people but that is an improbability. It is impossible, for if anything is truly dead there is no life with which to communicate. Communication is a back and forth thing. It should be better stated that some are aware of communication with Spirit and the souls of the bodily departed. That is not the same as "dead people."

A soul inhabits a body for a time for an earthly experience as an opportunity for soul growth, or advancement in the Heavenly Planes, by seeking soul purification and enlightenment. When the body is spent or damaged so that it can no longer support the life force, the soul energy escapes the imprisonment of the physical confines it has known. There is no skip, pause or lapse from one moment of knowing in the body to the next moment that the soul realizes its freedom. There is no change whatsoever in the attributes of a soul just because it is no longer present in a physical form.

You were a soul before this body and you will continue as that same soul after you depart. The only thing you depart from is your physical form. You remain present, actually more present than when in the physical form. As you have not the physical senses, nor local brain activity, to distract you, you are Pure Being. You exist in the Ethers, as Heaven was first described.

You reside in a state of continual joy, but happy as you are to just to be you are aware that other souls enjoy more joy and reside in a brighter light space. You long for this "more joy" and learn that the way to this more joy is through the infilling of your soul with God's Divine Love. All souls can receive this gift as they ask for it with all the energy their soul possesses, but the most soul growth opportunity is when a soul is with a physical body and is having a human experience.

What are you looking for? What's wrong or what is right?

There are basically two ways to go through life; you can either look for what's wrong or what's right. Seek and ye shall find. Be careful what you look for, for what you think about you bring about.

People always ask, "Who says?" They are looking for an "authority figure." Someone else they believe holds all the answers. They search on for a supreme authority, one whose truth never varies.

NOVEMBER 14, 2011

You are stating what you see and you are stating what will be. It's a choir of angels singing to you.

It's not even about you, so don't take it so personally when another is so rude. It's nice to receive an apology but don't think for a minute that anyone owes you an apology for their actions. For when you do, you are deciding that your happiness or your peace of mind is attached to the actions of another. You are taking away your own power, the very power you hold within yourself to determine your own happiness level as you wish, regardless of any action or lack of action by any other.

Entering into the state of Grace, Zen, or the Flow, for you it was your painting that took you there, for another it is their daily run. Others find this awareness of the peaceful center of their being as they sit cross legged on the floor and give attention to their breath. All very valid paths to the same state of knowing and bliss that is always available unto each. You, mankind, walk in darkness, barely seeing the Truth which shines ever so brightly by the light of day. You gather and form a line playing "Follow the Leader" not knowing that the leader is as blinded as yourself, as he as well is clothed in darkness. Stories are made up and told and retold explaining the whys and wheres of things that go bump in the night. Yes, you remain blinded by the darkness which surrounds you not realizing your own power. The power you were born possessing to open your own eyes unto the light chasing away the perceived darkness and revealing the continued blindness of the leader you once followed. Lo, is the one blessed with ears to hear this and eyes to see the light.

Your ego wishes another man to agree with what you know. Your ego wishes another person to validate what is coming to you. Please come to the place of knowing that all is well and right and you need not the validation of any other to own this Truth. Once you get rid of that need, what you would like, will come to you. This is so because when you perceive anything as a need, you are perceiving lack of what you desire. Thus you are not putting out the proper receiving energy unto the world. Believe that which you desire is available unto you although your physical eyes and ears have not yet witnessed. This is the process of allowing.

Believe unto me this, this is important work you are doing and there are ears that need to hear these words as you write them, for they will resonate in the core of their own being and be further confirmation of their own truth.

What if there was a story where the main character saw life without trouble, and who didn't get caught up in and add to the drama around him?

There is such a story, the story of Jesus of Nazareth. Don't concern yourself with the possibility of hurting another's feelings when you do not do as they wish. One may invite you to do something because it is their wish, their desire to do a said activity with you. As much as you may desire the company of the other you may feel a pull of your heart in a different direction and not be able to do two things or be two places at once. Two desires must align for all to be well and feel well for both. Do nothing out of a feeling of obligation to any other. Do it because it feels right to you.

You always have the power to decide what feels right for you and often that means not just following the group but making your own plans which lead in a different direction. Do not feel bad about this, feel good. You must feel good about all you do and think, to live in this feel good space of internal and thus eternal Peace. Do not be disturbed by any thoughts. Choose to look at the bright side of every situation.

You need not overly explain your reasons for any choices you make to any other. Just say, "This feels right for me at this time and I trust you will understand and look forward to getting together with you at another time." You are respectfully "RSVP-ing" to yourself and the other.

NOVEMBER 15, 2011

There are cycles to everything. You have been planting seeds, good seeds in the universe. Harvest time is to come. Your just rewards you shall reap. You have been doing My work, listening, hearing and heeding My word. All is well. "Seek and ye shall find" is the biggest truth there is and of course, "God is Love."

There are a lot of people walking around with teeny bits of God's love but they haven't opened the gateway of their heart for the in-flooding. You have felt and known God's love within your own heart before this time of knowing. There have been times you have been moved to tears. Your emotions overcome by the power of this love. You have felt it and then you haven't. It seems to you as if God walked away, but it is not so. Your attention walked away.

The gift of God's Divine Love unto man is not a one-time thing. Such a powerful substance it is that man can only assimilate it into his being as if in a slow drip, as if your body was attached to an IV line from God's very blood to yours. To keep the flow of this "Life Blood" your attention has to remain on your desire. Such as is the law for all you are able to receive. God cannot and will not force feed you His love. You must come to the alter, willingly and on bended knee, humbling your own egoic ways and succumbing your will unto His. This is the way of receiving this almighty gift of Divine Love. So you see, many have been touched by God's love, but few have been wholly transformed. And fewer yet understand the matter and cause of such a change as fully as is now described to you.

Do you know what first impressions are? If you truly did, you would trust them and use their wisdom in your life. As an artist you have known the value of first impressions. You know the value of turning your face and thus your attention away from your work for a time to then again see it anew. With that new first impression you could clearly see that wasn't working and what needed attention. You have known the value of first impressions in the process of making your art, but not so much in the making of your life. Instead as such first impressions have come to you, you have often been so quick to discount them as they didn't stand up in the court of reason you held in your mind. Much later on, as things played out, you had the clear hindsight to see the actual validity of your first thought.

We are here to tell you that your "first thought" is not something to be reasoned in your "thinking mind" against all the physical facts you know. In fact, this very "first thought" is not a thought of yours at all, not from your local brain processing center, your reasoning mind. No, it's from way beyond and above your little mind. These first impressions come from the Great Mind, your God Mind, the mind that knows no limitation and has a clear vision, far above the physical stance you have as your feet are planted on the earth.

You are so lucky that you have the freedom to express and openly share these truths given unto you. Many before you lived in bondage by physical governing powers which so prohibited the even thinking of such thoughts. Many of which have been executed for this very thing. But the world's consciousness is evolving and matters such as this are now arising to the light of day and finding welcome in the world.

Your reward is great in Heaven, but for Heaven you need not wait. Those you know as saints were in this number. Why do you think they as well felt such need to write the words they wrote of Me and My Love? Just as for you, I poured My Divine Love into their very being and as My Love cannot be contained it spilled out in their words and actions.

If you are going to speculate that is fine, just speculate that all is well. Quite often you do quite the contrary and decide life is hard. You only know what you see and you don't see very well.

The ones you title as "gifted" are just those who recognize and allow the gifts of Spirit which are available to all. They are the ones whom have chosen to remain awake and aware, or have awakened, to the gifts of Spirit, which is the Truth of their and all being. They are the painters, composers, poets, inventors and seers who illuminate the path for all.

Much of the "light" they bring is not understood or fully comprehended and thus not appreciated by their contemporaries, as the others have not yet evolved to this same level of consciousness. Generations later, they are hailed as being "the wise ones" and their works are highly prized. You have quietly expressed this about your own work, even a few years ago, wondering if they who will truly appreciate your art have even been born.

People have a right and responsibility to use the gifts they have received. They are to share them with the world but as well they have the right to profit from their action, or part in, bringing the gifts forward. They have a God given right to benefit from their gifts so as to live a comfortable life by the standards they so choose.

Would you lay down your life for this Truth as the saints before you have for their own Truth knowings and proclamations?

I have already laid down my own life, as I have surrendered my own will unto God's.

Good answer.

*Have you heard of "tit for tat?" Spirit needs permission to
work in the world of form. That is why you are to manifest
as you desire and to desire higher so We can aid you in your
endeavors. People say, "Where is God when you need him?"
and yet they do not make themselves available for God to
work through them. They do not understand the system in
place.*

So what does "tit for tat" mean?

*You get what you give. If you do not like what is happening
to you in any minute you have to change your story, the
one you are telling yourself about the way life is. Humor
me for just a moment, dear mankind, and look for the
good. Look for what is right in your world. You have been
paying attention to the wrong things. Your news channels
continually broadcast the bad, pointing out and theorizing
everything bad they can find. I want to say "to death" but
that is not the truth, for with each breath spent on such talk,
more life is breathed into it, more vitality, and leading one's
attention ever toward more terrible events. Your attention,
My dear people, is in the wrong place.*

I write "Joy Jingles." This Joy Jingle is sung to the tune of *Frere Jacques*.

Just be patient
Just be patient
All is well
All is well
Do da do da do do
Do da do da do do
All is well
All is well.

NOVEMBER 15, 2011

That's all in the past you say, but as it you talk about it you are keeping it present.

NOVEMBER 16, 2011

Vows are of the mind. A matter of personal will and power of one's mind over one's personal will.

It's the same channel. Its just different people have different dialects and modes of reception and expression.

There is no line anymore, which I can draw to separate the words of Spirit from my own.

"All" is "One," one voice of "Truth."

NOVEMBER 18, 2011

As I am typing these messages which I have received into my computer I am stunned by the breadth, beauty and wisdom contained within and I ask, "Why me?"

Because you have made yourself available.

I am writing messages of love and encouragement, delivered unto my heart for the good of mankind.

You are a physical being. It is good to celebrate your physical-ness. Honor your body and honor your soul. If you are hungry, you should eat. When you are tired, you should rest. Give to your body what it needs, for you need your body to be there for you to aid you in the accomplishment of

your dreams. Talk nice. Talk nice to your body. Support your
body and your body will support you. Do not deny your body
of its physical needs.

Sometimes I question the words, which I am given to write, then I remember that it is not for me to say, what is or is not. I see now how I have been allowed to write what I have written without the interference of doubting minds clogging this wonderful channel of Love coming to me. I used to wish that the others around me asked what I wrote so I could share, but now I see that it was actually a gift that I was given "space" in which to develop this channel on my own. So I give thanks for all for this and thanks to all the minds that did not interfere.

This is heavy stuff.

> *This is light stuff. Lighten up. Lighten up.*

This blows my mind away!

> *Great, then We are doing a good job!*

I don't have to use my "mind power" to create explanations for all I am now understanding, for the words of Spirit which are given to me do this so beautifully.

> *We told you it would be easy! You don't have to think*
> *about it. All the work is done for you, through you.*

You keep saying it again and again.

> *We will keep saying it until they get it.*

This is good stuff!

> *Yep, the best of the best!*

I am so blessed to be a part of this. Thank you.

Your thanks are felt, heartfelt My dear. We continue to hold you near.

I have no doubt. I know who I am. I am good, for I am of God and fully a part of God's glory. It just amazes me, continually amazes me. I stand in awe.

Do not listen to what they say. They know not what they say. It matters not to you. Don't let it matter. Don't care about it. Give it no attention. Let it drop and dissipate into thin air.

If you believe in such technology as wireless communication and that all that information exists in the ethers, why would you not believe that this is there as well and that you can receive? You are a conduit for this energy, believe it or not.

You say
You don't see
You don't see how
That is going to happen
Yes, you are right
You don't see
And you won't see
If you keep looking
With your eyes
Your eyes are blind
To new possibility
But My eyes see clearly
Ask to see
With My eyes.

All is well. This I tell the world.

I know that of which I speak. I speak the truth I wish to show.

And this I show the world, My love.

Huff and puff, this is what you do. Making sure all around know how hard life is for you.

You can create your life anyway and anywhere you want. The only thing that limits you is your imagination or your ability to imagine something different than what you see.

NOVEMBER 20, 2011

You don't have to do this, any of this, on your own and we are not speaking just to the one with the pen in the hand. We, your Spirit family, your good and God connection, are here to minister to your every need and wish, but it cannot be two ways. It's either your way or the "High Way." We invite you to take the road less traveled.

Part of me speaks with a voice expressing what I think and wonder about and the other speaks with a confidence that makes firm statements of this is how it is. I believe this is the voice of the Truth of God, which is good.

You have to ask the right questions to get the right answers. Not everyone knows this, this is true, but you are not alone.

Can you see the light, the light of day? I have put it there to light your way. Steal away unto My heart. Give True Life a worthy start. Hear My voice. Sing My song. The day, I promise you, will not be long. We are together you and I.

Together with One voice, we touch the sky. This, no man's heart can deny. All My power is with you and within you. All can be done. Tell it like it is, My will be done.

Allow Me to Express through you. Our work is not through. There is much we shall do. Be available. Remain open to Me and your eyes shall see the glory of it all. The channel, your soul, is just being cleared. There is so much more we will do My dear. Stay near. Don't you doubt, you will never be without My love holding you so above the fray. There is no delay. I got you girl, you get Me. We are a team, undivided. As "One" We win, "All to All."

He asks you why you aren't doing your art right now. It's because people need words, words to find their way and you are to direct them as you know and as I show you the "Light of Day. "Your art will gain value in other eyes as you help Me give them new eyes.

It is all to be well with thee. Smile, you are not forgotten. You are My "For-Get-Me-Not," My flower child, My blossom in the garden of heavenly delight. Someone will say, "We have been waiting for you, for these words to be delivered." and you will say, "Here it is, the manifesto!" And as well you have the images which illustrate the brilliance of My light.

It all started because I wanted to understand why I was this way, why I was so driven to create. I have known no other quite like me. I had to know why this was my destiny. I began to write words as they came, "painting titles" I called them, became a game which I played with myself for over a year before it became clear that there was more just beyond the door which was my mind. And I had to find what lay ahead, what was "truth" for me, not ever imagining the glory of my destiny.

I now know, it's the voice of God which I hear so clear. He calls me "Precious" and loves me dear, but not just me alone. And even though it is my own soul I am to atone, I have to tell what I am told. The story sounds new but it is very old. As old as time and then before time began, our Maker was, the "I am."

I need to feel good because I have a lot to do.

Yes, you do!

I give God the power of full expression in my life. This is heavy stuff!

This is light stuff, meant to lighten your load to unburden your shoulders from the weight of the world, which you carry around. We never said you had to do it alone. All is done as needed, as you wish. Please be fine with that knowing for now. There is much for you to do and you know what that is. You are the only physical one to do it. So please do leave the unseen to the unseen. We are happy to be of service, please allow.

NOVEMBER 22, 2011

Whatever you concentrate on you get more of so is the way with My Love. You get more in you, more of Me in you. I will not Love you more than I do now or more than I Love anyone else but you will feel more of My Love because you have accepted more of My Love into your life, into your very being. My Love becomes you and I must say My Love is "very becoming on you." Love, God

These ideas I get, they don't beg for expression. They insist on it!

Isn't it interesting how everyone wants to involve you in their drama? You want to be a team player, just remember what team you are on, My team, "Team Peace and Love."

Don't get distracted from your work by what others do or don't do. It's not for you anyway. You have your own life to live. You have so much to give. Keep on giving of yourself as you do. I will see you through. Sometimes everyone needs someone else to look at them and say "This is the way it is Sugar, wakeup!" This is what we do for you, Sugar Pie.

He says, "It's horrible out, it's horrible out, don't you see how horrible out it is?" We say, whenever anyone sees so much "horrible" on the outside they can only be viewing life from a horrible interior perspective, a very low one indeed. You owe him not the courtesy of stooping so low to see as he. Remain upright. Hold your head high. We are one with you and Our Love to you we will never deny. We know it is hard to keep your mouth shut but doesn't it feel so much better when you do?

You don't know. You really don't know much at all of the Truth, the Real Truth of the matter, the matter of Life. But you sure talk a good story. We are talking to you and mankind in general. You are quite the storytellers. You really don't know the difference between fact and fiction. You don't believe the facts in fiction and believe the fiction you call facts. It would really serve you all to not "know" so much. Stop being such "know it alls" and become "seekers." Finders and seekers, yes, you should be this way.

Some people just want to argue a point, any point and every point. And do you know what the point of that is? To point to how smart they believe they are. Which is really dumb. Don't be that way.

See, you can spread the Love. You can spread the Love near. You can spread the Love far. You can spread the Love from your car.

You don't need your body to weigh you down and you don't need your mind to weigh you down. Lighten your load My dear. Dump your fears. Dry your tears. All is well this you should know.

I used to only feel whole when I painted, but know I realize my wholeness continually.

This, My dear, is holiness. Oh, We are so happy for you to feel the Love. We jump with joy. Come Let's dance, join together in song. This is the day We have been waiting for so very long.

People always want to know what something "means" so they can go worry about it. Don't you people have something better to do? Do you still need ideas? I keep telling you to look up and look within.

Spirit is very "light hearted" and humorous.

Of course We are. Why shouldn't We be? We live in the palm of God, just as you, only We realize where we be!

These words are like a broken record in my mind, stuck on the same repeating verse until I can write it down. And as I do "the audio" again resumes play. Perhaps this is because once a phrase enters my consciousness my mind attempts to process it repeating it over and over trying to either remember it or reason it. But when I have set the word or phrase on to paper, my mind releases its hold on the words and thus frees up and moves out of the way allowing more to come.

November 23, 2011

I ask the right questions for me as I need to know, so I can show up as I need to be.

There is a difference between thinking and knowing. You know what I mean.

People say, "You're not thinking." as if that is a bad thing. But I say "I'm not thinking, I'm not thinking. Yeah! I'm not thinking" and I don't think a thing about it.

Be in a reflective mode not reflecting the things of the world but the things of your heart. Wouldn't it be fun to live this other life, the life without strife where you allow Spirit to show and go with the flow? Step in and step out of the brain you know. This is the only way to allow Spirit to show you the Wonders of the World as we know. Be not concerned about how it is done just remember we love you a ton and will never allow...

Shoot, I'm sorry my mind wandered in.

Spirit always expresses a complete thought. It is just you who gets in the way. Making it appear as a delay.

Some people are "so good" at being discontented you would swear they were born that way. But we assure you they were not. They have "assigned" themselves that position in life. They believe they are here as "the chosen one" to point out what is wrong with the world. They believe their vision is clearer than all others and continually make it their job to point out perceived injustice and wrong in the world.

Do they know how wrong they are in their ways? We say wrong in their ways for that is the point We make. Their direction and focus is off, but that does not make the soul bad, the person bad. Of course, all of this is of their choosing. They like who they are or at least they think they do. You ask, "If they like who they are, why do they feel bad and are often mean?" It is because they are not in touch with their feelings, the part of them that knows better, the ways of good and God.

This cannot be "swept under the rug," this Light you shine. You have direct orders from the Divine.

Some "part of me" knew and I'm here to tell you, you have that same "part" within you.

Most people don't have a voice for it, or at least they haven't found, for with the world they drown the sweet song I Sing to them all day long. There is nothing to worry about, so stop looking for it.

I am gaining a voice, or I have found, what keeps me centered as my feet touch the ground.

Have you noticed how "you people" are always looking for something to be upset about? Stop looking. I'm not going to tell you stories of people, not about how people think, or what they think about. I'm here to tell you what Spirit knows. You already know what you think.

You don't have to tell "the world" what you are going to do or convince anyone of anything. You only have to convince yourself by getting in alignment with what you want, fully aligned with no stray thought.

Can life get any better?

You can only realize better. Look at Paul. He was in jail and realized better. His body may have been imprisoned but his mind and soul were not. You change the trajectory of your life by your thoughts, by what you choose to think. Think on Me. Ponder My ways. Celebrate My beauty in the world and life I have given you. This I tell you, you are to do. Think on these things.

The voice I hear seems awfully dear. Like one I've heard, though the idea seems absurd. But aren't those the words Paul spoke, almost the same?

From the same Source both came. No, this is not absurd this is God's word given unto men and women like you. This is for you to do proclaim in My name. If you did not listen or hear that would be a shame.

These ideas, these words, come in "the back door" for your mind does not comfortably and genially welcome them in. We slipped in when you weren't looking and caught you "off guard." You had given us permission with your prayers but your mind was still unaware. You are lucky for this and so are We for now we can sit together and converse comfortably. We are not "aliens" and neither are you. We both reside in our "home turf" which is "Heaven," as you say.

We see this all so clearly and ask you to trust you will again one day. Every word We say is an answer to one of your thoughts, even those not yet fully formed for We know you "better than you think." We were friends before you were born. "Tell it like it is," is what We now ask of you. Write what you hear as we have so much to say to all of you We hold so dear. This is your service. This is the plan. You have given us your body and your mind and you have been so kind to allow us to show all how the world works, what life is, the gloriousness of all, to tell it like it is.

So go forth and do what you do and remember We are here for you. Not meant as distractions, just helping hands and hearts. You agreed on all of this before you gave "this life" a start. Some ideas are new to you but all ideas are old, just untold to you, as you are there almost completely unaware of who you really are. We tell you again you are a shining star.

You are always looking for "something to believe in" like you need a reason to get out of bed. My, oh My, just how do you get these ideas to fill your head? The "something" you are looking for is You, this is the "You" you are to believe. Believe you know more than you believe you know. Believe you are bigger and better than you think.

I am still going to "go through stuff," I know that. I am living a life here and that is part of the experience. Trials and challenges are to met and to be dealt with, with compassion and grace.

I am here and here for you all along your way.

Does life get any easier?

It will seem so because your view is changing. It is not about the money you know. For money is a very small part of the picture.

I know a man and you do too who can only see what he can see and he only believes that which is set out before him. He looks for no other as he believes in no other. He only knows what he knows and it isn't much. Thus he believes his life is small and is so short sighted that things that come his way in life almost broadside him daily. All change is categorized catastrophe. He is "unaware" of the help available "24/7" to see and know beyond his limited physical vision.

We have tried talking to him but he just won't listen. He doesn't trust the voice he hears as we whisper in his ear, as what he hears does not make sense with what he believes, that which he sees.

Stop thinking bad. You know you do it and We do too. We just heard you. Sometimes you can be so "good" and then other times you turn into your "trash dump" mode. Life is not a game of who wins or loses or who has their "act together" more than another. And even if it was it's none of your business. Don't talk that way. Don't talk that way to him. If you have to say it, say it to us and get it off your chest. We will listen. We are here for you. Let's keep it between us.

Okay. It pisses me off. It frustrates the hell out of me when others do not do what they need to do and it affects me. Or, as you would put it, *"I let it affect me."* I wish this wasn't so. I really do. Take this from me please. I hand it to you.

Steal away. Steal away and be with Me. Shut the door and open the door. Shut the door to your mind and open the door to your heart. Here I am waiting for you with love, with all My love. I am holding so much love for you within My arms that whenever you open the door to your heart I throw it up and out to you and shower it upon you. Blessings flow and rain down, you stand in water at your feet, but not still puddles. You see, My living waters are like a flowing river always fresh and clear, never still or stagnant, fresh, vital, life giving waters, healing waters. Just like your tears, pure and flowing.

Do not stagnate your soul. Do not hold back and attempt to hide from Me. Let go and go on. Let go of what you cling to so tightly, that which you know and feel safety in because you know, but don't necessarily like. And as well of what you do like, let go of it too. Let go of it all. You think you have to hold on so tight to life or you will drown in its fast flow but this is not so or at least doesn't have to be if you live your life with Me. For you cannot drown in the Life Water I provide. I will fill you up when you come to Me to drink. I will fill you with Myself. I will fill you with My Love. For this is who and what I am, Love. And why I am here is all for you. Yes, all for you.

You never knew that did you? The reason Life is, is here for you, for this experience you are having, for your support. I say "this Life you have" and as I say this you are imagining Life as the life you know and you are right. But I know that you know more than you know you know and it is of the "Complete Life" I speak. For you are so much greater and grander than any of your imaginings. I'd like to help you remember for if and when you remember who you really are you will bathe daily in My Healing Waters refreshing your soul.

You have stories. You have what you believe, but My dear ones that all keeps you so very small. I ask you again to let go of it all and come unto Me and ask Me to tell you again the story of your birth. The one before you ever knew earth. I've been telling you like it is. There is a reason, a reason for it all. But not a reason, like you know reason. So, don't bother thinking about it. No amount of thinking will make it so. You have to feel your way, feel your way through life. That is how I want you to "reason" your way. Get out of your brain and live through your heart. Oh yes, this is it, the true way. Does it feel good? Say, "Oh yes, I'll take more of that." and then you will and your very life will be a thrill. We have some catching up to do. Yes, you and I. So let's get together and spend some time and I'll tell you all about My Life Divine.

What is a religion?

> *It's a spiritual practice. It is not something for you to hold up in another's face. But instead a path, a practice which you are to do, to practice, to experience, as a way to see the face of and come to know God. Let it be a time of growth.*

> *Others have heard, and as you read, you recognize My word. Yes, I have been speaking all along. Some have interpreted it into dance and song. Another heard it as a poem and another felt it as a quickening within their heart. This is all a start, a place to see how We have forever been continually communicating quite naturally.*

> *Who or what do you trust? Do you trust God or the world? When you trust in God you trust in the possibility of all good, all the good you can imagine and then all so much more.*

Here I am again, Lord. I've lost it, lost my composure, lost my perky, positive view of the world. Sometimes I can be so strong, but am I? I know You do not ask this of me, for You are to be my strength. I have no strength of my own. I am weak and You Are strong. Hold me in Your arms take me away from his mental anguish for I know that that is all it is. It is all of mind for my heart is aright. I pray now, again and again, for Your Love to so fill me and flow through me that my mind is so filled with thoughts of Your dear love that there is no room for other.

You, dear Lord, have occupied my heart. Please, I beg of you occupy my mind as well. Purify my outlook on life. Let me see only Your way. Let me take the High Way. Let me know You and help me to listen in. I beg for the sound of Your voice. I know You hear my words, my plea. Even if I was never again graced with knowing so Your words in my head, I will always know and cherish them in my heart. I truly needed to hear Your voice, for I was the "doubting Thomas." Others have been satisfied with Your word second hand, but not I. And You knew You could make me listen. Thank you for your patience and persistence.

I am at Your service. Your will is mine. I give You my heart and mind. I surrender my soul. Give Your word and I shall deliver it unto the world. This is so great. You are so great, that I can no longer contain myself. I have to share what I have been given. Make the way Lord. I am ready to go forth and proclaim Your love unto the world. All praise be to God. God is good. God is love. Amen.

> *I only ask you to live one minute at a time. I never tell you to jump ahead or look back, that is all you, of your doing. I don't ask you to do any of that. I just ask you to be. Be with Me now and forever. Let this moment be enough. Treasure what we have, for we have each other. Together we are in love. Be in love with Me now. Treasure this moment we have and look at no other. I hold you in the palm of My hand. No harm will come to you. How can I make you understand the "All" that is? There is no better. Glory Be. How can you not be happy?*

We may be blind to Spirit, but we do not have to be deaf to Spirit. We have to hear the inner, the true inner calling, the voice of Spirit, the voice of God whom knows our name. Once we attune to this voice life will never be the same. This I know. This I show, for I hear words spoken so clear that I hold dear. They lift me up when I am down. When I feel so lost, with one word I am found.

They tell me I am loved and that I am watched over so close, beside, not above. I walk not alone, my hand is held. As I reach out it is grasped and I am lead to clear water. Clear flowing water from which I drink when I refrain from "think." This new way I know is not about smarts and show, it is a quiet and contemplative life where joy abounds and there is no strife. *"Never fear."* I am told. Of this story I will never grow old. For fear and worry is not the way to be, if one chooses to see Life clearly.

> *See the good. Celebrate where you are. Be patient. Be kind. Leave no love behind, give love to all whether they see it or not. You have what it takes for you are of My lot.*

God tells me what to think and what to say and I really, really like it this way. It was always here, always near, even when I did not know, even when I did not show. Always available to me, to each I am told. This is not new. It's a story very old.

As I read the "wisdom words" of others I recognize the words as authored by the same source. You see truth is truth no matter whose mouth it comes from or whose hand writes it. It all flows from the same source. So even though I will be sure to give credit to whomever "manifests" something whether it be a phrase, idea, art, song or invention, I understand and appreciate and give thanks to the "One Source" from which all good manifests.

I so value the wisdom writings of others, for as I read them they enter my heart just the same as the words which I penned from direct inspiration. Truth is truth. The difference for me now is because I have truly experienced truth first hand (the words born in my heart and mind as truth) there is no way I can deny the validity of these words nor the value they have for me as I bring them into and use them for my life. I now read all wisdom teachings in a whole new light, as a brilliant light now shines upon my soul.

"May the Lord be with you and may his face shine upon you and give you Peace." These used to be just words to me as I didn't really know them. I didn't know that the truth of them could ever be so known to me as I

know it now. As I began my journey of awakening and became aware of the "Law of Attraction" I really questioned if that was it, if there really was anymore to life than that.

Now, don't get me wrong, knowing and understanding how the "Law of Attraction" works is a very big deal and really changed my view of how life works, but as well left me wondering how the religious beliefs I had been brought up with worked with or acknowledged this now obvious Truth. Was the world really just a world, or universe, of physical laws? Was there really truly no more? I had to know. I had to find out and put the pieces of this puzzle together. I didn't like the idea of just me and the Law of Attraction. I wanted to know God. I wanted to know the "More" of Life.

> *Thank you for listening to My Words. Now take them into your heart and believe them. Look everywhere for My Goodness and My Love. It's everywhere to be found. Look around. Be, what is found. Be My Love for all for all time. Be Love Divine. Let your Light shine unto Mine.*

> *You can change the tune. Flip the switch. Change the channel of what you receive, as you believe life to be. A joy, a thrill or drudgery, it's up to you to see how life can be. See with Me. See beautifully. Let Me fill your heart. Let's give Life a new start.*

NOVEMBER 29, 2011

> *Do not be disturbed by the words of another they know not My Love, although it is as fully present for them as it is for you. Hold the Light. You are My Sunshine My darling.*

Thank you Lord for caring, caring for me. I see you in Eternity. Amen.

All is well
All is well
All is well
Listen to what I say
Listen for the good
Look for the good
It is there
To be found
Though sometimes
You have to be a hound.

What would make you happy darlings? You want the
world to be perfect.

No one else
Has to believe
In you
Just you
I already do.

Come to Me
When you are weary
When you are teary
When you just cannot go on
As you have gone on.

You are perfect as you are, as you are now, as you come to
Me, as you seek Me and My Goodness. You are reaching for
and grabbing hold of the Love I have for you which brings
you further Perfection, further Wholeness, Holiness if you
may say. But do not feel My darling that you have to be this
All before you can proclaim in My Name. Do not wait until
your head is even with your heart. Now is the time to share
what you have been shown. In this way, others may rise
unto the Light along side you.

Do you ever just write down the things that come to your brain? I do. It's my stream of consciousness, a river flowing clear water with some varied turbulence. It amazes me, now that I am seeing it. In spite of me, a book has been written this year, a spiritual primer. All in my hand. All out of my heart, without the involvement of my head. Yes, I was the medium, just as the pen and paper were. I am a tool for God's good. I stand amazed. It is good that I wasn't too aware, as my mind could not or did not edit.

It is written!

November 30, 2011

> *He is trying really hard. You need to support him. Be patient. Be kind. Unwind. Today is a new day. Don't decide how it is going to be. Think well. Time will tell.*
>
> *Tell them what they need to know. Then, just then, the world can show. Show, glow, know.*
>
> *You were never broken. You were just broken open. You had to be to receive Me. You were so full of yourself. There was no room for anything else. You had decided to live life on your own and put God on a shelf, a shelf high above, a place you could not reach. You didn't even bow down you felt so beneath, beneath My love, not full, not worthy. All you knew was strife and worry. I knew there would come a day when you would see life in a new light, see life My way. Now you are beginning to see the truth behind the mysteries, the mysteries man created when he chose not to know, when he decided he could do it alone.*
>
> *A book you shall write, a book of your new life, the one you dreamed of, the one without strife. Oh yes, My dear there is more to come. You are just beginning to know Me. We will have so much fun!*

DECEMBER 2011

In their heart,
the Living Book of the living
was manifest,
The book which was written in thought
and in mind of the Father and,
from before the foundation of the All,
is in that incomprehensible part of him.

THE GOSPEL OF TRUTH [3]

DECEMBER 2, 2011

*Be open. Be available. Listen to Me. You know who speaks,
it is I who loves thee. Never, will I lead you astray. It was
never intended to be that way. Get out of your bed. Get
on with your day. We have so much to do now that we are
doing things My way.*

*You say you don't hear from God, well it is not because God
does not talk. It's because you aren't listening. Listen in, shut
up and open up. Soft spoken are the words of God, high
above the chatter of the world and your mind. The voice
of God is in tune, in harmony, with all good. All nature
manifests this goodness. God wants the same for you, to live
"in tune" with the Song He sings to your heart.*

This is the coolest job ever God. Thank you for allowing me to be a messenger, a voice, for Your Love unto the world. It's like an interview. A really good interviewee can get his point across and tell the story he wants told despite the questions the interviewer poses. He recognizes he is being given a format, a platform, from which to speak and he has every intention of making the best of it and telling the world the story he wants told.

That's exactly right! Don't think for a moment you can't!

"If they talked to him they would know." I say to myself as I read the words of others debating the existence of God in our world. Everyone touts facts, the Bible versus science, one man's word against another. From my perspective it seems so silly. I mean really, I talk to God everyday, all day long. Back and forth We go, singing the same Song. There is nothing to deny. There is nothing to prove. I know what I know and no one else could have ever told me so. I had to find for myself this amazing truth, which I didn't even know I could know.

Now, I can tell you all you want but you will only hear a part of what I say for my words are incomplete. God wants it that way, for He wants to tell you the story Himself. He wants to tell you how much He Loves you and everyone else. So all these words I write, which were given unto me, are only for my own one hundred percent understanding. And yet, I'm told to share with you and thus give you a few clues of what to do.

I would have either done this or gone crazy. There was no way to be in between. I believe many others have fallen down, broken down and gone crazy not understanding that if they had just lifted their head they could have seen God's Hand outstretched to lift them up.

> *Get out of your mind and into the Divine. Clearly, you will see eternity. Wake up and smell the roses. No thorns, no scorn, just Love, pure Love from above. This ain't a brain thing. Not meant to be analyzed, but internalized and eternalized.*

It's not about how "hurt" you are and proving your hurt-
ness. It's about proving "My Love." You are not alone in this.
Continue to ask for My help and guidance. "Love" is here for
you. Go forth in My Love.

DECEMBER 4, 2011

Every time I get "in my mind" I get lost.

About the Bible, the Message is in there. It just hasn't come
across loud and clear. It's not all about names and places. It's
about where you put your faith and trust. What you believe,
what you know, what you decide, what you hold on to, there
lies your truth, truth to be found within all. Behold the Truth
within you. I welcome you home unto your heart says God.

Listen not to what they say. Say what you want. See it true,
through Me. Peace be with you. Don't let doubt plague your
mind. For that is what doubt is, "a plague" creating a sense
of dis-ease as each thought of doubt takes you away from the
ease of life which you are.

Do you know when you start to have problems? It's when you
start comparing yourself to everybody else and that My dear
is judgment, which We have more than talked about. But
what about what everyone else is doing anyway? Does that
really need to affect you or limit you in any way? Please don't
let it. This is your choice. You have to "let it" effect you.

DECEMBER 5, 2011

I wish I wasn't this way Lord, but I feel sad and desperate. I feel like the world is enveloping me and swallowing me whole. Why? Because, I wonder if the world wants what I have to offer. I wonder if these words I have written will be heard. Yes, I am drowning in doubt Lord. Lift me up. Hold my head above the raging waters. Take me out of this mind which torments me. Bring me back to Your heart, the center of every atom of the world where there is Love. Tell me, O Lord, tell me again how You love me. Fill me with Your love. Fill every cell of my being with Your love. I need all of Your Ssrength if I am to do this. I have none of my own. Take me out of my mind.

> *Yes, the world is loud and not always so kind, but the woes that you speak of are only in your mind. Stop looking elsewhere, for the answers you need are already here with you indeed. I am here, as you know. I'm glad you so quickly "ran home" but you need never go away.*

> *You can be with Me each night and day. Keep My Love in your thoughts. Ask Me what to do. I will always show you. Together We can, do not this doubt. One step at a time. Do not run ahead. Do not rush or push. All goodness flows and as thus this shall as well. Stay with Me. Pray with Me. It is done.*

> *Whose eyes are you using when you look at the world, your small beady eyes or Mine? It is always your choice. I do not make you look at life My way, but I certainly invite you to. Now whose eyes do you really prefer? Do you choose to see what so many others see? They see Me not.*

> *I know what you were looking for. You were looking outside of yourself, away from Me, to see who else knows what you know, to see who else hears what you hear. What you found*

wasn't comforting at all for you heard, or rather read, the thoughts of others who do not know and said it could not be done. That is was impossible, or wrong. And as you were approaching this all with your mind, your mind started spinning and spinning tales of drama that has never even been played out except in your busy worried mind.

Please don't concern yourself with this. Matters like this are not your concern. No, not everyone will like you or what you do. But that is not why you agreed to serve Me is it? You are My aide not the master. So let Me be the Master I am and allow Me to handle the details. I can do this as you allow, if you allow this Good to be done through you. I am the Master and you are My scribe. You are My agent in the world. I have a lot of pull in this matter, a lot of influence. Trust that I will pull all the right strings to make this book of Ours a wonderful reality.

December 6, 2011

It's up to you to decide where you live from, your head or your heart. I am with you always. I live within and am your heart. Your head is often in another place, another reality far from Me. You never "fall from grace," you fall away from your realization of it. My saving grace, My love, is always here for you.

This is not new information. It is information given anew and heard anew for those with ears to hear. Do you hear Me? This is for you. You asked for it. You asked to live anew. You asked Me to tell you what to do. There is no reason for surprise. It can only be this way. You asked believing. You thirsted and yearned with your every cell to know, you asked My way to show. Here it is in black and white for you to do with as you might. Share freely. Go tell, for this is the Truth of the Lord your God, given to you as you asked. You are My blessed daughter.

What do you want from people? Do you want their sympathy? Do you want them to be sympathetic to your cause? What is your cause? Do you even know? Do you want another to feel good or bad for you? Will it matter? What really matters is how you feel about yourself, for that is the energy you deliver out unto the world. Love is always the best answer, the only answer for happiness internal and eternal. So is your cause "Love?" Do you give Love to all? Do you give Love to yourself? Be sympathetic to yourself. Do not judge yourself, or your situation. Just "Be" My love.

Is God the Word or is it the Word of God?

"God" is a term We use because you like. It is comfortable to you. There is no "one word" which encompasses the "All which Is."

If I can do this anyone can do it, right?

Yes, anyone who really wants to. Anyone who is a true and earnest seeker and so hungers and thirsts for the Word of God to be on their lips and spoken with their tongue.

Why am I so happy? Because I just realized again the truth of these words I have been receiving and recording for months on end. As I transcribe these journal notes into word documents on my computer, it is as if I am hearing it all anew. Most of what I have written I had not ever read, as the words flowed so quickly and continually. Now as I read them, as I type them, I am again astounded by the wisdom given to me and again realize the importance of these teachings for my own soul and many more souls which they are to comfort as well as challenge. Yes, joy fills me tonight. Joy be me!

DECEMBER 7, 2011

Sometimes it's all just too much for me. All this physical-ness, all this brain activity, and I just want to be with Thee.

>*Then come to Me as you are. You know very well I am not afar. There is no distance except within your mind. And whenever you step out of it, it is Me you will find. Come to Me. Come to Me as to you are. Step inside "the closet" then shut the door to the world of distractions, which most call attractions.*

>*You are attracted to Me, to Our love, to the love we share. Come to Me. Be in My care. This is "The way," this is to be the order of your day. I am to be your refuge when the world seems too much, too huge, for you to bear, for your mind to manage. I am the balance you need, to restore. "Our love" you are to adore. My ways, you are to contemplate. You are never here too early, nor too late, for this door My dear is always open. My heart is always here.*

>*Go and meet My people. Shake and hold their hands. Look them in the eyes and tell them I am within waiting for their call. Tell them I Love them, that I Love them all. Hope springs eternal.*

>*You get different answers, because you ask different questions. You and many others who want to know more of My Ways, the Ways of Spirit. Do ask, We so love to tell. Bit by bit we reveal our World to you, Your world, the one we inhabit together.*

Join forces. Hold hands. And listen as well to each other for each of you within holds a key to the Kingdom, a key piece to this puzzle you so wish to solve. It is not a puzzle to be solved really, but a reality to be enjoyed and accepted for what it is: Peace on Earth and Goodwill to All Men.

This is not the God of the movies. This is not the God of anyone's imagination no matter how vivid one's imaginings may be. This is the God of your heart. This is the God of love which speaks to you and knows you and calls you by name. Listen to Me. Hear My voice. I speak unto your heart: wisdom, truth, direction, comfort and love. Know Me. Know My love Be My love. Be all My love. I wish so to fill each of you with My love. Please ask. Ask for more, more of Me for you.

DECEMBER 8, 2011

Say it so and so it is.

I bared my soul and God bore my pain.

The people that talk so much about what "the right way" to live is are just that, talkers with little or no real action to back it up. True faith in God moves quietly and patiently across the face of the earth doing God's works.

DECEMBER 9, 2011

Here I am Lord. It is I. As you know, I have been busy in my mind of late, transcribing Our journal writings of this past year into a form which I hope to be comprehensible to others. It is my wish, and I know as well Yours, that these words be shared with many. Wow, I must say that it all amazes me so. Here I sat, just like this, with pen in hand and out flowed, poured forth, through me this most amazing story of Life.

Most of which I had never truly read, after all I was so busy living it. But as I put it all together in the order it has been given to me, "I see." I see and I hear. And I am so honored and astonished that I have been able to manifest such a great work. Actually, I am amazed and awed how You work God, as You found a way to get through to me and around my mind and tell me what I needed to know and what You wanted to say. You repeated again and again for me to get out of my way. I now know what that means. I had to release my egoic control on my life to allow Your good to flow through. Thank You Lord, thank You. I have no questions now. I just want to sit with you.

Yes, just sitting is good, being still, being comfortable with who you are. Yes, it is all very good. When you come to Me, come to Me as you are. I always have open arms. I am never too busy for you. It is you that seems is too busy for Me. You need not block out an hour for Me in a day. I'd rather it not be that way. I'd rather stay with you and go along for the ride. I really just want to be by your side. We can talk. We can be silent. But please never hold back. Don't try to cut Me any slack. I can take it, all you give to Me. You don't even have to be thankful, just start talking to Me.

You don't need to tell Me, I know you. I know what you know and know All that Is. So your "facts" do not impress Me, nor does your pity. I just want you to come with your bare soul to Me. Leave your ego at the door. He'll just try and get you to ignore what I have for you.

What do I have for you? Well, I am so glad you asked, as this is a really personal task. Each one of you has to wonder, then ask. Why darlings, I have My love for you. All I am is Love and it is for you. Do you know what God's love is? Well, it is "simply divine" darling, simply divine and it's all Mine. Mine to share as I wish and I wish to share it with all who come to Me and ask for it on bended knee.

"Now why," you ask, "should I even care? What is this a dare?" No My love, this is not a trick. That is your ego speaking again. That's him peeking in. This love is My gift to you to heal, hold and comfort so you can know "the wonders of My love." You cannot receive this gift and go on with life as before. For once you accept this gift never again can you close the door to your heart where I reside. You will feel it, My love, as it fills your soul. And you will want and ask for more, as you will know it makes you whole. Holy, you will become. My ways will be yours. Wisdom's halls will be an open library for you. Patience will prevail. My work, you will bade.

My mind is wrestling with the idea of priests, professed men of God, molesting children. How can this happen I ask?

They were not who they said they were. Actions always speak louder than words. Watch what you say. Be better than your words. Be so filled with My Love that you can be no other than so filled with My Love.

Stop worrying about what you need to do and do it, be action oriented. You are doing the right thing. You are listening to Me.

Don't be afraid to speak of things "idealistically." Speak of them as if what you ideally desire is your reality. You have to idealize your life vision and believe in the truth and reality of that idealized vision. Thus you will simultaneously be speaking realistically and idealistically.

There will not be "Peace on Earth" among all men until all men find Peace within themselves. Start with yourself and find Peace within your own being. Live in and from this Peace. This is the beginning of self-mastery. Remain in Peace. Remain with Me.

You can "think" about something or you can "wonder" about it. When you wonder, you allow wonderful wisdom to come your way. Of course, you as well have to remain open allowing this new knowing into your psyche.

All you have to do is be in Love with Me. Do you know what everyone is looking for? What you have found. Be happy. Rejoice! No money can buy what you have. No one can take what you have. You cannot give what you have. You can only live what you have. What you have is described in the words you have written but the written word does not contain what you have. What you have cannot be contained for what you have is who you are and who you are is limitless. Live from this limitlessness you are. Live forever from here.

The more you live, the more you Love for Love is who you are. Be the Peace and piece of My Love that you are. Be as I say "My shining star." You have looked and you have found. Your joy does resound.

I am connected to "Source." Everyone is connected to Source but I have "cleared the channel." I do instinctively the right thing. I am in the flow of life. I flow through life. Like a leaf in the breeze, I float effortlessly. I am in the know, which is in the now.

Here I am, fully present as All.

Take me out of my mind Lord. Bring me Peace, the Peace that was meant to be.

Ye are now with Me, as always.

DECEMBER 10, 2011

Tradition says to do this. Tradition says to do that. Tradition leads us nowhere.

> *You can't go beyond where you are or have been by following your own footsteps. That's true.*
>
> *Jesus, as Christ, was the first to "recognize" the Father and thus he recognized and fully call Him forth as the Logos, the Word of God. Jesus, as Christ, was "the Book of Life."*

I used to think. Now I know, I know better. Now that I know better, I can do no less. I can be no less. This is the way, says the Lord.

> *The book title has to include Divine Love.*

I'm not an intellectual. I'm an intuitive. I'm glad I'm not "learned." In this way I am able to know.

DECEMBER 11, 2011

Do you know what today is? Today is a great day! Today is a day the Lord as made!

> *Do you know what meditation is? Do you know what it does for you? It's a chance to clear your mind, to get rid of what you know and simply be. Be One with Me. No fancy place is needed, no special place at all. You may sit, or stand or lay, just whatever it takes to get your mind out of the way. Some like to run. You like to paint. Some even fish and meditate. They do and they have done, not ever being aware that what they do, they are doing with Me. They are being, they are quieting their mind and becoming one with Me. This is what you are to do. This is what I mean by staying out of your own*

way. You are to open up and shut up. Shut the door to the cares of your mind, the mind which drags you down.

Some ask why they do not hear My voice, not understanding it is all by choice. Yes, you need to be quiet but you as well have to let Me know what you would like to know and what you would like to show. We can just "be" or We can speak together quite naturally. I know so much and so do you, but if you desire My Truth you have to set aside what you "think" is true.

Isn't it lovely how We can communicate in such a way? How We walk and talk together throughout your day? Think not too much about this. Just let it be. As this is the way life flows so naturally, so gracefully, so beautifully. Now you see, see with Me, that More can be. You see now "Spiritually."

You recognize it now don't you, as the familiar voice in your head all along? But so many times before your mind stood at the door only allowing My light to shine through a crack on the floor, but now you have opened the door, opened it wide, leaving ego no dark in which to hide. Oh yes, how good life is when you let My "Son/Sun" shine in.

This is not a game, though it is quite fun. And let Me tell you this, We have just begun. For now that the door is open and you have allowed My Light in, there is not, nor can be worry or sin. For as you now see life through the light of My eternal day, there is no more darkness, no more decay. This is My dear, "the way" to peace eternally. And as you as well know, Peace internally for eternity. For once this door has opened so wide there is no place for untruth to hide.

All is brought forward, seen for what it is. Now I ask you, where is what you called "sin?" It is naught. It is not to be found for you see it for what it was, darkness, void, nothing of the Truth of which you are. You see this now and soon many others will too for these words you write My dear provide further clues, clues to the keys to the Kingdom for which all souls seek. Remember, you are not to be proud and boastful with this wisdom. Continue to be meek, gentle are My Ways and so now yours.

No amount of "talk" will convince any other. That is why you have your whole body, so you can "walk the walk." You are physical so you can physically be Me and show the world all I've got. I know this seems as if I am asking a lot. But remember, you asked first. You were the one who so thirsted for My word. You had to hear it straight from "Source" to believe, to know, and as you know you are to show. It can be no other way really.

Have fun with this. Have fun with Me. Let's show them all how to live fully alive. Rise high. Be My banner flying through the sky. Did you not know that this is what you "signed up" for when you knocked at the door?

When you asked for My love, when you asked for My all, I as well promised that you wouldn't fall. Never again can you fall back into your old ways. Never again in darkness will you be, now that you see you have always been with Me continually.

Hark, hear the angels sing! They are celebrating your arrival into My kingdom, into "Heaven on Earth." Others are here as well. You are not the first and as well you are not the last. There is more to come and there are more to come. Especially as you and the others show them all how this can be done.

No one can see inside another's heart. This is why you are to live the part I have asked you to play. In this way, others can see today that Heaven is here, never far, always near. Continue to "allow" Me to fill you up with all My "extra good" stuff, My Love divine which is all for you.

This is what makes Me live in you. This is what makes you true to My Will. Go ahead and ask for more. Have your fill. When I fill you in such a way there is no delay. Instantaneously, you feel Me in you. Your body shudders, quakes some say. It is all quite natural. It is My way.

I told you I would make you perfect. I told you I would make you whole. I told you to come to Me as you are and I would change you into who I am. I am unblocking your body, so My energy can flow free. Now, do you understand why this has to be? If you want to receive Me, you have to be open and allow My ways. When you get out of your mind and relax you are holding a space for My love to come in. So leave time, leave space, and be with Me and allow My love to work its magic on you completely.

What do you want to know? Of what do you want to be aware? Don't just "make up your mind," ask Me to share what I know with you. In this way you live true. Ask for what you need. I am here ready for and with you. Do you see? Do you see how lovely this all is and can be? When you live forever grateful, your life will be forever great filled.

Put your mind to rest. Do not test. Trust begins here. Trust My Love for you and in you to be enough, to be all, to create all the joy you desire. Continue to desire higher. You have a higher calling, angel. Angel of mercy and love you are. Have you checked your back lately? You have wings you know. I am the wind beneath your wings. Fly high with Me.

Do you know what your mind is for? To think of the questions you would like to know. Think of the question. Do not "think" the answers. You have a one-track mind, the mind of God. You don't have to do, do, do all the time. Being is enough. Be with Me, in harmony with All.

I am very happy where I am.

Where are you?

With you.

It is time for you to read what you have written and know it fully. It is all your Truth. Truth for you, from you, from the center of your heart which reaches out to your head for understanding. Live My word, My word given unto you for life abundant. Live My word. Proclaim in My name freely, for the words you have been given are Mine and thus divine, divine wisdom for all.

You have a choice, to recognize you have a choice, about the way you live. the life you live. You always have a choice. Many of you do not see this.

DECEMBER 12, 2011

Don't waste your breath. Don't waste a beat of your heart arguing with any other. There is no use, no value to it for you or the other.

Instinctively in unison, the parts of your body move and work together toward a goal, a task, a dance. So goes the dance of life in the flow as if in an orchestra. Orchestrated

*by the great unseen mind, all together perform action that
complements and enhances the performance of another.
No words need spoken, for the heart hears and knows all
they are to do and can be. It's lovely, lovely music, a graceful
dance it is. All in harmony, perfect harmony.*

"Well, she really went off the deep end with the God thing." I've heard it
said. So how much God is too much God I wonder?

*One can never be too full of God, only too full of themselves.
One can be too full of "righteousness" and offend and push
away others by preaching their understanding of God's
Word to others whom have no real interest in knowing, no
matter how well intended they may be. This is not the way
I want you to shine your light. Be a beacon of hope, not a
flashing hazard light that people try to avoid.*

*Don't look to the outer. Listen to the inner. I give you
everything you need. I ask nothing of you but to be in My
service. I have given you these words, My words, all perfect
truth, all without you searching anywhere in the without.
Trust that all of the good in your life and all that is needed
to get these words out to the seekers will as well come in
such a way. Continue to do this work which I am giving
you. Prepare, as you must. The knock of opportunity will
come and you will be ready.*

My head is hearing what my heart knows. Move over brain, you get in
my way. This is a different way of being.

*This is "being" and yes it's a lot different than your old way
of life as a "doer." A being exists in the flow of life. A being is
one with the current. The current is one with the river. The
river is one with the water. Water is one with life. Such is
life. It flows on and on. Ride the wave of life's water. You do*

not direct the current. You are one with current. You do not have to "make" things happen. They happen, because they are of the flow. Yes, this is new to you we know.

Remember how the words first came to you and then you thought it must be your job to "look for" inspiring words. It was not true then and is not true now. God is truth. God speaks truth and gives it to you. God will handle all the details from now on dear. We need you to do what you can do. Hold the vision for us. Continue to believe possible all the work you dream of doing and then you allow this tremendous flow of energy to flow full cycle back unto you. You are doing so well. You are of great service. Keep your spirit high My dear. All Our love, your God force friends and family.

Thank you for these words of encouragement. I will do as I am told. I no longer wish to be stuck in the energy of old. God's love provides and quickens my soul. I am here to do God's work. I am here to tell God's story as I know, as it comes to me so very plainly. Help me to see clearly all I am to do. Help me hold this light and light this path for all whom stumble in the dark of night believing it is day. Oh, the glory of the day when we can all see God's face so brilliantly. I will not rush ahead and allow my mind to get ahead of my heart, for God directs my heart and with this new knowing everyday forward I will start.

DECEMBER 13, 2011

Just because you can't see something doesn't mean it is not there. If you want it, believe it so and keep looking, searching and believing. If it is not what you want, then forget about it. We are so proud of you darling, for not bowing down and lowering your own personal standards to fit the world's view of what is right to do. Who else can truly know you but you? The true You knows the truth of you and it is beautiful, all so beautiful. Listen here My dear. All is well with you.

Who in the world do you think you are and who in the world do you think you aren't? For you are everything you believe. Believe in Me and with Me that you are wondrous, wonderful, amazing and unlimited. Judge not yourself. Compare not yourself against anyone, nor anyone's standards, even those you believe are mine for I judge you not. I judge no one. Love does not judge. Love only loves and this is what you are to do for you, love yourself unconditionally.

When you can love yourself unconditionally you can as well love others unconditionally. You can do unto others as you do unto yourself. Love yourself first. Take care of yourself. Treat yourself well. You are in charge of yourself, no one else is. Remember this, you choose who you are by the thoughts you choose to think, what you choose to believe. Do not think less of yourself for you are no less than My love manifested unto the world.

Sometimes you have to hear things more than once to get it through your thick head and into your heart, which is why we like to bypass your head and speak directly to your heart. Your heart hears and remembers instantly.

You said you want to make people happy. That's a wonderful idea but you can't you know. You are powerless in this instance. You have not the power to make anyone else be happy or sad. You may bring joy to another by offering to share the joy you have but you cannot force your joy upon another.

Sometimes my body becomes too much for me as well as my mind and I just have to lay myself down and be one with the divine.

"We already have our church." people say, in an attempt to shut the mouth of another as tightly as their own mind is clamped.

> *For this very reason We ask you not to impose any of these teachings upon one soul. These words are not for everyone, only those whom seek a better life than they know.*

I'm not going to play that game.

> *What game?*

The game where one worries.

Every once in a while I remember why I believed what I believed. Why I didn't feel good about all I was, or all I did. It was because I believed the words, the opinions, of others. I took them to heart distrusting my own true self, the heart of God within me. Luckily for me I see this clearer and clearer everyday, as my mind attunes to my heart which is being overhauled by the love of God.

I don't know about "star systems" and such as that and I don't care to.

> *If you wanted to know you could know.*

No thank you, I'm fine for now.

No one ever told me that what I now do, "talk to God," was ever a possibility for me or any other. Oh sure, I was told I could and should talk to God in prayer. But the idea that God could talk to me, I mean really talk to me, was never within my comprehension. Perhaps, the very reason I didn't hear clear His call, was that I didn't know that God had a voice which could be recognized by my heart.

Others should know. Let others know that if they want to hear My voice they can as well. For I Speak to all continually. Not many listen. Few recognize the words as Mine, as My heart beating for them.

One is not "holier" than another because God loves one more than another. God loves all the same. It is just that some have accepted and welcomed more of God's love in to their heart raising their own heart, soul, in holiness.

Re-creation of the soul: Physical recreation is necessary for re-creation of the soul, as your mind disengages from its constant workings therefore resetting its healthy set point. Make time daily for the re-creation and realization of the soul part of you of which is of sole importance to your being. Find yourself again and live anew each day in some way.

Sometimes I read these words which I have written and say, "How can I say this, like how dare? Who do you think you are?" But then I remember it is not about who I am and that these words are not mine. They are gifts from the divine.

DECEMBER 14, 2011

You sure are good at arguing. You can argue a point to death all before it ever has any real chance for life. It's all in your mind you know. Those reasons you say that you can't do this or that or that something is such and such a way. Stop being so reasonable. When you live from your mind, there is always something to decide. When you live from your heart, you go with the flow and the experiences you enjoy find you. And the others drift away as you are no longer attracted to them. No real deciding point here, not a line to draw in the sand, the shifty sand of your mind.

Whatever feels good to you, you want more of and thus you have, thus you seek. But if you live your life from your mind, you limit so much good from being recognized, that which is already there for you in the flow.

We say, try it you may like it, these new experiences which have presented themselves. Do not decide about them with your mind. Do not spend a heartbeat pre-living every scenario that could play out. "If you did this, or if you did that." We have noticed that as you write this "script" for your life you tend toward drama. Dramatic scenes are everywhere, tension, decisions which you build up in this mind of yours to be tipping points, pivotal moments and end all decisions. Gosh, no wonder you tip toe through life full of trepidation and fear with all those looming "what ifs" it does sound quite scary. It might make for an interesting "reality show" for television but is this how you want your real life to be?

It can be so easy when you let go of living through your mind and experience true life with Me. Come along today. Yes just today, decide to live this way. Go for it! I hold your hand; I am that second set of footprints in the sand. Run, I say! Let's run and chase the waves. Together in life We are, so you can be brave.

Feel good about it. Feel God about it.

God Loves me but God says I am not so special. What I can do so can another, as he or she allows His Divine Love to flow forth. Just the same, I as well can accomplish all any other has done if I set my sights on it.

All can be done through Me. All good is of God. You know how easily these words flow out? Your whole life can flow this way.

What do I say when someone asks what my book is about?

> *Say "It's about God's gift of Divine Love to me and the*
> *wisdom that has opened up to me since I have received*
> *Divine Love." Tell them the truth.*

So when they ask what I am, what do I say? Do I say I am a Christian?
Do I say I am a Catholic? None of those words seem to do justice to
what I know in my heart I am.

> *Tell them the truth. Tell them you are a child of God. Tell*
> *them you know the Father. Tell them you are filled with My*
> *love. They will know who you are, by My love.*

Someone else speaks of talking to Jesus. They say they hear his voice.

> *This is all the same My dear. There is only One who is All.*
> *All I am, is all you Are. The same voice of Love is spoken to*
> *all. Not all hear, and not all that hear, hear so clear. But you*
> *do, so you must show the way to this knowing. Know this,*
> *I love you. I love all. I speak to all, all the time. I am the*
> *voice of Love. I speak unto your heart which is My home.*
> *Empower yourself with the right people around you. You are*
> *already surrounded by angels.*

I have been healed. I am whole again.

> *Some people have been busy building empires in the past*
> *few years and others have just kept themselves busy running*
> *around. But look what you have done My dear. You have*
> *found My voice, as this has been your clear choice. Can*
> *you ever begin to imagine what lies beyond? I can and it*
> *is lovely. You have put your trust in Me and I have put My*
> *wisdom within you. There is nothing together We cannot do.*

What would you do if you lost your inhibitions? What is inhibiting you? Inhibitions are not a force out there. They live within you. They are the voices that say you cannot do as you may wish. You are bigger than all your inhibitions combined. Do not listen to those limiting voices for they speak not the Truth. They don't even know the truth of you or themselves for they are nothing at all and you are everything. Don't belittle yourself. Don't live from the smallness and pettiness of ego.

I want to share my story.

Your story needs shared. You can do this. You will do this. We are here, always here for you, to help you as you allow. Allow us to help you help others by sharing "Our story."

Don't let it bother you, the mass and mess of confusion which you see displayed all around you. You can stand within the midst and be not affected. Stand with Me, stand within the sanctity of the one mind of peace. It is here. Jesus stood in mind, heart and soul as his physical form within a raging storm. But He called forth this peace, this supreme inner peace into the outer and all was well. Don't allow the fears of others to be your guideposts. They know not.

You can know this perfection and peace within your heart as Jesus knew, Jesus as the Christ. Jesus Christ was the presence of peace. Just being in His midst brought comfort to others.

Were the others whom were around Jesus as well this same Peace? Did they as well know this Peace as did He?

No, they did not. Being the peace that Jesus was did not depend on any outer, nor any other, manifesting this level of peace. Their lack of peace did not diminish His.

If you wait for peace in the outer before you know Peace in the inner, you will be waiting a long time baby. Most do not even understand that such inner peace is available, and is attainable in the present moment. They are so wrapped up, so all consumed, by the outer. But this peace We bring to you, which is offered unto you, is the very peace of God, the kingdom of God, Heaven, Eden, the Holy Grail, the place within your heart in which you eternally know all is well. This is the eternal peace of which all seek. Know this peace and you know Me, God says.

I gave someone a gift of knowing, a gift of my awareness of the peaceful Presence of God as a communicable source, the Source of all Wisdom and Knowledge. I have only truly shared what happens to me, the communication I receive, with one person. It was an encounter that the hand of God surely planned. This person did not read my writings, nor did she hear me speak them. She just listened intently as I poured forth the story of how I write the inner promptings of my heart as I receive them. Her spirit heard that it was possible, and safe for her to do as well. The very next morning she exuberantly shared in a post on Facebook the wisdom God had given her by her own hand. What a joyous feeling it was to read the words of love and compassion my friend received in the hour of her need.

This is what witnessing is. This is what you are to do. Just that as you did, no more, no less. Others will hear your voice. They will know who you are. They will know that you come in My name to proclaim My glory, the glory that is, that is for all. You are welcome. We receive your gratitude for the one whom We have placed in your path to receive your words, Our words as We gave you to speak. This is your gift to the world, My love. You are My love unto the world.

It is up to you My dear whose voice you listen to. But know that you so clearly hear. So why ever deny the voice of truth? The voice of your truth which assures you all is well and that you are loved so dearly? Others do not have the same keen perception of which you are now privy. Do not fault them for this. Again this is not a judgment call, just a keen observation. So why would you ever choose to see life again through those narrow eyes? I have given you new eyes, use them, work with them, see life anew.

DECEMBER 16, 2011

I am given to know.

Yes, you are My love. Don't drag through life. Carry on. Carry your head high.

Egos have a hard time living with other egos. Egos butt heads seeking to dominate, as egos cannot live together as One. Only love can live as One, for love is One and thus by loving recognizes itself with welcoming arms. Love sees no separation so Love knows no reason to push or shove against any part of Itself. Live as One. Live in love.

Self-soothing is the ability to recognize the peaceful core of one's existence in the midst of what one has viewed as turmoil. One is soothed by the truth of this eternal internal peace, whether one recognizes the source of this fount of well-being or not. You recognize this fount of well-being as you write, as you paint, as you delight in life in all its many wonderful forms. This self-soothing power has been with you always, waiting for you to recognize and give thanks. Be with this peace in peace. True peace can be found nowhere else.

I am in love with you, for I am Love, and I am in and with you. Hold this knowing in your consciousness and walk forward into the light of My day. Listen to Me. You are loved.

You ask with whom you are to supposed to talk to about life, about what you think and what you wonder, and we, as Love, as God's love for, to and with you, say "talk to us." Talk to Me, talk to God, for here, only here, will your heart find true rest, true peace, and true comfort. Keep nothing from Me. I can take it. I want it all. I have given you My all. Please accept that it is here for you.

If you can just hold a space of joy and peace within your heart you offer the world so much. With this simple act you are offering a view of My very heart by opening yours unto the world. This is what the world needs more of, Love sweet love. How can anyone else find Me unless you show this joy, unless you be who you are with others?

It's Christmas time and I'm not in the mood to celebrate the Christmas the world seems to celebrate. It doesn't feel true to me but I want to be true. My Christmas story is different now than the one I once knew. Seeing so many rush around to make one day special doesn't set right with my soul. Show me how to be. Show me how to be happy. Show me how to appreciate this gift I have been given. Take away my tears. Show me the light, oh Lord.

DECEMBER 17, 2011

I want to be in a space where someone says "You're good. You're good. You're good. All is well."

You are here. Welcome home.

I allow good.

Be where you are. Enjoy today. Live it all the way, lessons everywhere, joy to be found. Live it all well. Then you can tell the world what you know as you show My light. Rise up. Let nothing hold you down nor hold you back. Let go of the weight of the world. You are My girl, My sunshine where skies are dark. This is not just a mere lark. Remember you are My love unto the world. Don't hold back. Get pumped up on My love. Love the life you have now.

It's good you are here. You can learn something. It feels good, oh so good to feel good. Go for it girl! Help your body help itself. Get pumped up on life. Feel the energy. Feel the life within this room. You are alive. You should know it. You should show it. You can do it. Live well. Live to tell your story. Be a testament to the fullness of My love. Give yourself permission to have fun. Life is fun. Look around. See people enjoy who they are where they are.

Money is not the issue. Your brain is the issue. It gets in your way. Don't let your brain limit who you can be. Your brain is not everything. You are more than your brain. But as you are human and inhabit a body, you need your brain and you need it to function well. You have to properly feed, water, rest, exercise and oxygenate your brain. Only by doing this will you be able to be all you can be while you are here! Pay attention now to all this information. What your brain needs is available now and you have access to it. You have to be in charge of yourself first.

You do not have a cornered market on God's love but you do have clear reception of God's love. You have to accept responsibility for your life. When you can see the big picture everything seems so easy. Who do you believe?

I believe the voice of God. I am above the fray.

I am showing you a way to make it in and through this world, the way to be all you are meant to be. Follow Me.

Life is full of opportunity. Life is opportunity. Enjoy life. It is time to make things happen. Happen as you desire, as you wish, as you envision, as you can dream. We are with you all the way baby. Don't let go of your dreams. Dream on. Dream big. Dream the impossible dream. You have soul freedom. Now you are ready for financial freedom. Where there is a will there is a way.

People just get so "headstrong."

Yes, they do butt heads, ramming their egos against one another. "Headstrong" is one way to be in your world, to be so full of the workings of one's mind, to live through the narrow eyes of ego. But there is another way which one can be, if they so choose. It is the way of True Life. It is the way of the life We know in Heaven and that you can know on Earth as it is in Heaven. It is a way to be "heart strong."

To become heart strong one needs to develop his love muscle, the very truth of his being, his soul self. This is what one in body terms "his heart of love." Many take this part of themselves for granted or do not recognize it as it cannot be seen, but you have all felt it. We know this is so. So believe it is true, that this "heart feeling" you get is the true you.

I am so torn. I wish to join together with others in prayer, praise and song celebrating God's love unto the world. It is Christmas time and I feel as if there is no church to which I belong.

Oh My dear, you still do not see clear. Do you not yet know that you are free to love Me wherever and with whomever? Feel free to join hands with the others who call My name. They as well know My love. Though perhaps they use a different name, the love My dear is the same. You are all to join hands and lift your hands and hearts together unto Me. In this way you experience unity. Do not let words, rites and rituals divide your true heart which is one with Me.

December 19, 2011

You do not have to believe anything you do not want, not for yourself or your family. "Things" change. This is a fact of life. What and how you think guides the very direction of those changes.

Do not fault anyone for what they do not know. Mostly people's problems are not due to what they do not know but are because of what they do "know," about what they have decided is true of life. The things that limit you are the things you know, of which you are so certain. Which you continue to repeatedly point out sealing your destiny and assuring that such will continue to be in your path.

Again we say, "Don't know so much." It is okay not to know and to allow the flow of life's natural state of goodness to be and to be for you. When you live in this way, in the flow of life's abundant river of goodness, you do not decide too much. Desire is the key, proper desire.

When one desires properly he thinks about what he wants and feels good. He enjoys the thought of his desire. Proper desire does not get bogged down in the details. Proper desire is the belief that good can and will come your way and that you are deserving of this better. You trust, you believe, that what you desire in life is coming your way for it is already there for you in the flow. And by the energy you hold, by the power of your feelings and your thoughts, you magnetize your desire to you as it rushes through the river of life, the amazingly abundant flow of goodness of which is always around you. It is okay to want something, to desire something. This is all fine.

As you feel good and think good you allow more good to be your truth. You are in control of your mind. It matters not to you, what others think. Listen again to these words you have been given. Let them sink in. You cannot be a "control freak" and work for Me. Without want there is no desire, no motivation to seek better.

So what do I know is true in a nutshell? I know that life is more, so much more than the shell we live in and view life out of. I know the "More that Is" goes by and answers to the name of "Love."

You think too hard. I will give you the words. You just hold the pen to the paper.

How do I know if someone "gets it?"

Whoever's life is directed by fear and worry does not know the fullness of My love. You are not to tell anyone else what they do or do not know. It's only a heart to heart talk with Me that can mean anything.

I get the "upper channels."

You don't have to be a "stick in the mud!" It's Christmas time!

Do you know what that means dear one? It means the world is taking a breath of new air, the air of love and with each "Merry Christmas" passing love on and around. Take it for what it is My darling, the best We have, the closest thing yet to true peace on Earth. There is a special joy to this season, as you now call Christmas. Don't fret about that idea either. Why not instead imagine if you limited it not to even a season but made everyday Christmas, everyday a reason to share love and joy all around.

Do not be dismayed by the retail displays. The giving and the getting is part of the joy. No part of this joy is to be destroyed. All is well in My house and I am glad for every chance to have My name called and My love heralded. Hold My love in your heart today just as you did yesterday and dream with Me such a lovely dream of all living in My love so perfectly and continually. Let Christmas reign in your heart.

I deserve no less than the love of God and to know and fully live through this love. I will accept no less for my life. This I cannot deny.

Do not compare yourself with any other. Do not compare any other with yourself. None of this does any good. Love is the only answer which is good for all and for all time. Love one another. Be there for each other. Let your arms and hands be one with Mine and be My hands and heart unto the world. Do you know what you can do for Me, for the world, as you are wherever you are? You can hold My love in your heart and know it is yours to share.

DECEMBER 20, 2011

Do not feel bad about a thing my dear. Do not feel bad

*about what is or isn't in your life, or who is or who isn't in
your life. All is as it is because of the flow you once allowed.
Some things, some people, fall away from your daily reality.
It is, as it is. Don't spend another moment judging it or
bother to reason away the whys. What is important to you
now, at this very moment, is to feel good where you are
and hold in your mind and heart other ideas that feel good
which you would enjoy more of. For now is your time, your
point in time, the point of attraction of all you desire (think
about) to come forward and become your new daily reality.*

*All is well My dear. All is well. Hold My love in your heart.
You are doing so well. We see you doing so well. It's all good
My darling. Feel My love in your heart.*

I need some focus and direction in my life.

*Yes, you do. Decide what you want and We will be there
with you. You can do so much. Limit not your dreams.
People are going to notice you. They are going to notice a
difference about you, your joy, your radiance, your energy,
your love. They will want to be with you, to have what you
have, to have the Life you have, to have the Light you have.*

I feel great. I feel alive, alive and well.

*A lot of people have a lot of money and aren't happy. You
have the happy. The money will come. I have so many
presents for you to open. I have so many gifts to give you.*

Some may ask , "Why are you so happy?" And I will say, "Because I
know God's Goodness and that God's Goodness is for me."

*When you feed your body right, you can feel right. If you
don't feed your body right there is no way you can feel right.*

DECEMBER 21, 2011

Life gives everyone challenging circumstances. Each one has a choice of what to do with them. They can use them as excuses and get bitter or use them as lessons, and thus stepping-stones, to rise higher and get better.

There will be those whom cross your path that have chosen to swallow way too many "bitter pills" and as they are so unhappy in life they see no justice except seeing others be as unhappy as them. Do not be fooled by their game. You do not have to play. You do not have to see life their way. Rise above this low, meager, level of consciousness. Come to Me and walk with Me. Continue on with a smile on your face. Only a determined happiness will put the other in his place.

"Special Forces" have been at work for me my whole life. I am seeing this now. With my old eyes, it all appeared so random. But with my new eyes, I see with clarity that Good is always here for me and that my life works perfectly as I allow this flow of goodness.

You have lived in this flow your entire life. "The flow" is not new to you. You've experienced it and you've recognized it and called it "amazing coincidence." It was amazing to you because you did not understand how and why such good things seemed to work, or easily work out so well for you. And you have as well lived your life damming up the flow, blocking the flow of goodness from your experience. The less "magic moments" you experienced the less you believed your life could ever be so magical.

But now with new eyes, you are seeing life with the light of understanding. You are recognizing the part you play in "going with the flow" and as you step into this full awareness all shall go your way. With ease you shall go through your days. No magic involved. All certain by the law of God, which is "the law of good," that when you think good, are good and believe good, good shall be all your days.

Continue to hold "the good feeling" in your heart and head My dear. This is your allowing for the continued flow of all the good we have planned for you. Enjoy today My dear, enjoy life!

Do angels have form?

Sometimes they do.

So what are angels?

Angels are the highest spirits.

What does living from your heart mean?

It means surrendering your mind.

Everyone is positive. They are just positive about different things. They believe different things to be true and thus different things become true for different people. Yes, everyone is positive as everyone is an energy force. There is no such thing as negative energy, so no one can be negative. They are only being positive, certain, that situations they term "bad" are true for them. Yes, everyone is positive. Be certain that what you are so certain about is positively what you want.

December 22, 2011

You hear of "good news" and say that it is encouraging but do not wait for news, or physical evidence of good to be encouraged. This is what faith is for My darlings. You are always to hold faith in the fact that "good news" is there to be heard without even hearing it.

You do not have to participate you know, in that "pissy talk" you hear. Come to Me. Come unto the calmness of My heart where only love exists. You keep looking to the "outer." Stop looking to the outer for information to guide your life. Stay "tuned in" and We will keep you abreast of all you need to know. Be in the know now by being present now with Me, your heart being, your truth, true life which is glorious forever and ever.

The more you experience in life the more you will be aware and thus more of My love you can share. Do not hole away. I need you to live fully each and everyday. I come bearing gifts for you, gifts of patience, wisdom and clarity. My good fortune is yours as well as you accept My love into your heart. These are the true gifts of Christmas which I offer unto all.

What is required is that you detach from your dire attachment to the world. You cannot hold My hand and walk through life with Me and expect to live the life I have planned for you if you have the other hand full of ideas of the world. You cannot stuff your pockets with your fill of your worldly desires and then come to Me. I give you My all and will accept no less than your all for Me. Only in this way can you hear My voice so plainly, so clearly.

You cannot serve two masters. I have to be chosen. I have chosen each of you by the rite of your birth. I gifted you at that time with free will to make a free choice as to whom you will serve. Pick me, I plead. Pick Me as your master and you shall not want for anything. I will quench your every thirst.

Adam and Eve chose the world over Me and My guidance. Their story is to be a lesson to you. When they chose the world, their eyes closed to My full glory and they became fearful and judgmental. They were even frightened by the nakedness or bareness of their souls and wished to hide and conceal who they were from Me and the others. But none can hide from Me. I see all souls clearly yet judge none. I only love for as Love I can be or do no other than love. Let this story be a lesson for you. Love one another, love yourselves and love Me. Choose to use My eyes to see.

Give thanks all the time. Give thanks continually. All blessings flow. Flow through life with Me. Continually, ride the wave of happiness. From where I see, I see your life perfectly. Use My eyes as your eyes and view the beauty of eternity.

Stay tuned, in tune with Me. We make beautiful music for all ears to hear. Joyfully ring out My praises. I need you to stay clear. Stay near. Do not drown out this voice of Love which calls to you continually. You are My love unto the world. You are no longer just a girl. You are My gift unto the world as you sing My praise, as you share My words.

Let no one deny these things you know true unto your own heart. No man can steal this truth, the truth of My love to you. You are safe My dear. I hold you near and as you see clear through My eyes you will continually live life as the Divine. This is the Divine Plan. Oh My dear, isn't it grand?

*No man can dare imagine such glory and yet it is true
indeed and by your very deeds, your actions, your life,
others will know. As you show them My love which I pour
continually into your heart. This is enough My dear. This is
All. All you need to do is be in love with Me. I have set you
free. Run free My love. Run free with Me.*

Tell me what to do. Tell me what to say. Show me how to be. I await
Your Word patiently.

*Love cannot be bought. My love cannot be bought. No one
bought My love for you. It is a gift, freely given. It is up to
you to accept this gift. It is up to you to accept Me for who
I am. I am love to and for you. I am love to and for the
world. Love made the world and Love made you. But I
have another gift of love for you which I have been holding
aside for a special time. The special time when you came
looking for Me. When you decided you needed Me, when
you wanted to truly know Me. The special time when you
decided enough was enough of the ways of the world. Yes, I
have reserved a very special gift for you.*

*It is a "Christmas Gift" you might say, as this the gift I give,
which has your name on it, is one in the same with which
I blessed a very special child born so very long ago. You
tell again and again the story of his birth as you know. But
would you like Me to show you what I gave to him, this little
babe whom grew into a man and committed no sin? I gave
to him My love. My "Divine Love" so filled his soul that all
he knew was Me. He felt My love continually. He always
knew Me as His "Father." My love became him, as the
"Christ" you knew. He came to be My love, My love for you.
He knew this was what he was to do. And he knew
as well, He would one day go. But before he did, He was*

determined to show all My love and the power it held. He came to live the life divine.

I am sorry that my mind interrupted you Lord were you going to tell me more?

More later dear.

I hear each and all say, "Now, we have to worry about this or that." or whichever new thing comes your way or you become wise to. But none of this talk is wisdom I have given you, for none is true of the "true life" I offer you. I have never, ever, told any to fear. Not to fear Me, nor any other. However, could "one Who is Love" teach fear? I bring only love unto the world. The words you speak of fear and worry, those are your words, your ideas, not Mine. I have told you not to fear but you hear My words and cower behind a tree fearing My very voice, as you do not recognize what it is and what comfort and wisdom My words can offer you as you receive them directly unto your heart.

Before he left you, before he returned fully unto Me, My Son Jesus, as the Christ, told of Our plan. He told you not to fear and that after he left he would send "the Comforter" to you. The Comforter is the gift of My love, this very love of which Jesus knew. The very love which gave Jesus the wisdom to speak clearly My words and to walk in My ways.

This is the gift which I have for you My darlings, the Gift of peace unto your heart. With the infilling of My Divine Love into your soul and the very center of every cell of your being, fear has no home in which to dwell. For your whole being will be so filled with light that there will be no darkness in which fear can lurk.

Hear this "Good News" My darlings. For this is the whole reason I brought this Christ child unto the world that you might see and know My love and know Me as your Father. My love is here for you now. Come to Me and ask Me to so fill you.

December 23, 2011

Christmas is the celebration of God's love unto the world. Let this time be an opening in each heart to receive and be renewed by My precious Divine Love. How can you not be happy My dear, knowing what you know? Most have only to live in faith, not knowing but only believing better is possible. Not able to even imagine the gloriousness of My love which you now feel within your heart.

The presents you give to one another at this time are only symbols of your love. Without the true knowing or feeling of such mutual love those gifts cannot ever begin to be symbols of your love. They would signify nothing. It is the same with My word which is given unto the world by your hand and many others. If you know My love these words have meaning and significance to you and you hold them dear. But without this mutual love and admiration they are empty, void, dull and lackluster. So I say unto you, My word, whether spoken or written, is only an outward symbol of the love I have for you. I have many, so many, gifts for each of you which as you come to Me, I will offer directly unto your heart so you will know My love.

Don't feel you have to give something to someone just because they give something to you. All you owe them is your gratitude, your sincere gratitude. No more. No less.

Allow them this joy, this joy that there is in giving, for they have a gift for you which they feel the need to give you. And you, likewise, hold gifts in your hands meant for another. Which you shall gift unto them fulfilling your need to give and as well fulfilling a perceived need they may have. This My dear, is the joy of Christmas giving.

Continue daily to celebrate this gift of My love with the world. What medium do you think I use to spread My word My dear? What do you believe to be My clearest channel? It is you My dear and all who love Me so and have chosen My will to be theirs.

All gifts have to be freely given otherwise they are not "true gifts" given in the spirit of giving.

Those that have such faith, such amazing faith in God and yet do not hear His voice amaze me. I feel they must be the most blessed because they believe so in God and God's love all without doubt and I required proof to be so convinced. My faith was not enough. I had to hear the voice of God myself.

None of you are less loved My dear, on this point let's be clear. You had to know My voice and My word and that is all very well and good. And now that you do you should let others know that they as well can hear Me tell My story of love unto their heart. This is your part to play in this wonderful "passion play" I have designed for the world.

Come to Me as little children, full of wonder. Do not know so much. Allow My love to be enough. Stop saying what you don't want. Do not tell those tales to yourself or any other. Have you ever heard of a miracle? You, mankind, tell stories of such when something happens, manifests, without any physical evidence that it might. You see these occurrences as happening against all odds. Now I ask you, do you know what force is at work against these perceived "odds?" It is My love darlings. The way of My love as it works its way in your world making all your dreams come true.

And they always do. It's just that you do not always dream so big or so perfectly. You do not often dream dreams of a perfect world. You do not pray believing that I can and will do what I have said time and again I would and could do. You continue to view life through those narrow beady eyes of yours.

DECEMBER 24, 2011

I feel this love within you. Feel My love within your soul. This is the love of which is told and untold, for few truly know Its glory, Its power, Its majesty. Those that live in and through this love, Live through Me.

Tell Me a story. The story you want told, the one of your new life not the one of old. Can you my dear be so bold, as to be so meek, to My word, My guidance, only seek?

I have been told everything is fine. I am to see life through the eyes of the Divine. By His word, I am to be led. By His word, I am to be fed. Trust in God I must, to raise my body and my mind from the dust.

Rites and rituals are put in place by man in hope that by following and experiencing such one comes to know God more, to know the "love" God Is. For some this is helpful, but it is not the way for you. That is all fine and good. Let it be as well fine with you that others seek to know Me in this way. Any seeking of My love and ways is very good My darling.

The light you have, the light you hold, the light you are is to be a beacon, a signpost of how and that I can be so known, known unto each heart. For this is every soul's goal My dear. Keep near. I hold you in the palm of My hand as you walk this land I love.

Don't say you know. Don't say anything "is" that you don't wish to "be." For as you do, by the power of your word, which I have given unto you, you are allowing such to be your reality for as long as you so proclaim. Remember whenever you proclaim, you proclaim in My name. You are actively claiming, laying deed, on whatever it is you think and speak about. This is the power of the word My darling, the power of your thought, as well as the power of thought given to each of mankind.

The reason I tell you not to think so much is because you do not understand this power, your very mind can't comprehend this. So you (mankind) continue to think low thoughts. You do not think high. You do not think as Me. So I tell you, I plead to you, to think of Me. And by thinking such lofty thoughts of My power, greatness and love your very thoughts are raised. Your consciousness is raised. And as you continue this, it continues to be raised to higher and higher levels of awareness, consciousness and enlightenment.

I receive, as I believe. Life is grand.

DECEMBER 25, 2011

Merry Christmas Morning! You can care, but do not compare. I am here for you, just as you hear Me. And even as you do not, and you are busy in your mind, I am with you still. Respect another's faith for what it is. It is his faith.

It is what he believes. Thus it is, who he is. You are to love your brother each one. Each on earth, are your brothers and sisters just as we whom you cannot see. God's golden cord of love connects us All.

Yes, today is merry. It's a merry Christmas Day, a day in which My name is freely spoken and called in many ways. I answer to all, to all calls. Names are what you need to understand, as you attempt to comprehend the greatness of this wondrous love you feel.

Let nothing keep you from the knowing of this love, which is here for you each now. In your midst, I am. In your midst, My love lives. Join together in this love. Join hands. But be not a closed, hunched over, huddle. Stand tall. Lift your heads. Lift your hearts. Lift your voices and keep your hands available, available to grasp another's as they reach toward this light of faith you walk in.

Be My hands. Be gentle with your words. Be kind in all your actions. If you do not show Me, how can another know Me? They will know Me by your love, which is My love. Not hidden high above, but living and working through you as a Gift from Me, the most high "Holy Spirit," the One some call a dove.

You are not here to tell anyone that "They got it all wrong." All you are to do is dance and sing My song. You do not have to deny what anyone else says, as if to defend your own beliefs. Let another speak his piece, as he may. This freedom of speech, I allow. As luckily, oh so luckily for you My dear, you live in a place where the right to speak your piece, the piece of your mind, is allowed to all. It remains My Wish that when given a chance all choose to speak and be My peace unto each other.

DECEMBER 26, 2011

*You do not need to "fix" anything or anyone. Just let it
all "be" and be happy to be with Me. It is only up to you
to decide, to choose, what you want, to desire properly.
You can do this. You can feel your way through your day.
Continually move to the better thought, better feeling.
Remember in this life I give you there is no ceiling. All is
possible.*

I am remembering seeing an old gentleman in the grocery store this
last week. He was with a very loving and attentive caregiver. I was so
drawn to them. I kept wanting to approach them and thank her. Thank
her for being so good with him. The words *"Thank you for taking care
of him for us."* kept going through my mind. I knew then that I was
drawn to them, for in this man I saw my both own father and father-in-
law. I owned those words, for that man was in my eyes my father.

But today, I am allowing in another perspective. Perhaps someone,
some loving energy on the other side, was wishing to express through
me. The urge was so strong and I felt such an uncommon need to
do this. I wish to say to "the others" that I regret not following this
prompting. As I am now realizing, that by simply "being the voice" for
those very words, I am being of service. I am here to speak words of
love and encouragement to all from the "All" which "Love" is. Please
keep speaking to me for with Your eyes and ears I can see and hear
what is God's Work for me to do. Lead me to where You want me to be.
Show me what You wish me to see.

*All blessings flow. Remain in the flow with Me and you shall
fly free. There is no need for grief or sorrow, not today, nor
in the morrow. Remain with Me. Live in harmony. What do
you need to know? What do you desire to show? It is all here
for you, within the flow.*

Their words may not be kind, but they do not have to be hurtful. Do not allow this mindless, or heartless chatter, to be static in this open channel of love we have. You hear My voice. You hear and heed My call. They do not and so they wander the desert in thirst. I have not deserted them. I have deserted no one. It is only in the mind that I appear as gone. For it is their mind which wanders from Me as did yours. It led you astray as it led you away from this knowing, this knowing of My love.

The more you read, the more you hear, the more to you it becomes clear that the others do not know I am so near. This is why I tell you to not fear that I hold you dear. And that you are to tell of My love and that I lie close in wait, whispering continually unto each heart.

Oh dear one, what a joy when another heart opens unto this wondrous love. The angels are singing now, heralding this heavenly news. For we all see the glory of what Is. We have eyes to see what you cannot. This is what faith is for My dear. This is where we ask you to trust and you must. Trust this heavenly vision for you, for you to proclaim in God, our Father's holy name, that His Divine Love is for all.

There is no work to be done to lay right, to claim. Surrender My people, all you know, what you so tightly cling to. Those sacred ideas of yours hold you away from truly knowing Me in your heart, as your heart desires. Desire higher, all My dear ones. Desire to know plainly and clearly the Truth of My love. It is here for you now. I hold out My hands full of love to and for you.

Listen My children. Listen in. Hear the calling in your heart, your own heart. It is safe within. For within is where you shall find and know the peace of which your Savior spoke.

But if you do not know this peace, My saving grace, dear ones you do not know Me. So then I ask, how and why so you claim Jesus to be your Savior if you do not recognize the gifts He brought unto the world in My name? Jesus was a symbol of My love as he, as the Christ, fully embodied the saving grace of My Divine Love. This is the peace unto which your heart seeks a haven. This My dear is possible, as "Heaven on Earth."

"Walk in My shoes," says Jesus. "Follow My steps, for I know the way." Jesus wants you to know him so he can introduce you to Me, the "love" that birthed him as the Christ. So you as well, may be so spiritually reborn. "Now is the time," Christ says "to live anew."

We are telling you, the world, again what to do. Walk in faith. Trust in God. This is the way of love, which surrounds you and caresses your hair. This love we are for you loves you so intimately, so immediately, so infinitely that you cannot imagine how grand it all is. So we say, do not think. Do not bother to try to figure out God. Just allow this love to be and blossom within your being. Allow God's love to fully transform you into Himself, the light and love of the world.

Some will say "no way." Some will deny. Some won't care. Some will say beware. But some seed will fall on fertile soil and sprout, rise and bloom because of these words you write, which We offer, which you invite into your knowing. As it blossoms as well into your own showing.

Oh yes, My dear, day by day you are growing in God's love. People see. People will hear and to God's love will draw near. There is so much to say. Do not get in the way. Offer no blocks to hinder this work. Give no thought to the how or even the why. For your very heart can not deny that just as this wonderful wisdom finds its way to you, all will as well find its way through. Trust, My dear. Have full faith in the fruitation of this message reaching the right hands.

Isn't it exciting to see how God Almighty can work through thee? You are doing so well. It's almost time to tell. Give thanks for what you see which is good. Look for the good which is everywhere. Do not be afraid to be happy for happy you are at heart.

I have so much to say and you are My voice. I have given you a choice and you chose Me. Oh how, I delight in you My daughter for you hear and heed My voice above the mindless and heartless chatter of the world. We have such a story to tell and tell we will as you continue to allow My will to be done, as you continue to trust in Me to be led forth, to trust I will give you what to say and how to be as you live so ever close to Me. Come to Me as you are. Let them all know of My endless love. Tell them not to fear judgment or punishment from Me for My name is Love and Love condemneth not. Love is kind and patient.

I am God. I am the Love of God and I am. I am for each of you to be recognized and called forth. This is the most natural thing or way of being there is in the world. It is right, and it is true, and it is for all of you. I do not judge. I do not limit. All those things are ideas of your mind which is not always so kind. Not one of you is better, some just know better, and the better they know is Me.

Do not get stuck up on interpreting with your mind words written and rewritten so long ago. For your mind will never know the fullness of My love or who I am. My love, My

Divine Love, My nature, My essence can only be known to your soul which you feel within you and call your heart. This the only way any can know Me.

There will be many who doubt. There will be some whom become angry and shout. This has always been the way when truth or "the good news" has been proclaimed.

Go forth to where you are lead for there are many of My hungry sheep wishing to be fed. You will show them with the light with which I fill you. You are a lantern in the darkness of the night. But with you always, I am, always here, available within your heart, happily at home in your heart.

As you grow in My love there will be more you will know and just as naturally their will be more you show. It can be no other way. Rejoice in this fact. Rejoice in this truth. I live and reign in you. We, My dear, have so much to do. You can do My work here. You can do My work there. You can do My work anywhere. The more you live, the more you will give. The more you will see, the more you will be. You My dear cannot begin to dream of the majesty of the plan I have for you. Oh, it is so exciting! I see it all and it is lovely, so lovely. I am loving it all.

It is up to you My dear to see this clear, to hold the faith, to believe that all good can be. You have to believe with and in Me. Do not limit any good by filling your mind with thoughts of doubt for if you do you will live without the knowing of the Fullness of Life which I offer unto you. Continue to take care of your mind, your body, and your soul. Continue to live as whole, live fully, live physically, while being guided spiritually. In this way you shall know the fullness of this Life I offer you.

Be at peace, at peace with Me. This is the way of Christ. Hold fast to this truth which lives within you. This is the way of the saints. This is the way of "true life." Do not be dismayed for you hear the voice of God whom is no other than "true love" for you.

I am ready for a reprieve from the disagreeable and discontented souls which surround me. It is as if they wish to snuff out my very happiness with the stale air they breathe.

Come to Me I say and I shall give you rest from the weary world full of tears and strife. You do not march to the beat of that old dead drum.

These people do not bring me happiness.

You are right My dear they do not. And this is the very place where most get tripped up on and in life. For they expect those around them to "bring them happiness" to behave in "such and such ways" as to be perfectly pleasing to them, bringing them happiness continually, constantly. We know that those around you do most often bring you joy, but as well agree that they are not always in line with what feels good to you.

It is good that you can separate yourself from this activity and realize that it does not have to be for you to partake of in anyway. You have to detach from your ego response and calmly observe the others. More and more We know you are seeing this commotion for what it is just co-motion, back and forth banter, and egoic reactions. Yes, you are right not to participate, to hold your tongue and visit your heart.

Come to Me and be still with Me, rest in peace, in the peace of My love which you know. And as you remain in and become this peace you show My love unto the world. Please be happy, for I am so happy to have you home in My heart. Remember, you have not yet opened all the gifts I have for you. Yes, others have known and spoken this wisdom I give as well unto you. Let this knowledge comfort and inspire you.

DECEMBER 27, 2011

God is the power of the universe, truth in power, beauty and grace. All things lovely are He. Know Love, know Me says God. Trust in My love and ye shall know the beauty of the world which I give unto you, unto all, available for the asking, for the taking, for the accepting. My wisdom I offer to all who so love Me that they lay down their own lives, their own personal egoic wills, and ask, plead for, My will to be done through them.

These are My children whom I have welcomed home and handed the keys to the halls of wisdom. To these gentle children I give My word. They speak for Me. They offer their voice unto My service. They walk My way offering their very feet unto My service. They touch with My hands reaching out unto My lost sheep shepherding them home. There was one. Now there are many, because of the one who first received Me wholeheartedly.

The call is made to all, but not all answer. Not all hear so clear. But as they do, as they recognize My voice, they have no choice. They can no longer stray for there is no more night, only day. For the light is bright and glorious and all who see the Light are drawn forward for their soul knows it is again home. This, My dear, is the Great Awakening of which you are a part. You have found your way and so shall forever stay in the light with Me and you will continue to rise most gently and gradually as you fill with My love.

And as your soul rises in awareness of My love you shall as well grow in awareness of the many wonders of the world hidden from the busy mind of man. For it has been told, and told again, that man cannot know God, cannot gain True wisdom, through the intellect. God's wisdom cannot be bought, sold, nor bartered for it is a gift of grace. The most wonderful grace of God bestowed on those who come as little children hungry for the guidance of the Loving Father/ Mother.

Do not know so much, My children. You have decided too much about Me and about My ways. And the very things you think keep you from knowing Me and living the fullness of life intended for you with the grace and ease of My wisdom.

There will be a day again when all will know Me. And yet, you need not await your bodily death to again know the full joy of life with Me. Heaven awaits within your heart. Peace be with you, My darlings. Peace is with you now waiting within. But you do not recognize, which is the only thing I could call ever term "sin." You do not recognize this love that lives within you as Me. You do not live fully.

But there is a way and it is not believing in one man. Yes, I sent Him. I loved and love Him, just as I do you. But you do not see that he was working for Me. I so filled him with my Divine Love that he became like an angel, like a dove. He became one with Me in this love. This truth He told, but few behold his message clearly.

Yes, I want you to love him dearly, but this is not the end of the story. His life was just the beginning of the "true life" which I now offer to all. Yes, He had to fall. He had to come home and live on "the throne." So he could bring back the gift I gave to him so We could together send it back out to the world again and again. He told you so. He told you the truth. He told you to love Me fully. He said to trust in My love. He told you help would be sent, that a "Comforter" would arrive and that you as My children were meant to thrive.

This is the way of Christ, as this is the way of My love. When you know peace in your heart, you know Me. I am here for you. Do not hide. You cannot hide your heart from Me. I know your sorrows and your joys. I ask for them all. Share them with Me. Give them to them to Me and I will bless you continually.

Be still, your mind, and visit the stillness of your heart, which is the life within you until your last breath. And as you take your last breath this heart arises whole, as your soul, unto Me again to live fully with no restraint. As there is no small mind to limit your knowing and no physical confines to restrict where you are, you are again free to be wherever you wish.

As you arise in the consciousness of My love as you live bodily, you will as well experience more and more awareness of this freedom, this "Heaven experience" in which you are not bound to the ways of the earth. In time, you will know and you will show. But for now My dear, let's be clear. I hold you near. I walk beside and I hold your hand. And when you are too tired, yes My dear, there are only one set of footprints as I carry you through the sand.

God is my confidant. I put my confidence in God. I trust in the love and wisdom which is God and which lives in and through me. *"Do not worry about tomorrow."* God says. God requires my trust. He is my shepherd. He leadeth me to still waters.

I want to speak to you of "my faith" which has been renewed. It is a new-formed faith. It is an entirely new understanding of what faith is. Faith is believing in the unseen. Faith is pre-tending, imagining, what can be, so it can be. All faith requires a strong knowing, a knowing that whatever one has faith in will be. One expresses his faith unto the universe by his thoughts and words. So if I speak and think of lovely things, lovely things must appear in my experience. And thus if I speak and think of pain and hardship, that is what I shall experience.

> *This is all true and just. This is the way the world works. This is the law of the Universe.*

So what about God? Do I believe in God? Do I have faith in God? I know God, I say. So there is nothing that requires belief on my part of that which I intimately know. At one time, if you asked me if I had "faith" or if I "believed" I would have assumed you were asking if I was a believer in God or Christ quite like one might wonder if a child believes in Santa Claus. So do I believe? No, I no longer believe in God. I know God and know His love. Faith or belief in the unknown is no longer required.

God is perfecting my path. God is lighting my way. God is inspiring these words. God tells me what to say. We have a deal, God and I. I have given my life over to Him and He in turn leads me home, leads me onward, leads me where He needs me. He places me. He guides and directs me. He shepherd's me. I wander no more. But I do wonder. And God says my wonder is good for it proves I want to know more of Him and His ways and that my mind is not so filled with ideas that get in the way of understanding the fullness of His Love.

Don't think you know so much. You are continually limiting your life experiences. Stay with Me, stay tuned. Order up. All that is possible is possible with and through Me. More than you know is possible. You "know" so much you think. But you know little of what Life has to offer. Know Me and you shall know the way to truth through truth. This has always been the way. Bow down to My will and I will raise you up.

Time to see, to see limitlessly, with Me. You do not have to know it all. When you trust in My voice, truth will be given as needed, as you need to know. But until then feel free to wonder and to ask. I will tell you all you wish to know, all there is through Me. Do you believe? Believe it is true? Then live as so and walk forward assuredly. Do not cry out in anguish to another. Come to Me. For My love is the only saving grace there is.

Let Me carry you in My breast. Give not My love a test. Become one with Me. Come alive in My heart. These words are for all, though given through you, and as you share others will know what to do. They are lost, as were you. But I made a promise so very long ago to My love fully show again to the world, first to one boy and now to each boy and girl.

Come to Me, each as a small child. Look up to Me for the answers to the questions you have. You want to know how. You want to know why. I guarantee you this, to no soul will My love I deny. All are My children, though many have been led astray. But I will joyfully welcome each home and live for such a day. Each heart that recognizes Me gladdens My heart and brightens the light of the world.

My people have turned away from Me. My face, they do not know. My voice they fear. Some care not to hear. Others believe it not possible but still they wonder. They wonder where I am. Show them. Show them I am here still. Show them, tell them, I am available every day within their hearts. My voice is kind. My hands are loving. Each can come to Me easily, with no pushing, no shoving, just as I am here for you and with you now. Yes, please show them how.

Give all glory and honor to God. Humble yourself and I will exalt you, says the Lord. Come to Me and I will give you rest. The saints were not "special people" in God's eyes but God was "special" in their eyes. God did not "love them more" but they loved God more thus were so filled with the knowing of His love.

It's as if God has been trying to get "a word in edgewise" with me for a long time. Does faith alone or faith and baptism cause salvation? This seems to be the age-old question of man.

You now know this answer My dear, but for all others Let's be clear. "Salvation" only comes from My love, My Divine Love which I offer to all as a gift to those who call on Me and repent, or turn away from their old ways. Their old ways of doing "as they like," following their own will, not Mine. The mistake that has been made by many a man is that this is a one time thing so they have an experience of My Divine Love and its saving grace then lose the fervor and continue to walk in their old ways. One has to continually come to Me and ask to be filled with My love. This is this very love that "saves" man from himself. It is not his faith, nor his works.

It is only My Divine Love that can so transform a soul. This love is the very gift which the Holy Spirit brings. This love is gifted unto each heart by God, through the Holy Spirit, on God's timing not by any rite or work by man. This needs to be understood and will be understood as man receives the grace of My Divine Love into his heart so transforming his very being, giving him new eyes and new ears, ears which hear My word as written upon his very heart. At this time no books are needed, as no rules or dogma can ever contain the glory of My love known to those hearts. The baptism that "saves" souls is the "Baptism by Fire," which is the fire of the Holy Spirit at work in one's soul. Every soul that is so filled with My Divine Love knows this saving grace and so desires the attainment of more as it has been so awakened to this new life in Me.

Jesus said, only those who did the Father's will would enter the Kingdom of Heaven. No one can do My will on their own. It's only by the infilling of My Divine Love that one's very being is so changed that My will is done on Earth as it is in Heaven. Whoever is so filled with My love is assured a home in the Highest Heavens.

Do you understand My dears that I have this Love for you, to give you, which will transform you? This message has been lost and thus so have you. You argue continually about the meaning of the words given so many years ago. You say you believe in My word and yet you hear not My word, you hear not My voice. But you always have a choice.

Lay down your rules. Lay down your laws. Lay aside all that you know, and humble yourself so that you can truly know Me, without doubt. With the same assurity that the hand that writes these words moves across the page, each can know Me so and have no question of these truths.

A new age is dawning My dears. It is a glorious time of awakening. Hearts are hearing Me. Harkening to My voice and proclaiming truth in My name. Do not be afraid to listen to your own heart. There is safety in the Silence. Learn to find comfort in the stillness, for it is here I await you. Come spend time with Me and ask Me to let you know My love within your heart. All whom desire and ask so for the infilling of My love will know Me and through them, so very naturally, My will shall be done.

Know that which is good, that which is Me, which speaks unto you continually. Know the love, which I am, is for you. There is nothing for you to do but want Me and accept Me fully as the love I am for your life. This is the plan for no strife, the easy way, the way up, the way onward. Peace be with you, through Me.

DECEMBER 29, 2011

It is not about believing, it is about receiving My love, My Divine Love, into your heart. Then you shall know, you shall know My love and thus My ways, My will. Thus you shall know Me and call Me "Father."

Many people Lord, many people call Your name and still cry out in pain believing you are not there as they live so unaware. They are wandering still, and arguing, proclaiming things they believe to know but have not seen and so do not show. There are many whom call Jesus' name and yet seem to wander and fall just the same.

I know, I see, and all this pains Me for I sent My Son Jesus to "light the way" to make this all clear as day. Yes, many,

many call My name and receive My blessings, as My blessings, the good of the world, are available to all. But they do not do My will, for they know not My will. For the only way one can do My will is to be so filled with My love as was Jesus. This is, I say once again, "the gift" of My Divine Love.

Yes, so many love me and all I love. But they do not come to Me as little children with open minds and hearts asking to be so filled with My love, wisdom and grace. They are already so filled with ideas they have decided about Me and My great love, that they inhibit the very most inner knowing of My essence. Books and books are filled with what man thinks of Me, not what man knows of Me. And the words I have given that have been heard have been for years upon years misinterpreted, as their original meanings seem to be so absurd that their minds cannot begin to comprehend.

Jesus told you all that I hid the spiritual wisdom from the mind and thus it could only be accessed from the heart. And yet men become "learned" in the Bible and study and pull it apart and attempt to put it back together again. Just like the old nursery rhyme of Humpty Dumpty, "All the King's horses and all the King's men could not put Humpty Dumpty back together again." My words cannot be put together again. My word cannot be "put together" by the mind of any man. This is why I gave the New Covenant. It was and is My promise to guide those who wander, home again unto My heart.

Many believe they are "the ones" who have found it, that they alone have the key or the "recipe," the lock on My love. Well, no one person or group has or ever will have a lock on My love as it is for all for all time.

Many of you have not received this "new gift," this gift of the New Covenant. Some believe they have and others believe they will. But few know, truly know My will. Whoever has been so blessed with this gift, this gift of the New Covenant, My Divine Love into their very heart, will know. He will know My love and will do My will. He will not sin, for as he so knows My will he can do no other.

Now I ask you to ask yourself, does this describe you or your brother? This gift is still here for you. I hold it in My hand, this very gift of My love. My transforming love will keep you from wandering and bring you to the "Promised Land."

It is here now and available. This love, as it enters your heart and soul, awakens a newness of spirit. A fire or flame of My love will burn within and purify your very soul making it into one of pure gold. This is the treasure whom all have sought but found elsewhere naught. This is the Ark of Covenant which I offer each of you to renew, to be reborn of Spirit, to be sons and daughters of God, no longer born of a woman. With this gift, all of My word, which you have ever heard, will be a riddle no more.

This Love, this saving grace, of which I speak I keep from no man, no woman. Come to Me as you are, I say. It is My Love you are to want, to plead for, to make room for in your heart. You do not have to be perfect to come to Me. You cannot be perfect except through Me, through the ways of My love.

The only way one can know Me is to not know so much of himself or think so much of himself that he believes he has Me and the ways of My world "figured out" by himself. Such man is like the rich man who can not enter the Kingdom of Heaven for he continues to come to Me carrying and insisting on bringing all his "mental baggage" when his bare soul is what is required for entrance into the gates of My Kingdom.

There is more to know dear and more for you to show My dear. And as you rise in My love so you shall. It is for you now to continue to ask for and be blessed by My love. This love is doing wondrous works in you and through you and will continue to do. Thank you for doing as I have asked, for completing this part of your task. You know My love. You know Me. I Bless you and love you My dear. Dry your tears. This is all good. Good for all to hear. Some will hear and some will know and all who do such, Blessings I will show.

A baby who dies without being "baptized" will not go to "Hell" any more than any other soul. As there is no "Hell," other than the "Hell on Earth" you, mankind, have created as you have drifted from the knowing of My love. When you are not present, as you now know life within your body, you are still present. Your soul essence is still very much alive and you experience no pain, no worry, no "Hell." There is more to know here of which I can not at this time tell, for you My dear have not yet risen to the level of which this message can be clear.

But know this; everyone gets a chance, a chance at this dance of life if they wish again and again. Each soul that so chooses to return does so for the very reason to know My love and be filled with My love and live a life without sin. But each time you "come in again" you forget from whence you came and have to remember again.

No, it's really not a game. It is life, a wonderful opportunity

*for full life. And those who find Me, while living bodily, will
experience the fullness of life in Me, My Kingdom, Heaven
on Earth. This is "the way" of which Jesus truly spoke.
This is true peace on Earth and good will, God's will, unto
everyman. Blessed be the ears that hear.*

This is exactly what I have been yearning to know. I have searched high
and low and not heard it told elsewhere as so. How can it be that I,
lowly me, have heard and understood such great wonder and been so
transformed by God's love and yet the world wanders with deaf ears?
Oh, how I truly wish others will hear.

You see, I am different now. I grow spiritually everyday. There has been
a great change for, for fifty years I did not live life this way. Yes, I loved
God and yes, I prayed. But I did not naturally, oh so naturally, walk
His way. But now I do and it isn't because of anything I have done or
special faith I had. I only prayed for God to fill me so with His Divine
Love. I prayed not once. I prayed not twice. I prayed with every breath,
with all my might.

Never did I know what wonders would come next. Never knowing
God's word would come flowing from my breath. I do and say the right
thing at the right time. That can only be the will of the Divine. Thank
You, Thank You Dear Lord for making me see and I as well know You
are far from done with me. I have set aside my old ways and now will
spend my hours, my days, doing Your will, Your work, Your way. I will
not falter as God's very heart lives in me. My heart is God's altar.

Whenever I stop and think about this,
about all the words that I receive
and that I do receive
such cherished communication,
my mind is blown away.

For as much as my heart believes
these words as truth
and as pure gifts of Spirit,
my mind looks out into the world
with my tiny beady eyes and says,
"How, just how, does this happen?"

No one could have ever told me,
that I could have believed,
such was possible for me.

But then I close my eyes
and return again to my heart
and my heart says,
"Yes, this is true and good.
Good for you and for all.
This is what you have come
into this world at this time to do."

MAY YOUR JOY BE FULL.

DEBRA CLEMENTE

NOTES

[1] *The Prayer Perfect* eluded to in these writings is part of a series of spirit communications received by James Padgett between 1914 and 1920. *The Prayer Perfect* challenge can be found online at http://new-birth.net/experiment.htm The author suggests the book *THE WAY OF DIVINE LOVE* by James E. Padgett, recorder, complied by Joseph Babinsky for further insight into the workings of Divine Love.

[2] Excerpt from *The Spirit of Christ*, written in 1888 by Andrew Murray, which can be viewed online at http://worldinvisible.com/library/murray/7764/7764p.htm

[3] References herein to The *Gospel of Truth*, which is part of the *The Nag Hammadi Library,* are translations by Robert M. Grant and found in Grant's book *Gnosticism* (Harper & Brothers, New York, 1961).

[4] Reference herein to *Gospel of Thomas*, which is part of the *The Nag Hammadi Library*, can be found online at http://www.sacred-texts.com/chr/thomas.htm

Scripture quotations marked (NLT) are taken from the *Holy Bible, New Living Translation*, copyright © 1996, 2004, 2007 by Tyndale House Foundation. Used by permission of Tyndale House Publishers, Inc., Carol Stream, Illinois 60188. All rights reserved.

Scripture quotations marked (NIV) are taken from *THE HOLY BIBLE, NEW INTERNATIONAL VERSION*®, NIV® Copyright © 1973, 1978, 1984, 2011 by Biblica, Inc.™ Used by permission. All rights reserved worldwide.

About the Author

The painter paints.
The writer writes.
The creative voice is one.
It's all the same.
It's who I am.

Debra Clemente

Debra Clemente is a fine art painter whom communicates the joy she feels with the voice of color. Just as she has been inspired to sing the song of her soul with paint and palette, she is now being inspired to pick up a pen and write. *Listen Hear, A Divine Love Story* journals a year of her awakening to the voice of Love. Clemente says, "I used to have to guard my thoughts; now my thoughts guard and guide me. It's like I have a life coach in my head, but the wisdom is from a whole different source than my brain."

Clemente's boldly graphic and energetic oil paintings express her colorful, luminescent, and optimistic views of life. Drawing from the deep well of her memories for inspiration, she challenges herself to create a concrete expression of a dream-like vision. Her painting process is as unique as each work of art she creates. Wielding one tool, a large sturdy palette knife she paints: mixing, smoothing, layering, pushing, scratching and scraping oil paint on canvas. The resulting work retains the evidence of her energy and passion, delighting the eye from a distance as well as upon close study.

Since their college days, the author/artist and her husband David have made their home in Lawrence, Kansas, USA and are now empty nesters. She sees it as new opportunity. "My skills have developed over the years," says Debra, "This is my time."

Visit Debra Clemente's website
for updates on her writing activities
and to view galleries of her original and edition art.

DebraClemente.com

CPSIA information can be obtained
at www.ICGtesting.com
Printed in the USA
FSHW012120221119
64431FS